LIVING ON DEADLINE

LIVING ON DEADLINE

The Amazing Adventures
Of a Southern Journalist

JAMES L. DICKERSON

SARTORIS
LITERARY
GROUP

SARTORIS LITERARY GROUP
Metro-Jackson, Mississippi
www.sartorisliterary.com

Will Frost,
Father of Robert Frost

Some Traditions
Die Hard

Robert Frost and his poetry are associated with rural New England, especially New Hampshire and Vermont, but he began life as a city boy in San Francisco, where he often roamed the streets with his father, Will Frost, a confirmed walker who was known to pack a Colt revolver in his belt as he made his rounds. Will was one of the more eccentric editors at the *Daily Evening Bulletin*.

Will often took his son with him to work at the newspaper. One of the poet's earliest memories is of his father placing his revolver in his desk drawer, where the sound of rolling bullets could be heard whenever the drawer was opened or closed.

**From Sartoris Literary edition of
Robert Frost's *New Hampshire*,
winner of the 1924 Pulitzer Prize**

CONTENTS

James L. Dickerson, age two, on Central Avenue,
Greenville, Mississippi, not far from the home of Shelby Foote,
where the journalist was writing his first novel *Tournament*.
Foote went on to become an acclaimed Civil War historian.

Chapter 1

Night Train to Chicago

WE HAD JUST PULLED THE MUSTANG into the Ole Miss Service Station to fill-up with gas, the radio blaring the Animals' "We Gotta Get Outta This Place," the speaker pulsating with hypnotic bass guitar runs, when suddenly the music was interrupted by an urgent news bulletin.

"Martin Luther King was shot and killed this evening in Memphis."

The deep-throated announcer did not sound the least bit upset about the news. The monotone delivery was all very matter of fact, followed by a commercial for a local coin-operated laundry owned by a wild-eyed Klansman who once garnered national attention by writing a book that claimed he had scientific evidence African-Americans were actually apes wearing human clothing. I had once met the man in his laundromat. Looking into his depraved eyes, as he tried to sell his book to me, chilled me to the bone. I wondered if it was he who had killed Martin Luther King.

Hearing the news, my wife, Ina, and I looked at each other, speechless. We had been in an emotional free-for-all for several weeks over President Lyndon Johnson's speech in which he said he would not run for re-election. That seemed to clear the way for our favorite candidate Robert Kennedy. Now this! Would nihilistic idealism become the pulse beat of youth or would it sunder the American soul? As Dylan once said,

"Times, they are a-changing."

Before we had a chance to say anything to each other about the news bulletin, we heard the booming voice of the pasty-white service station attendant who suddenly appeared at my window.

"That bastard got what he deserved," he said. Around twenty, he had the pot belly of a sedentary man in his sixties. He grinned and lifted up his shirt to show off a revolver embraced by several rolls of fat. He looked past me, his eyes riveted on Ina's long, tanned legs that contrasted nicely with her white shorts. "I might have to kill me a nigger, too."

Not really expecting a response from us—he was just showing off, judging by the twisted smirk on his densely freckled face—he took a step or two and began washing the windshield, the pearl handle of his pistol bumping into the glass with each stretch of his pink, hairless arm. I hoped the pistol would accidentally fire. From the way it was positioned, an accidental discharge would be devastating for his hopes of fatherhood.

My grandfather once told me to never argue with a fool with a pistol stuck inside his belt. I took that advice and didn't debate the issue with the attendant. Instead, we hurried home to get more news on television. Students at the University of Mississippi, we lived in a sparsely furnished mobile home located in a trailer park on the outskirts of town.

Ina was eighteen and I was twenty-one. We met in Spanish class. Because we both were late the first day, we had to sit on the dreaded first row. She was a stunning blonde with a sweet smile who did modeling for ads for the campus newspaper, and when she sat down and our arms brushed together on the arm rest I felt a mild electrical jolt. We made a date to go to a pizza joint the next night and neither of us ever returned to the Spanish class. Other times we went to Papa Kiamie's to pick up his locally famous barbecue sandwiches.

We consummated our relationship in a mobile home on Old Taylor Road, which had been William Faulkner's favorite place to ride his horse. Because Ina's maiden name also was Taylor, we figured our union was ordained by the stars. When you are eighteen and twenty-one, you tend to embrace coincidences as proof of one thing or another. Not so much so when you get older. Then life seems painfully random.

INA AND I DATED for a passionate eight weeks, with me learning for the first time about something called spermicide foam. Once I drove her to the town square and parked in front of a drugstore and waited outside like a lookout in a gangster movie, furtively watching through the store window as she picked up the box and took it to the pharmacist to check out. She looked so damned grown up. I was so impressed. She left the store almost at a run and jumped into the car as fast as she could, with me pulling away from the curb, her door still wide open.

"I was so embarrassed," she said, pulling the door shut while looking back over her shoulder as we made our getaway.

After eight weeks of this—I can still remember the blissful shock of seeing a beautiful eighteen-year-old woman walking around my house with familiarity—she decided she must be pregnant. Because she was too young to get married in Mississippi—twenty-one was the minimum age at the time—we drove over to Jasper, Alabama, where we found an Episcopal priest who was willing to marry us. Within a couple of weeks of getting married, she discovered she was not pregnant after all. Oh, well.

We were both passionate about civil rights and against the Vietnam War—and that was a strong aphrodisiac. It was us against the world. We slipped into that groove and rode it for all it was worth. Of course, there was no shortage of students at Ole Miss who didn't see eye-to-eye with us on those issues. We didn't care. It was 1968, the worst year in American history since the Civil War. Not until 2021 would we see its likes again. That afternoon after leaving the service station, we watched on live television as America descended into chaos over the assassination. Riots broke out everywhere. In Memphis the National Guard was called in with bayonets and armored vehicles. Police violence against Blacks was rampant. They were beaten and chased with bayonets.

It is funny how relationships work. Together you are stronger than

11

Now it's Pepsi . . .

for those who

think young

BOTTLED AND DISTRIBUTED IN THE OXFORD AREA
BY THE PEPSI-COLA BOTTLING COMPANY
OF TUPELO

One of Ina's modeling gigs at Ole Miss

you are individually. We talked all night. By morning we knew what we had to do. That afternoon I packed an overnight suitcase. We ate dinner in silence. There wasn't much else to say. What happened next changed our lives forever.

Ina walked me to the door. She lowered her head to hide her tears. I reached out and lifted her chin with my fingertips. It pained me to see her sadness. We kissed and embraced, and I walked to the car and tossed my suitcase onto the backseat and drove away. She watched from the door as my taillights disappeared in the distance. In those days the drive from Oxford to Batesville was on a two-lane highway. The night sky seemed unusually dark, not a moon or star anywhere in sight. It was the first time I had been away from Ina since we were married. Not far out of Oxford, a car pulled up behind me, tailgating my car. I slowed down so it could pass, but it didn't seem to want to pass. I had seen enough horror movies to know this was not a good thing.

Someone was following me. That much was obvious. But who? Was it that service station attendant? Or was it law enforcement? Perhaps it was the FBI or the KKK? So far I knew that whoever it was did not want to pass me. But did they want to keep up with me? My speedometer went to 140 miles per hour. I had never driven the car that fast, but I had pushed it to 105 miles-per-hour several times.

I floored the accelerator.

Seventy … 80 …90 … 100 … 110.

The V8 roared like a rocket, eating up the headlight-illuminated road.

I turned the radio up full blast. Otis Redding's new hit "(Sittin' on) The Dock of the Bay" was playing. God I loved that song. It gave me a sense of peace. At first, the car behind me fell back several car lengths and I thought that was the end of it. But after a while it suddenly began closing on me, finally, pulling up within ten feet of my back bumper. The car blinked its lights several times, whatever that meant. I held steady at 110.

Fortunately, there was little incoming traffic.

A couple of times, coming down from a hill, the undercarriage bumped hard against the pavement as the highway dipped and then lifted up into another hill. Still, the car behind me pressed on.

Soon I would be entering Batesville. I wondered what was going to happen when I arrived at my destination. I saw lights ahead and began to de-accelerate. The car behind shadowed me like the souped-up cars do on a racetrack.

Up ahead was the turnoff to the train station. I wondered if the car behind me would drive on past, or turn when I turned. My heart was pounding. It was all like something out of a suspense movie. Sure enough, when I turned onto the street that went to the train station, my pursuer turned as well. I saw the train station in the distance. There were no cars in the parking lot, but the lights were on inside. The Panama Limited would be stopping in ten minutes or so on its way from New Orleans to Memphis and points beyond.

I pulled off into the parking lot and stopped. The car behind me continued about hundred yards up the street and stopped. It was not what I had imagined. It was a late-model four-door sedan, perhaps a 1968 Plymouth VIP or a 1968 Ford LTD, the type of car that Klansmen and FBI agents drove—and the occasional retired librarian.

I could see the waiting room was empty, but I was afraid to go inside. I stayed in my car, my eyes glued to the car up ahead with its lights still on. I was just sitting there, waiting, listening with a pounding heart to the radio. The Beatles' new hit, "Hello, Goodbye" was a welcome diversion.

I PARKED AT THE TRAIN STATION so I could see both directions, north and south. The mystery car was still north of me, its lights still on, the exhaust still sputtering moon-sparkled clouds that quickly dissipated into the darkness. I kept thinking someone would step out of the car. That never happened. I had questions about the driver. Was he young? Was he old? Did he wear a fedora? Did he have on a Klansmen hood? For some reason I preferred he wore a fedora.

Finally, I saw the train light approaching and heard the train whistle.

14

I got my suitcase out of the car and then locked the doors. A lot of good that would have done if the man in the car was a car thief. It was a convertible. All he would have to do is cut through the canvass top.

I made my way to the platform and waited for the train, clutching my ticket at my side. First, I felt the planking on the platform tremble; then I heard the engineer braking the powerful locomotive, the metallic sounds cutting through the night air. I looked at the parked car. No change.

Slowly, the train rolled into the station, finally stopping about a dozen railway cars from where I was standing. However, as soon as the train came to a complete stop a porter opened the door and deposited a step for me to use to board the train. The porter spoke to me, but didn't tell me where to go. I turned left and kept walking until I found a place to sit. The seat next to me was vacant. I moved over to it because it was by the window. Within minutes the train began pulling out of the station.

The parked car with its lights still on began moving as well. There was no one sitting on the passenger side and it was too dark to get a good look at the driver. By the time the train reached its cruising speed, the car was gone.

Before long the conductor came along and asked for my ticket. An older Black man who wore glasses, he looked at my ticket and in a rich melodic baritone voice said, "Chicago Union Station—the end of the line." He peered over the top of his glasses to look me over. "Why you going to Chicago young man?"

"It's sort of a business trip," I answered.

"Business? You don't look like no businessman to me. How you make your money?"

"I play in bands."

"Is that right?"

I nodded.

"Ever been to Chicago?"

I nodded, no.

"Well, you be careful in that city. There's sure enough some wickedness going on there. Don't try no rock and roll attitude while you're there. Know what I mean?"

"I'll be careful."

I felt I had a pretty good idea who was in the car that followed me to the Batesville train station. My high school friend, Charlie Sudduth, had warned me that things like that were likely to happen. Growing up we both had been supportive of voting rights for the Black citizens of our hometown of Hollandale. Like me, he got death threats. His father, Chuck, was a television repairman who had a business in an alleyway off Main Street. In his shop, prominently displayed, was a black-and-white enlargement of a photo of Charlie's mother, Kathy, standing on a roof in a tiny bikini holding onto a television antenna. She was a striking woman with dark hair who had a movie star figure and because of those assets teenage boys in town found excuses to visit Chuck in his shop for the sole purpose of staring at the image, hands in pockets, while carrying on small talk.

Kathy Sudduth was unique in our hometown because she had joined the U.S. Marines during World War II and had been designated as a recruitment "poster girl," because of her great beauty. While Charlie was coming of age, she worked for the U.S. Postal Service. By the time Charlie and I went off to college, Kathy and my mother lived across the street from each other and developed a close friendship.

"Whatever you do," Charlie once warned me, "Don't file for conscientious objector status with the draft board."

"Why?"

"Because the FBI will follow you everywhere you go. They follow you at night and tailgate you with their lights on bright. Once they followed me, two of them, into a café and sat on either side of me at the lunch counter. One of them even reached over and dipped one of his French fries into my ketchup. Both of them had on those fedora hats."

Of course, during that hellish drive from Oxford to the Batesville train Station his warning was all I could think about. *"I mean it—don't file. I am afraid they are going to shoot and kill me. I don't want that to happen to you."* Now I was pretty sure the man in that car was a FBI agent.

* * *

It was difficult sleeping in the coach with so many people, coughing, laughing and getting up to go pee while making spasmodic little grunts that probably pulsated in unison with the ones being made by their bladder. Mostly, I thought about my new bride, Ina. Surely, the men in hats would leave her alone. She had had a run-in with a Mississippi highway patrol-man several months earlier while driving her Mustang (yes, we were a two Mustang family) home to visit her mother in Meridian. About a dozen miles out of town, she was blue-lighted by the patrolman.

She pulled over and looked for her license.

The officer sauntered up to her window with a grin on his face.

"What'd I do, officer?" she asked.

"Speeding. I'll need to see your license."

She handed him the license. He looked it over and said, "Looks in order. I see from your decal you go to Ole Miss."

She nodded yes.

"That's where all the rich girls go."

"Well, I'm not one of them. You're not going to give me a ticket, are you?"

"Well," he said, pausing. "I don't have to."

"What do you mean?"

"Tell you what. I live just up the road. You follow me home and I'll forget about the ticket."

She glared at him, not believing she heard him right.

"So, what do you say?"

"What if I take the ticket and go home and report you?"

The patrolman laughed. "They wouldn't believe you."

The patrolman got into his car and pulled around her Mustang and honked his horn, waving. Ina pulled in behind him. When he braked and turned left onto a gravel road, she sped past the turnoff, watching the rearview mirror to see if he followed her. He didn't. She laughed telling

17

me the story and explained that she took a different highway back to school. I laughed with her, grimacing on the inside, worried that he might be looking for her the next time she went home.

SEVERAL TIMES I dozed off and was startled awake by dreams of suspicious looking men in hats looking at me from across the railway coach. *Maybe I should get myself a fedora and blend in.*

The overnight train ride aboard the Panama Limited, except for its brief exposure to the bright lights of Memphis, was uneventful, like traveling through a dark tunnel, with lights from rural farms sparkling like distant stars. Memphis fairly exploded with light because the station was downtown and streetlights illuminated the ride into the city and the ride out as well. Once we left Memphis there was little to see from the windows except your own reflection. I fell asleep, soothed by the clickety-clack of the wheels, not awakening until we pulled into Champaign-Urbana. I looked for things to tell Ina about that stop because I knew she had been born there, but there was nothing to see other than late-night dreariness.

MY EARLIEST MEMORIES in life are free-floating sensations, fragments of scents, colors, sounds, and textures, and not actual recollections. Combined they gave me a sense of wellbeing while held by my mother. It was not until my mother was ninety-six that she provided me with the key to unlock the actual memories of those things I already carried deep within my heart. They had resided more than seventy years in her memory, locked away in a safe place; but when I heard the explanations from her they defined the nameless, sometimes fragile, feelings I had carried for the same exact number of years.

Because I was diagnosed with whooping cough at the age of three months, my mother was told by the doctor that only fifty percent of the children my age with the disease survived. Furthermore, the doctor explained that if she left me in the crib on my back or stomach, I would not be able to breathe and would die gasping for breath. My only hope, the doctor explained, was for Mother to hold me in an upright position throughout the night so I could breathe through the suffocating mucous that obstructed my throat. There was absolutely nothing medical science could do, he said—it was in God's hands.

At the time my father, James L. Dickerson, was stationed at a U.S. Army base in Austin, Texas, where he awaited orders to be shipped to the South Pacific to serve in the U.S. Army Air Corps. My mother had the support of her parents, two brothers and two sisters, but that was not the same as having her husband at her side for support.

Because of what the doctor told her, she held me for twenty-four hours a day in her lap in a rocking chair, sitting up straight, with her loving arms wrapped around me as if I were a toy doll. I seem to recall from some distant place the smell of honeysuckle wafting in through the open windows, the sound of her sweet soprano voice as she sang to me, and the slight *thump thump thump* of the rocking chair, the back-and-forth motion helping me to breathe. But mostly there was the music. Mother's favorite song to sing to me was, "You Are My Sunshine," written by Louisiana Governor Jimmie Davis. No one ever sang it as well as she did.

You are my sunshine . . .

Sung in Mother's sweet, soprano voice, the song became an anthem to celebrate the love of a mother for her son. I would hear the words of that song wafting throughout the house from time to time until I went off to college. In the years between, she sang other songs to my younger sister, Susan, especially Hank Williams' "Hey Good Looking, Whatcha' Got Cooking," her notes soaring above his whenever it was on the radio.

Of course, Mother couldn't hold me for 24 hours a day, no mortal human could do that, no matter how much they loved their baby.

"Honey, do what you have to do," the doctor explained. "But don't beat yourself up if it doesn't work out. The Lord works by his own schedule."

To be safe, Mother and her best friend, Mitzi, held me every night, all night long. She was afraid that if she went to sleep, I would suffocate, so whenever I cried, which was often, Mother and Mitzi cried with me. And whenever I slept, they took turns sleeping, so that one person would always be awake to hold me. They were a tag team hell-bent on saving my young life.

Night after night she sat with me, rocking in the dark, and singing softly to bolster my spirits as the electric fans stirred the air, moving it from one side of the room to the other. Scents of honeysuckle crept about my bedroom, day and night. Frequently, Mother's sister, Marcie, drove the sixty miles from Greenwood to Greenville, to hold me all night so that Mother and Mitzi could get some sleep.

Perhaps because of that I developed a lifelong bond with Aunt Marcie. It was like having a second mother. Though it would be inaccurate to say I can remember those terrifying bouts with whooping cough, I can recall the sense of hope I felt cradled in Mother's, Mitzi's, and Aunt Marcie's arms as an oppressive world settled in around me in the sweet-scented darkness of rain-soaked Delta nights, where unknown dangers always lurked just an arm's length away. I would not be alive today without the kindness of generous and loving women.

My first life lesson was that the world was an unfriendly place on the day you are born and only gets worse from that point forward.

WHAT AWAKENED ME in the morning was the train braking to enter the station ever so slowly, the long, drawn-out screech of metal against metal cascading lightly through the air. It seemed to take forever for the train to finally roll to a complete stop. I looked at my watch. Straight up 9 a.m. I stood and pulled my suitcase down from the rack and fell into line behind an elderly Black woman who was singing softly to herself. I turned and looked at the line behind me. There were no men in hats. A relief. I did wonder if they were smart enough to remove their hats, only to decide that they probably didn't know I was smart enough to know about the significance of their hats.

Finally I stepped off the train onto a platform, thinking *I can't believe*

I am in Chicago. I followed the other passengers because they seemed to know where they were going. After a good deal of foot shuffling, we emerged into a gigantic room that had a ceiling that must have been a mile high. The room was called Great Hall and it was truly magnificent. I walked slowly across the marble floors, everyone else walking much faster than me. I was stunned by its grandeur. Soon I was on the sidewalk outside, where everyone seemed to abruptly disperse like magic.

So there I stood on a sidewalk in downtown Chicago, clutching a small suitcase in my hand. At this time the morning before, I was having breakfast prepared by my wife in a Mississippi trailer home park. *It was only a bowl of cereal. However, it should be noted that shortly after we were married she decided to bake me a cake, but because she did not know what kind of cake I liked she baked three cakes—one chocolate, one lemon, and one vanilla.*

My appointment was not until 2 p.m. My first task was to check into a hotel. I saw one whose name I recognized, perhaps a Marriott or a Holiday Inn, and I stepped off the curb, only to hear brakes screeching and someone yelling at me to go to the corner. I chuckled, thinking *they wouldn't last two minutes in Mississippi with that rude yelling,* and I made my way to the nearest corner and crossed the street. The hotel had a brightly illuminated front with lots of glass. It looked clean and safe. I pushed open a large glass door and strode over to the reservations desk and dropped my suitcase to the floor with a thud.

"I'd like a room for tonight."

The reservations clerk shook his head and said, "Sorry, but we're all booked up. Next time you'd need to call us about a month in advance."

No one likes to be told no, especially me. I snatched up my suitcase and returned to the street. I looked in both directions. I saw some marquees that looked like they could be hotels, but I wasn't sure. There was a cab with a driver pulled over to the curb.

"What's the matter, buddy" said the cab driver. "Can't decide?"

"I just got off the train and need to find a place to stay tonight."

"Where you from?"

"Mississippi."

"Jump in. I'll take care of you."

I opened the backseat door, tossed my suitcase in and jumped inside the cab. The driver peeled away from the curb and lurched into the traffic. After a short distance he turned off the main street, then turned left, and then right, his speedy turns sending my suitcase banging into my side each time he veered in a different direction.

Finally, he turned into an alley and stopped outside a hotel that had only one small door. "Here you go," he said.

"Is this a hotel?" I asked.

"Sure—it's hard to get a room in the big hotels without a reservation. They'll take good care of you here."

I paid the driver and just stood there and watched as he drove away. The door creaked when I opened it and stepped into the hotel lobby, a room about the size of a barber shop back home. The floor was carpeted, not marble, and it had a brown, musty smell to it. I approached the reservations desk and was greeted by a dark-complexioned man with darting eyes and a bushy black moustache.

"I'd like a room," I said.

You betcha. Sign here. That'll be seven dollars."

I paid in cash, counting out seven ones.

He slid a key across the counter to me and said, "Room 303. Turn to the right after you step out of the elevator."

The elevator was tiny and whined all the way to the third floor. None of the lights on the control panel ever came on. The hallway was deserted and stone cold silent. The moment I entered the room I was blasted by a musty order that seemed to match the dark, stained carpet that was bunched in places. I tossed my suitcase on the bed and immediately went to the window and pulled the blinds. To my surprise there was no view of the Chicago skyline, just a brick, windowless wall.

Suddenly, there came a knock at the door.

Oh, no, I thought. *This can't be good.*

I opened the door and faced a Black man in his thirties wearing a severely wrinkled hotel uniform. Before speaking, he handed me a copy of the *Chicago Tribune.* It had two coffee stains on it. "This is your complimentary copy of the paper," he said, smiling broadly. His dark brown eyes radiated a dulled brightness. "That means you don't have to pay me for it."

"Thank you," I said.

"Anything else I can get you?

"I don't think so."

"I can get you a pretty girl."

"What?"

"You know, a girl to mess around with. Twenty dollars. Or if you'd like more than one, I can send up three for fifty dollars."

I'm in a whorehouse!

Recovering, I said, "I appreciate that, but I have an important meeting this afternoon and need to get some rest before I go. It's one of those life or death things, if you know what I mean."

"Yes sir," he said, saluting me before he walked away.

I closed the door, and slid the chain lock.

Then I stretched out on the bed, chuckling to myself about another hotel where I once had a weird experience. This time in Oxford.

I was only seventeen when I enrolled at Ole Miss for a summer semester my freshman year. I was assigned to the university's first high-rise dormitory for men called Kincannon Hall. My first roommate, who went by the name Billy Bobbs, was my age and a fellow refugee from the Mississippi Delta. We grew up with the same life experiences. He had a girlfriend named Ann from his hometown who enrolled at Mississippi University for Women. Once she drove over for the Ole Miss Homecoming football game against Vanderbilt. With her she brought her roommate Beverly, a knock-dead gorgeous brunette with long hair.

I fell in love instantly, something Ole Miss students do on a regular basis. We went to the game together, which Ole Miss won 21 to 7, thanks in part to star quarterback Jimmy Weatherly, someone you may recognize as the songwriter of Gladys Knight and the Pips' big hit, "Midnight Train to Georgia." After the game, we went to a party at Billy's fraternity house.

Later, I took my date back to her hotel, a somewhat seedy establishment named the Henry Hotel. Its nondescript entrance was in a downtown alleyway. Instead of a doorman, they had an empty Coke crate that propped the door open. As my date and I entered and started up the stairway (there was no elevator), we heard the desk clerk loudly clear his throat. We stopped and turned and looked at him.

"We don't allow no dating in this hotel."

"What?"

"The girl can go up, but son, you need to turn your smart ass around and hit the road."

My date and I looked at each other. Her eyes suddenly lit up, prompting a smile. Then she said, "I had a good time."

"I did, too."

We looked at each other, wondering what might have been.

"Son, I ain't just whistling Dixie. Time for you to leave."

I turned and left with a sense of defeat, uncertain if my date ever made it to the top of the stairway, and vowing to never again give the Henry Hotel my business.

Apparently, Chicago hotels had a business plan that encouraged "dating" in their rooms. I had no intention of signing on for that service, but I couldn't help but wonder how many rejections they would accept from me before sending up a guy in a pinstriped suit with a tommy gun.

Chapter 2

Chasing Bobbie Gentry

BY MID-AFTERNOON, I was standing outside the entrance to the Canadian Consulate. My heart was racing. I considered turning around and returning to Oxford, but that would have solved nothing. At least this way I had a fighting chance to live as a free man.

Following the assassination of the Rev. Martin Luther King, Ina, and I knew we had no choice but to leave America and flee to Canada. My request for a draft deferment to attend graduate school to study psychology was rejected by my draft board, which was headed up by a man from my hometown who had placed me on his enemies' list because of my support of civil rights—and because I had refused to testify against a Black teen I had known was innocent of trying to steal my lawnmower. He was a white supremacist who served as the grand dragon of the KKK and he used his authority on the draft board to demand sexual favors from anxious mothers fearful of their draft-age son's future.

My draft board also rejected my request for a deferment to serve in the Peace Corps, this after I already was accepted for overseas service. In violation of federal guidelines, it routinely refused to accept conscientious objector applications on the grounds of conscience or religion. There was no way I could go to Vietnam and slaughter women and children, as I had witnessed occurring nightly on television news as napalm, a chemical weapon that was first used with flame throwers and subsequently dropped from bombers, was used on villages mostly inhabited by women, children and old men. Certainly, I had no intention of being ordered on such a mission by a white supremacist.

Don't aim at anything you don't aim to kill, was my grandfather's advice. If I aimed a weapon, it would be to kill targets other than women and children.

I entered the building and made my way to the office, where I took a seat in the waiting room. I was dressed in a light tan, linen suit, the style at Ole Miss in those years, and wore a button-down-collar white shirt set off by a colorful necktie. Perched on my lap was the hand-tooled Mexican briefcase that had been a gift from Mother. Inside the briefcase were the papers I thought I might need if the visit progressed to the interview stage. I had made an appointment, but when I called I really didn't explain why I had an urgent need to meet with the Canadian consul general.

The secretary was middle aged, but I think she was flirting with me, or it could have just been my imagination. I already knew from the hotel that Chicago women were plentiful and available. Hell, three for fifty dollars was amazing. Almost anyone could afford that.

I didn't have to wait long. She rose from her desk and walked me to the consul general's office. He was a jovial, red-faced man with a vigorous handshake. He looked intelligent, which is to say he didn't wear a baseball cap, and he seemed to be one of those men who perpetually have a cool breeze circulating about them during the summer months.

"So, what can I do for you today?" he asked after I was seated. "You have come a long way to see me."

I paused before I spoke, weighing my words.

"I would like to request political asylum."

Ina Taylor Dickerson at age 18

"Oh," he said, somewhat taken aback. He stared at the briefcase on my lap. "That's beautiful work. Was it done in Mexico?"

"Yes sir. A gift from my mother."

"Outstanding . . . so tell me why you want political asylum. You know, there are other options. You could simply drive across the border and notify Canadian border agents that you would like to apply for landed immigrant status."

"OK, I'd like to hear more about that."

"Sure, but first I'm curious why you chose Canada??

"I have a family member there—my father's sister married a Canadian. She's from Virginia. The Blue Ridge Mountains."

"Good to know," he said, pausing a moment. "I'm wondering about the reason for your relocation."

"Yes sir," I said. "I'm against the Vietnam War."

"I see. I've been under the impression you have numerous options, such as conscientious objector status . . . or the National Guard . . . or the

Peace Corps . . . or some kind of alternative service."

"Yes, that is true in most places. Not in Mississippi. The National Guard said they didn't have any openings. I was approved for service in the Peace Corps, but my draft board would not allow me to serve. I suggested alternative service and they said no to that, too."

"What about conscientious objection?"

"I didn't apply because a friend did and he was harassed and followed by the FBI. So, I knew that was a waste of time. Why apply for something that is only going to put you on an enemies' list?"

"My, my," said the Consul General, shaking his head.

"My friend and I were both in our teens when the Freedom Riders came to our hometown to register Black residents to vote. We both voiced our opinion that they should be able to vote. After all, at that time, the population was 50 percent Black. The white 50 percent totally blocked them from voting. We thought that was wrong and said so. Because of that the police chief told my mother that if I didn't stop siding with the Blacks I would be shot. Mother was horrified."

"Did that have a bearing with the draft board?"

"At that time, our draft board member also served as the Grand Dragon for the KKK of our area. My friend and I became targets of the draft board because we supported voting rights for Blacks."

"That is despicable," said the Consul General, his already red face flashing even brighter red.

"It's even worse than that. The draft board member I told you about approached the white mothers who had draft-age sons and told them, point blank, he would spare them from the draft if the mother slept with him."

"Oh, my God."

"He approached my friend's mother and she told my mother about it. I asked Mother if he had contacted her yet and she said no, but I don't know if that was the truth. She probably wouldn't have told me if he propositioned her."

"I see—so how do you feel about the war itself?"

"I consider it illegal and immoral. The Vietnamese did not attack us. We invaded their country, siding with an artificially created regime in the South whose goal was to prevent the reunification of the South and North. Even so, if that was all it was I might could have found a way, but there is more to it than that. For the past several years, I have been an avid reader of everything published about the war and every night I watched television for news of the war. More and more I heard about war crimes against women and children."

"All very understandable," said the Consul General. "But I also suspect you may have a more personal reason."

I looked at him, wondering if he could read my thoughts. Finally, I explained "Yes sir, you are correct. If I live in Canada, they will have no reason to harass my mother."

The Consul General seemed moved by that and said he understood. Then he shifted gears and asked me how I planned to make a living in Canada after my graduation in May.

"I have a double major—one in psychology and the other in English. I figure I will look for a job related to psychology, perhaps social work— or try to get a job as a writer, perhaps at a newspaper."

I see. Have you had anything published?"

"Yes sir." Then I proceeded to tell him about my meeting the previous August with recording artist Bobbie Gentry, whose hit record, "Ode to Billie Joe," was a Number 1 record at the time, and how that meeting resulted in my first story in a magazine published by the journalism department at the University of Mississippi. As I told the story, the Consul General's eyes sparkled.

On August 5, 1967, "Ode to Billie Joe" debuted on the Hot 100; three weeks later it bumped the Beatles' "All You Need Is Love" out of Number One and prevented Diana Ross and the Supremes' "Reflections" from moving up. Bobbie was stunned by the record's success. So was Capitol Records. No one had a clue it would sell.

Bobbie Gentry on the day the author interviewed her.
Photo by Young's Studio, Houston, MS

In September, accompanied by her record producer, Kelly Gordon, Bobbie returned to Houston, Mississippi, for a homecoming celebration. By that time, everyone in the country wanted to know about Bobbie Gentry. "Ode to Billie Joe," with its mysterious reference to something being flung from a river bridge, had intrigued the nation.

I was a student at the University of Mississippi at the time and had enrolled one semester for about twelve hours of journalism. I asked if I could cover the event for the magazine and, in the process, write my first published story. I was given the assignment, but warned that one of the journalism professors also would be going in search of an interview and I wouldn't stand much of a chance against a seasoned professional like him.

"Go ahead," said the professor, smiling. "It'll be a good lesson for you."

"Thanks," I said, without the least bit of sarcasm.

A media contingent befitting a presidential candidate descended upon tiny Houston. Gentry's producer was inundated with requests for interviews. Newsweek was there. So was Time. The wire services. Who is this Bobbie Gentry, they demanded—and what's the deal with that song? Inquiring minds wanted to know.

The producer turned down all the media requests, saying Bobbie just wanted to enjoy the homecoming celebration. I was among those turned down by Gordon, and if memory serves, I was not too happy about that.

"Absolutely not—she is not going to do any interviews for you or anyone else. We've got the big boys here—Time, Newsweek, and so on—so I can't give you something I didn't give them."

Later in the day, when everyone, including Bobbie, was seated in a banquet hall, I rose from my table and approached the singer and asked for an interview. Bobbie looked me over for the longest time. She had heard the question, clearly, but something was preventing her from giving the answer Gordon had instructed her to give. I could not take my eyes off of the singer. There was a connection there neither of us understood. Finally, Bobbie nodded, the words following at a slower pace.

"OK," she said. "Meet me after the reception and we'll talk then."

Strikingly beautiful—and more attractive in person than in her photos or on television—she quickly proved that she could handle herself in an interview situation. The interview took place in a Holiday Inn room loaned to us for this purpose. A Mississippi highway patrolmen stood at attention against the wall. Others lined up next to him, including Gordon. The interview was surreal. She sat in a chair next to the bed. I sat on the bed, with her deliciously blonde female roommate curled up on the bed behind me. The roommate looked over my shoulder as I looked at my notes. Every time I turned around and looked at her, she smiled sweetly.

I asked all the obvious questions and a few that were somewhat in left field. Bobbie didn't care. Frankly, I think she was glad to finally be talking to someone about her record. There were things she wanted to say. When I ran out of questions, but didn't want the interview to end, I lobbed a desperate inquiry her way and lamely asked, 'So what's your favorite fruit?"

I regretted the question the moment I asked it, but before I could poke fun at myself Bobbie broke into a broad grin and answered, "You are hoping I will say banana, aren't you?"

I cracked up. Everyone in the room joined in the laughter.

To the producer's great relief the interview ended without Billie Joe's secret being divulged. Bobbie did admit that her songs were drawn from her own life experiences.

"I find writing easy, and I can do it almost any place," she said. "However, I prefer creating in solitude, probably because I have lived most of my life alone. I try to write wherever I am. My writing is largely autobiographical, so I find that keeping notes helps me to remember."[1]

Afterward, Bobbie and I talked a few minutes in the parking lot.

"Where do you go from here?" I asked.

"Memphis. To the airport."

"I'm going that way. Want a lift?"

She thought a second or two before saying, "Sure."

We walked over to my convertible and I opened the passenger door for her to get inside the car.

Suddenly, I heard this desperate, "no, no, no, no," and turned to see her producer running across the parking lot with an expression on his face I had never seen before or since. His eyes never met mine; they were entirely on Bobbie.

"Where are you going?" he demanded.

"Airport," she said.

"Oh, my God. No!"

He grabbed her by the hand and led her away the way you would do a child. Bobbie looked over her shoulder and smiled. The look on her face told me she never intended to go to the airport. She was in a power struggle with her producer. I thought, That'a girl!

Several years after that interview took place I was visiting my mother when the subject of the interview arose. She was a fan of Bobbie Gentry

32

and loved the song "Ode to Billie Joe."

"You know she's from Greenwood, Mississippi," I said.

"Really." She paused a minute, thinking. "I don't recall any Gentrys when we lived there."

"That's not her real name. Her real name is Streeter."

"Streeter!" she exclaimed. "You know who that was, don't you?

I shook my head.

"Roberta Streeter."

"Oh," I said, the memories flooding back to me.

I recalled playing outside with my cousin Martha. I was around five, so that would have made Martha six. Before long a little girl about my age came out of one of the other apartments and joined us. Roberta Streeter was her name. She had dark hair like me and I took to her right away. At one point, Martha went inside, leaving us alone.

In a conspiratorial tone, Roberta said, almost breathlessly, "Do you want to see something?"

I said, "Sure."

Roberta led me inside, moving quietly through the dark shadows of the house, almost tiptoeing, and without either of us saying a word, we made our way past a gauntlet of oscillating electric fans that purred with quiet efficiency, sending loose currents of cool air scooting through the house. When we entered the back bedroom, where a woman was lying on the bed, she looked up at Roberta and smiled.

"Hi, honey," she said; then she looked at me, surprised to see me in the room.

"Who's that?'

"That's Jimmy."

Roberta swept her arm out toward the woman, saying proudly, "See!"

I looked at the woman, who was cradling an infant to her breast. I had seen infants before, but I had never seen a female breast. I stared at the woman's breast, seemingly paralyzed; then I heard Roberta say, "Let's go back outside." I slowly backed out of the room speechless, as Roberta broke into one of those skipping gaits of which little girls are so fond.

Eventually, Roberta moved away from the Greenwood area. She went with her mother first to Houston, Mississippi, then to Palm Springs, California, where she attended high school. After studying music at the Los Angeles Conservatory of Music and philosophy at UCLA, she did secretarial work for a while; then she put together a song and dance team in 1966 and struck out for Las Vegas to prove herself as an entertainer.

By the time I interviewed her in August she had changed her name to Bobbie Gentry and she was the hottest singer in America, hotter even than the Beatles and that's saying a lot.

I COULD TELL THE CONSUL GENERAL was impressed with my story. We talked for a while and he said I would meet the qualifications for landed immigrant status once I entered that country.

"We could use more people like you," he added, smiling warmly.

He opened a desk drawer and removed a sheet of paper and an envelope. He thought a moment, and then he started writing. When he finished, he put down his pen and carefully folded the sheet of paper and placed it into the envelope, promptly licking the envelope to seal it. Then he handed it to me.

"When you cross over into Canada," he said, "Give this to the officer in charge at the border."

I put the letter in my briefcase and he rose from behind his desk. As we stood facing each other, he gave me a hearty handshake and said he hoped I had a safe journey back to Mississippi. What a high that was! I left thinking, *I hope to God all Canadians are like him.*

Moments like that can stay with you forever.

When I returned to the hotel, my "newspaper" man greeted me with a grin and a reminder that his was a full service hotel. I called Ina as soon as I was in my room. My optimism about my interview was contagious. Soon she was jumping up and down in our mobile home. *Free at last, free at last. Finally we would be free at last to live our lives in freedom.*

Suddenly, there was a hard knock at the door.

"Excuse me—there is someone at the door."

I placed the phone on the nightstand and went to the door and opened it. There stood a young girl in pigtails. She reached out with a rose. "You can have anything you want for twenty dollars."

I took the rose and reached into my pocket and pulled out two dollars and gave it to her. "Is that OK?" I said.

She took the money, looked at it with disdain and walked away.

"Who was it?" asked Ina when I returned to the phone.

"Oh, just some girl selling flowers."

* * *

The train ride back to Mississippi was uneventful. When the train pulled into the Batesville station at 3 a.m. it was drizzling soft rain. The train stopped and dropped me off, the only passenger to depart, and headed south to New Orleans. I stood there on the platform and watched it pull away. The parking lot was empty but for my Mustang. I looked around. There were no other cars in sight.

I got home about 3:30 A.M. Ina was standing in the doorway, her slender curves framed by the backlight. She was looking for me, tears streaming down her pretty face while holding our calico cat Hadley, named after Ernest Hemingway's first wife. I parked the car and started running toward her, clutching the letter in my hand as I ran in the rain.

I kissed the tears away and we stayed up all night talking, our eyes occasionally wandering to the dresser where the mysterious letter was propped against a clock. We couldn't hear it ticking, but we knew that the second hand was moving with blind urgency.

We possessed everything we needed for the boldest adventure of our young lives each other, rock 'n' roll, and two V-8 Mustangs. She was eighteen. I was twenty-one. Soon we would leave not just Mississippi, the only place either of us had ever lived, but the United States of America, for the first time, ever.

**Tennessee National Guard round up Black Memphians
after the assassination of Martin Luther King, Jr.
Photo courtesy Mississippi Valley Collection
University of Memphis**

Chapter 3

Brave New World

ONCE THE SEMESTER ENDED, we loaded up our two cars and headed for the Mississippi Delta. With us was our calico cat, Hadley, who rode in the car with me, something I am certain she did not appreciate. Once I came home from class and she leaped onto my shoulders, clawing and biting my flesh with wild abandon.

Other times I have awakened at night to see her creeping toward me from the foot of the bed, her demonic eyes glowing in the dark. I've always heard that calico cats have a high incidence of mental illness. This female cat was a raging psycho and then some.

Because I elected to not attend graduation ceremonies, the university agreed to send my diploma to my mother's address. I felt a deep sadness as we drove deeper and deeper into the sun-bleached Delta, a carpet of cotton plants rolling out as far as the eye could see, knowing we may never see any of this countryside again. Growing up in the Delta, I could not go in any direction without slicing through two-century-old cotton fields. Depending on the season, the fields were virginal white, deep green, or barren brown. I wondered what it would be like to drive on highways on which cotton did not grow on either side of the road. We had absolutely no idea what grew on either side of the highways in Canada.

37

Waiting for my diploma, we had endless conversations about THE LETTER. Should we open it to see what he had written? The intrigue and uncertainty of it was killing us. We held the envelope up to the light, searching for clues. We saw nothing. We wondered if we could steam it open the way they do in the movies and reseal it in such a way that no one would be able to detect our intrusion. But no, that was too risky. What if we couldn't trust the Consul General and he wrote something that blocked our entry into Canada? On the other hand, there was the possibility he had written something very favorable. If so, it would make our entry into Canada so much better.

Finally, we decided to trust our instincts and not open the letter. It took forever for my diploma to arrive. Mother was weepy the entire time. She was not singing "You Are My Sunshine" during that time, at least not in my presence, but clearly she was feeling the sentiments of the song. Once the diploma arrived, we learned we would not be leaving in two cars. Ina's mother wanted to keep Ina's car in the United States. So, before leaving, we took everything out of both cars and chose what things we could take in one car. The day we left branded me with an indelible memory of the tearful anguish on Mother's face as she half hugged us, half pushed us out the door, weeping uncontrollably. Saying goodbye is so hard, especially if you think it is forever.

The first day on the road we drove as far as Crawfordsville, Indiana, where we spotted a motel that resembled, a little too much to be honest, the infamous Bates Motel in *Psycho*. There we spent the night, awaking whenever a car pulled into the parking lot and a car door opened and slammed shut. Neither of us slept that night. The next morning we got an early start, taking secondary roads in case someone was looking for us.

After we crossed the border from Michigan, entering Sarnia, Ontario, on June 3, 1968, I pulled over as requested. A border guard walked up to our car and I asked to speak to the agent in charge. He turned around without comment and went into the building. Moments later, an older man, who walked with rigid authority, approached our car.

"What can I do for you?" he asked.

"I have something for you," I said, handing him the letter.

"What's this?" he asked, surprised.

"I don't know."

"Who's it from?"

"The Consul General in Chicago."

"Oh … very unusual."

He opened the letter, read it and then re-folded it and put it back in the envelope, creating a wall of silence that lasted at least thirty seconds. He leaned over and looked inside at Ina and smiled. Then he stood up and said, "So, you would like to apply for landed immigrant status?"

"Yes sir."

"Both of you?"

"Yes sir."

"I'll get the paperwork for you." With that he turned and went back inside the building, returning minutes later with some papers and a clipboard. "I'll come back in a few minutes and pick those papers up."

It didn't take long to fill out the forms. We merely stated that we had not come to Canada as visitors, but as immigrants who wished to establish domicile. When the agent in charge returned he explained that landed immigrant status meant we could not vote in Canadian elections, but we would qualify for government health insurance.

"If after five years you would like to become Canadian citizens you can request the paperwork from the Department of Immigration," he explained. "Meanwhile, as landed immigrants you are free to go wherever you like. There is no requirement for you to check in with the government for any reason. Any questions?'

"No sir."

"In that case, you are good to go. Welcome to Canada."

"Oh," I said. "Don't you want to go through our car?"

"No need for that."

"I've got a shotgun and pistol that belonged to my father."

He laughed.

"You are allowed to have guns in Canada. Good luck to you, eh?"

I can't imagine what was in the letter. Whatever it was, it worked to our advantage. Thank God for the kindness of strangers.

Not knowing exactly where to go, we drove to Toronto and checked into a motel with a view of Lake Ontario. I think we chose it because we saw a Faulkner's Insurance sign nearby and considered that a welcoming omen. We paid in advance for a week's lodging at the motel and promptly purchased State Farm car insurance from Mr. Faulkner himself.

"I am a fan of yours," I said tongue in cheek.

"Well, thank you," he said, not as baffled as I figured he would be. "I was the top policy man for Toronto last year."

The first day or two we were at the motel—it is hard to pinpoint individual days when you are on the run—we awoke one morning and turned on television. To our horror we saw that Robert Kennedy had been assassinated. We were devastated. I had attended a speech Kennedy delivered at Ole Miss in 1966 and I was greatly impressed by him as a person and by the goals he expressed for America. Watching the news coverage, we felt guilt, anger, and a spiraling sensation of powerlessness. It was a terrible way in which to begin a new life.

THAT FIRST WEEK IN TORONTO I called my father's sister, Aunt Claudia, who had married a French Canadian named Vince Sirois. They invited us to their home for dinner. Vince was vice president for logistics for Exxon Canada. After dinner that night, he took us to his luxurious downtown office and showed us around. The office was on the top floor of one of the city's tallest buildings and the view of the city was very impressive, especially at night.

Despite the friendliness of the visit, it was somewhat strained because before leaving Mississippi we had asked if they would be our sponsors in Canada. They declined because they feared it would reflect badly on Vince as an Exxon Canada executive. We never let on we were bothered by their rejection. My father's family was from the Blue Ridge Mountains of Virginia, where years later the popular television show "The Waltons" was set. My aunt not helping us would have been viewed as an outrage by the Waltons. We were not outraged, just disappointed. I encountered Aunt Claudia twenty years later at a family reunion in Virginia. We did not speak and I noticed that my favorite uncle shied away from his sister while I was at the gathering as a show of support for his brother's son.

We lived in Toronto for most of the summer. It was the biggest city either of us had ever seen. That first week we rented a basement apartment in the home of Nazi Holocaust survivors. The home was in Downsview, a middle-class suburb with a large Jewish population. The Jewish family we lived with cooked knishes for us, which neither of us had ever had, and recommended even more new foods at the local grocery, items such as wax beans, which resembled albino green beans, and acorn squash, which didn't resemble any other squash we had ever seen. Our Jewish hosts said they had tried to enter the U.S., but were told there was a limit on the number of Jews they could admit. Why would Americans send their sons to fight the Nazis, they wondered aloud, but turn away the Jewish victims of Nazi persecution? We explained America had both a dark and an enlightened side, and the two had been at odds ever since the Civil War.

We were stunned at how friendly everyone was once they found out we were Americans. I would have thought our Southern accents would have instantly branded us as Americans, but that was not the case. As a matter of fact, I went to a post office to rent a postal box and when the clerk heard me speak, he said, "You must be from the Old Country." I had no idea what he meant by that and readily nodded yes.

"I thought so," was his response.

THE CANADA DAYS! They seem so very distant now, but in 1968 I was an American expatriate living in Toronto. How I loved that city! The bold expansiveness of it. How it took my breath away to stand in the valley of such splendid architecture! The women in the South were beautiful, but the women of Toronto were beautiful in a more sophisticated way. I did not see a single pickup truck with a gun rack, or a drooling redneck wearing a baseball cap the entire summer we spent in the city.

June 1968 was an exciting and vibrant time to be living in Toronto. Just as the preceding April had been a pivotal point in American history, due to the assassinations of Martin Luther King and then later Robert Kennedy, it was a pivotal time in Canadian politics. Prime Minister Pearson announced his intention to step down as leader of the Liberal Party, which meant he would be retiring as prime minister. Newcomer Pierre Trudeau entered the race for the top Liberal leadership position. After barely winning the race, he called for an election on June 25.

You might say Pierre Trudeau was the Mick Jagger of Canadian politics. He was forty-nine and handsome, with charisma in abundance. An intellectual, he avoided the politics of social appeasement and pursued hot-button progressive issues. Newspaper headline writers described public excitement over Trudeau as "Trudeaumania," primarily because of the throngs of young people who flocked to his public appearances. He was a "rock star," and on top of that he was single, making him Canada's most eligible bachelor.

Print and television media frequently called Trudeau a "swinging bachelor" because of his active dating life. One of his most high-profile relationships was with actress and recording star Barbra Streisand. Weary of public criticisms of his private life, his third year in office he married Margaret Sinclair, who was twenty-nine years his junior. He was initially attracted to her because of her engaging "flower child" approach to life. He would come to understand that it was but a short distance from "flower child" to "wild child." Unknown to Pierre when they married, Margaret had a bipolar disorder and it greatly affected her moods and her behavior. In the 1970s, she had an affair with U.S. Senator Ted Kennedy, and was reported at one time to be involved with Mick Jagger. Despite her unpredictable behavior, they didn't divorce until April 1984.

With Trudeau heading up the Canadian government there was

excitement in the air throughout 1968. Of great interest to me was his position on American war resisters relocating in Canada. It might be useful here to explain the differences between a war resister and a draft dodger. In those days, a war resister was someone who opposed the war in Vietnam for religious or moral reasons and either fled the country or went to prison. A draft dodger was someone who dodged the draft by unscrupulously obtaining a deferment from the draft, whether by bribery or deceit. President Donald Trump was a draft dodger. I was a war resister who readily supplied my draft board with my Canadian address. I wasn't trying to dodge anything. I just refused to participate in a war in which the killing of women and children was commonplace. There was much about life that I did not know at the age of twenty-two. What I knew with absolute certainty was that I was killing no one on behalf of a KKK Grand Dragon.

What especially endeared Prime Minister Trudeau to me was his willingness to provide a safe haven for war resisters in Canada. In an interview with the *United Church Observer*, he said: "Those who make the conscientious judgment that they must not participate in this war and who become draft dodgers have my complete sympathy, and indeed our political approach has been to give them access to Canada."

On day one, inspired by the imagery of a political rock star holding the door open for me, I got busy right away looking for employment. I went in two directions. I sent out letters to various Ontario Children's Aid Societies inquiring about work as a social worker, my qualifications based on my psychology degree—and I sent out letters to newspapers and book publishers. I told the latter that I hadn't written a book, but planned to do so in the near future.

To my surprise, I heard from Jonathan Lovat Dickson, one of the executives at Longmans Canada, a prestigious book publisher. He invited me to drop by his office, which I did. Dickson and another editor showed me around the office and then we sat down to talk about writing. They didn't have any editor positions for someone who had never edited anything in his life. But they were impressed with my story about Bobbie

Gentry and encouraged me to write about my new experiences in Canada.

We stayed in touch for several years, talking shop and exchanging ideas, but I never got around to publishing anything with Longmans. Still, it was a magnificent start and introduced me to the openness and generosity of the Canadian people, qualities that would surprise me time and time again. My overtures to the city's two main newspapers were mostly ignored, but in time I landed a job at the *Toronto Star* as a book critic. Ernest Hemingway had worked for the same newspaper as a European correspondent. My first review for them was of Budd Schulberg's *The Four Seasons of Success*. The review, which was my second published work, and the first for which I received a check, began:

The Four Seasons of Success is a revealing collection of anecdotal sketches by novelist Budd Schulberg about his sometimes fleeting, sometimes solid friendships with such writers as Scott Fitzgerald, Nathanael West, Thomas Heggen, Sinclair Lewis, William Saroyan, and John Steinbeck. Bound together by the recurring themes of the disastrous effects of success American-style, the six sketches show how each were affected, and sometimes destroyed, by the success-failure syndrome of the Great American Literary scramble.

Reaction to that review quickly led to others, beginning with Louis Nizer's *The Implosion Conspiracy*, and Mohamed Heikal's *The Cairo Documents*. That, in time, led to editorial writing opportunities at a smaller newspaper and books to review for the *Baltimore Sun*. My first book to review for the *Sun* was Joe Eszterhas's *Charlie Simpson's Apocalypse*. He went on to become a superstar screenwriter in Hollywood, the writer of the Academy Award nominated film *Basic Instinct,* and author of the best-selling book *American Rhapsody*. As fate would have it, our paths crossed some twenty years later when he generously sent me a recipe for a cookbook I was writing entitled *Last Suppers* and then again in 2001 when he wrote an endorsement of my book, *Colonel Tom Parker: The Curious*

Life of Elvis Presley's Eccentric Manager.

* * *

One sunny day I took a long walk downtown. I hadn't walked for very long when I came across a legless man at the street corner. He had stubs for legs and well-worn leather pads on the stubs. As I approached, I saw him slug a man in the groin with his knotty fist, hard enough to knock the man's hat off his head, and then chase him up the street, bouncing up and down on his stubs as his victim ran for his life. The vet could move pretty fast for a man with no legs.

I stopped a man on the street to ask a question.

"What's that all about?" I asked.

"Him? He's a pissed off veteran. He's been doing that for years. The police just leave him alone. Good luck."

As I approached the man he glared at me.

I stopped on the corner, waiting for the light to change. I smiled and nonchalantly said, "How you doing?"

The man's grizzled face went from noncommittal to blistering rage before he lunged for me. I started running across the street, against the light, causing a car to swerve to avoid hitting me. Right behind me was the legless man, his leather-padded stubs popping against the pavement. His face swelled into pure rage. Even though I was not within range, he swung his arms at me, throwing wild air punches that never landed.

There were others on the sidewalk walking toward me, but they seemed unconcerned. They smiled and continued walking in the direction of the legless man, and he paid no attention to them as they passed. Somehow they had acquired immunity to his madness. How incongruous it was for me to be running for my life from a man with no legs, weaving in and out of the stylishly dressed pedestrians on the busy sidewalk.

After running about two blocks with the man pursuing me like an out-of-control lawn mower intent on cutting my legs down to nubs, I turned around and saw the legless man sitting on a street corner, leaned into a light post, panting. I waved goodbye and continued walking.

The author with his the V-8 Mustang he drove to Canada

Chapter 4

The 1000 Islands Beckon

AFTER A TWO-AND-A-HALF MONTH job search for positions related to my psychology degree, I received a letter from the Children's Aid Society in Brockville, Ontario, informing me that they had a job opening. They enclosed an application and invited me to submit it for consideration. Within a week, I was invited to Brockville for an interview. It was a city of about 20,000 people located east of Toronto on the banks of the scenic St. Lawrence River, where the city serves as the gateway to the 1000 Islands tourist region. The river, which is crystal clear for most of the year, is recognized as the international boundary between Canada and the United States.

I arrived early for the interview and took a spin around town to get a feel for the place. I realized, just from the architecture, that it was a very old town, with stately homes built in Classical Revival, Gothic Revival, and Georgian styles with plentiful gables, dormer windows, and two-story bay windows. I did not discover until much later that it is one of the oldest settlements in Ontario, originally populated by British subjects who fled the American Revolution, fearful for their safety if they remained in the Colonies. I felt as if I had driven my car into a different century and parked in the Twilight Zone, where I expected to hear Rod Serling's seductively resonant voice introducing me to the townspeople.

I reveled in the quaintness of the main street, filled as it was with three and four story buildings, many with dates on the facades going back to the 1890s. North of the main street were tree-lined streets filled with old houses, many of them quite large and imposing in their turn-of-the-century architecture. The apartment buildings, car dealerships and industries were even further north. I felt oddly comfortable there, but it took years to figure out why. I grew up in one of the most conservative areas of the South. Brockville was one of the most conservative areas in Canada. The town felt like a well-worn shoe, despite the fact that the two conservatisms were radically different. In Mississippi being conservative meant being racist. In Brockville, conservatism was based on economics and a British/Irish heritage and had nothing to do with race. Indeed, I would soon learn that the president of the local Children's Aid Society was a Black man, in fact the only Black man who lived in the town.

I parked on the street outside the offices of the Children's Aid Society, which was located about a block from the St. Lawrence River. Before going inside, I strolled down to the river. Across the water was New York. It was an odd feeling to stand in Canada, where I was protected, and gaze into New York, where I would soon be wanted by the law. I couldn't see much from where I stood. Just a solid line of trees.

I returned to the building and entered the office, encountering a receptionist who greeted me warmly. She called the office of my interviewer to let him know I was there. Within minutes, Reg Barrett emerged into the waiting room, offered his hand for a handshake, and identified himself as the staff supervisor. He was immaculately dressed in an expensive looking suit that was set off with a brightly colored necktie. I wore a beige linen suit of the type you see men wearing in all the movies about the South and a bright red necktie given to me by my grandfather. I was dressed to play the role of Atticus Finch in *To Kill a Mockingbird*.

Reg explained the mission of the agency and told me the job opening was for the position of "home finder," which meant the person in charge of interviewing and approving foster parent applicants. As a son who grew up without a father in the home, finding homes for children in need of homes seemed a perfect fit. In the year 1968, bachelor and master degrees in social work were uncommon. My bachelor degree in psychology was a good fit and entitled me to be licensed by the Ontario government as a qualified social worker. Reg asked about my background, my marital status—I didn't tell him my wife was only nineteen—and my views on parenting. The only shocking question he asked was the final one, "When can you start work?"

Driving back to Toronto, I marveled at the good vibes I had received in Brockville. I had entered that quaint village on the river with no job experience, outside of rock 'n' roll, working in my grandfather's store, and working one summer for the highway department, and I had left with a job offer, a pension plan and free medical care. All of a sudden Canada looked like the Promised Land—a place we could live free and follow our dreams. To my amazement, Reg never asked why we moved to Canada. He didn't have to. The answer was obvious and on television news every evening.

Within the week, Ina and I were in Brockville, looking for a place to live. Luckily, we found an upstairs, three-bedroom duplex apartment in a stately old home at 40 Pine Street, about two blocks from the river. You couldn't see the river from our apartment because of the trees, but you could if you stood on the street corner. Our immediate problem was that our furniture, meager as it was, was still in the States. It would possibly take a month to arrive. Luckily our landlord owned a downtown hotel and loaned us a couple of hotel mattresses to sleep on.

There we were 1,100 miles from home, neither of us having lived anyplace other than Mississippi, potential fugitives trying to blend into a foreign culture that so far had embraced us with open arms. We had cooking utensils we had brought with us, but little else. On my first day of work I left behind a wife who had no place to sit but on one of the mattresses loaned to us—no radio, no television, no telephone. We had only one car, so she had no transportation but her feet.

49

Thankfully, we were only two blocks from Main Street That allowed her to walk downtown to shop for items we needed, at least items that could be carried back home. However, when you are nineteen and bursting with energy, carrying a couple of packages is no big deal.

My first few days at work were spent in orientation. At the end of the week I was asked to do my first interview for my "home study," a written report that analyzed the couples' relationship, their sex life, family relationships, their work history, their attitudes on parenting and their health history. The couple who were applying for foster children were in their mid-twenties. I was twenty-two. For me, it was all about asking questions and writing down their answers. At the end of the interview, I was in awe that I had been handed so much responsibility.

On Friday, at the end of that first week in Brockville, Ina and I ate dinner while sitting on our mattresses in our otherwise bare bedroom, enjoying a home cooked meal she had prepared. We sipped on iced tea and gazed at our newly installed telephone. Life was sweet!

As we sat there in introspective silence, enjoying the moment in our first home that did not have wheels beneath it, I could not help but think how lucky I was to have her there with me. The silence of two people is so very different from the silence of one.

EACH DAY BROUGHT exciting new discoveries about our new homeland. The three television networks that dominated television viewing in the U.S. were available to Canadian audiences. We watched NBC, CBS and ABC news programing, along with the dramas and comedies we enjoyed in the U.S., but it was Canadian television, CBC and CTV, that most often engaged us. We were hungry for Canadian news so that we could better understand the country and its people. We subscribed to the local newspaper, the *Recorder and Times*, along with both Toronto newspapers, the *Toronto Star* and the *Globe and Mail*. We loved the cleverly written dramas that appeared on CBC television and immersed ourselves in discovering things we didn't know about Canadian culture.

Shortly after our furniture and books arrived from the States, we had our first visitors. One evening, after hearing an unexpected knock on the door, I walked down the stairs to the entrance and opened the door. Standing before me were two men, probably in their late twenties, dressed in business suits. They quickly introduced themselves as members of the Royal Canadian Mounted Police, Mounties for short. I invited them in and they followed me up the stairway. Ina was standing at the top of the stairs, looking somewhat fearful.

"Ina, these men are Mounties. They would like to talk to us."

She led the way into our newly furnished living room. I sat on the couch next to Ina and they sat in chairs across the room, facing us.

"We're sorry to bother you," said one of the officers. "But we are required to visit you and ask if it is your intention to remain in Canada."

"Yes," I answered.

"If you stay more than six months, you will need to apply for status as landed immigrants."

"Already have," answered Ina.

I handed our port-of-entry identity cards to one of the men.

"We applied when we entered Canada back in June," I said.

The man I handed the cards to examined them and smiled and then handed them to the other man for inspection. He looked them over and stood to hand them back to me. The other man stood and said, "Welcome to Canada. Let us know if there is anything we can do to help you."

We all shook hands and I escorted them back down the stairs and said goodbye to them. When I returned to the living room Ina was standing at the window, looking out into the street. She turned and said, "They were nice, weren't they?"

"They were," I answered. "And they didn't even ask about our reason for being here."

Ina shrugged. "I guess they liked us."

* * *

In the early 1970s, after we had been there a while, Royal Canadian Mounties contacted one of my co-workers, David Rice, to inform him they had received intelligence that an American black ops team across the river in New York had plans to enter Canada for the purpose of abducting me and returning me to the States.

Without informing me of the threat, Rice and other townspeople, including off-duty Mounties and custom agents, kept a clandestine watch on our house so that they could repel the abduction. I was never told of the threat, even after it evaporated, and I did not learn of this high drama for another forty years, when my friend and his wife, Debra, visited me in Mississippi. I was stunned to hear the story.

If I had gone for a nighttime walk during that time, as I often did— and spotted cars filled with men, some with baseball bats and shotguns— I naturally would have assumed the bats and guns were meant to injure me, not protect me. It was such a *Canadian* thing to do: To do the right thing, quietly, without appreciation, because they felt an obligation to protect a man who protected their children. It was the Canadian way.

David waited decades to tell me about the good-hearted Mounties and custom agents until they had retired or passed away so that they would not get in trouble with higher-ups who might be tempted to prosecute them for their kindness to me and my family, especially since it involved sharing classified information with David.

I had overseen adoptions for Mounties, and I had responded to calls from law enforcement officers on a regular basis at all hours of the night, but I had no idea they were keeping tabs. It was my job to treat them fairly and with respect. They must have figured it was their job to protect me and my family from harm. For that I will be eternally grateful.

In contrast to our positive experiences in Canada, we were horrified in 1970 by the student killings at Kent State University by National Guardsmen. The students were unarmed. They were simply expressing their right to protest America's involvement in the Vietnam War. An honor student at Kent State, Allison Krause was shot in the chest and killed by a trigger-happy National Guardsman while protesting the invasion of Cambodia. I wrote a letter of condolence to her family and received a reply from the woman's mother, Doris Krause, who wrote, "How sad to have to give up one's homeland because of such differences in beliefs. I do not recognize the world any longer. It has changed beyond all nightmares."

We cried when we read her letter.

A month or two after our initial encounter with the Mounties, I received an induction notice, ordering me to report to a U.S. Marine Corps base in Washington State. In a letter to my draft board, I politely declined the invitation, but re-stated my willingness to report for any alternative service they could arrange that did not include killing innocent civilians. They never wrote me back. That did not surprise me. Klansmen, regardless of their government rank, are not known for their writing skills.

Stories of Canadian compassion and support began to emerge every few days in newspaper and television stories. Prime Minister Trudeau solidified his position on American war resisters in 1972 after a delegation of American Mennonite leaders travelled to Ottawa to meet with him about war resisters. Before they left, they presented Trudeau with a written brief on the subject. Later, after reading the brief, Trudeau spoke to the Mennonites again and explained that the views they expressed were "close to [his] heart." When we heard statements like that our hearts soared.

In early 1970, Ina and I returned to Toronto to attend the Canadian production of the rock musical *Hair*. It was a sold-out performance with the biggest advance sale of any show ever in Toronto. One of the stars of the show was Gale Garnett, who had immigrated to Canada with her parents from New Zealand by way of the United Kingdom. In 1965 she won a Grammy in the United States for her 1964 smash hit "We'll Sing in the Sunshine" which was a Number One hit on both the Cashbox and Billboard charts. She was very impressive in *Hair* and Ina and I left the Royal Alexandra Theatre thrilled with the creative energy that permeated Canadian society at almost every level.

That evening we went out to dinner and afterward went to a Yonge

Street bar to listen to a blues band. During one of the intermissions, I invited the singer, an African American, to sit with us for a drink. I was particularly interested in talking to him about a song he sang titled "Hi-Healed Sneakers," recorded by Tommy Tucker. Three or four years earlier, my Ole Miss band had backed Tommy Tucker at Memphis's Club Flamingo, where I played the same B-3 organ that Booker T. Jones of Booker T. and the MGs used while working out the riffs of their hit instrumental "Green Onions."

Not long after we returned to Brockville, I got to work on my first teleplay, inspired by our trip to Toronto. I was a big fan of the thirty and sixty minute dramas on CBC, so I set out to write a thirty-minute teleplay that would target CBC. The story was about an ambulance driver and a medical attendant who were in the process of transporting an elderly man from the north Canadian bush to a Toronto hospital. At one point, they stop to get gas and eat dinner, but before they go inside they check out their patient who they found to be sleeping soundly. After one too many beers, they go into a strip club next door to the restaurant. After even more beer, the driver takes one of the dancers outside to have sex with her in the back of the ambulance. Those plans fall apart when the driver discovers the old man has died. From that point on their journey becomes a most unusual road story that sees the old man suddenly come back to life at a most inopportune time.

In April 1971 I sent the script to no one in particular at CBC. I received a response from the supervisor of the national script department, acknowledging receipt of the teleplay. A few weeks later, I received a letter from Phyllis Ashton, an editor at the CBC script department informing me that she had been unable to place the teleplay with any of their producers. However, she ended her letter with the following invitation, "If you are in Toronto at any time we should be happy to discuss your writing with you, if you would be good enough to telephone or write for an appointment."

I didn't want to seem too eager, so I let a month go by before contacting her for an appointment. Then I boarded a train to Toronto. Entering the sacrosanct CBC script offices was a pretty heady experience for me. I didn't have to wait long before being escorted to Ms. Ashton's office. She was dressed in black and had a somewhat grim countenance. We had a very amiable and encouraging meeting during which she made suggestions on how to improve my teleplay. She also gave me the name of an agent she felt I should contact about representation.

Once I returned to Brockville, I reached out to the literary agent, but I was advised he was no longer taking on new clients. I decided to put the teleplay aside for a few months so that I could finish my first novel, *Come Slowly Eden.* I queried several U.S. publishers about reading the manuscript. Most, such as Simon & Schuster and Putnam, replied they would not read it unless it was submitted by a literary agent. I contacted New York literary agent Howard Moorepark, who represented the mystery writer known as Ellery Queen, and he responded: "I should be glad to read the complete novel. Let me know to whom it has been submitted and I am curious to know which publishers declined to read it because it was not submitted by an agent? . . . Publishers are always hopeful, like agents and authors. The trouble is that many things get read by some little neophyte fresh from Vassar or Smith whose knowledge of literature is academic and whose knowledge of history and life is minuscule."

I responded and a month or so later Moorepark wrote: "I read *Come Slowly, Eden,* and I'll be glad to see what I can do with it."

With my novel now in the pipeline, I returned to the teleplay of "The Graveyard." I submitted it to Ms. Ashton at the end of December 1971. Three months later, I received a response from her. "We sent your second version to one of our television producers but it was turned down . . . Please keep in touch and let us know how you are getting on."

Because I couldn't get the storyline out of my mind, I wrote a short story version of "The Graveyard." It was accepted for publication by the *Cimarron Review,* a literary publication published by Oklahoma State University; it was published in July 1973.

ON THE DAY my son, Jonathan, was born there came a heavy snow, so much that I was unable to drive to the hospital. I walked through eighteen inches of new snow, with below-zero winds stinging my face. The doctor was in Ina's room when I arrived. Her eyes were closed and he motioned for me to step outside in the hallway so that we could talk.

"Her blood pressure went very high," he explained, shaking his head. "I thought we were going to lose her."

"What's wrong?" I asked, feeling a surging level of impending loss I had not experienced in many years.

"She has toxemia," he said.

"What's that?"

"Her pregnancy created toxins that got into her bloodstream and poisoned her."

"Is she going to be all right?"

"I think so, but you can thank God for that."

I sat with her until she awakened. She looked at me, smiled, and said, "Good morning," although it was late in the afternoon. I didn't quibble.

"How are you feeling?"

"I've got a pretty bad headache. How is Jonathan?"

"They tell me he is doing just fine."

"That's good," she said, nodding off to sleep.

As soon as Ina was able to go home, the three of us settled into our new, two-bedroom apartment. Not knowing exactly what to have for her at home, I bought her a ten-pound wheel of cheddar cheese. Not such a good idea as it turned out. I have no idea what I was thinking. Everyone loves cheese, don't they?

On his first night at home, Jonathan cried all night. On the second, third and fourth nights he also cried all night, his cries sometimes escalating into blood-curdling screams. After about two weeks of that, we took him in to see the doctor. He examined him and said he was just fine, not to worry. He said it was important for us not to pick him up when he screamed as it would set a bad precedent. We took him to a specialist who said his problem was caused by a painful hernia. He underwent surgery and the crying stopped. The physical pain went away quickly, but the emotional pain lingered for years, well into adulthood.

AS A SOCIAL WORKER IN CANADA, my weekdays were spent interviewing couples who had applied to be foster parents or who wanted to adopt an infant (infant adoptions were added to my caseload). At that time, single individuals were not allowed to adopt or keep foster children. I was only twenty-two, but I had the lives of hundreds of children in my hands. In retrospect, I am amazed that they gave me—or any other twenty-two year old—that responsibility. If my assessments of individuals and marriages were not accurate, children could be abused or raised in families destined for divorce, thus adding more pain to the children's lives.

Although my weekdays all had a nine-to-five sameness to them, my weekends, on those occasions when I was on call, were filled with the unexpected. Once I received a weekend call at 2 a.m. from the provincial police who said they needed my assistance for a possible hostage situation. I was a bit groggy after being awakened by the telephone.

"What did you say?" I asked.

"It's a possible hostage situation."

"Are you sure you have the right number?"

"I'm sure."

He went on to explain that the grandfather of two boys, seven and eight, had taken them from their mother's home and refused to return them. His son and the children's mother had recently divorced and he did not feel she provided a suitable home for the boys.

The mother called the provincial police, who visited the grandfather's home to investigate. He refused to open the door and told them to get off his property. Under Canadian law, specifically the Child Welfare Act, the only individuals who could enter a home without a warrant were social workers who worked for the province. The police knew they would never get a warrant in this situation, especially at that time of the night, so they called me and gave me directions to the house where the children were being held. I quickly dressed and told my wife goodbye, her only words being, "What? What do you mean hostage situation? What did you say?"

When I arrived at the two-story house, located in a rural area in which there were no other houses in sight, I found a half dozen police cars, parked in such a way as to make a circle around the house. All had their headlights and spotlights shining on the house.

I was greeted by the officer in charge, who apologized for awakening me. "We know this fellow," he explained. "If we had gone in with a warrant, knocking in the door, there would have been a gunfight. He's hot tempered. We figured you might could de-escalate the situation and get the boys out without problems."

"I'll do what I can," I answered, now fully awake.

I was never much for public prayer, but I was praying like crazy inside my head because no one had ever taught me how to de-escalate a potential gunfight. I would have to make it up as I went along. What I learned from the experience is that if you give a person in crisis credit for what they have done right and give them hope for what they have done wrong, they will de-escalate by choice.

"If there's a problem, we are authorized to enter the house to protect you," said a grateful law enforcement officer.

As it turned out, I was a pretty good de-escalator and the situation was resolved and I returned home in one piece. Who knew social work packed such an adrenalin rush. I know what you are thinking. No, I was not packing heat when I entered the house. Yes, I was thinking that a cool song title for the event would be "The De-Escalation Blues!"

IN MID-1974, when the U.S. Congress was in the process of impeaching President Richard Nixon, the procedure became confusing to Canadians. What did all this talk of impeachment mean? A.C. Runciman, the managing editor of the Brockville *Recorder and Times*, one of the most conservative newspapers in Ontario, asked me to write an unsigned editorial explaining the process and taking a position suitable for a Canadian newspaper.

I wrote an editorial that ran under the headline, "Nixon may have miscalculated Senate support." The editorial explained that Nixon had accepted his inevitable impeachment in the House of Representatives but felt that the conservative Senate would not convict him if he was able to maintain tight control of a large block of conservative Republicans and Southern Democrats. Like his 'secret plan' to end the war in Vietnam, this not so secret plan to remain in office was also based on political manipulation.[2] To escape conviction, Nixon counted heavily on Senator James O. Eastland of Mississippi, to vote with the Republicans. Nixon did not resign until he realized that Eastland, a Democrat who was chairman of the powerful Senate Judiciary Committee, would not risk losing his chairmanship, a position that brought the senator prestige, power and wealth, by voting for Nixon's acquittal in the Senate.

The Recorder and Times thus became the first newspaper in Canada to forecast Nixon's demise. The editorial was unsigned and thus represented the viewpoint of the newspaper, and helped turn the tide against Nixon among Canadians. There was no deception by the newspaper. The editor shared my views, and published it as the newspaper's opinion because he agreed with what I wrote.

I grew up less than twenty miles from Eastland's Delta plantation and knew the planter would never risk losing his chairmanship by going against fellow Democrats, who year after year elected him to that important position. I knew Eastland was only out for himself. He was as corrupt as a politician could be. How do I know? My mother and grandfather once met with Eastland to see if there was anything he could do to bring me home. Eastland said it was doable, but it would cost them a lot of money. In other words, he solicited a bribe. Mother and grandfather told him to go to hell. Driving home from that meeting, my mother heard her father curse for the first time in her life.

"That sorry son-of-a-bitch," he said, fuming with anger.

Mother had much the same thoughts, but she sat quietly, allowing her father to vent his anger.

* * *

After Nixon resigned and Gerald Ford became president, Ford announced an "earned re-entry" program for war resisters who would perform alternate service. Most war resisters in Canada rejected the offer, but Ina and I had a spirited discussion about whether to return to the States under those terms. Ina didn't want to return. She was very much against it. But Ford's offer was what I had told the draft board all along I would do if given the opportunity. I would look insincere if I didn't. Besides, my grandfather was getting along in years and I wanted to see him again. It also would present an opportunity to make amends to my mother, whom I had devastated by leaving the country on such short notice.

So, we decided to do it with the understanding we would return to Canada once my service was over and we had spent more time with our families. Unlike the first time we went to Canada, this time we would be able to return to the States on holidays or any other time we wanted to.

I sent a letter to assistant U.S. Attorney Al Moreton, whose office was in Oxford, and notified him that I would be accepting President Ford's offer. His response was to ask me to give him a call once I returned so that we could set up an appointment for a face-to-face meeting.

My second letter went to Pic Firmin, the managing editor of the *Delta Democrat-Times (DD-T)*, the Greenville, Mississippi newspaper I had grown up reading as a child. It won a Pulitzer Prize for editorials written about civil rights and the World War II era concentration camp across the Mississippi River in Arkansas. The camp had been built for Japanese Americans who had been born in the States and therefore were American citizens. I told him I would be returning soon and would like to apply for employment at the newspaper.

In a letter written in October 1974, he responded that they had no openings at the moment, but "you never know what might turn up." He said the editor Hodding Carter III was out of town at the moment, but he would discuss my employment when he returned. Then the U.S. Air Force veteran continued: "I hope the President does the right thing on 'amnesty' insofar as he can, politically. It's obvious that he does not intend to do the right thing insofar as he can as a moral being, which is not amnesty but an apology to war resisters, GIs, parents, etc., all Americans and mankind. I could go on and on, as I seem to do daily because there is no lack of people around here of the other viewpoint with which to argue, but I won't. Instead, I invite you to write a story (your story) or series of stories about the subject for publication in the DD-T if you feel up to it. Let me know what you think, then I'll let you know how much—if very much—I can pay you."

I responded that there was a chance the charges would be dropped altogether because the U.S. Attorney's office had dropped charges against other war resisters from Mississippi, but if that was not to be the case I would be free for employment after I completed my service. As far as writing my story, I explained that I did not think it would be a good idea before or during my public service.

Firmin wrote back that he understood my reluctance to comment publicly at this point, adding, "I do hope that you put it all down in print at some time in the near future, if not for the DD-T, then for another publication . . . I hope there is a 'probation' in your future. Keep in touch and call me when you get home."

Ina and Jonathan in Canada

Chapter 5

Circling the Wagons

IN NOVEMBER 1974 we loaded up our four-door Mazda sedan (we had gone through the Mustang convertible and the MG-B convertible), getting the Mazda because we needed a backseat for the car seat for the baby, and drove from Brockville to the international bridge west of the city. Shortly before leaving, we ran an ad in the newspaper to find a home for our dog, and were surprised one evening when the mayor knocked on the door to see the dog. When we told him we were moving back to the States, he begged us to stay, using every argument he could think of. It was difficult saying goodbye to so many good people, and to the river, which had seduced us with its ever changing moods throughout the year.

As we approached the bridge, we pulled off the highway to take a photo of the sign that announced the route to cross the bridge into the United States. After we crossed the river bridge and entered into the United States, we pulled into the U.S. custom's lane and stopped in line as the motorists ahead were approached by U.S. border officials one at a time. When it came our turn, I lowered the door window to talk to the official.

"Do you have anything to declare?" he asked.

"Yes, I have a pistol," I answered.

"Please turn your engine off and remain in your car."

The official walked away and returned moments later with a form on a clipboard for my convenience. I filled out the form stating that I owned a .22-caliber nine-shot revolver. As I was completing the form Ina opened the glove box and retrieved the pistol, with four-year-old Jonathan leaning over the seat watching her every move.

I handed the officer the clipboard and the pistol.

"Unloaded?" he asked.

"Yes."

"We are required to send it to the FBI for a ballistics check. If it comes back clean, we will mail it to you at the Mississippi address you gave us on the form."

As we drove away, I turned to Ina and said, "I sure hope it comes back clean."

"What do you mean," she said, a look of concern on her face.

"Well, my dad bought it from a Greenwood cop who took it off a Black man he arrested."

"Oh, my God!"

"I wouldn't worry about it."

"I can't help but worry. That gun may have killed somebody."

I took her face in my hands and kissed her sweetly.

We were soon on our way. I must admit it felt a little strange to be driving through New York State, the staging area for the black ops team who had to abandon their plans to kidnap me, with no one chasing us. We travelled through New York to Pennsylvania, and from there down into Virginia and Tennessee, finally to Memphis and straight down the Interstate into the Mississippi Delta.

It was late in the day when we pulled up in from of my mother's home. She came running out to greet us with open arms and a huge smile. Many hugs later, we all went into the house where Mother's new husband Dick Caldwell was waiting. Within moments my grandfather and his new wife arrived. It proved to be a glorious homecoming. After a sumptuous meal of all my favorite dishes, we made plans for a Thanksgiving homecoming to which other family members would be invited.

The next day I phoned Assistant U.S. Attorney Al Moreton to notify him of my arrival in Mississippi and to set up a time for our first meeting. He was cordial when we spoke and we agreed on a day and time for the following week. I would learn that he was an Ole Miss graduate who had worked during the civil rights era as an administrative assistant to U.S. Senator John C. Stennis. In that capacity as a senator's "boy," he would have been a go-between the senator and others with whom he did business. He might not have known the "business" but he would have known the cast of characters. Stennis was not the racist that Senator Eastland was, but both men worked tirelessly to prevent Mississippi's Black citizens from having voting rights—or, more accurately, any human rights at all.

Within a few days I was sitting across the desk from Moreton in his office in Oxford. He shook hands with me and explained the program, but largely seemed disinterested. To my surprise, he said I should let him know when I found a job and give him details of what I would be doing. It was clear that neither his office nor the State Selective Service Office in Jackson would be very much involved in the process. That was because they didn't want me to find a job.

Watching him shuffle through papers, I couldn't help but wonder how much he would have received from Senator Eastland if my family had paid the bribe requested by the senator. Certainly, he would have received something because he was the individual who would have to drop the charges. He would get a little something under the table for that.

Exchanging pleasantries with him, I pondered the possibilities of what an investigative reporter could unearth on his operations. I had wanted to be a writer ever since I wrote my autobiography at the age of twelve, but now I knew that when the program ended I wanted to become a journalist for the purpose of exposing corrupt public officials, whether through editorial writing or investigative reporting. Moreton may have represented the federal government, but in my opinion he was no better than a sweetly perfumed grafter.

On the way back home from the meeting, I decided I didn't mind being on my own. He would have only hindered my progress. I applied for a job at the local county welfare agency, which had social workers and and eligibility workers for programs such as Aid to Dependent Children (ADC) and Food Stamps. Within a couple of days I was called in for an interview. The director of the agency told me he had no social work positions open, but he could offer me a position as an eligibility worker in the food stamp program. Both the director of the welfare department and the supervisor of the food stamp office were aware of the circumstances of my enrollment. The supervisor of the program was a retired U.S. Army officer, a woman who was most agreeable to having me on the staff. It didn't take long for us to become good friends.

Around this time, I received word that the Klan was up in arms over my return. I quickly received back-channeled threats. The Klan persuaded the local VFW chapter to sign a petition, asking the county welfare director to fire me. I found out about this from my hometown mayor. He was in bed sick at the time and he asked me to visit him at home. He told me that the core group—one of them was a highway patrolman and the others were farmers—had solicited his support. He turned them down because his son and I had been friends in high school, and because he did not want to anger my grandfather, who was known to have a pretty stout temper. He gave me their names. These were uneducated, no-count individuals who had no concept of right and wrong. Once I had their names, I knew the lives of myself and my family were in grave danger. Violent murder ran in one family like eye color runs in others.

A few days after my talk with the mayor, I signed in at work and learned that I had been fired because of the Klan protests. I called the *Delta Democrat-Times* to speak to Pic Firman but learned he had left the newspaper and taken a position as the editor of the *South Mississippi Sun*. Then I asked to speak to Hodding Carter III. He invited me over to the newspaper, where we met in the conference room. I gave him all the details, with him taking notes the entire time. At this time Carter was one of the most revered newspapermen in the South. Clearly, it was a story he was going to write himself. That evening, when I told my mother and her husband about my conversation with Carter she became very upset. She feared publicity would cripple my step-father's dry cleaning business. I promised to speak to Hodding.

After the threat to myself, my wife and my son became apparent, I purchased a .30-30 caliber, lever action Marlin rifle with a six-shot magazine. That meant I could load six cartridges into the magazine, pull one into the chamber, and then insert another cartridge into the magazine, giving me seven shots in all without reloading. To make a point to local Klansmen, I purchased several boxes of cartridges at a local hardware store for my new rifle and double-ought buckshot shells for my shotgun. I knew word would get out that I had accumulated enough ammo to carry on a small war. There was a misconception going around that to be against war, you had to be a pacifist. Not true.

I spoke to Hodding the next day and he reluctantly agreed to shelve the story, but said he wanted to make some telephone calls to convey the story privately of Klan interference in what was a federal program. Behind the scenes, he was successful in saving the integrity of the program. Because of his efforts, the State Welfare Department offered me a similar position in Issaquena County, the poorest, blackest county in Mississippi. There I would be in charge of a two-person food stamp program. Our office was located in the courthouse, one of only a few brick structures in the entire county, one of the others being the post office. There was not a single stoplight in the county. You can't get any more rural than that.

In the mid 1800s, Issaquena County was designated as the second richest county in the United States. That was because of the great wealth generated by the rich bottomland which was planted in cotton and harvested by more than seven thousand slaves that called Issaquena County home. During that period more than ninety percent of the county's population were classified as slaves. By the time I arrived on the scene, the percentage of the county's 2,500 population that was Black was around 65 percent. Almost all of the Blacks in the county worked on the plantations, which meant they only had income during "chopping" and "picking" seasons. The chopping was to remove weeds from around cotton plants; the picking, of course, was to harvest the cotton.

Financially, that meant that for almost six months of the year Black families had no income at all unless the women in the family worked as domestics, cleaning and cooking in the white homes. The nature of the lives of Black workers in Issaquena County was the reason the food stamp program was created. In the off season, Black families had very little to eat. I saw few children who did not have distended bellies or look hungry.

Prior to my arrival at the food stamp office, eligibility determinations were made on the conservative end of the scale. I took the program in the opposite direction and gave a liberal interpretation of the regulations. I never once broke the rules, but I saw to it that no one went hungry in Issaquena County. The director of the Mississippi Department of Public Welfare office also had supervisory responsibility for the food stamp office, so I worked for him. To my surprise, he said nothing about my liberal interpretations of the rules. That was because he approved of them. He knew that if he had done what I had done, he would have been fired.

I had a certain amount of immunity because I was in a federal program that no one understood and after what happened at the previous food stamp office that attracted Hodding Carter's attention state officials didn't want to rock the boat. Besides, if the poor were being fed, they could just blame it on me when the Klan came knocking, which of course eventually happened. Truthfully, most of the white families in the county were happy to see me feeding the poor.

Hodding's intervention was a godsend because it put me in the position to meet and befriend a man who would soon become a close friend, Arthur "Bubba" Lawyer. Three years earlier he had been elected sheriff of Issaquena County. He went on to serve seven additional four-year terms. When he retired in 2003, he was undefeated.

One day an obese, slovenly Klansman from my hometown, nicknamed Juicy, showed up in the county and proceeded to encourage my lynching. The sheriff heard about it and set out to find him. He had a description of the car, so when he found it, he blue-lighted the car and pulled the fat man off the road. According to what the sheriff later told me, the fat man twisted and turned to get out of the car, huffing and puffing, a big grin on his already profusely sweating face.

"Hey sheriff!"

The sheriff did not return the greeting. Instead, he snapped, "What you doing in my county?"

Juicy was beside himself with what he felt would be a well-received report. When he got nervous, he sweated profusely. His faced looked as if it had been sprayed with water. "I been getting your folks organized against that new food stamp worker you got."

"Is that right?' said the sheriff. He walked straight up to Juicy (he was a good twelve inches taller) and he wrapped his mighty arm around the fat man's shoulder, pressing down, pulling him into his side.

"Tell you what, Juicy. We like James Dickerson in this county. If you don't, it's best you never come back—know what I'm saying?"

The fat man got in his car and hightailed it out of the county and was never seen there again.

I never told the sheriff that he had another reason to send the fat man packing. I didn't withhold the information out of compassion for Juicy, but because it was an embarrassing story to tell. One day, when I was around ten years of age, I went to the barber shop to get a haircut. The barber shop was next door to the fat man's office. The two businesses shared a common restroom. On this day, the barber shop line was long and after a while I felt the need to go to the bathroom. I went into the back room and approached the bathroom, only to be startled by the fat man stepping from behind a stack of boxes.

"I'll show you mine," he said, grinning, "if you'll show me yours."

Stunned, I froze in my tracks.

"What's a matter boy? Cat got your tongue?"

I whirled and ran out of the back room as fast as I could.

If Sheriff Bubba had heard that story he might have left his county and hunted the fat man down and whipped his fat ass just on principle. The sheriff was an honest man whose slogan was "Just do what's right." And he always did that and more!

Sheriff Lawyer was a true-life hero. He defied every known stereotype of a Mississippi sheriff. Like Sheriff Taylor in the Andy Griffith Show, Lawyer never carried a gun. He didn't need to. His character was as visible and unyielding as a two-by-four slab of pine.

Bubba and I spent a lot of time talking. Not about politics, or the Vietnam War, but about life in general. My observations about his sleepy little county often made him laugh. His observations about life outside his county made me laugh. He was full of surprises. Once day he stuck his head into my office and asked if I was busy. There was no one but me and the clerk in the office, so I asked what he had in mind.

"I need you down at the courthouse," he said, grinning broadly. "Come on."

I followed him down the hallway to the courtroom. It was filled with restless people. Murder trials always attracted a full house.

"Go sit over to the side," he whispered—and I did as he instructed.

Then he was recognized by the judge.

"Your honor, I have been called away for an emergency in the north part of the county. I have appointed Mr. Dickerson here as the bailiff. He should be afforded the same considerations you would grant to me."

"So granted," said the judge, pounding his gavel.

Sheriff Bubba walked over to the defense table and whispered to the attorney so that his client could hear. "You need to do whatever Mr. Dickerson asks you to do. He's not wearing a sidearm but he's a mean sumbitch so don't rile him, you hear."

Both the defense attorney and the accused murderer nodded.

On his way out, Sheriff Bubba walked past me and winked.

I sat through another hour or so of the trial, during which the prisoner was convicted of murder and sentenced to death on the spot .

All of a sudden, without warning, the bushy-eyed judge slammed his gavel down hard, eyes glaring at me. "Court adjourned," he growled.

I stood and said, "All rise."

And the judge hurried from the courtroom.

The prisoner walked ahead of his lawyer to the door. He never said a word during the trial, but his body language was most common throughout the testimony and said more than he ever could have with words alone. The deputy was waiting for him just outside the courtroom door and slapped cuffs on him. The prisoner turned and looked at me, expecting me to say something official, but I just walked away in the opposite direction.

I proved to be a great bailiff, if do say so myself.

* * *

Once Sheriff Bubba invited me to lunch at his home with himself and his lovely wife, Delores, who originally was from my hometown. After lunch he showed me around his "den." It was a rather large room in which the walls were lined with gun cabinets. He was a collector of firearms of all kinds. He had rifles, shotguns, and pistols of every description. I suddenly realized that everyone in the county knew he was an expert with firearms and owned enough guns to fight a war. It was yet another reason why he didn't feel the need to strap on a gun.

One day I borrowed my grandfather's yellow Ford to drive to Issaquena County because Ina needed our car for an appointment. When I arrived I parked in my usual place outside my office and went inside. Moments later Sherriff Bubba appeared in my office and asked me to go outside with him to the parking lot.

"Did you know about this?" asked Bubba, leaning over to point at my grandfather's car.

I followed his hand to what looked like a bullet hole in the vicinity of the right rear wheel. The hole was about the size a bullet from a deer rifle would have made.

"Damn," I said.

"You didn't know?"

"No."

"Didn't hear anything?"

"No . . . wait a minute I ran over something and there was a loud bump. I figured it was a rabbit or something."

"I wasn't no rabbit you hit, and I don't know for sure if it is a bullet hole, but come with me."

We went into his office and he reached into his drawer and slapped a .25 caliber automatic pistol down on his desk. "Why don't you take this?"

I picked up the gun and examined it.

"Where'd you get it?"

"Took it off a man who wanted to kill his wife with it."

"I see. Thank you."

"Thank you for what? I don't see anything."

Sheriff Bubba just sat there, grinning.

I wanted to ask if this was what it looked like—a license to kill—but I knew that saying the words would ruin everything. Sometimes you've got to hold your cards until someone makes a play. Instead, I inserted the pistol into my pants pocket without further comment. It was small enough to be unnoticeable.

One bitterly cold weekend during my third year at the University of Mississippi, I accepted an invitation to join my grandfather, my Uncle Rex and his son Rex Jr. at a deer camp located on federal forest land located a few miles out from Oxford. I joined them at what appeared to be a tent city. There was a large, circus-sized tent, and numerous small tents. My grandfather gave me my .308 caliber, bolt-action rifle that my Uncle George had loaned me; he had brought it from home, along with a box of ammo. The other hunters offered my grandfather and myself one of the individual tents, but he declined, saying he preferred to stay in the large cook tent because he knew the cook would keep the fire going all night.

The cook was a loquacious Black man, probably in his sixties, who never ran out of hunting stories to tell from the old days. That first night we turned in early, sleeping on army cots piled high with woolen blankets. We were very comfortable, but throughout the night we heard random cries of, "Damn, it's cold!" rolling throughout the camp from inside the unheated tents. They were sounds that made my grandfather grin.

The next morning, the cook—I think his name was Moses—gave us plate loads of eggs, bacon and biscuits, along with a warning that he needed meat to cook for dinner. After breakfast, my grandfather and I went our separate ways into the woods.

I walked a while and then found a place to sit next to a towering oak at the top of a hill. At the bottom of the incline was a clearing through which went a trail I knew had been made by deer. After a while I heard leaves rustling in the distance. I leveled my .308 bolt action rifle down the hill toward a clearing where a good-sized doe was meandering along a well-worn path. With my heart pounding, I put the sight on her front shoulder. Slowly she walked, dipping her head, foraging for food. Slowly, I followed her every step, holding the rifle steady. She had no idea I was at the top of the hill.

I continued to follow her until she disappeared into the brush. She was a beautiful animal. I did not pull the trigger because in those days it was illegal to kill a female deer or fawns. Even then, I did not kill women or children, no matter the species. If I had pulled the trigger, it would have been a sure thing. I was a marksman, so good that the carnivals that passed through my hometown banned me from their shooting booths after I once cleaned the trophy shelves of one of their booths with my shooting.

I have my dad   and my Uncle Luther Webb—to thank for that.

My dad taught me to shoot a .22 caliber rifle early in life, probably around five. After my dad died, I went to Virginia every summer so that I could be around his brothers and sisters. Uncle Luther was married to Dad's sister, Hattie. Uncle Luther owned a stone grinding mill that was built on a beautiful mountain spring in the Blue Ridge Mountains. A giant water wheel powered the grinding stones inside the mill itself where mainly corn was ground for animal feed and for meal for cornbread.

On the third floor of the mill was a window that overlooked the stream. One day Uncle Luther handed me a pump action .22 and told me to shoot the corn cobs when he tossed them into the air. I tried, but I missed every corncob he tossed.

"Here, let me show you," Uncle Luther said.

With the rifle in his right hand and two corn cobs in his left hand, he tossed the corn cobs high into the air and proceeded to shoot both in half before they hit the water below.

Over the course of the summer I learned to do the same thing.

Years later, when out hunting squirrels, I taught myself how to fire my automatic .22 like a machinegun by inverting it and rocking my finger inside the trigger guard. I would stand on the banks of canals and fire my rifle that way, making my shots splash in a straight line like a machine gun, the shots literally walking up the middle of the canal, probably firing fifteen rounds in less than four seconds. If you are a teenager, that is a thrilling discovery to make. If you are a grown man, that is a fond memory to have. If you are a married man with a wife and child to protect, it is a comforting skill to have.

Every evening after dinner, despite the threats that remained, I continued a tradition I had begun in Canada. I went for a long walk. Unlike in Canada, I strapped on a pistol holster under my jacket and I walked along the highway, and I meandered up and down the dark alleys into downtown, knowing damned well I could defend myself if I had to. In Canada my job was to analyze behavior and write predictive scenarios for those behaviors. Using those skills, I calculated the person most likely to ambush me was the highway patrolman who had plotted and signed petitions against me. In his case, I favored the hypothesis that he would pull his squad car up ahead of me to block the alley. Then he would get out of the car with a shotgun, which I would catch a flicker of in the moonlight. When he moved to bring the shotgun up to his shoulder, I would draw my weapon and squeeze off two shots, corncob style, before he got his shotgun fully into position. Thankfully, it was a plan I never had to execute. My proficiency with firearms was well known to the people who knew me. I will never apologize for being good with a gun.

AFTER TWO YEARS in Issaquena County, I resigned my position at the food stamp office and said my goodbyes. The following day I called U.S. assistant attorney Al Moreton and notified him I had completed the program. He said he would be in touch.

Meanwhile, I received a letter from E. W. St. Clair, Commissioner of the State Department of Welfare, accepting my resignation. To my surprise his response was cordial: "I would like to take this opportunity to express to you our appreciation for the work you have done for the Department during your time with us. We are glad you have enjoyed your association with this agency, and we value highly your continued interest in our work."

A few days later I received a letter from Moreton. Opening the envelope I assumed it was my certificate of completion. Instead of the certificate, there was a letter stating that he had gone before a judge and requested he dismiss the case because I had completed my agreement and newly elected President Jimmy Carter had issued pardons for all Vietnam era war resisters. It was Moreton's way of saying that my two years of working on the program at $533 a month was all for nothing. I had neither solicited a pardon nor accepted a pardon. In 50 years of reporting, I have never encountered a government official of lower ethics.

For two years, the entire time I worked in the food stamp office, I had written book reviews for *Delta Democrat-Times* arts editor Ben Wasson. He was impressed that I had written reviews for the *Toronto Star* and the *Baltimore Sun*. For many years, Wasson was the only book critic in the state, just one of many things that made the newspaper distinctive.

While a student at the University of Mississippi, Wasson had befriended William Faulkner. Later, while living in New York and working as a literary agent, he sold Faulkner's novel *Sartoris*, to Harcourt, Brace & Co., which had just published Wasson's first novel. *Sartoris* was the first Faulkner novel set in the fictional Yoknapatawpha Country. When Faulkner went to New York to finish his masterpiece, *The Sound and the Fury*, he did so in Wasson's apartment.

Wasson was a delight to work with, not so much for his personality, because he was at times crotchety, but for his personal ties to Mississippi's literary past. One time, when I came across a review of Mississippi writer Stark Young's letters, I sent Wasson a note asking if I could review the book. The author of *So Red the Rose,* the first best- selling novel to come out of Mississippi, Young had lived in New York City for a time, where he served as the drama critic for both *The New York Times* and the *New Republic*. I was also eager to review the book because it had been written by Ole Miss English professor Dr. John Pilkington, my favorite professor at the university.

I will never forget the day I stumbled into the Ole Miss cafeteria, haggard and bleary-eyed after my band had performed in a Black nightclub in Memphis, and encountered Dr. Pilkington entering the building. Although I was dressed in a burgundy blazer and wearing a pink shirt, a mode of dress he had never seen me wear in his classroom, he offered to buy me breakfast, perhaps intrigued by the life of a rock 'n' roller. More likely he had hope of civilizing me.

Wasson responded that it was too late for him to obtain the book from the publisher, but he was happy for me to review it if I could get the book. I did, of course. Within Wasson's note to me was the type of comment I always looked forward to from him: "Stark Young was a very good friend of mine in earlier days in New York City and I regret I didn't keep the few letters—charming of course—he wrote to me."

The most important book I reviewed for the *Delta Democrat-Times* while I worked in Issaquena County was Joseph Blotner's comprehensive biography of William Faulkner, aptly titled *William Faulkner: A*

Biography. I desperately wanted to review the biography, but since Wasson had been such a close friend of Faulkner, I naturally assumed he would write the review. Then came word he was ill and couldn't do the review. He asked if I would. I'm sure Blotner received more erudite reviews of his masterpiece, but I doubt he had any reviews by daily newspapers that gave the book as much space as the *Delta Democrat-Times* gave my review.[3]

While I was writing the review, my wife Ina and I got into a discussion about the writer's characters. One of the mysteries entertained by Faulkner scholars up to that point was where Faulkner got the family name for his ne'er do well, redneck family called Snopes. Ina and I tackled the question the way one would a word puzzle. Before long we had the answer. Rearrange the letters in Snopes and you get the word peons, minus the second "s." This was included in the review, which no doubt mystified the publisher as to how a solution to this mystery could have emerged from the Mississippi Delta when it had been such a long-standing contemplation in the ivy-lined buildings of English departments across the South.

Issaquena County also was a launching pad for my writing career with *The Commercial Appeal* in Memphis. One of the things that caught my eye in Mayersville was an old country store which was a stone's throw from my office. Originally named the Red Star Store and Saloon, it was built on the banks of the Mississippi River in the early 1900s. On my daily lunch-time walks I occasionally saw a young couple going in and out of the store. It clearly was not open for business. Intrigued, I asked Sheriff Bubba about the building. He told me it was owned by Jim and Lorraine Mabus. Jim, who was known by his friends as Diamond Jim, worked for his father who owned one of the big farming outfits in the county.

One day I went by to introduce myself and they invited me into their home. Outside, the store was weatherworn and appeared deserted. Inside, it had been remodeled into a modern home. I was impressed. They were a young, attractive couple and their renovations were spectacular, so I asked if they would mind if I pitched an article about their home to *Mid-South*

*Magazin*e, a weekly publication of *The Commercial Appeal* in Memphis.

I interviewed them about the house, shot a number of color images of the building inside and out, and submitted it to the magazine. The article was accepted for publication, bringing Mid-South attention to the home and making me a local celebrity.

I left Issaquena County only because it was time to move on to new adventures, but I returned several times over the next year in my capacity as a newspaper reporter. Several years later, I was surprised to receive a holiday greeting from Sheriff Bubba Lawler. He had a difficult time tracking me down. On the card he wrote, "You move around as much as a sharecropper. Let me know what you are doing."

Without trying to learn anything, in Issaquena County I had stumbled across the bedrock requirement of good journalism, namely to interact with the community in which you live in such a way as to develop friendships and news sources that you can trust and—in the case of Sheriff Bubba—admire for their courage and honesty.

Chapter 6

Delta Democrat-Times

MY FIRST FULL-TIME JOB as a journalist was with the legendary, Pulitzer Prize-winning *Delta Democrat-Times* in Greenville, Mississippi, for a time one of the best newspapers in the South. From the time I first met with Hodding Carter III in 1975 until I was free to accept a position at the newspaper, two years had elapsed. My life during that time was fairly static, but the newspaper had undergone several big changes. For starters, Hodding left the newspaper—and Greenville in general as it turned out—to accept a position with the Jimmy Carter administration as spokesman for the U.S. State Department.

In his absence, Hodding and his mother, Betty Carter, who was publisher of the newspaper, hired David Ethridge to be the executive editor. Ethridge had newspaper experience, but his most recent experience had been with the Democratic National Committee as a writer and as Terry Sanford's press secretary when the North Carolinian ran for president in 1975. Ethridge was only thirty-seven, but in his photographs he looked closer to fifty-seven. I surmised he must have had a rough life.

I exchanged several letters with Ethridge about employment at the newspaper, beginning with a freelance submission, an updated article about Mississippian Bobbie Gentry and her recording career. Ethridge replied: "I have looked over some of your work. Your piece on Bobbie Gentry was good but we had already given her what seemed to be eight pages, so it never really had a chance of getting off my desk. Drop me a note shortly before you will be available and we can get together and talk."

Six months before submitting my resignation in Issaquena County, I wrote to him again, prompting this reply, "I still don't have anything available now, but if you'd like to come by and chat, that would be fine." Finally, with just a month or so to go before I would be unemployed, I wrote to Hodding at the State Department. It was at this point I learned that Ethridge had either resigned or been fired. In his letter to me, Hodding wrote, "What I would suggest is that you get in touch with my brother, Philip, who will be phasing in at the newspaper, and go over the possibilities with him . . . Keep in touch."

Philip Carter owned a weekly newspaper in New Orleans, the *Courier*, and another weekly named *Gris Gris* in Baton Rouge. Before becoming a publisher, he worked as a reporter for *Newsweek* and the *Washington Post*. He had solid credentials as a journalist. After Ethridge left the newspaper, he was asked by his mother to take over the *Delta Democrat-Times*. It created quite a disruption in his life—it meant renting an apartment on Main Street and commuting to New Orleans and Baton Rouge on weekends to take care of business there—but no son of the late, Pulitzer Prize-winning "Big Hodding" was going say no to a family request that involved the family legacy. To do so, would be like forgoing red-eye gravy on biscuits. It just isn't done in the Delta.

Quoted in a 1980 *Christian Science Monitor* profile on Hodding, Philip said of his brother: "Hodding has never been less than complicated. He's alert, intelligent, persuasive. He has an extraordinary theatrical presence and a basic sense of decency . . . He has an enormous lot to say."

Philip displays many of those same qualities, but without Hodding's need to stake out positions on serious issues. Hodding has a temper. Philip is more laidback. In pop culture terms, I would describe Hodding as Chuck Conners in the "The Rifleman" and Philip as James Gardner in

"Maverick," ever willing to deflect trouble with a sense of humor.

My family was always devoted to the *Delta Democrat-Times*, even before I was born. My maternal uncle, Rex Turner, started delivering the newspaper in 1941, at the age of fourteen. An electronic genius—he later would become one of the first ham radio operators to bounce a signal off the moon—he built a radio from scratch and attached it to his bicycle so that he could listen to music while he delivered newspapers. An enterprising reporter for the newspaper spotted him one day and interviewed him for a feature article, providing my uncle with his first brush with celebrity.

My grandfather religiously subscribed to the *Delta Democrat-Times*, which arrived late in the afternoon, and *The Commercial Appeal*, which arrived early in the morning. By the time I was old enough to read, both newspapers had won Pulitzer Prizes for their support of basic human rights. As a youth I did not always understand the issues that Hodding Carter wrote about on the editorial page, but I understood enough to know that his thinking ran counter to the opinions of many people in my community (by then I lived in Hollandale)—and, for some inexplicable reason, I was drawn to Hodding Carter's writing, impressed both by the clarity of his thinking and the fearlessness of his actions, even when it meant he and his sons had to hide in the bushes outside his home with loaded shotguns to intercept marauding nightriders.

Big Hodding was one of my first heroes, along with my grandfather. The only time I was ever disappointed in the *Delta Democrat-Times* was when the newspaper got word that I owned the only set of groundhogs in the entire state of Mississippi. A photographer called and asked if he could come over the next day and photograph the groundhogs. Within minutes after putting the telephone receiver down, I was off to get a new shirt for my photo session—and, at the insistence of my mother—a haircut, topped off with the barber's infamous Rose Hair Tonic, which was about 70 percent alcohol. I told all my friends my picture was going to be in the newspaper, and I hardly slept at all that night.

The next day, when the photographer arrived, he was accompanied by the Hollandale High School Homecoming Queen. As my spirits deflated faster than a marble rolling off a kitchen table, he explained that he thought a beauty queen would make a better picture than myself. I accepted his decision with good grace—he promised to spell my name right—but there are no words to express the embarrassment I felt, not just because I had told my friends what turned out to be a lie, but also because, while working in my grandfather's store, I'd recently sold the Homecoming Queen a Wonder Bra and I could not look at her posing with my groundhogs without wondering if she was wearing it, thoughts that made my face blazing red and baffled the photographer.

There came a time when Big Hodding handed off the editorship of the newspaper to his eldest son, Hodding Carter III, a summa cu laude graduate of Princeton who served two years in the Marine Corps before joining the staff of his father's newspaper, first as reporter and then as managing editor, and, finally, as editor in 1960, when his father retired after penning some twenty books and leading the newspaper—and his community—through some of the roughest years of social unrest imaginable. However, long before Hodding III became editor, he wrote award-winning editorials for the newspaper, editorials that I read in high school and then later as a student at the University of Mississippi. With time, Hodding III also became my hero.

So, while I feel it was Hodding who was responsible for me getting the job at the newspaper, it was Philip who actually hired me and became my first newspaper editor as a staff writer. After mailing in book reviews to various publications over the years, including the *Delta Democrat-Times*, it was nice to actually have a desk inside a newspaper building. I was given some news assignments, but mostly I was an enterprise feature writer, which meant that I looked for stories on my own. The great thing about being a journalist is the opportunity it gives you to investigate issues that always have interested you.

IN THOSE DAYS in the South, Black families lived in close proximity to white families. Today white families stay as far away from Black families as possible. Behind my childhood home in Greenville, often called Mississippi's liberal oasis, was an alley that contained numerous shanties that were occupied by Black families. On her way to work each morning, Mother had noticed a young girl who lived in an alley down the street toward the levee. One day she pulled over and stopped and asked if she'd ever kept babies.

"Not white babies, but I've kept Black babies," the young girl explained. "I have a little baby of my own."

"Can you come by the house tomorrow so we can talk?"

"Yes ma'am."

Sallie Mae Elle was just eighteen, but she was very mature for her age—and she had a smiling face that radiated love. Mother had a satisfactory talk with her and hired her as my new babysitter. For some reason, I took to her right away. Unlike the previous sitter who frightened me, I wanted Sallie Mae to hold and cuddle me. She did so with a sense of wonderment. Times being what they were she probably had never touched a white person. Now she was in charge of one.

It didn't take long for Sallie Mae to become a revered family member. She was the reason I became the first white person to integrate the public parks in Greenville, although you won't find any plaques there celebrating the occasion. Technically, I didn't integrate the parks, Sallie Mae did, but I was the vehicle through which the integration took place and that has always made me feel special.

I was three when history rudely knocked on the door.

One of Mother's neighbors stood in line at her teller's window at the bank. Although normally high-strung, the woman seemed more agitated and ill-at-ease than usual. Twisting and turning from side to side, she took turns kicking her legs from one side to the other and then holding that pose for a long moment. Her body language radiated anger. Her eyebrows had been shaved and redrawn with a black mascara brush, a custom at the time among some whites, but it didn't make her look more attractive. Instead, it made her look angry, even when she was not.

Mother smiled when the woman stepped up to her window, waiting for her to put money or paperwork on the counter. But the woman, who was there to ambush Mother, was not there on banking business.

"There's something I need to tell you," she said, leaning over into the window.

"What is it?"

"Did you know that nigger you hired is bringing her little boy up there to play with your baby?"

Mother wasn't sure she heard her right.

"What did you say?"

"Your little boy is playing with a nigger in the park." The woman paused a moment and then smugly added, "I thought you needed to know."

She whirled and stormed out of the bank without waiting for a response from Mother.

After work Mother spoke to Sallie Mae about the neighbor's accusations. "Sallie Mae, have you been letting your little boy come up here to play?"

"Yes 'ma'am," answered Sallie Mae. "You don't want me to?"

Sallie Mae had a beautiful face. When she smiled, she lit up the room, and when she frowned it nearly broke your heart. Mother looked at Sallie Mae, who had been caring for me for two-and-a-half years and who loved me as if I was her own child, and she thought about the morally twisted, self-righteous neighbor standing in line to share the bad news about Sallie Mae—and it was no contest.

"No," Mother said. "I think it's a good idea—a very good idea."

As a result of Mother's decision, Sallie Mae and her son and I became the subject of controversy in Greenville because the city park was a place Black children were prohibited from visiting. We played on the swings and slides, and we chased each other across the rich, Delta grass that was soft as a cotton quilt when we tripped and fell into its fragrant folds rolling over and over again, oblivious to the hatred directed toward us.

Mother never explained to anyone why she did what she did. She asked her father, Audie, if he thought the police would arrest her. He laughed and said he didn't think so. "They'd better not."

FOR ONE OF MY FIRST STORIES at the *Delta Democrat-Times*, I stumbled upon a church baptism at Lake Washington, which was located about halfway between Greenville and Mayersville. It was by accident that I came across a well-dressed Black man sitting on the back fender of a truck reading his Bible. When I saw him, I pulled off the road and parked and walked toward him. As I approached, he called out, *"Look at that!" He firmly thumped his finger against the Bible. I looked at where he was pointing. It was St. Matthew, third chapter.*

"Read that, then I want to show you something."

I did as he asked and he took the Bible from me and put it away and grasped another Bible that he earlier had parked on the back bumper.

"How come one Bible says it one way and another Bible says it a different way?"

I told him I couldn't explain it.

"Ain't the Bible always supposed to speak the truth?"

"Yes sir," I said. "It is supposed to."

"But it don't."

"Different people wrote different chapters. Some were better at it than others."

"The Lord should've written it himself. He can read and write, can't he?" [4]

As we talked, the Rev. Elijah Lewis, Jr. drove up in a pickup truck, followed by a church bus and about a dozen cars. It was early Sunday morning and members of St. Peter's Missionary Baptist Church of Mayersville were at the lake for a glorious baptism.

After Rev. Lewis led the group in prayer, he waded out thirty feet into the water and turned around. From there, he preached to the congregation, his voice booming with conviction. The preacher took a child in his hands and lowered her into the water so that she was now out of sight. My heart skipped a beat. Within moments, she was raised from the water, gasping for air, an enormous smile on her face, causing me to let out a sigh. It brought back memories of my own baptism in the Hollandale Baptist Church, with me going under water, thinking . . . *What if I don't come up?*

For a subsequent story at the *Delta Democrat-Times* I chose a topic that had been in the news recently and greatly interested me. In the late 1970s, the Charismatic Movement was on the ascendency in the United States. In the first century A.D., disciples of Jesus Christ gathered on the day of Pentecost, the King James version of the Book of Acts records, and "began to speak with other tongues as the Spirit gave them utterance."

For the newspaper, I did an investigative series that ran on Page One.[5] The first story took readers to a meeting of charismatic followers who had gathered in a private residence. They were a racially mixed group. The service began with lots of singing and continued for at least ninety minutes. Throughout the singing those in attendance clapped their hands.

Once the singing stopped, everyone gathered in a circle and linked hands and prayed. Afterward the leader of the group moved over to the Black woman who had been playing the piano and he placed his hands on her head. Suddenly, she began to chant ecstatically, surrendering herself to blossolalia, which one dictionary defines as a spiritual "gift of tongues." Her arms rose skyward and her feet pumped against the floor with the rhythm of her excitement. Her words sputtered out in no language I had ever heard. She was followed by a man who took the floor to testify as to his former wickedness.

A Catholic priest who had been sitting in the back of the room raised his arms and began to speak in a language unknown to me. Was it Latin? I don't think so. He was possessed. When the meeting was over everyone formed a circle and joined hands. They sang out, using the Hebrew word for peace, "Shalom, shalom, shalom."

To my surprise, Philip Carter wrote an editorial commenting on my series of articles, saying they were "highly enlightening." He went on to write: "[Dickerson's] articles have drawn numerous letters to the editor signed by local members of a variety of Christian denominations, including the Pentecostal Church. American Pentecostalists, as one writer pointed out, have been practicing charismatic Christianity in this country for many decades. What that letter writer probably felt no need to emphasize was the fact that—aside from the ignorance or occasional private intolerance exhibited by members of other denominations—American Pentacostalists are not persecuted for their beliefs. In the United States, government is not merely neutral on the subject of religion. To a degree that most of us take completely for granted, American law and the Constitution enshrine the right of every American to worship—or not to worship—as he sees fit."

NOT LONG AFTER my lake baptism story, I was asked to travel to Indianola to cover a press conference at the Sunflower County courthouse organized by Mississippi Governor Cliff Finch. I had no way of knowing it at the time, but he would become the prototype for Donald Trump. He was two years into his first term and was being coy about whether he would run for president against President Jimmy Carter, something he had suggested he was thinking about doing. He did and lost by a huge margin.

After parking in the courthouse parking lot, I went inside and started up the stairs to the second floor, where I had been advised the press conference would take place. Lo and behold, as I started up the stairs I encountered the governor walking down the stairs toward me. He had on a metallic gold suit and wore a metallic gold necktie with a starched white shirt. His dirty blond hair had been tinted golden presumably to match his suit, but it looked orange.

I knew who he was, but I pretended I did not.

"Is the press conference over?" I asked.

"No," he said with a surprised look. "It'll start in a few minutes."

"Is the governor up there?"

He stopped for a split second, almost losing his footing, but then regained his balance. He shot me a look of bewilderment, as if he were lost in a maze, and he said, "He'll be there in a few minutes." I subsequently learned that he almost always had a look of bewilderment. I proceeded up the stairs and when I made the turn I glanced back and saw him wandering about, apparently looking for a restroom. I entered the room where the press conference was scheduled and counted about one hundred people there. Not a large crowd for a sitting governor. He wasn't my first governor. When I was a teenager, my Uncle Hilton Waits of nearby Leland, who was speaker *pro tem* of the House of Representatives, took me to Jackson with him to serve as a page. The Speaker, Walter Sillers, had experienced a heart attack while out of the country, so that made my uncle the acting Speaker. The highlight of my service was meeting then Governor J. P. Coleman. At that time his office was located in between the House and Senate chambers on the second floor of the capitol.

One day I walked into the governor's office and asked the secretary if I could see him. "Do you have an appointment?" she asked.

"No ma'am," I answered, holding up a blank piece of paper. It was then that the emerging Sam Spade in me first appeared "I'm a page in the House and I need for the Governor to sign this paper."

"Oh," she said. She got up and stuck her head into the office and told the governor that he had a visitor—a page from the House with an important paper. He apparently said yes—I didn't hear his voice—because she stepped back and waved me into the office.

"Son, is that the paper you need me to sign?"

"Yes Sir." I handed it to him and when he looked over both sides and looked puzzled, I added, "I'm a page in the House and I was hoping you would sign an excuse for me for being away from school.

He handed me back the blank sheet of paper.

"Son, I can't do that. Wouldn't be constitutional." He saw the disappointment on my face and then said, "I'm sorry."

That night I had dinner with Uncle Hilton and told him about my meeting with the governor. He frowned and said, "I've got a meeting with him at ten in the morning. Meet me outside the office."

I got there about fifteen minutes early. Uncle Hilton showed up a minute or two before ten and greeted me warmly. He opened the door for me and said, "Come on in, we have an important meeting."

The secretary greeted him with "Good morning Mr. Waits. The governor is waiting for you"

The secretary looked at me and smiled.

We walked into the office and found Governor Coleman sitting behind his desk with his feet up on his desk. He was wearing nylon socks, which were the rage at the time, but he had a good bit of hairless leg between his socks and his trousers. He didn't get up to shake hands with either of us, but he greeted Uncle Hilton with a big smile.

"I see you brought your assistant. I had the pleasure of meeting him yesterday."

"He's a member of my family and he's serving as a page in the House."

The Governor looked at me with what I would call a weary smile.

"He's a fine boy. He came in yesterday wanting me to sign his school excuse, but I can't do that because I don't have the constitutional power to do it."

"It's just to show to his teachers and classmates. He's already excused to be a page."

"I know that and for me to sign that paper would put me at odds with the constitution."

"State or federal?" Uncle Hilton asked, losing patience.

The Governor laughed and reached to pull up one of his socks.

Uncle Hilton put his hand on my shoulder and directed me to the door, which he opened with his other hand. His face and the top of his bald head were red with anger. "I'll see you at dinner tonight—fried chicken sound good to you?"

"Yes sir," I said.

* * *

When Governor Finch entered the room, his eyes were unusually bright and jumpy. I wondered if he perhaps had enjoyed a drink of whiskey in the restroom.

"I've come here to tell you some of the good things about Mississippi," he said. "I represent the finest, the most generous people in this country"

He went on to say he was pleased to announce that the state was now third in the nation for the rate of increase in per capita income.

"We used to be laughed at," said Finch. "But now we're on the move."

Before he could move on to another boast, a woman in the audience questioned that Mississippi was third in the nation on per capita income.

Embarrassed by the question, Finch rapidly back peddled, acknowledging that Mississippi was still 50th in per capita income. However, he explained he was referring to the rate of increase, adding that was important even if it didn't move the state out of 50th place. No one in the audience clapped.

Before wrapping up his speech, he invited everyone to come to Jackson to visit him at the Governor's Mansion. "I'm coming back to visit you more often," he threatened. "So you might as well get ready. I might want to spend the night with some of you."[6]

Writing this book all these years later, I could not help but to compare him to Donald Trump. Both voiced populist sentiments, both left orange impressions anyplace they put down their head, and neither had a clue about how to govern. Finch out-rednecked Trump in two instances. He carried around a metal lunchbox—some said he mistakenly thought it was a man purse—and he spent one day a week at a local supermarket bagging groceries to show he was a common man. He certainly was that.

ON AUGUST 16, 1977, a fateful day in American music, I was driving along a tree-lined boulevard in Greenville on my way home from the *Delta*

Democrat-Times, when I heard a bulletin on the radio that Elvis Presley was dead. My mother and step-father were in Baptist Hospital in Memphis when Elvis was brought into the emergency room. My step-father, Dick Caldwell, was there as a patient. The same day Mother learned of Elvis' death, she learned my step-father had a brain tumor.

The next morning I picked up a copy of *The Commercial Appeal*. Four-fifths of the front page was devoted to coverage of Elvis's death. "Death Captures Crown of Rock and Roll" read the banner headline. Inside was another full page of news stories and photographs. Elvis' personal physician, Dr. George Nicholoulos, told reporters that night that a heart attack was the possible cause of death. Elvis had been found face down in his upstairs bathroom at 2:30 p.m. Fire Department medical technicians tried to resuscitate him on the way to the hospital, but got no response. At 3:30 p.m. hospital emergency resuscitation teams pronounced him dead. By 4 p.m. a crowd of 150 people had gathered at the hospital. They all had the same question: "Are you sure there's no mistake?"

There was no mistake.

The following day I returned to the newsroom and learned Philip was writing an editorial about Elvis. That's good, I thought—no controversy there. I had always felt that music was more than something to dance to. It is a healer, an instigator of change (as I learned during the Vietnam War years) and a means of communication of some of the deepest feelings we have as human beings.

I didn't see the editorial until the following day. I was shocked to see that Philip had written that Elvis was "white trash" and reflected poorly on the state. I couldn't believe it. Philip was entitled to his personal feelings, but he had put the newspaper on record as sharing those feelings. It didn't take long for the switchboard to light up. Complaints, one after another.

Then the threats started coming in. By the end of the day Philip was uncomfortable with his downtown living arrangements because of public access to where he slept at night. That put him at a disadvantage when it came to self-protection. He could spend a few nights at his mother's home, but that would put her at risk and be a first choice for his enemies.

Philip announced to the newsroom that he was going to write a second Elvis editorial, this one retracting his previous "white trash" comments, after which he planned to take a few days off and return to New Orleans. After Philip left, managing editor Sallie Ann Gresham approached my desk and asked if I'd like to be the editorial writer in Philip's absence.

My first editorial was about lawyers. I figured I couldn't go wrong there. I don't recall what my position was, but since I don't much care for lawyers I might have suggested that lawyers be required to perform public service to obtain a license. My second editorial called for the complete overhaul of the food stamp program. I was troubled that an individual in need of food stamps would have to pay for a portion of the stamps. For example, to receive one hundred dollars in stamps, they might be required to pay seventy-five dollars. I thought that was absurd. If they had seventy-five dollars, they would spend it on groceries. I suggested they simply be given the twenty-five dollars in stamps for which they were eligible. The government was trying to nickel-and-dime families that typically had incomes of less than three thousand dollars a year.

I don't recall how many editorials I wrote, but one day Betty Carter, the most elegantly gracious lady you would ever want to meet, and one of my favorite people, took me aside and told me she thought I was a little too liberal to be writing editorials for the *Delta Democrat-Times*. I wasn't offended. I figured the assignment was too good to be true, anyway.

FROM RELIGION, my focus as a journalist shifted to death and dying. I researched and wrote an investigative series of Page One stories on the subject. The first story dealt with two recent deaths in the community. One instance involved a 65-year-old woman who was diagnosed with inoperable lung cancer. Her husband had preceded her by ten years, his death attributed to lung cancer.

Because they had no children, she began her journey alone. For three months she lived a relatively normal life at her home. When the time came for her to be hospitalized, she took her bag of knitting with her to the hospital and spent her final days knitting and watching television. Two weeks after entering the hospital she went into a coma. The nurses did what they could to make her comfortable. However, sometimes they gathered in her room on break and spoke as if she were not even there. To their surprise, their chatter was abruptly interrupted one day by the woman, who opened her eyes and spoke to them.

"Please be quiet! It's time for me to die and I'd like to say a little prayer first."[7]

The stunned nurses watched as she recited a short prayer. When she finished speaking, she relaxed and died quietly without a struggle.

As that story demonstrates, people are often quite aware of their demise in the final moments. Often terminally ill patients in comas emerge from unconsciousness long enough to converse lucidly with loved ones in the final moments of their life. Sometimes when individuals in comas are disconnected from life support they will not die as long as there are people in the room looking at them. They will cling desperately to life until their room is cleared so that they can die in peace. If you ever find yourself in a room with a loved one who is dying, be sure to ask if they want you to stay or leave the room. You may be surprised at the answer.

For my second story in the series, I looked at the psychological implications of death and dying. Many people die while experiencing great anguish and emotional suffering. That need not be the case. A person's response to death is determined by his or her philosophy of life. The important thing for those around dying persons is to allow them to deal with the emotions associated with dying. They should be encouraged to talk about their death, no matter how frightening that may be to loved ones. It is their death. They own it. Let them talk about it.

Chicago psychiatrist Dr. Elisabeth Kubler-Ross performed a great service when she wrote a book titled *On Death and Dying*. In the book she lists five stages encountered by the terminally ill, beginning with denial and isolation, in which the patient denies the diagnosis and goes from doctor to doctor in search of a more favorable diagnosis, followed by anger about their situation, and then progressing to bargaining, depression and, finally acceptance. Sometimes people get hung up on a particular stage and never go past it. Those who go through all five stages, asserts Kubler-Ross, die with "peace and dignity."

In his book, *Life After Life*, Dr. Raymond Moody, who has a Ph.D. in psychology and a medical degree with a focus on psychiatry, has written about numerous "life after life" experiences. He presents a typical case that is based on points of likeness with many of the cases he investigated:

> **A man is dying and, as he reaches the point of greatest physical distress, he hears himself pronounced dead by his doctor. He begins to hear an uncomfortable noise, a loud ringing or buzzing, and at the same time feels himself moving very rapidly through a long dark tunnel. After this, he suddenly finds himself outside of his own physical body, but still in the immediate physical environment, and he sees his own body from a distance, as though he is a spectator. He watches the resuscitation attempt from this unusual vantage point and is in a state of emotional upheaval . . .[8]**

Medical science has an excellent track record of reporting on what happens in the weeks, days and minutes leading up to death, but it has little to contribute to the discussion of what happens immediately after death. Dr. Hollis Burrow, a pathologist, told me that people don't die in real life the way they do in the movies. "Ninety-nine percent don't make any last minute statements or confessions. And those that die suddenly just drop over."

Brain death follows clinical death within a matter of minutes. Cellular death follows brain death by as long as two hours or more. Different types of cells die at different rates. One of the startling aspects of death comes with the realization that someone who has been beheaded may have a conscious awareness of dying—perhaps even continuing eyesight—even as the severed head lies on the ground or in a basket. That is yet another reason why beheading is such a horrendous act. As a dying person, you may have an awareness of your surroundings for as long as ten minutes after your heartbeat ceases.

The series of articles on death and dying attracted a lot of reader interest. Most of the comments were appreciative of my efforts to lessen the mystery associated with death, but not everyone was happy to see the articles in print. I received complaints from people who said the details of death upset them. I received death threats. How ironic would that have been? You write a series of informative stories about death—and someone kills you for doing it.

About a week after the series ended, I read that a Florida cardiology instructor at the University of Florida medical school, Dr. M.B. Sabom, released a study of cardiac patients who had reported life after life experiences. Assisting him in the study was a psychiatric social worker named Sarah Kreutzier. Impressed by what I read, I requested an interview with him for a follow-up article to my series on death and dying.

Dr. Sabom told me that when he began his study he was skeptical of reports of life after death experiences and resolved to answer his own questions about those reports by interviewing fifty men and women who had suffered cardiac arrests and then been resuscitated. Eleven told him that they had sensations of leaving their bodies.

Sabom tabulated two different types of episodes. First were those in which patients described instances of leaving their bodies. Second were those who reported going a step further to enter into another environment. Explaining the latter group Sabom said: "They tended to drift off into calm, peaceful places where they often met dead friends and relatives. A white light emanated brightness and warmth—and a few had playbacks of major events in their lives."

Dr. Sabom said the interviews had an impact on him because none of the individuals he interviewed said they were frightened by the experience. "Some even said they didn't want to come back. You'd expect a dream at that time to be a nightmare, not something pleasant—it leads me to believe that it's more than just a hallucination."

While I was working on the article, *Delta Democrat-Times* publisher Betty Carter told me she had a story to tell me, but she didn't want her name used for privacy reasons. I had no problem with that. Mrs. Carter was a legendary figure to me and I couldn't wait to hear what she wanted to tell me. Truthfully, I felt honored she would even talk to me.

To my great surprise, she told me she herself had had an out-of-body experience in 1938 while pregnant with twins. However, she miscarried and lost enough blood that doctors were concerned about her survival. She went into shock and the doctors issued a call for blood from the community. Despite her doctors' efforts, she began slipping away.

"At some point, I found myself floating up near the ceiling," she said. "I looked down and there I was in the bed. There were three doctors and several nurses standing around the bed. 'It's 107,' I heard one of the nurses say—and I thought, well, I'm dying—but then I thought to myself, I can't die because there are things I need to see about. The next thing I knew I was back on the bed inside my body"

I included her comments in my story, which ran on Page One, and cited unnamed sources, but for many years I never told a soul that Mrs. Carter was the unnamed source. I previously wrote about her conversation in a book I co-authored titled *Devil's Sanctuary*, but before publishing the information I contacted her son, Hodding, and asked for his permission. His response was gracious: "I think Mother would like for it to be used; her reasons for reluctance at the time are, like her, no longer with us."

I STAYED IN TOUCH with Sheriff Bubba Lawler in Issaquena County. Sometimes we talked about the people there that I knew. Other times he had news tips for me, such as the day he learned that a large field of marijuana was growing in an isolated part of the county. He called his favorite reporter and I drove out and shot his photograph standing in the marijuana field.

Lawler didn't stumble onto the marijuana patch. . Two state narcotics agents walked into his office one day and told him about it. They refused

Sheriff Bubba Lawler in marijuana field.
Photo by James L. Dickerson / Delta Democrat-Times

to tell him how they knew about the marijuana and they refused to disclose the name of the informant. It was information that would have helped him make an arrest.

"They could have been a lot more helpful if they had told us more about it," Lawler said.

With no information about how the field was discovered, the only thing the sheriff could do to apprehend the criminals was to stake out the field in hopes of nabbing them when they showed up to inspect their crop. At that time the plants were four feet in height. After maintaining surveillance for six weeks, with no one showing up, he decided to harvest the crop. By that time the plants were seven feet high.

"We thought it'd be better to go ahead and harvest it," he said. "We were afraid someone would get it while we weren't there."

With the help of his deputy and two inmates from the county jail, they pulled up the marijuana plants, shook the mud off the roots, and loaded the forbidden crop into the back of a pickup truck. Altogether, the crop weighed in at eighty-six pounds. Before they left, Lawler left a note nailed to a tree informing the pot farmers where they could get their crop. No one ever showed up to claim it.

On another occasion the sheriff called to let me know an escapee from the jail had set fire to the town's only store and it had burned to the ground. Now residents of Issaquena County had no place to buy groceries. They had to drive to another county to do that. The escapee was caught and transferred out of the county for his own safety.

I told Sheriff Bubba I was going to drive out and take a photograph and I asked if he would put out word that I was coming so that I could get an image of townspeople standing next to the ashes. He was happy to do it. After all, it was his town and his burned down store.

When I arrived there was quite a crowd waiting for me. Most of them were happy to see the best damned food stamp man they'd ever had return to the county. I got them to gather at the remains of the store. These were the days before the arrival of digital cameras, so I didn't know what I had captured until the film was developed and editors chose an image for the newspaper. They ran the photograph above the fold on Page One with a headline that referenced the anger the townspeople felt over losing their only store to an escaped prisoner.

However, if you looked closely at the photograph you could see that almost everyone in the photo was smiling. They were so happy to see me again that they were grinning ear-to-ear, despite the tragedy. It was a hilarious example of what can happen if the layout editor writes a headline without looking at the accompanying photograph.

BY THIS POINT in my career as a full-time journalist (the first year), I had decided to focus on an investigative approach to my efforts, whether as a reporter or an editorial writer. When people talk of investigative journalism, they often focus on political or corporate corruption, but I feel there is a broader canvas that accommodates investigative journalism. By that I mean the investigation of ideas, beliefs and social and economic

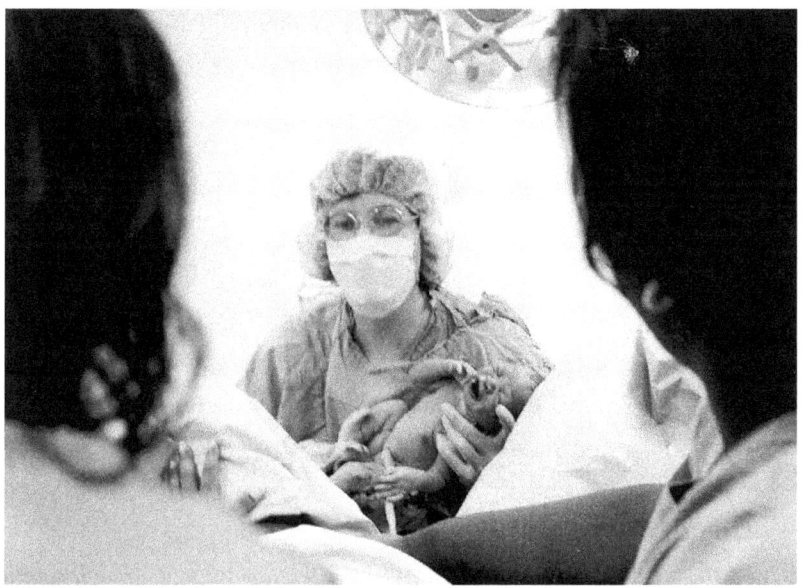

Author snaps photo of actual delivery.

trends. It can involve criminal acts, but it also can involve distorted thinking and the immoral manipulation of public policy.

When I wrote investigative features for the *Delta Democrat-Times* the stories were usually run on Page One in a series of articles. When I wrote features that involved my own photography, I was usually given a full page on Page Three to accommodate both photos and text. One of those stories that generated a lot of interest—and hate mail directed toward me—was an investigative look at a new midwifery program in the Delta, specifically in my hometown of Hollandale, where clinic doctors had introduced a midwifery program to serve the desperate need of minority residents in the area. I was given permission to interview the midwives on staff and to attend a birth.

I did the interviews I needed for the story and then waited to hear that a birth was about to happen. That call came at around 11 p.m. I was asleep and the telephone rang in the dark. After much groping, I found the ringing telephone and answered. It was the clinic letting me know that a pregnant teen and her mother had agreed to allow me to attend the birth for the purpose of taking notes and photographs. Having never seen a birth, I had no idea what to expect.

I arrived at the clinic and was greeted by midwife Kaye Thackerson, who then introduced me to the soon-to-be mother and her mother.

"There are stirrups on the table, but they are kept pushed to the side," I wrote. *"Cheryl's (not her real name) legs—parted at about a 60 degree angle—are not fastened down. This is a natural childbirth. That means Cheryl will play an active part in the delivery of her child. She will not be put to sleep with an anesthetic. Nor will she be strapped down to the table."*

Suddenly, things began to happen.

Once the baby's head came into view, the skin was bright blue and the umbilical cord was wrapped around the baby's neck. Unless something was done quickly the baby would die.

Quickly, the midwife yanks the baby from the birth canal, then baby spinning, hands darting at lightning speed, she frees the child from its bondage. There is a long pause. Then emerging from the stillness came the cry of a healthy baby girl.[9]

Exhausted by the tension of the delivery, and my own efforts to be there yet "not be there," I went home and went to bed.

"How'd it go?" asked Ina, wide awake.

"Baby girl," I said, already slipping into sleep.

The story ran with a full page of photographs and text.

In the newsroom the day after the series began, the telephone calls started coming in. Some of the callers were upset with me because I used such words and phrases as "birth canal" and "legs parted at about a 60 degree angle." I have never apologized for realism. If someone doesn't like real life they should check out and bask in the constant glow of hellfire. Those calls didn't bother me. Racist calls did bother me. I was called every name in the book because the mother in the story was African American. Over the years, I have received a number of death threats. All have involved race in one way or another. I have decided that to be a good journalist you must have the survival instincts of a bootlegger and the moral compass of a priest.

* * *

After a while, Pic Firmin emerged again. He told me he had suggested to *Facing South*, a syndicated column out of North Carolina that they should check out my stories. They did and asked me to start writing for them on the side. My first column was shaped from a full page of photographs and text written for my Page Three slot at the newspaper. It was based on a visit to the home of Mrs. Dorothy Phelps, a legendary Deltan who lived in a grand house in Nitta Yuma. My story began:

At mid-morning there is a disquieting stillness in the house. A door opens. A cold wind pushes its way into the hallway, pulling the door shut with a bang. Ten thousand staring, unblinking eyes are waiting inside. They peer out from the tops of shelves, around partially opened doors— and every last one of them is as blind as a ten penny nail.

The door creaks as if to shake off the cold.

Mrs. Dorothy Phelps slowly makes her way up the staircase of the Nita Yuma plantation house where her husband, Henry, was born more than 60 years ago. She is leading a visitor to the most important room in the house.

With a sweep of her hand, she introduces the speechless visitor to the inhabitants of the house—5,000 equally speechless dolls. It is surely one of the largest doll houses in the world.

ONE DAY I WAS AT MY DESK in the newsroom, typing away on a story, when I felt someone looking at me. I looked up and saw Philip Carter intently staring at me from across the newsroom. I made eye contact with him, prompting him to say, "I need to get you interested in news."

Facing South

a syndicated column:
voices of tradition
in a changing region

Dorothy Phelps: "It's the number one hobby."

NITTA YUMA, Miss. – At mid-morning there is a disquieting stillness in the old house.

A door opens. A cold wind pushes its way into the hallway, pulling the door shut with a bang. Ten thousand staring, unblinking eyes are waiting inside. They peer out from the tops of shelves, around partially opened doors – and every last one of them is as blind as a tenpenny nail.

The floor creaks as if to shake off the cold.

Mrs. Dorothy Phelps slowly makes her way up the staircase of the Nitta Yuma plantation house where her husband, Henry, was born more than 60 years ago. She is leading a visitor to the most important room in the house.

With a sweep of her hand, she introduces the speechless visitor to the inhabitants of the house – 5,000 equally speechless dolls. It is surely one of the largest doll houses in the world.

Mrs. Phelps reaches for one of her favorite dolls and sits down in a rocking chair. She holds the doll close, with great tenderness.

"When I was three, I had a lot of dolls," she said. "One day my cousin and I were talking. He said it was so nice to go to Heaven that we gathered up all of my dolls and buried them.

"A month later my cousin decided they couldn't go to Heaven since they hadn't been baptized. So we dug them up – but it was too late, they had all gone to pieces. I've felt guilty ever since."

Mrs. Phelps has been collecting dolls since she was six, providing a home for wayward manikins, many of which came from as far away as China, Europe or South America. The oldest doll, she said, was made in China in the 1700s. The modern dolls were made in the United States and Europe, during the 1920s to the 1940s.

Most of the dolls were given to her by her husband, who is co-author with her of a book about the plantation settlement of Nitta Yuma. Many of the other dolls came from friends and relatives.

"I try to name them after the person who gives them to me," she said. "But some already have names when they're made. Oddly enough they say the first dolls were not made for children. They were made for religious purposes or to demonstrate new clothing styles."

One of her favorites is a large china doll which she said was made shortly after the Civil War. "My husband and I went to an auction, but my ankle was hurt and I couldn't get out of the truck," she said, her voice suddenly growing very soft. "My husband brought it over to the truck and gave it to me – it's a sentimental doll."

Another favorite is the Scarlett O'Hara doll. "It was made right after they did the movie and it's dressed in the original clothes of 'Gone With the Wind,'" she said. "I've had it for years, many years."

Some of her most valuable dolls, she said, are those with black faces.

"They would make a lot of white dolls and only a few Negro dolls," she said. "They would have the same features, but just a few of them would be black. In the old days, most of the black children played with white dolls. The first dolls were manufactured in Europe and that could be a reason they didn't make so many Negro dolls."

The single most valuable doll she has is a religious doll called Saint Theresa. Kept apart from the others, it is on display beneath a glass cover. "She can be found in any encyclopedia," she said. "And I couldn't put a price on her."

Mrs. Phelps said men who see her doll collections are every bit as excited about them as women. "They just throw up their hands," she said. "You know they say men and boys collect dolls, too. It's the number one hobby all over – but men generally collect toy soldiers, mannish things."

That brought Mrs. Phelps to the subject of Teddy Roosevelt.

"I have a lot of teddy bears in my collection – you know they were named after Teddy Roosevelt," she said with a nod. "My daddy knew Teddy Roosevelt. One day they were at a banquet in Nashville. Teddy Roosevelt picked up his cup of coffee and said, 'Ah, good to the last drop.' And, don't you know, that's where that Maxwell House Coffee jingle came from."

– JAMES DICKERSON
Delta Democrat Times
Greenville, Miss.

FACING SOUTH welcomes readers' comments and writers' contributions. Write P.O. Box 230, Chapel Hill, N.C. 27514.

You've got to understand that Philip was a likable person—and I like him to this day—but that was a hell of a way to communicate with me. When he said that the other reporters turned and looked at me. I was embarrassed and said nothing in response. What I did do was make up my mind I no longer wanted to work there.

I was hired as a feature writer at a time when all the other reporters had assigned beats such as cops, the environment, city government, the county supervisors, courts, etc. There were no beats open for news reporting. Philip could have talked to me in private and asked if I had any interest in replacing any of the beat reporters. I might have said yes. It should be obvious to the reader at this point that I have always been open to trying new things. The truth was that many of my features for the *Delta Democrat-Times* were investigative news stories. The story about the midwifery program is a good example. No one outside of my hometown had any idea the innovative program even existed. Its creation addressed a major healthcare problem in the Mississippi Delta.

After the incident a staffer sidled up to me and whispered that Philip was cutting staff on his two Louisiana publications and wanted to move his feature writer into the popular slot I had created on Page Three. As it turned out, the female feature writer Philip had in mind was buddy-buddy with Sallie Anne Gresham, my managing editor.

When I went home that day I wrote a letter to John Emmerich, the moderate editor/owner of the Greenwood *Commonwealth,* asking about employment opportunities. The newspaper was sixty miles away and offered the added benefit of being the actual city of my birth. Emmerich immediately called me and said he didn't have an open position but would create one. He asked what I wanted to do. I said I wanted to write features and editorials. He offered be a five dollar a week raise and that was good enough for me, so I reluctantly resigned my position at the Greenville newspaper and relocated my wife and son to Greenwood.

With apologies to Woody Allen, journalists and sharks have one thing in common: both have to keep moving to stay alive.

James L. Dickerson in Delta cotton field

Chapter 7

Greenwood Commonwealth

JOHN EMMERICH was the son of J. Oliver Emmerich who founded the *McComb-Enterprise Journal* in the 1940s in McComb, Mississippi. Through the 1940s and 1950s, J. Oliver Emmerich opposed civil rights, but as the abuses against Black Mississippians reached intolerable levels he changed his mind and became a supporter of civil rights. He was one of the first newspaper publishers in the state to use courtesy titles for African-Americans, and when violence took place against the Freedom Riders who came to Mississippi to register Blacks to vote, he editorialized that violence could not be condoned.

Not surprisingly, after growing up in that atmosphere, John Emmerich attended Ole Miss, where he obtained a degree in journalism, and then relocated to Paris where he studied at the Sorbonne. Following that he received a Nieman Fellowship to study at Harvard University. Before becoming the editor-publisher of the *Commonwealth*, he worked for *The Baltimore Sun, The Houston Chronicle*, and *The Minneapolis Tribune.* In short, John had outstanding credentials as a journalist.

Before moving to Greenwood, Ina and I received an invitation to move into a duplex apartment owned by my Uncle George and Aunt

Marcie. Ina got a job at a bank, Jonathan was enrolled in public school, and I began work at the *Commonwealth*.

On the first day, I spent most of the morning in John's office with the door closed, with him talking about the newspaper. He had served as a lieutenant in the Korean War, but he did not bring up the Vietnam War, not then, not at any time I worked at the newspaper. Neither did anyone else. It was as if that war never happened.

After a general discussion about Greenwood, the demographics of the city, and its history, we got down to business. John told me that he wrote all the editorials and didn't see that as anything I would be needed to do. *Swish*....the sound of air deflating my balloon. Then he informed me that since they already had an arts editor that would have to be something in the future. *Swish*......another deflation. "While we like your features and would like to see more of those, we also need you to develop sources and help out on the news side."

I nodded, thinking . . . *this is not a great start.*

Then John began doing something I have found to be a common trait among editors. He began thinking out loud.

"It has always bothered me that Hodding could get outstanding job applicants from all over the country, many from Ivy League universities," he said, addressing no one in particular. "Why can't I do that?" He didn't wait for an answer. "It's a mystery to me. Our politics aren't all that different. I just don't get it."

I knew why, but I didn't really think he wanted to hear it from me.

After that meandering conversation, I stepped out of his office and was shown to my desk by the managing editor, Claudia Martino. I sat at my desk while everyone else worked on stories. I rearranged the items on the desk several times and looked around the newsroom several times without ever making eye contact with anyone. I was the invisible man. No one was looking at me. No one asked me any questions. What they did do for the remainder of the day was bring me employment papers to sign. The following morning I told the managing editor I thought I would spend the day driving around, checking out the community, and reacquainting myself with the layout of the city.

I was born in Greenwood, not because my family lived there—Mother and Father lived in Greenville—but because Mother wanted to give birth in a hospital where she could be near her sister, my Aunt Marcie, a registered nurse who lived in Greenwood. After I was born, I was taken home to Greenville, where my family lived until I was three, at which time we moved to Greenwood, where my father operated a department store named Mays that had an area set aside for World War II army surplus items. I can't explain why, but I really liked the way army surplus smelled.

I drove around downtown, looking for landmarks that might bring back memories. I found where the department store that my father managed had been located. The store was gone, of course, but sadly the storefront had been changed to suit new tenants and brought back no memories. However, two doors down I saw the Crystal, a restaurant where my father and I often ate lunch, sitting on stools at the counter. How proud I felt sitting next to my father in the restaurant.

The railroad tracks in front of my father's store divided Greenwood into Black and white neighborhoods. Across the street and over the railroad was another street that was lined with businesses, most of which catered to Black customers. My Uncle George had a furniture store there named the Mule Barn. It sold less expensive furniture to Black families. I drove over there to look at it because I had not seen it in many years. Behind the store I saw a blacksmith shop where a group of men gathered around two men playing checkers on an oversized custom-made wooden checker board. I watched the game, taking photographs, and then talked to the men once the game was over with the intention of writing a story for the newspaper.

From there I drove west to the last house that I lived in before moving away. The house was still there—a small, two-bedroom house with a detached garage. There was a small front porch where I often posed with my father for photographs. There were no cars in the driveway, indicating perhaps that no one was at home, so I parked in front of the house, my memories overtaking me like a sudden rainstorm.

MY FATHER AND I often went on long rides together in the country. It was during one of those rides we drove out to the Greenwood airport that he confessed he was saving money to purchase an airplane, only he made me promise not to tell Mother since she did not like for him to fly. The stories of him stunt flying with his U.S. Air Corps buddies under the Mississippi River Bridge at Greenville gave her nightmares about him crashing into the pylons and drowning in the river.

Other times, Dad took me out in the country to teach me how to fire a .22-caliber rifle and a 20-gauge shotgun. I still have both guns. They are not instruments of death to me. They are symbols of a father's love for his son. We never went hunting for game, but once while hiking in the Blue Ridge Mountains, he helped me shoot an aggressive black snake that charged us, refusing to give way to us on our wooded path. The snake was not poisonous, but its bite could have left behind a nasty infection.

Dad was patient and loving and always made me feel safe. Sometimes we went to the movies together, just the two of us, usually to see the latest Roy Rogers or Gene Autry feature. Once we went to the picture show to see a Tex Ritter movie, only to our surprise Tex Ritter himself stepped out on the stage in front of the movie screen. He did some tricks with a rope and fired his pistol (I didn't know they were blanks; I thought Tex was firing live rounds) and at one point he brought his horse up onto the stage, the horse's shod hooves banging against the wooden floor like thunder. My father and I talked about that horse and the gunplay for days. It was a bonding moment for us that still exists with me.

My father genuinely loved children. Growing up, I thought all dads were like that, but now I know better. He not only spent time with his own children, he always made a big fuss over his nieces and nephews, especially Aunt Marcie's children, Martha and her younger sister Janet. July 29, 1953 was my cousin Janet's fourth birthday. To celebrate, Mother and Aunt Marcie planned a party at the same city park across the street from the graveyard that I walked through on my way home from school. I really didn't want to go to a birthday party for girls at which there would be no boys but myself, so I asked my father if he would take me fishing. We had gone fishing a couple of weeks before at Third Bridge Lake and I was eager to return. Father hadn't planned on going fishing, but I kept saying, "Please, please, please," until he relented and said yes. He told me I could invite my friend Richard to go with us.

When told of the fishing trip, Mother's only comment to my father was the same as it always was each time we went fishing: "Don't let my baby boy drown."

"Don't worry. I'll take good care of him."

"You better."

Because Richard's father had just purchased a new outboard motor he hadn't yet tried out, our fathers decided to make it a father-son affair. We drove to the lake in Father's car, a two-seat roadster that had a tiny backseat that was perfect for two seven-year-old boys.

The last thing Mother said to my father was, "Don't let my boy drown. Remember my dreams."

"I won't," he said softly. "I promise."

The lake was about a thirty-minute drive from Greenwood, on the other side of Sidon, a small crossroads town. Once we turned off the main highway, the dirt road wound several miles through cotton fields and swampy forests before it dead-ended at the lake. Before Father got out of the car, he did something I had never seen him do: he tucked the car keys behind the sun visor. Usually, he kept his keys in his pocket.

We fished on the bank of the lake for a long time, using live roaches and crickets for bait, but the fish were not biting that day and no one even got a nibble. Finally, when it became obvious that we would be taking home no bluegill bream or bass to fry up for supper, we decided to rent a boat and go for a ride, using Mr. Cooper's new outboard motor. They had two types of boats—sixteen-foot military surplus boats that rode deep in the water and had plenty of room to walk around in and fourteen-foot, lightweight skiffs that barely skimmed the surface of the water. We chose the skiff because it was the only boat equipped to take the outboard motor.

The boat had a seat at the stern, where the outboard was attached, and Mr. Cooper and Richard shared a seat there. Midway up the boat was a seat on which my father and I sat. It was a wooden cypress boat and every time we moved our feet, it clanked with dull thuds, sending sound waves rolling out across the water.

The son of the woman who owned the boats, who was a year older than Richard and me, helped us into the boat and then untied it so that it could drift away from the dock. Mr. Cooper had a hard time cranking the motor. He adjusted the gasoline flow each time he pulled on the crank. We drifted quietly out into deep water. Again and again he yanked the crank.

Suddenly, the motor started with a loud, sputtering roar and sent the boat lurching forward. We looked back at Mr. Cooper, who was frantic because the motor had started at full throttle and he didn't know what to do about it. When we turned back to the front of the boat, we saw the bow bounce up and then slap down hard and dip beneath the surface of the lake, allowing water to pour over the front seat. The boat was sinking.

We panicked and stood up, all four of us, and I felt my father's arms around me as he grabbed me and leaped into the water.

"Hold tight," were his last words to me in the water.

I could not swim, but my father was an expert swimmer. Mr. Cooper and Richard were right behind us. Even though the boat was made of wood and should have floated, it sank out of sight beneath the muddy water. There was nothing near us to hold onto. I felt my father's arms tighten around me. You would think there would be a lot of screaming and thrashing about in a situation like that, but the lake was stone-cold silent. No one uttered a word. The water was surprisingly warm, like what you would expect in the bathtub. There was a sense of turning, floating beneath the surface, and reaching out, the soft pressure of the water holding me in in suspension.

Watching from the dock was the eight-year-old boy, now frightened out of his mind. He jumped into a boat and paddled in our direction. Father held me close against him in the water, keeping the two of us afloat. The rescue boat reached Mr. Cooper and Richard first. As the young boy helped Richard into the boat, my father and I treaded water, about thirty feet away, neither of us saying a word. I had water in my nose from when we first jumped into the lake and I gasped for breath. The water tasted like rust and made my throat burn.

Then something extraordinary happened. We slipped beneath the surface, floating about in complete darkness. With my father's strong arms wrapped around me, I fell into what felt like a soundless, motionless, endless cocoon that enveloped us like something in a dream. The daylight, with its flickering rays of hope, was sucked out of the cocoon.

In an instant I was back on the surface with my father and felt him throw me toward the outstretched arms of the young boy in a boat. Abruptly, without warning, I was airborne, floating through the air toward the boy and Mr. Cooper, a sensation so unlike anything else that I'd ever experienced that I can remember it to this day. Still in the water himself, Mr. Cooper clung to the boat, a look of stunned horror on his face.

I felt a sudden surge of adrenalin as the young boy grabbed hold of my shirt and my arm and pulled me into the boat. When I looked back to find my father, he was gone.

The young boy paddled us back to the dock, not knowing what to say, looking straight ahead as if he was alone in the boat. Mr. Cooper ran to the house with the young boy to get help. But the boy's mother said she was there alone and could not swim. Neither could Mr. Cooper nor Richard nor I. The only person in our group who could swim was Father.

Mr. Cooper called the sheriff's office and frantically asked them to send help. Throughout it all, I stood on the edge of the dock, shivering, helpless, more scared than I'd ever been in my life.

"Daddy!" I called out, peering down into the water, hoping to see his smiling face. "Daddy, where are you?"

When the sheriff finally arrived, we pointed to where my father had disappeared. The heavyset deputies all stared helplessly at the water. Incredibly, none of them could swim either. I expected them to jump into the lake and save my dad. After a while, Mr. Cooper walked away from me to have a private conversation with the deputies. When he returned, he said, "Let's go find your mother, son."

We walked back to the car and got inside. When Mr. Cooper realized he did not have a key to the car, he asked if I knew if my dad kept a second key hidden anywhere. I pointed to the sun visor and within minutes we were on our way back to town, the rancid, Delta dust billowing high into the treetops behind us.

Mr. Cooper knew about Janet's birthday party, so he went directly to the park. As we got out of the car, I saw my mother's head rise above the children and look our way. She saw Mr. Cooper and Richard and me, but not my dad. There was a sudden look of panic on her face. I could see the fear in her eyes. Only a few steps from the picnic table, Mr. Cooper stopped and grabbed me by the shoulders, leaning over to whisper in my ear, "You go tell her, son." He forcefully shoved me in her direction.

I broke into a run, my arms outstretched to my mother. I cried out, my voice cracked and forlorn, "Mama, daddy's dead! Daddy's dead!"

Mother took me in her arms and squeezed me tight, looking back at Mr. Cooper, who remained in the distance. She could tell by his face that it was true. The other women, including Aunt Marcie, approached Mr. Cooper and asked what'd happened. I watched as he talked to them, their bodies deflated by the bad news. For years after that, Janet met Mother in tears every time she saw her, crying that if she only had not had a birthday party that day my daddy would still be alive.

By late afternoon, our house had filled with people, all seemingly talking at once. Aunt Marcie, who had the face of a saint, held my three-year-old sister, Susan, and talked to her, speaking in soft, measured tones, gently rocking her from side to side. Mother was in the bedroom with the other women. They gathered around her, not exactly sure what to say.

The author and his sister, Susan, at their father's grave

Whenever they spoke, evoking common sense, or what Daddy would have wanted, or the grace of God, it was not what she wanted to hear.

"Please, just leave me alone!" she cried out, her voice cutting like a knife through a room filled with caring people. "*I just hurt all over*. My chest hurts. My shoulder hurts. How will I ever live without him?"

WHEN I RETURNED to the newsroom that day I was somewhat shaken by the painful memories the city brought back to me, many of them repressed for years. Claudia had a couple of news stories for me to write based on press releases. I did those and then had my photographs developed of the checker game and wrote the story. They gave me three-quarters of a page inside for the story and photographs. After the story ran, the Associated Press picked it up, along with the photograph, giving me my first AP story and photograph. It went to every AP newspaper in Mississippi.

I spent the rest of the day going through back issues of the newspaper to determine if any follow-ups were needed for previous Page One news stories. A couple of unusual stories caught my eye, both of them alleging the rape of white women by Black men. Don't misunderstand. Mississippi has a history of black men raping white women. However, I had been aware of an alternate history by the time I was a teenager. I once took a girl on a date to a movie theater only to hear her tearful confession that her father made her have sex with Black men for money. Then there was the planter out from Hollandale who took his young wife to parties given at Black tenant houses, only to leave her alone to dance with shirtless Black men in exchange for a marijuana stash.

One of the cases that got my attention took place in a small town several miles from Greenwood. I told Claudia I was going to visit the town the next morning and poke around to see what was happening. She grimaced, a gesture I did not understand until much later. Here's the story that had been told to the newspaper by the police: Two white women in their late teens were walking along a street when a Black man driving a limousine forced them into the car and drove them out into the country and raped one of the women. The alleged victim told someone about the incident and the Black man was arrested and charged with rape.

The original *Commonwealth* story did not give the victim's name, but it was not difficult to find out the names of all three individuals involved from local residents who were not shy about providing information to me. In conflict with the police report, I was told by one source that the rape victim had recanted after her friend told her she was going to tell the truth if the victim did not. This alternate version of the police story was that the women willingly got into the limo and were driven outside of town where the driver parked in a secluded spot and asked one of the women in the rear of the limo if she would trade places with him. With the friend sitting in the front seat, the driver proceeded to sweet-talk the other woman out of her clothes so that he could have sex with her. When they returned to town, the driver stopped and let the women out on a street corner. They waved goodbye and turned to see a white man who knew their fathers standing in the shade. When the women went home, fearful of what the man in the shade would tell their fathers, they claimed they were abducted.

Armed with two accounts of the incident, I stopped off at the police station to talk to the chief. If you've never seen a man wearing a pistol explode, believe me, you never want to do so. It is not a pretty sight.

"Don't you write no story on this," the chief bellowed, his face flashing beet red like a stoplight.

"The truth has never hurt anybody," I said, thinking *Sheriff Bubba, you may have a road trip in your future*. Having a cop for a friend is the best insurance policy a reporter can have.

"It's gonna hurt *you*," he yelled. "I'm going to put *your* ass in jail."

"For asking questions?"

"No, for disturbing the peace."

"Haven't you ever heard of freedom of the press?"

"What's your editor's name?"

I gave him the general manager's name because he, not John Emmerich, directly supervised the news staff. He went into his office and closed the door. *The poor man has no idea what is happening in Mississippi between white women and Black men. Either that or he does know and the thought of it is driving him crazy.*

When he came out of his office, he was grinning.

"Looks like your editor saved your ass," he said.

"Yeah?"

"You are free to go."

On my way back to the newsroom, I stopped by the courthouse to request court files on the other rape case that attracted my attention. In this instance, a young white married woman, who worked at a downtown store, was allegedly abducted in a parking lot by a Black man and driven just outside town where she was raped beneath a bridge. The man was arrested and charged with rape. He claimed they had spoken inside the store where she worked and she had agreed to meet him in the parking lot. He admitted they had sex on the grass beneath the bridge, but he claimed the intercourse was mutual. He also said she accompanied him on another day to a deserted cotton gin where they had sex on a mound of freshly picked cotton. If Freud had developed a concept involving interracial sex in the South surely it would have involved sex on a mound of freshly picked cotton. You can't get any more Freudian than that.

When I returned to the newsroom, I was invited into the general manager's office to talk to him behind closed doors. He said he had received calls from the police chief and the court clerk that I was "stirring up trouble." I told him I was researching follow-up stories.

"I don't want you to do any more investigating into those stories," he said. "That's all in the past. We don't want to be stirring up any trouble."

So, that was the end of that. As it turned out, I would leave Greenwood without ever knowing if the black man had been put to death or released from jail.

My purpose in the first story was to show how easy it was for a Black man to be accused of rape and how the accused man in this case would die in the gas chamber if the conflicting stories were not reconciled in a public way. As it turned out, I would leave Greenwood without ever knowing if the Black man was put to death or released.

As far as the second case was concerned, it was my understanding the accused man had been found not guilty by a jury. There were things I read about the trial that made me wonder if the case had a deeper cultural context than was apparent on the surface. As a social worker, I had learned that human sexuality is complex and not at all what it may seem to be.

In the 1970s in the Mississippi Delta, local government, store owners, and preachers all shared an unspoken commitment to protecting white women from Black men. That is ironic because the truth was that white women in the Delta had begun eyeing Black men as potential partners, primarily because the decline of leadership skills in the South among white males was beginning to become more and more evident as white males turned their back on education as a means of self-improvement.

WORKING FOR A NEWSPAPER in the South during in the 1970s was discouraging, not so much because you knew that people would report you to your editor if you ever asked questions that threatened "Mississippi values," defined as anything that presented Black residents in a positive light, but because you knew your editor likely would pull you off the story. Over the years, Mississippi has produced some outstanding journalists, but that greatness was not derived from covering up the truth.

With the realization that I would not be allowed to do investigative stories, the bedrock of my journalistic psyche, I decided to focus on something else I very much enjoyed doing: being both a journalist and a photojournalist on feature stories that would tell "truths" of a different sort. Finding features like that outside the city meant driving around a lot, talking to people in country stores, or sometimes just spotting something on the side of the road that grabbed my attention.

One such feature story I wrote and photographed was about a natural springs east of Greenwood near Winona that had once attracted people from all over the South seeking miracle cures for a variety of ailments and diseases. Stafford's Wells had been closed for sixty years, but Mrs. Lois Rolph, who currently owned the facility, planned to clean out the bricked wells and once again offer the water for sale. At the turn of the century the water was placed in jars and sold for twenty-five cents per gallon.

I do believe that it was with this story that I first began using my signature, three-beat feature lede. The story began:

If you are having a problem with your liver, you are advised to drink the water on the west side of the road. (beat 1)

But if your kidneys are keeping you awake at night, you are advised to drink the water on the east side of the road. (beat 2)

That's according to Mrs. Lois Rolph, who owns Stafford's wells, a former mineral water resort that once attracted health enthusiasts from all over the South. (beat 3).

I believe good writing requires intellect, creativity and a sense of rhythm. The three-beat lede provides an irresistible rhythm that will work every time to ensnare the reader. It is similar to the format of popular songs you hear on the radio—two verses and a chorus. It's all about the beat. The reason you can remember memorable lines from a narrative is because the rhythm of the writing enables the lines to dance into your memory. As a writer, what you are saying to the reader is, "Come dance with me." Of course, some features don't lend themselves to a three-beat lede. In those instances, a memorable quote will provide a decent entry into the story.

I continued to do a mixture of news and features because that is what John Emmerich wanted me to do. One morning I came into work and he pulled me aside. At that time in Greenwood's economic development the largest non-agricultural employer in the city was Baldwin Piano. In 1961 it had relocated its piano factory to Greenwood from Cincinnati, Ohio. The plant did not actually make finished pianos. It made the wooden frame-work and cabinets that enclose the mechanical workings of their pianos. I don't recall the details of the problem, but something big was happening at the plant that was unsettling the employees. The reporter who usually covered the plant was unable to obtain information about whether the plant would be closing, so John asked me if I would give it a try.

I spoke to the plant manager, if I recall, but he didn't know anything more than what he already had told our reporter. So, I did what I always do when I want to get the best information possible. I went to the top. In this case, I telephoned the corporate headquarters and spoke to an executive who repeatedly dodged my questions until I invoked an interviewing trick I had learned as a social worker when I was attempting to obtain information from couples about prior marital separations or breakups. I call it the "white space" effect. It is especially effective when speaking on the telephone. In the case of the executive, the next time he responded and gave an incomplete answer to my question, I did not respond, leaving perhaps 30 seconds of dead air, or white space, in our conversation. Most people feel uncomfortable with white space in a conversation and possess an instinctive urge to fill the space. The executive was no different. Finally, his level of discomfort became unbearable and he blurted out the information I needed for my story. Silence, when weaponized, can be used as a form of mind control.

It's been forty-three years since I wrote that story, so the exact issue that was involved escapes me, but my story did calm fears that the plant was about to be closed, putting many employees out of work. John Emmerich was thrilled. Some time prior to this story he had attended a conference on employee morale and returned with the idea of creating a "Super Scooper Award" for reporters he wanted to honor for distinguished reporting. Soon after my Baldwin story, John assembled the staff in a private dining room of a hotel for a free lunch and news of the next Super Scooper Award recipient. Before I disclose the winner—although you may already have guessed—I must explain that the entire staff felt the award was an idiotic thing to waste time on. Personally, I could not hear the name of the award without breaking out into laughter because every time I heard the words I envisioned a reporter with a dog scooper gathering poop. To me, the symbolism was hilarious.

To my eternal regret, when John announced the winner for the award was me, I broke out into laughter, prompting everyone else at the table to laugh, except John Emmerich who looked truly stunned. I instantly felt remorse. I truly liked John. I knew what it was like to be a moderate and live in a city populated with right-wing dodo birds waddling about, pooping on the ideas of others. No one has ever accused me of possessing an abundance of tact. It is a weakness, I suppose, that I am that way, but for those who don't like in-your-face honesty, fuck'em.

With an anguished, almost tearful, face, John told the group he was just trying to be a better employer by giving the award and treating the staff to lunch. Abruptly, he terminated the meeting and muttered something about the award not being appreciated. I made a mental note to withhold all future criticisms—at least until I found a new job, which I immediately started searching for. I got along well with John, except when I insulted him, but the staff seemed to resent me being there and I really didn't try to foster any friendships, except with the managing editor, Claudia, who often expressed appreciation of my work.

Despite my blunder at the award luncheon, John continued to confide in me. One day the newsroom buzzed with news that the husband of a very attractive Greenwood socialite had been killed in an automobile accident, after being hit head-on on a two-lane highway just outside of town. John took the news hard. He literally began to wring his hands and pace. Noticing John's discomfort, a reporter whispered something to me that I am not going to repeat. I have no idea if it was true or not, and I had no interest in pursuing the gossip. However, the next day John called me into his office and closed the door and asked if I would do him a personal favor. How could I deny him a favor after the way I had hurt his feelings at the Super Scooper luncheon?

"I guess you've heard about that horrible accident?" he asked.

"I have."

"The collision sent the steering column into his abdomen, spilling his guts all over the car."

I grimaced.

"There is a book of mine with a personal inscription on the back seat of the car." He paused a minute, looking intently at me. "Would you mind going over to the wrecking yard to retrieve that book for me? I need to get it back. You can park nearby and watch, and then run in and get it when no one is looking."

I was speechless, but I nodded, wondering why he would ask me. Was it because he trusted me or was it because I was a social outlaw? For whatever reason, he assumed I would have no problem stealing a book from the back seat of a bloodied car for a man who signed my paycheck.

If so, he was correct.

Later that day, I staked out the wrecking yard and parked in the shade of a tree and waited until I saw what appeared to be the only employee go into the office. Seeing that, I made a mad dash for the car, opened the backseat door, and snatched the book from a pile of debris, my heart pounding. Then I ran like hell back to my car, where I quickly inserted the book into a large manila envelope and drove back to the newsroom.

I did not look at the inscription.

John's office door was open, so I walked in and handed him the envelope the way I had seen drug dealers in movies pass kilos of cocaine to buyers. Then I turned and left, his voice cascading over my shoulder, following after me in a haunting but grateful tone, "Thanks, Jim."

Was I the one he trusted the most at the newspaper?

I had met John's wife, Celia, a couple of times, and she impressed me as a very nice person. A former Ole Miss cheerleader who went on to receive a master's degree in history from John Hopkins University, she was an unrepentant liberal who worked for civil rights and community development. History will leave her standing alongside Betty Carter of the *Delta Democrat-Times* and Hazel Brannon Smith of the *Durant News* as one of the most important women in Mississippi journalism. At the

Commonwealth, she sold ads, wrote a popular column, and served as a sounding board for her husband's proposed editorials. Because of her standing in journalism, I felt a little guilty about my participation in the book heist. They had a son, Wyatt, that I never met, and a twenty-year-old daughter, Melanie, whom I met when she returned home from college that summer. She once asked if she could spend the day with me as I made my rounds. I said no. If you are a thirty-two-year-old married man, the last thing you ever want to hear yourself say to a pretty twenty-year-old college woman who wants to spend the day with you is, "Sure, why not?"

As luck would have it, thirty-two years after meeting Celia, I reported to a classroom at Millsaps College in Jackson, Mississippi, to teach a course on writing. I sat down and looked over the crowd of gathered students and thought I saw a familiar face. I asked everyone to take turns giving their name and informing the class why they were enrolled. When it came time for the person who looked familiar to me to give her name, she said, "I'm Celia Emmerich and I want to write my memoirs." She paused to laugh. "But I'm not sure what to do with it after I write it."

I smiled broadly. So did she. It was no accident she took my class.

"Do you think anybody would be interested?" she continued.

"I would be," I said.

In the years after I left the Greenwood *Commonwealth*, she had explored the world, travelling to the Himalayan Mountains while in her Fifties and sailing the Maldive Islands while in her Sixties. I felt certain she had the kind of life experiences that would be of interest to book lovers. I subsequently wrote about Celia in a column for the *Jackson Free Press*:

When the class concluded, I noticed she stayed seated while I gathered my papers. Once everyone was gone, except for a promising children's book author, named Tony, she fished her walker from its hiding place, snapped it open and proceeded to the door.

Tony and I walked her to the elevator and asked how in the world she ever made it to the third floor with that contraption.

She smiled but didn't answer.

"Can you make it down the front steps?" I asked, concerned.

"Oh, sure," she said.

Tony and I were not so sure.

Tony took her walker, and I offered her my arm for support and ever so slowly walked her down a very steep stairway. Once at the bottom, with her behind the walker again, we scooted across campus to the parking area, where her son, Wyatt, was supposed to pick her up. Unfortunately, he was not there yet.

"Why don't I wait until he comes?" I asked.

"No need to do that," she said, nodding in the direction of two strapping male students who quickly volunteered, "We'll be here a while."

I left her in good hands and looked forward to seeing her again in class. I wanted to hear more about her memoir. But that was her first and last day in my class. The semester ended with no word of Celia's whereabouts.

Later, I came across her obituary and learned that something had happened that sent her to the hospital. Shortly after she returned home, she collapsed of a fatal heart attack. She died quickly, the same way her husband died, which I suppose is a blessing. I was glad I had her as a student, if only for one day.

FOR A WRITER, memories are like onions. You can peel off a layer, but there are a dozen more to replace the one you discarded. Among the memories I have held onto over the years are those associated with a little girl named Grace Mangum. Grace and I were born at the same Greenwood hospital only two months apart, which makes me the oldest. The year we were born there were two people living in Greenwood who went on to achieve fame—mystery writer Mickey Spillane, who lived there with his first wife, Mary Ann Pearce, and Bobbie Gentry, whose hit "Ode to Billie

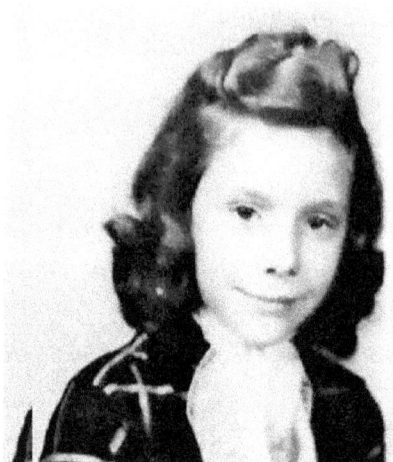

Grace Mangum and James L. Dickerson in 3ʳᵈ Grade

Joe," made music history. Grace went on to become a prominent bronze sculptor and had two sons, Jake Turner, who became a world traveler and successful businessman, and Mike Turner, who achieved comic book fame before passing away at a young age (his book *Witchblade* was made into a TV series). Our lives did not intersect until after my father died and my family moved to Hollandale, a town of around three thousand people.

I entered the third grade there emotionally battered by my experiences at Third Bridge Lake. The boys in the class made fun of me because I didn't have a father. Over and over they chanted:

"Jimmy doesn't have a daddy!" "Jimmy doesn't have a daddy!"

The only classmate who took up for me was Grace. Each time the boys misbehaved, she chastised them, vigorously shaking her index figure at them to show her disapproval. If that didn't work she did not hesitate to kick them on the shin, while screaming her displeasure. Not only was she a beautiful child, she was absolutely fearless. She was the Wonder Woman of her generation.

For Valentine's Day one year I gave her a large box of candy I purchased at the drugstore with money I earned working for my grandfather. The box was pink and had a twelve-inch palomino pony raring up on top. It was wrapped in pink cellophane and had a huge pink bow. I knew she would like it because we talked about horses a lot when we got together after school. I have a memory of us riding a horse bareback together: her with the reins, me with my arms around her waist.

I had no way of knowing—and indeed it took me more than sixty years to learn what I am about to tell you now—that Grace herself had a tortured road on her way to that third grade classroom. The previous summer her parents believed her to be too skinny. Friends told them that their daughter, too, had been too skinny. To help her put on weight, they sent her to a facility in Sanatorium, Mississippi, named the Preventorium. It was opened during a tuberculosis outbreak to protect vulnerable underweight children from being exposed to the disease while the institution helped them to gain weight.

So, at the age of six, Grace was dropped off by her loving parents at the Preventorium for the summer. In later years Grace referred to it as a "concentration camp." In fact, it was every bit as hellish as the fictional mental institution in the movie *One Flew Over the Cuckoo's Nest*.

"Before that happened I had never even spent the night away from home," Grace said in later years. "When I arrived, they took me from my parents, put me in a little room, put a bowl over my head and cut off all my hair. Then they took off all my clothes and put me in a pair of white shorts. There was no explanation. Then they shoved me out a door into a big outside area in the back. I saw some kids in the distance. They all seemed pretty traumatized, too. I didn't know anyone and I had no idea what to do. It was scary."

Visitation with her parents was allowed only on Sundays for two hours. If they brought her a toy, it was taken away after her parents left and put in a communal location they called the "brown house." Each day the children were allowed to go into the brown house to choose a toy to play with. The only rule was that the children could not pick a toy given to them by their parents.

"Every night in the dormitory we had to get in our little cots with

125

metal guard rails. You had to sleep on your back with your arms eight inches away from your body and your legs eight inches apart. The supervisors (both male and female) would come around, fuss at you and adjust your position if it wasn't exactly correct. I slept in the same white shorts I wore during the day. In fact, those white shorts were all we wore the whole time we were there. Many indignities were experienced by the children. I've got a feeling I was touched inappropriately, but can't be positive, as I blocked out a lot of memories of that place."

Grace and I both had been to hell and back. It was perhaps natural we find each other and become friends. Actually, from the Third Grade through the Sixth Grade she was my girlfriend. We played together at recess and did things after school, such as going to movies. I can remember going to the Roosevelt, the local movie theater, at least once to watch a heralded western.

On other occasions Mother drove us to Greenville to go to the movie theater there. We were sitting in the matinee audience at that theater when *The Fly*, starring Vincent Price, was making its first theatrical run. Sometimes Grace's parents took us on Sunday drives together, with us sitting on the back seat holding hands.

One day I still remember with great clarity was the day I kissed her while we sat together in her father's recliner watching television. It was our first kiss. It did something to Grace because she jumped to her feet, and said with some urgency, "Let's go outside."

I did as she asked and stood exactly where she told me to stand. I could not imagine what treat she had in mind. Suddenly, she turned on the water to the water hose, picked it up and pointed it at me, soaking me from head to foot. It was her way of cooling down my boyish passions. I told you, she was a smart kid. Hearing the commotion outside, Grace's mother came running out the door with a horrified look on her face.

"Grace, what were you thinking?"

"I don't know," she said, looking at me, daring me to tell her the reason why. "It just sort of happened."

With eyes sparkling like jewels, she bit her lower lip and twisted her mouth into a mischievous smile. Her mother gave me towels to sit on in the car and immediately drove me home so I could get out of my wet clothes. I wore that wetness like a badge of honor. She was embarrassed to explain the situation to my mother. However, I could tell by the way Mother looked at me that she suspected I might have provoked Grace. Mother could read me like a book.

Our friendship flourished until the end of the Sixth Grade school year. That was when the school superintendent asked my mother, Grace's parents and another girl's parents if they would like for us to skip the seventh grade and proceed directly to the eighth grade. My mother declined because she felt it would not be in my best interests. I have always agreed with that decision even though it had the unintended effect of separating Grace and me. Not far into the seventh grade, the bullies who had made life miserable for me by teasing me because I didn't have a father, resumed that activity once Grace was no longer there to keep them at bay. Watching this behavior and not understanding why I didn't fight back, the superintendent went to talk to my mother.

"I just don't understand why he won't fight back," he said.

"That's because I asked him not to fight at school," said Mother. "He promised me he wouldn't."

"I suggest you release him from that promise. I think if you do, you will see a big change in the situation."

That evening Mother had a talk with me and released me from the promise. The next day, during recess, one of the bullies, Jimmie Patterson, started taunting me again about not having a father. This time I tore into him like a tornado, whipping him from one end of the playground to the other. After that we became best friends and remained so throughout high school. As a result of Grace skipping a grade, I almost never saw her. She made new friends and the following year she joined the band and became the top baton twirler in the state. Grace and her parents moved away at the end of tenth grade and I did not speak to her again for sixty years.

Main Street of Webb, Mississippi / Photo by James L. Dickerson

THE MOST POPULAR full-page feature I did while at the *Commonwealth* probably was the one about Webb, Mississippi, a small town north of Greenwood. One day I overheard a conversation in a check-out line about Webb being the "beauty queen capital" of Mississippi. Needless to say, it peaked my interest. I telephoned a couple of public officials in Webb to ask if the rumors I had heard were true. To quote one official, "Hell, yeah. Come on up and check out our beautiful girls."

Who could resist an invitation like that?

Early one morning I drove to Webb (population 751) to scope it out and gather some names of the town's beauty pageant winners. When I returned to Greenwood, I whittled the list down to three: a former Miss "W" (Mississippi University for Women) and second runner-up to Miss Mississippi; a Miss Clarksdale; and a Miss Delta State University. I contacted all three women and asked them to meet me in Webb on an appointed day and time—and I asked them to please wear a swimsuit.

"Are we going swimming?" one of the woman asked with a skeptical giggle.

Before the women arrived I spoke to the police chief and asked if he minded blocking one end of Main Street while I took a photograph. No problem, he said, adding, "It's for a good cause."

The women all arrived at the same time. We parked on a side street, where the women stripped down to their swimsuits in full view of shoppers. Then we all walked out onto Main Street. At the closed end of the street I saw the squad car parked, lights flashing. I explained to the women that we would go out into the middle of the street and I would get ahead of them with my camera.

With everyone in place, I asked them to start walking toward me.

I didn't ask them to link arms, but they instinctively did and it looked great. Out of the corner of my eye I saw several passersby on the sidewalk staring at us, as if we all had escaped from a lunatic asylum. I kept snapping the shutter of my 35 mm until I thought I had what I needed. The result was an intriguing photograph that is now considered a classic, a throwback to a lost era. You couldn't take a photograph like that today. The protests from women's groups would be deafening.

Finally, I said, "That's it"—and watched with amusement as the women quickly fled to their cars as if they had been caught skinny dipping by a troop of Boy Scouts.

For the interview, all three women were willing to discuss hot-button topics (at least in the Seventies) such as premarital sex, marijuana and sexual harassment. I'm not sure if Greenwood has yet recovered from those frank discussions. By the standards of the Seventies, the women were fearless.

The photograph was taken in 1978. Forty-one years later I decided to use the image of the women on Main Street on the cover of a book of photographs *Mississippi on My Mind*. I checked with *Commonwealth* editor Tim Kalich and he had no problem with me using it for a cover. He called the photo a "classic." I also wanted to let the women know about it in case they had any objections, so I tracked them down to tell them about the project. Sadly, one of the women had passed away. Another was married and worked as a church mental health counselor. The third woman was married and worked as a high school principal at a Baptist school.

ALL THINGS CONSIDERED, my favorite story while at the *Commonwealth* is an interview I did with author Willie Morris. I had followed his career for years. A native of Yazoo City, Mississippi, he left the state to attend the University of Texas at Austin and then continued his education by studying history at Oxford University as a Rhodes Scholar. When he returned to the States it was to become the editor of *The Daily Texan*, a bi-weekly newspaper with a liberal viewpoint. By 1963 he had joined the staff of *Harper's m*agazine as an associate editor. Within four years he was tapped to become Editor-in-Chief. Under his leadership *Harper's* became my favorite magazine while I was a student at Ole Miss.

My devotion to the magazine, only increased when *Harper's* became an outspoken opponent of the Vietnam War. Under Willie Morris's leadership, *Harper's* published in its March 1968 issue the longest magazine article ever published, "The Steps of the Pentagon." It was written by acclaimed novelist Norman Mailer, who wrote about participating in an anti-Vietnam War march on the Pentagon that resulted in him being arrested and taken off to jail. The magazine article was expanded into a book titled *The Armies of the Night*, which went on to win both a Pulitzer Prize and the National Book Award. The article and the book were notable for becoming known as the most successful attempt to-date at narrative non-fiction, a type of journalism that utilizes the tools of the novelist—dialog, identifiable plot movement, and compelling storytelling—to elevate journalism to an art form. Because the magazine piece was published three months before Ina and I left Mississippi to make a new life for ourselves in Canada, the article—along with editor-in-chief Willie Morris—provided the intellectual stimulus for our decision.

Since leaving *Harper's*, Willie Morris had written a coming-of-age book about growing up in the South during a time of great social upheaval. *North Toward Home* was described by the *London Sunday Times* as "the finest evocation of an American boyhood since Mark Twain."

When I was told Willie Morris was coming to Greenwood to deliver a speech at the annual Arts Festival about his recently published book, *Yazoo*, which was about school desegregation in his hometown of Yazoo City, I arranged to interview him at the home of his sponsor well before the event commenced. We sat in the upstairs room of a stately house on Grand Boulevard. At forty-four there was still a boyish glimmer in his eye. He smiled, indicating his pleasure at having his own pool table in his quarters. After that he laughed and said his flight from his home in Bridgehampton, New York, "was like a Greyhound bus. We made five stops between Richmond and Memphis."

One of the things on Willie's mind on this day was his surprise reaction to his return to Mississippi. "You never get it out of your blood," he explained. "You have all these memories associated with it. It haunts me to see some of these old landmarks. Coming into Greenwood, I saw things that hadn't changed much since I was a child. That Billups' service station at the edge of town was there when I was four."

I asked him what he was working on now and he said he was hard at work on his second novel, tentatively titled *Taps*, and a book about his friendship with James Jones, the author of *From Here to Eternity* and *The Thin Red Line*. It told the story of how when Jones was in the hospital dying, Willie stayed at his side, often sleeping on the floor of the hospital room. Knowing that he was at the end of his life, Jones asked Willie if he would please finish his work in progress for him, a novel titled *Whistle*. Willie readily agreed. The friendship book was published toward the end of the year, but he would not live to finish his novel *Taps*. It eventually would be completed by his second wife JoAnne Pritchard Morris and published posthumously in 2001. It was a book he had labored over for more than a quarter century.

I didn't know it at the time, but when *James Jones: A Friendship* was published in October I would end up reviewing it for my new employer, the *Tallahassee Democrat*. By then I had resigned my position at the

12/2/79
Bridgehampton

Dear Jim,

I was touched by your splendid review, and impressed also by the writing and the insights. I showed it to Gloria Jones, who sends you her best.

Best of luck with your writing. Stick with it.

Taps is a ways off, but I feel good about it.

Very best —
Willie Morris

Letter to James L. Dickerson from Willie Morris
Photo from James L. Dickerson Collection

Greenwood Commonwealth, primarily due to frustration with the newspaper, but also out of dissatisfaction with everything associated with my birthplace. Bad memories have a way of catching up with you. Third Bridge Lake seemingly shadowed me everywhere I went in Greenwood. I sent Willie a copy of my review of his book and he responded with a delightful letter. We stayed in touch via letters.

In 1980, he returned to Mississippi as writer-in-residence at the University of Mississippi. Over the years, Willie wrote fewer books about social issues and more about purely human issues. His book, *My Dog Skip*, was made into a movie, and his book *Good Old Boy: A Delta Boyhood*, was made into a movie for public television. By the time of his unexpected death in 1999 of a heart attack, he had become a beloved figure in Mississippi, his liberal viewpoints on human rights largely forgotten.

The same day my interview with Willie Morris was published inside the newspaper, I had a photograph and news story on Page One. State Senator Charles Pickering had flown into the Greenwood Airport to be interviewed by me and a television news crew regarding his candidacy to occupy the U.S. Senate seat vacated by Senator James O. Eastland. With Pickering were his wife and two daughters.

"This is strictly a media event," he admitted. "We didn't ask any of our supporters to come out to the airport."

Pickering's opponent in the Republican primary was Thad Cochran, who won the primary and went on to defeat his Democratic opponent. After his speech to me and the camera crew, he and his family got back on the plane and flew away to his next "media event."

This, my friends, is how the media is manipulated in America, and how leaders are chosen and elevated by party politics. The newspaper buried an important interview with Willie Morris inside the newspaper, while putting my fake photograph and fake news story on Page One, above the fold. Morris had more than 200 people show up for his speech, an attendance which was real.

Trader Jon's historic Pensacola bar was considered the western
anchor for the Florida Panhandle. The author's first *Facing South*
syndicated column was about this legendary topless bar.
Photo of owner Martin Weismann by James L. Dickerson

Chapter 8

Tallahassee Democrat

IN THE SUMMER OF 1978 I took my family to Florida on vacation so that Ina and Jonathan could visit Ina's mother and younger sister on our way to Disney World in Orlando. I had written the *Tallahassee Democrat* in May about employment opportunities, but they had not responded. While we were in Pensacola I stopped by the *Pensacola News Journal* to see if they had any job openings. They didn't.

On our way to Orlando we stopped off in Tallahassee to visit relatives. They had owned a bookstore there they closed after they retired. They pointed to a box of books in the corner and said, "Help yourself." I chose a 1933 German language reprint of Adolf Hitler's *Mein Kampf*. It was in pristine condition. At worst, I figured, it would someday become a collector's edition and at best might someday come in handy.

It took a few years for the latter to occur, but it did while I was interviewing a hard-core, underworld bodyguard. After noticing the rather large swastika on the man's forearm, I told him about the book.

"Oh, man," he said, his eyes on fire, "You're not shitin' me, are you?"

"Not at all."

"I tell you what, if you will just let me touch it, I will be your friend

135

forever."

"I'll see what I can do."

"Thank you, buddy."

After visiting the relatives, I parked Ina and Jonathan at the motel while I dropped in unannounced at the *Tallahassee Democrat*. I walked into a rather large newsroom that was filled with desks. On the left were the reporters' desks. All were unoccupied. None had dividers between the desks. On the right, the desks were all occupied by individuals staring at computer screens. I figured they were editors—and I was correct.

"I need an editor," I boomed out in a large voice that I imagined belonged to Humphrey Bogart's Sam Spade.

The managing editor just happened to be walking by.

"I'm an editor," he said, a look of confusion on his face. "What can I do for you?"

I explained why I was there.

The managing editor looked at his watch and waved the city editor over to where we were standing. He withdrew his car keys from his pants pocket and jingled them toward the city editor.

"We're going to take Mr. Dickerson to lunch," the managing editor said.

We got into the managing editor's car and drove to a nearby Chinese restaurant and were seated in a booth. The two editors sat side-by-side across from me, staring at me as if I were the lunch. They asked me a lot of questions, we ate lunch, and then we returned to the newsroom.

"When you get back home, send me some clips," said the managing editor.

We shook hands and parted company.

I don't remember much about our trip to Disney World, only that I was in a hurry to get back home to bundle up those clippings. The process didn't take long. About a week after I sent off the clippings, I received a letter offering me a position on the staff of the *Tallahassee Democrat*. They were prepared to boost my salary from $130 a week to $175 a week.

It was June and school was out, so I handed in my resignation to John Emmerich and we loaded up a U-Haul truck and hired a man to drive it to Florida. We found a second floor, two-bedroom apartment and watched with amazement as the driver, a Black man in his fifties and about five feet tall, unloaded the entire truck in no time at all. The last item on the truck was a refrigerator, which he strapped to his back and carried up the stairs and into the apartment without even breaking into a sweat.

I began work at the *Tallahassee Democrat* in the latter part of June 1978. I was hired as a general assignment reporter with a promise that I would be able to do features later. In fact, the city editor already had one in mind. Tallahassee had bragging rights on three New York fashion models, one of whom was the daughter of an editor in the sports department. The city editor wanted me to write the story. For the moment, however, it was placed on a back burner.

The first story I wrote for the newspaper ended up being on Page One. I was thumbing through the newspaper looking for ideas when the city editor asked me to go to the airport and meet someone named Darth Vader.

"Who's Darth Vader?"

"You don't know who Darth Vader is?"

I shook my head, no.

"He's the villain in *Star Wars*."

"What's that?"

"The movie—never mind, just go to the airport."

"What does this Vader guy look like?"

"You'll know him when you see him."

"Are you kidding me?"

"Trust me. You'll know."

Star Wars had premiered in the summer of 1977, but we were living in the Mississippi Delta where there was only one movie theater within an hour's drive. I don't think it premiered in the Delta. I was working at the *Delta Democrat-Times* and reading the newspaper, front to back, every day and I never saw anything about a movie named *Star Wars*.

When I arrived at the airport, the parking lot was filled and it was difficult to find a parking space. The inside of the airport terminal was packed with hundreds of people, mostly parents with children. I was there only a few minutes when someone dressed in a black costume with a black plastic helmet walked into the room, breathing loudly as if he was on a hospital ventilator. The lobby erupted with screams.

I sidled up to Mr. Vader and tried to talk to him, but he would have nothing to do with me. There was a Florida State University student standing next to me, so I talked to her.

"I'm just a Star Wars freak," she said. "I tried to get some of my friends to come out here with me, but they just laughed and said, 'you have to be crazy.'" She had seen the movie seven times. "We'd love to hear him breathe." By then Mr. Vader's breathing had stopped because he was too busy signing autographs.

Darth Vader's arrival was part of a publicity stunt for a local theater that was hosting the re-release of the movie. I made a mental note to go see the movie and take my son.

When I returned to the newsroom, the city editor gleefully shouted out across the room: "Were you able to find Darth Vader?"

"Hell yes," I answered.

The city editor and everyone else in the newsroom had a big laugh. On July 3, 1978, the day before Independence Day, I wrote three stories that were published in the July 4th edition and when the editor returned after the holiday he singled me out for praise. Three stories in the newspaper *was* a good day by any standard. I can't take too much credit, however. I hadn't been there long enough to develop any sources, so the stories were pretty much a reaction to events over which I had no control. There's that—and then there's the fact my desk was at the front of the newsroom where I was easy prey for any editor who had received a telephone tip and was looking for eye contact with a reporter.

Basically, a general assignment reporter takes on stories that do not fall within well-defined beats such as cops, courts, education, politics, and so on. Because the stories are all over the coverage map, you never encounter the same people twice, so it is not a beat in which you can develop sources.

I think it was during this time that I went to the county courthouse for a crime-related story, when I briskly rounded a corner and physically ran into serial killer Ted Bundy, who was in jail after his arrest for murdering sorority sisters at Florida State University. Accompanied by several deputies, he was carrying a stack of files in his manacled hands; my collision caused him to drop them. When it happened I noted that the hand of one of the police officers went to the handle of his holstered revolver.

I apologized and leaned over to gather up the files. It was not until I handed them to Bundy that I recognized the face and soulless eyes that had been on television and in all the newspapers across the country. He accepted the files without saying a word and proceeded down the hallway with his escorts. Wish I had a photograph of that look he gave me. I don't think I will ever forget it. Tallahassee is like that. Shit happens when you least expect it, without rhyme or reason.

Bundy confessed to thirty murders and investigators think there may have been as many as seventy more. He could be an affable fellow when he wanted to be and he had the gift that most true psychopathic personalities possess—a disarming, somewhat boyish, smile. Unable to charm his way out of a death sentence, he was executed in Florida's electric chair in 1989.

Walking away from the courthouse, I had a disturbing thought.

I just pissed off Ted Bundy. What were the odds of that?

Being a good reporter is all about beating the odds.

WITHIN A FEW WEEKS after arriving in Tallahassee, I wrote the type of human interest story for which I became best known. It was about a Sopchoppy (population 457) mother who dropped her daughter, aged eleven, off at a favorite swimming hole on the Sopchoppy River south of Tallahassee during a Fourth of July celebration while she worked in her church booth not far away. As the day wore on, Betty Green was in her church booth when a child came running up to her, hysterically calling out that her daughter, Lisa, had drowned in the river.

Mrs. Green rushed to the riverbank to find Lisa flat on her back while being administered to by two ambulance personnel.

"They said she was dead," Mrs. Green explained to me. "But they worked on her until she started breathing again."

Lisa was taken to a Tallahassee hospital, where she stayed three months, paralyzed because she had suffered brain damage. Before the accident Lisa was a vibrant child who was very much involved with church activities. Her favorite things to do were to play the organ, tambourine or drums during services.

"She was very mature for her age," Mrs. Green told me. "The church was her first love."

Unable to afford a private nurse, Mrs. Green had to quit her job to take care of Lisa, leaving her husband as the only breadwinner. She thought she was over the worst of it. Lisa could neither speak nor move, but Mrs. Green refused to give up hope.

Unfortunately, hope gave up on her.

Six months after the river incident, Mrs. Green and her husband separated, a result of the stress associated with caring for Lisa. Despite the separation, her husband, who was a cook in a Tallahassee restaurant, continued to provide her with enough money to live on so she would not need to apply for public assistance. More bad luck followed.

Three months after the separation, Mrs. Green learned that her two-year-old daughter, Swanzetta, had developed cerebral palsy and had lost the ability to walk. Then her eight-year-old daughter, Trina, developed respiratory problems and her twelve-year-old son, James, suddenly suffered a sixty percent hearing loss. Not long after that, Mrs. Green gave birth prematurely to a girl weighing only three pounds. The hospital had to keep the baby several weeks to bring her weight up to five pounds so she could be released. As bad as things were, there was still more bad luck headed her way.

One night, while they were asleep, their mobile home in Sopchoppy caught on fire. Mrs. Green awakened the children and picked Lisa up in her arms and got everyone out safely before the house trailer was destroyed by the fire. Mrs. Green lost everything she had, including Lisa's wheelchair and hospital bed. As a result of the fire, Mrs. Green and her children moved in with her sister in Tallahassee. When I heard that, I grabbed a photographer and went to visit her at her sister's house.

Mrs. Green sat on the edge of Lisa's bed and interacted with her, mother and child communicating by means of their expansive smiles. It was easy to see from Lisa's beaming face that she adored her mother—and vice versa. My story ran on Page One under the headline:

FAMILY CAN'T SHAKE DISASTER,
BUT TRUSTS TO LOVE AND PIETY

Within hours after the newspaper hit the newsstands, countless readers began offering their help. I telephoned Mrs. Green to get an update and wrote a follow-up story that ran on Page One under the headline:

SHE'S WAKING UP FROM NIGHTMARE

After the first story ran, a first-year nursing student at Florida State University, offered to spend two days a week helping Mrs. Green care for her children. The owner of a home care business donated a wheelchair. A man donated an air conditioner. "I couldn't bear to sit in an air-conditioned office while that little girl suffered in the heat." Someone opened a Betty Green fund at a local bank. And so on until Mrs. Green's needs were met by a caring community.

"I couldn't believe it," Mrs. Green told me. "People are reaching out the best way they know how. There's a big togetherness about it. Everything that happened was for a reason . . . If it weren't for my children, I'd give up."

BY SEPTEMBER, THE MAYHEM in the general assignment beat had slowed down to the point where I could focus on the fashion model feature that was scheduled for a full page section front and a half-page jump inside, complete with full color photographs of three very attractive young women. The hook on the story was that three recent graduates of Leon High School in Tallahassee had found success as fashion models in New York City. Interestingly, none of the women knew each other in high school. All three had had incredible success since leaving high school. The headline was uninspired but effective:

HELLO, BIG TIME!
Fashion world sparkles
For Tallahassee models

Rosemary McGrotha, nineteen, daughter of *Democrat* sports editor, Bill McGrotha, was home to visit after completing a series of photographs for *Vogue* magazine. She had only been in New York for six months. Previously, she had appeared in *Cosmopolitan* and *McCalls*. She also had done brand endorsements and commercials for Gucci, Clairol, Versace and Donna Karan. She was represented by Trump Model Management.

Rosemary was interviewed at her parents' home in the dining room. We sat across the table from each other, me with my reporter's notebook, Rosemary with a dazzling smile. She wore her hair parted down the center, looking every bit the cover girl. She placed her arms on the table in such an open, relaxed way that I knew she was comfortable talking to me.

The ultra-exclusive world of modelling in New York City, with all its built-in nuances, came as quite a shock to Rosemary. She learned that some of the highest paid models showed up for sessions with a list of demands that were incorporated into their contracts. The most outrageous demand she heard about was the one that models be allowed a certain number of naps during each session.

"God, I wonder if I'll ever be like that!" she gasped in horror.

"I don't know," I answered. "What were you like in high school."

"All through high school I was taller than most girls. I never dated that much. I always felt awkward because of my height. After school I usually went straight home to watch television or take a nap."

"There you go," I answered. "Now you know."

Rosemary's bright, optimistic face very much reminded me of a high schooler I once had a date with named Mimi Cefalu. From the nearby town of Leland, she was tall and had long, dark hair. We were seventeen, if I recall, and had double-dated on our first out-of-town adventure. She went on to become a very successful New York fashion model. However, on this particular evening we had driven to Vicksburg to attend a Civil War-era riverboat stage play at which we were allowed to throw peanuts at the actors.[10] The most memorable part of the date came afterward, when we went to the Vicksburg National Military Park overlook. It was a beautiful night with a full moon and we gazed across the Mississippi River all the way into Louisiana.

During a pause in our conversation, I moved toward Mimi to kiss her, suddenly realizing in a panic that I was not tall enough to reach her lips. Seeing my dire situation, Mimi, bless her heart, quickly came to my rescue with the words, "Why don't you stand on that rock." Obviously, the Good Lord made teenage girls smarter than teenage boys for a reason. They had to be smarter for the species to survive.

Susan Smith, twenty-two, became one of the top models in New York, working for *Mademoiselle*, *Vogue*, *Cosmopolitan*, and *Harper's Bazaar*, earning over $100,000 a year. Originally signed by John Casa, owner of Elite, she ended up with the Eileen Ford modeling agency. When I interviewed her she was pleased with her success, but she found the journey to the top frustrating. "When you first start, you have to knock on a lot of doors," she said. "Then, if it's slammed in your face, you have to pick yourself up and wipe away the tears. There's no easy way."

Elizabeth Shiell, twenty-two, had just signed a five-year contract with Wilhelmina modeling agency. By the time I interviewed her, she had done various photographs for *New York* magazine, swimwear photographs for *Newsweek*, and television commercials for Catalina sportswear. One of the first lessons she learned was to throw modesty out the door. "You're showing clothes all the time that reveal a lot of skin," she explained. That can lead to unwanted overtures from photographers. "This one guy told me that if I'd spend the night with him, he'd put me on the cover of *Seventeen*. If a photographer starts talking sexually to me, I back away. Who needs it?"[11]

AFTER THE FEATURE on the models was published, I was given a beat covering the area west from Tallahassee to Pensacola, south to St. Marks, north to the Georgia state line, and east halfway to Jacksonville. That was something I wanted because it allowed me to do features, cover news events, and do investigative reporting in the wild and woolly Panhandle. I had volunteered to do editorials as well, but the editorial page editor, an aging man with frown lines permanently chiseled onto his face, would have no part of that, especially from a "youngster." For the most part, his editorials read like retreads from the 1950s.

My new beat allowed me to spend most of my time outside the newsroom, and that suited me just fine. My next story was straight news. I discovered that the St. Marks Yacht Club and several individuals had filed a $30 million lawsuit against three companies—an oil transport company, an oil buyer, and a tow company—for allegedly spilling 13,000 gallons of crude oil into the beautiful St. Marks River. As a result, the director of the Florida Department of Natural Resources called St. Marks the dirtiest port in the state. Here is another example of my use of the three-beat lede (with apologies to Native Americans):

ST. MARKS—The historic port of St. Marks is under siege.

But not by the likes of hostile Indians, pirates or yellow fever as in years past.

This time the villain is oil—black, sticky crude oil that has polluted the river and beaches and earned St. Marks a reputation as the dirtiest port in Florida.

Environmental issues are a big deal for river and coastal communities who depend on those natural resources for their livelihood. The plaintiffs said through their attorney that should they be victorious in the lawsuit they would distribute any financial judgement among the residents of the area who had been affected by the oil spill.

I have no idea whether the editorial page editor ever wrote an editorial based on my news story, but there was really no need for him to do so. I had addressed the issue on the front page of the newspaper. I began to see news stories in a different light. As long as they are well-documented and accurate, news stories can be every bit as effective at bringing about change as cranky editorials that lean toward the opinionated marker on the scale. Don't misunderstand me because I'm not saying news stories should be slanted. I'm just saying the unvarnished truth in a situation in which individuals are alleging abuse at the hands of government or corporate interests will allow readers to decide which side they want to support. Facts are the best way to change minds, whether in a news story or in a passionate, desk-thumping editorial.

Sometimes I responded to brief news stories sent in by our correspondents from all over the panhandle by following up and developing them into Page One stories, and other times I simply hit the road in an effort to get to better know the residents of the Panhandle. For example, I had been reading stories from our correspondents in Liberty County, which was about forty miles from Tallahassee, about an upcoming school board election. I decided to make my first visit to Bristol, the county seat. Because half the county is occupied by the Apalachicola National Forest, the drive to Bristol was one of the most desolate journeys imaginable. There was no place to stop along the way.

When I arrived in Bristol I was pleased to see that the county courthouse was a two-story brick structure. I had halfway expected it to be in a log cabin. The county was 77 percent white and 18 percent Black, but I stayed there several hours and never saw a single Black person. With a population of around 3,000 in the 1970 census, it was the most sparsely populated county in Florida. The desolation had me hoping James Dickey had not used Liberty Country as a fictitious locale for his 1970 surrealistic novel *Deliverance*.

There was a country store there named Hoggly Woggly (after Piggy Wiggly), so I parked my car and went inside feeling very much like the only stranger in town. I pulled a soft drink from the icebox and sat atop a wooden barrel to engage in conversation with the locals, all of whom eyed me with a great deal of suspicion. At first, I mostly asked about the huntin' and fishin' in the county, hoping I hadn't stumbled into one of James Dickey's Deliverance situations. They had a lot to say about both topics. Finally, I worked my way around to the reason for my visit.

"So what's going on?" I asked.

"Not much."

"I'm surprised. I thought a town like this would have something going on."

"Well," a man in overalls said. "We've got a red hot election."

"Really."

"Yeah. There's a school board election and some are pretty hot about that."

"What's there to get riled up about a school board election?"

By then I was snacking on cheese and crackers.

"You see, the schools are just about the only employers in the county. If you work for one of the schools and get on the bad side of a school board member you're in trouble."

Passing the story from person to person, they told me about one school board member who got into an argument with the man running against him. One day he went out to check his mail and when he opened the door to the mailbox a rattlesnake jumped out and bit him on the arm and he almost died. Not one to take abuse from anyone, he set out to arrange a series of misfortunes for his competitor. At that time, they were the only two candidates feuding, so pretty soon it got out of hand. Shots were fired into homes from speeding pickup trucks as other candidates got into disputes with their challengers.

"You ought to come back next week for the school board meeting."

"I think I will."

"Write it up in the paper so we can read it and find out what's happening in this county."

"I will."

The following week I set out for Liberty County to see what all the fuss was about. Only for this trip I had a passenger. The automatic 20-gauge shotgun that had belonged to my father. I packed the magazine with double-ought buckshot. I wanted it just in case things got out of hand.

When I arrived at the courthouse I was disappointed not to see any of the people I had chatted with in the Hoggly Woggly. The school board meeting didn't disappoint. I quickly discovered that there were two factions. One side, led by the superintendent of the schools, Laquita Shuler or "Skeet" for short, wanted to do all the hiring and firing. The other side, represented by a majority on the board, thought they should be doing all the hiring and firing.

The superintendent's detractors began calling her "Little Hitler." The inscription on a marble plaque on her desk seemed to support that title: *I am not arguing with you. I am telling you.*

However, the dispute was complicated by sociological issues. Skeet was the first woman ever to hold the post of school superintendent. Bristol was not what I would call a center for progressive thinking. How Skeet was ever elected is beyond me because of decades of opposition to women holding power. Did the fact she was female contribute to the battle lines on the issue? That would be up to voters to decide. Certainly one casualty of the dispute was the county's Head Start program. When the superintendent and the board couldn't agree over who should be the director, the superintendent shut down the program, laying off all its employees. After that happened, the governor and the courts, state school officials, and a grand jury got involved to try to get them to settle their differences. When that failed, the governor gave them sixty days to settle or face removal from office. The two parties still refused. When the sixty days was up, the governor threw up his arms in a gesture of futility and did absolutely nothing because he knew any orders he issued would be ignored. The last thing the governor wanted was to be subpoenaed and have to travel that long, lonely road to Bristol.

New elections for the school board were held the day before I arrived. Unfortunately, the races were so close that winners could not be resolved until 384 absentee ballots were counted. The meeting was pretty chaotic, with some people expressing fears that the absentee ballots might not be honest. Cries of fraud were still in the air as I left the meeting to walk back to my car. As I opened my car door, I noticed a parked car several car lengths behind mine that was filled with five or six people.

As I pulled out into the street, I saw that the car filled with people also pulled out. Gradually they pulled up behind me as I made my way out of town. I slowed down. They slowed down. The street I was on was also the highway that would take me back to Tallahassee. It was dark and I became concerned about the drive home. As I saw the city limits in the distance, I floored the accelerator and then eased up. The car behind me did the same. By that point they were about a half car length behind me, their lights on bright, obscuring my view in the rearview mirror.

I floored the accelerator again, so that when I was a full car length ahead of them, I suddenly braked hard and turned right into the parking lot of a butane gas distributorship. The office was dark. The other car stopped on the road, with the faces of several men visible in the passenger windows, front and back. I drove in a circle around the lot and headed back toward the stopped car, my headlights on bright this time, revealing the faces of the men.

Then I stopped, certain they couldn't see me over the brightness of my headlights. I lowered the side window, grabbed my shotgun and stuck the barrel out the window as I pulled the bolt to inject a shell into the chamber. Then I hit the release, the hard metallic sound of the bolt slamming shut, is familiar to anyone who has ever hunted. It is a distinctive sound that can be heard for several hundred yards. Once that sound penetrated the night air, the car peeled off at a high rate of speed, turning left off the highway before leaving the city limits. With my heart pounding, I set out for Tallahassee, driving the entire way on a two-lane highway without a single pair of headlights ever appearing in my rearview mirror. Do I recommend that newspaper reporters carry a gun? No, I don't. Most would have no idea how to use one. I sometimes do because it is not in my DNA to ever be a passive victim. I haven't surrendered to bullying since the third grade.

I missed my deadline for the next day's newspaper, but my story ran the following day on Page One with the bland headline: **LIBERTY COUNTY SCHOOL ISSUE STILL UNSETTLED**. Sometimes what happens while gathering news is much more exciting than the news itself. Sometimes you have to write a book before the truth can be told.

IN OCTOBER 1978, I was dispatched to St. Marks, Florida, to cover a story about two missing nineteen-year-old men who had disappeared in a small boat in the Gulf of Mexico. The two young men were fishing about two miles from the St. Marks lighthouse when their motor suddenly went dead and could not be restarted. As I later learned, all they had to eat in the fourteen-foot boat were two sandwiches and three soft drinks. They drifted for the remainder of the day, with land nowhere in sight.

That night they were awakened by a ferocious storm that threatened to sink their small boat. By the time the sun rose the next morning they felt certain they would be rescued. However, as the day wore on and they finished the sandwiches and soft drinks, they began to lose hope. They became convinced they were going to die a horrible death. They started talking about their lives, all the things they had done. And they talked about their mothers a lot, sharing stories.

On the morning of the third day they saw a high-flying aircraft overhead. They waved, but the aircraft did not seem to see them. Three hours later another aircraft appeared. Again, they stood in the boat and waved. This time the aircraft banked and flew directly over them.

Back at the marina at St. Marks, the families waited impatiently for word about their sons, two cousins named Richard and Brinson Colson.

Brinson's mother, Eddie, had been at a baby shower earlier Saturday—before she had learned of her son's disappearance. Now, Monday afternoon, she sat near a window wringing her hands from the tension.

"Look how still the leaves are," she said. "I've never seen it so calm here."

Richard's sister, Beth Garner, walked outside.

"When I have to cry, I go somewhere and hide," she said. "I don't want anyone to see me."[12]

Time passed. The telephone rang and someone announced that the Coast Guard had found the men forty-three miles out at sea and they were alive. I was sitting at the lunch counter, pampering a cup of coffee.

I saw a boat captain enter the room and whisper to one of the mothers. She smiled and made eye contact with me. Then she waved me over.

"This nice boat captain has offered to take us out in his boat to meet the boys at sea, away from the prying eyes of the media. Oops ..." She paused. "No offense."

"No offense taken," I said.

She leaned over and whispered. "Would you like to go with us?"

I instantly agreed. Florida was a very competitive media state. There were reporters from all over the state at the marina, both television and print. The invitation offered me quite a journalistic scoop. I would be the only reporter on hand when the men were reunited with their mothers. The captain left the room and then, one by one, the mothers and I left, trying not to draw attention to our movement.

The captain's boat was small by ocean-going standards, but no one seemed to care. I was a little uneasy about getting onboard the boat, but I knew I had a job to do, so I overcame my fear of water. Once everyone was aboard we left the dock and followed the river down to the ocean and headed for open water. The boat had a rickety puttering sound to it like the boat in that Humphrey Bogart film the *African Queen*. It didn't take long for the shore to fade away to nothing but a vast sheet of water on the horizon. I was uncomfortable, but pleased to be a part of the journey.

Suddenly, without warning, the puttering engine abruptly stopped.

"Oh, no," said the captain.

He had a sick look on his face.

"I forgot to fill up."

Everyone looked at each other; no one was sure of the consequences.

"What happens next?" I asked.

The captain rubbed the back of his neck, a look of concern on his face. "Well, mostly we got to wait to be rescued."

"What!" exclaimed one of the mothers. "You mean our boys will get back and their mothers won't be there to meet them?"

"Sorry," said the captain.

"When will we get back?" a mother asked.

"Soon as they send someone out to rescue us."

"How long will that take?"

"I don't know."

About that time a Coast Guard cutter sped past in the distance. The mothers waved with wild enthusiasm, hoping someone would see us. No one waved back.

As we bobbed about in the small boat, all of us were seated now, waiting. I won't deny that the thought occurred to me that perhaps I should never get in another boat for as long as I live. I prayed that nothing would happen to capsize the boat. Why were death and water becoming so much a complement to my life?

There was a brilliant blue sky overhead, with not a cloud in sight. It was quite cool by Florida standards, the temperature hovering in the low seventies. *What a wonderful day to be saved*, I thought ... *or die*.

Suddenly, I saw a small speck on the horizon.

"Look," I said. "They must have realized we were out here."

The captain stood and squinted, blocking the sunlight from his eyes with his rugged, hook-and-fin scarred hand.

"Yes, they are coming for us. I know the boat."

In less than twenty minutes our rescue craft was alongside, the deck hand barely able to stifle his laughter as he tossed a rope to the captain.

"Are our sons back yet?" asked one of the women.

"Yes ma'am," said the deck hand.

"Are they all right?"

"Yes ma'am—a little sunburned but all right."

As the rescue craft towed us back to the marina, not much else was said. Everyone was reflective—not only about the rescue of the boys, but about our own rescue.

When we pulled up at the dock, there were cheers and broad smiles, not just at our folly but for the reunification of mothers and sons. One of the boys was lying exhausted on an ambulance stretcher, but the other boy was standing, apparently in much better condition.

"It was like a nightmare out there," one of the boys told me. "Last night we gave up all hope of being saved."

I left the mothers basking in the glow of their reunification with their sons and drove back to Tallahassee so that I could write the story in time for the morning edition. It was Page One, of course—with the headline:

SCARY SEA VOYAGE HAS HAPPY ENDING

WITHIN WEEKS, the newspaper sent me back to Wakulla County, to the small town of Crawfordville, only a few miles from St. Marks, to cover another death and dying story. The county was a scenically beautiful area of the state that had a dark social undercurrent that could knock you off your feet and pull you under when you least expected it.

One Sunday morning, a young mother was attending services at the Tower Holiness Church, holding her ten-month-old baby named Angel in her lap, when her twenty-six-year-old husband, wearing a dark blue suit, entered the church and cautiously approached her pew and quietly asked her to go outside with him. She refused.

"No, no, no!" she screamed, creating a scene. Then she turned to her mother and said, with desperation in her voice, "Take me home, Mama." The word "Mama" echoed throughout the church like a stone skipping across a pond.

Clutching her baby girl in her arms, she hurried out of the church, with her mother close behind. Also following her out was her husband. As she opened the car door, her husband pulled a .38-caliber pistol from his pocket and shot her once in the back. She fell to the ground still holding her baby, but then turned, and faced her killer, the baby rolling to the side.

The mother's fifteen-year-old sister desperately lunged for the gun when she saw him point it at the baby, but she missed the mark and fell to the ground and he re-aimed his pistol and shot his wife a second time as she stared at him with a blend of fear and loathing, slamming a bullet into her chest. Then as the stunned congregation and minister watched from the church steps, he put the pistol to his head and paused as if he were posing for a picture.

"He looked right at me," the pastor later told me. "I could see him making up his mind. He leaped several inches off the ground and pulled the trigger while still in the air."

The day before the murder-suicide, the husband had visited the jewelry store where the pastor worked to tell him his wife wanted a divorce. They had only been married three months. Without saying a word, he placed a bouquet of flowers and his wedding ring on the counter and left the store. It was a sign of something, thought the pastor. But what?

I turned in the story, which ran on Page One,[13] and then I focused my attention on the horrendous fallout of the murder-suicide. What was to become of Baby Angel? At first everything seemed fine. The mother's mother and her husband took Baby Angel and became her legal guardians.

Several months later, I drove out to rural Wakulla County to check on the grandmother and Baby Angel. They lived in a small, clapboard house. The outside walls were covered with tarpaper, but the inside walls were covered with family photographs.

I found Baby Angel sitting on her toy chest, her bright-blue eyes flashing at her grandparents. Above her was a photograph of a ship being pounded on all sides by an angry sea.

The grandparents were a hard-working couple—she was a nurse's aide and he was a crab fisherman—but a string of misfortunes had made it difficult for them to do much more for Baby Angel than provide for her basic needs. At the time of my visit, the grandmother was out of work because of an injured back. The grandfather's rusted crab traps were not usable. It would cost twelve hundred dollars to replace them.

Their only source of income was $120 a month in food stamps and a $54-a-month welfare check for Baby Angel. They were surviving, just barely, in quiet desperation that, frankly, pulled at my heart strings. What disturbed me was that if Baby Angel had been orphaned by a stranger, she would have been eligible for as much as ten thousand dollars from the Florida Crime Compensation Commission. If her mother had been killed by Baby Angel's natural father, or if the young mother had ever contributed to Social Security, she would have been eligible for Social Security benefits. But because she was orphaned by her stepfather she was ineligible for benefits.

"They've got the very life of that child in their hands," said the grandmother of the government. "There's no justice. This is a little person without anybody but us to look out for her welfare. They (the government) have a moral obligation to help."

In a Page One story[14] that included a large image of Baby Angel, I laid out the story for the world to see under the headline:

HELP SCARCE FOR ORPHANED ANGEL

I stayed on the story. There was no way of influencing the Social Security Administration. They were beyond the reach of mere mortals. But I did have hope I could influence state officials who were more accessible.

When I interviewed an official with the attorney general's office he shocked me by saying that he would not recommend to the three-member Florida Crimes Compensation Commission that Baby Angel be provided compensation as a crime victim. The only way for individuals like Baby Angel to get help, he said, was for the Legislature to change the law to include them in compensation guidelines. Said one official: "There is no provision in the law for compassion."

In time, the law was modified to provide services to children like Baby Angel, but it was not a quick process and Baby Angel and others suffered in the interim. Today, the Florida Bureau of Crime Victim Compensation can provide benefits to a "guardian applying for a minor child victim" or "any other person who was dependent for principal support upon a deceased victim or intervener."

I still dream about Baby Angel looking up at me with such hopeful eyes. How many millions of times a day must God have the same experience? How many times a day must God's heart be broken by the wretched excesses of the human race?

IN THE LATE 1970s, the Florida Panhandle had a lot in common with the Wild West of another century. Every other day, it seemed, life suddenly erupted into gunfire, fistfights or lawsuits. One day I got word that Port St. Joe, a city of 3,600 residents located on the Gulf Coast about 100 miles from Tallahassee, was in the midst of a festering civil war. Someone was going to get hurt—and bad. I quickly learned it was a complicated story that would require me to scrape layers of deception away from a public façade to get at the truth, the way you would scrape old paint from a building before applying a new coat.

At the center of this story was a former Florida state senator named George G. Tapper (1916-1982), who once served as chairman of the Senate Transportation Committee; his background was as a wealthy Port St. Joe businessman who owned a construction company that was adept at receiving government contracts for work done in the Panhandle. Opposing Tapper in many of his endeavors was a county judge named David

Taunton. *Time* magazine once labeled him the "Robin Hood" of Gulf County because of his tendency to side with society's downtrodden. He had a PhD. in philosophy from Florida State University and enjoyed a work history as a logger, school principal, coach, pastor and newspaper editor. He and his wife, Abigail, were beloved because of their decision to care for foster children. Over a period of forty-four years, they cared for over four hundred children. Taunton, who died in November 2019, outliving all of his enemies, is remembered as the longest serving Gulf County judge in history.

The point at which I entered this story was during one of Taunton's many re-election campaigns. Running against Taunton was Tapper's longtime personal attorney. At the center of the campaign was the Municipal Hospital, a city owned facility that was operated by a Board of Trustees rumored to be backing Taunton's opponent. This story initially crossed my desk as a tip that there were mysterious and unexplained deaths at the hospital that were the fault of a "foreign" obstetrician named Dr. Anila Poonai. Furthermore, the tip alleged, the hospital privileges of Dr. Anila Poonai were revoked and her license to practice medicine in Florida was suspended.

I had one side of the story. I placed a call to Dr. Poonai to request an interview so that I could get the other side. Both she and her husband, Dr. P.V. Poonia, agreed to be interviewed by telephone. I learned the Doctors Poonai had attended the Seth G. S. Medical School in India and had settled in Port St. Joe because medical care was so desperately needed in what was essentially a rural area. I began to wonder if this story was a racial issue. Because I was born and raised in Mississippi, I knew people in the South considered individuals from India to be neither white nor Black, but rather exotic members of a "foreign" bloodline.

As a result of the hospital's complaint against Dr. Anila Poonai, she was charged by the Florida Board of Examiners with eight counts of malpractice, including sterilizing a twenty-four-year-old woman without her permission, sterilizing a twenty-six-year-old woman and destroying a six-week-old embryo, and failing to perform emergency procedures when she was asked to do so. Mrs. Poonai denied those charges and stated that it was all a conspiracy between the hospital and the Board of Examiners.

Mr. Poonai attributed his wife's problems to the fact that he was approached by a man, whom he didn't want to publicly identify, and told that he would deliver the "heads" of the hospital officials who were attacking his wife "on a silver platter" if Mr. and Mrs. Poonai agreed to endorse Judge Taunton's opponent in the election. The Poonais refused to do that.

At this point, it was still, "he said/she said," but I now had a story.

By working the telephone, I obtained the names of two potential sources that agreed to talk to me if I protected their identity. One worked in the courthouse; the other worked in the hospital. Now, I was ready to drive to Gulf County to do in-person interviews. It took about two hours to make the drive from Tallahassee.

My first interview with the unnamed source from the courthouse was done at an office complex. It took place after hours and all of the offices but one were closed. As I walked up the steps, I spotted a police car slow down and then stop, watching me as I went into the building. I did not realize until that moment that I had been followed. It was stupid of me not to have checked my rearview mirror to make sure I was not being followed, but since only two people knew I was coming—my two sources—it did not occur to me to take extraordinary precautions.

Once inside my source's office, I questioned her about Mr. and Mrs. Poonai, the hospital, Judge Taunton, and others. She concluded her comments by saying, "They're trying to destroy the judge. He's a fine man who always has done right by this county. I'm afraid they might kill him if what is going on is kept secret."

After that interview, I interviewed the hospital employee at a different location. She told me she was being harassed by hospital officials for voicing support for Mr. and Mrs. Poonai. She provided me with names, dates, and places and I advised her to be careful about talking to others.

I drove back to Tallahassee and arrived home about an hour after dark. The next morning I met with my editor and we agreed this was not the kind of story we could provide daily updates about, unless the news involved a court action of some kind. I spent the next day digesting the information I had gathered. Then, the following day, I drove back to Gulf County to again interview both of my unnamed sources. This time I went to Wewahitchka (referred to by locals as WeWa), a small town in northern Gulf County. It was the county seat until 1965, when that designation was transferred to Port St. Joe.

As I entered the city limits, I noticed a sheriff's car in the rearview mirror. I tuned left, the deputy turned left. I turned right, the deputy turned right. It was obvious I was being followed. With the deputy still on my tail, I pulled into the back parking lot of the old courthouse, where the sheriff's office was located, and parked next to a police car. The deputy pulled in behind me and parked on the other side of the lot. With the surprised deputy sitting in his car glaring at me. I walked into the sheriff's office, which actually was the office for the county jail, and waved to the desk personnel as I passed by.

When I entered the office of the courthouse source, the first thing that caught my eye was the sight of her sitting in a chair, weeping. Standing over her, trying to comfort her, was a man who himself appeared to be distraught.

"What's wrong?" I asked.

"This is my husband," she said, wiping her eyes with a tissue. "He works for a company that is controlled by Tapper and he was told that he would have to transfer to another county or lose his job." She dried her eyes and continued: "I will not be driven from this county!"

Also present was my source from the hospital. She, too, was terribly upset. She told me her husband had been out of the county for treatment in a hospital and while he was there he was approached by representatives of the Port St. Joe hospital and informed that his wife had undergone a hysterectomy by Dr. Anila Poonia that involved the abortion of a fetus.

The news prompted him to accuse his wife of being unfaithful to him. She responded by filing a lawsuit against the hospital. Then came the shocker: Two days before this meeting, her husband was killed in a mysterious one-car auto accident.

About that time the telephone rang, prompting my courthouse source to pick it up and say "Hello."

There was a moment of silence.

"Why?" she said into the telephone.

More silence as she listened.

"Why?"

Suddenly, she hung up the telephone, her face quite pale.

"I have just been warned not to discuss the hospital issues to anyone over the telephone. I was told my phones are being bugged."

At that point, everyone just looked at each other in stunned silence.

I left the courthouse, leaving behind two weeping women and a distraught man. I immediately sought out Dr. Anila Poonai and asked her about the mysterious automobile accident.

"Police said he lost control of the car while intoxicated."

"Do you believe that?"

She looked at me with a blank expression. She said she didn't want to discuss it further. I left her and went to my car. After unlocking the door and getting inside, I checked the glove compartment and made sure my loaded revolver was still there. Then I headed back to Tallahassee.

A day or two later, I telephoned my two unnamed sources at their home numbers, hoping those lines were not bugged as well. Neither answered the telephone. No surprise there. They had good reason to be afraid. Source relationships are like romantic relationships. Some end badly. Others simply fade away.

I was at a dead end about what to do next, when early one morning the telephone rang (yes, this was before the time of cell phones and rings that could whistle Dixie) and a man on the other end said he could help me with the story if I would come to Port St. Joe and meet with him.

"What's your name?" I asked.

"I'll tell you that when you get here."

"Okay. Do you have information about the Poonais?"

"It's bigger than that."

"Do you work for the hospital?"

"No—I'm part of an organization."

"You act like it's a secret organization."

"It is. Don't bring anybody with you."

"Okay"

The man gave me directions. It was all very mysterious.

The next morning, bright and early, I set out for Port St. Joe, with adequate protection riding shotgun (certainly not sanctioned by my editor and I don't recommend new reporters do it either). In those days U.S. 98 was a two-lane highway all the way to Port St. Joe, which meant it was a slow drive that was punctuated with big logging trucks periodically accessing the highway, necessitating frequent braking on my part.

I followed the directions and arrived at an industrial site. There was no office I could find where I could check in, so I kept following directions until I reached a building with the number I had been given written on it. It wasn't the kind of place where you knocked before entering and I opened the door and continued down the only corridor, past clanking machinery and hissing steam, until I saw a bright light at the end of the corridor.

At that point, the corridor opened into a large, brightly-lit room where two men were seated in metal folding chairs; one man was white and the other was black. The room was sparsely furnished and had an oil-stained concrete floor. It resembled a secret chamber you might see in a science fiction movie. As I approached, the Black man stood and extended his hand, stating that he was the president of the local NAACP. Then the white man rose and extended his hand, explaining he was the Grand Dragon of the Ku Klux Klan. I recognized his voice from the telephone conversation we had. Both men were dressed in work clothes, so I surmised they both were employed at the facility.

My eyes darted over to the Black gentleman and he said, "Yeah, I know what you thinking. We've got a big problem here in Port St. Joe and we've joined forces to try to set things right."

This was a sight I had never before seen. The Klan and the NAACP in partnership. Blend that with the hissing and clanking sounds of that old building and you can perhaps imagine how I felt. The closest thing I can today compare it to is the *Mad Max* movie that was released two years after this meeting. Clearly, I had stepped into an episode of something entirely surreal. I put my right hand in my pockets, and griped my largest car key between the second and third fingers of my hand in case I needed the key as a weapon.

As I recall the meeting, both men were concerned about the city erupting into violence over the hospital dispute. Feelings were running high. They felt that by working together they could lessen the tensions. They wanted me to know that all the surface noise that was taking place was not the only "news." Neither man wanted race to be an issue. They saw old-style Panhandle politics, not race, as a threat to medical care in the city. I relaxed the grip on my car key. They wanted me to know Blacks and whites were working together to support the Poonais and Judge Taunton, who turned down my requests for interviews. I suppose that was to preserve the impartiality of his court. I suggested to my new sources that if they needed to communicate with me they should not call on a telephone, not even a pay telephone. Instead, they should drive to another town and call from a pay telephone or drive to Tallahassee and talk to me in person in the newsroom.

I continued to look for ways to develop this story in a way that would not get anyone else killed—or get the newspaper tied up in a lengthy lawsuit. If I had been given the time to make my story airtight—my editor was addicted to my daily news stories and did not want them to stop—I think I could have written something that would have brought justice to those injured by this massive political hospital scandal. By the way, Judge

Taunton won reelection by a landslide and the year after I left the *Tallahassee Democrat*, the following headline appeared on Page One of the Port St. Joe *Star*:

DROPS CHARGES AGAINST DR. POONAI

"Dr. Anila Poonai, a Port St. Joe physician, has been ruled innocent of six malpractice suits brought against her by the Florida Board of Medical Examiners," reported the *Star*.[15] Dr. Poonai was quoted as saying: "I'm relieved that this part of our fight is over. The charges were concocted by doctors at Port St. Joe Municipal Hospital who are trying to run me and my husband out of town."

Yes, that and so much more.

Before writing this chapter for the book, I did new research and found that Mrs. Poonai had passed away and Mr. Poonai had closed his practice some time ago. I obtained a couple of telephone numbers for Dr. P.V. Poonai, but both numbers were disconnected.

I spoke to a local lawyer named Tom Gibson who filled me in on the missing pieces. Apparently the Poonais never regained their privileges at the Municipal Hospital, but since the hospital was unable to get their licenses revoked they continued to practice medicine in the city. Municipal Hospital did not fare so well, according to Gibson, who said the hospital underwent numerous bankruptcies over the years and experienced liens placed on the facility by the Internal Revenue Service. In the end, the hospital closed and the building was torn down. The original owner of the land sued to have it returned, but the city won the lawsuit and sold the property to a newly formed hospital named Gulf Pines. It closed after a few years and a new facility named Ascension Sacred Heart Hospital opened in 2010 and seems to be thriving today.

The embattled land upon which Municipal Hospital existed was sold to a company that built a residential development with neatly laid out neighborhoods. It just goes to show that all things come to pass. The issues that had people so upset in the late 1970s no longer remain in the collective memory of the city's residents. It is as if nothing ever happened.

If there is a moral to this story it is that Page One headlines sometimes end up buried beneath new housing developments.

This story had a profound impact on me, however. From that point on, the word "source" was more than just a word to me. It never occurred to me that my source's home or office telephone might be tapped. Of course, it was tapped and what they heard from our conversation confirmed their suspicions that they were sources for the *Tallahassee Democrat*. From that day forward I took it for granted that the telephones of my sources and myself could be tapped, so I became careful about what I said and never again referred to meeting places on the telephone. Sometimes reporting is a life and death matter. If you are a reporter, forget that at your own peril.

IN DECEMBER 1978, I received word three days after Christmas that David Duke, Grand Dragon of the Knights of the Ku Klux Klan, planned to hold a rally in Perry, Florida, a town of 7,000 about fifty miles east of Tallahassee. The rally was set for early February. I was beginning to understand that the Florida Panhandle was quite similar to Mississippi in its racial politics. The town itself was named after a Confederate colonel in the Civil War.

In late 1922, during the Perry Race Riot, a mob of whites hanged a Black man named Charlie Wright and attacked the black community after Wright was accused of murdering a white schoolteacher. After the lynching, passions were still running high, leading to the shooting and hanging of two additional Black men. Left unsatisfied by the lynching, whites burned down the Black community's only school, churches and several family homes.

By 1978, Blacks made up about half the population of the town. It was just the sort of community that David Duke liked to visit and exploit. I gave Duke a call at his Metaire, Louisiana, headquarters to find out what he had in mind. "We hope to organize more and more white people," he explained. "We're trying to get across to the public about what is happening to the white majority. They've become second-class citizens."[16]

Duke said he wanted the Klan to become a political organization "like the National Association for the Advancement of Colored People." He had no idea how I felt about the Klan. That's because real journalism is not what you see on television with hosts arguing with their guests. That's what I'd like for young journalists reading this book to understand: when writing a news story, keep your opinions to yourself. Ask tough questions, but don't ask them in a way that reveals your personal feelings. Never argue with the person you are interviewing.

A year or so after my story ran, I read a story in *Playboy* written by novelist Harry Crews, who was born in Georgia but died in Florida.[17] He traveled across the country in 1979 with David Duke for a while and wrote about the experience. Explaining why he took the assignment, he wrote: "I believe that the decade of the Eighties will be the bloodiest of times, with men set against one another for real and imagined evils, urban guerrilla warfare such as this country has never seen, schools with as many police in the hallways as students, the National Guard standing duty in front of grocery stores and more, much more."

Crews said he didn't believe Duke, who once taught English in Laos for the U.S. State Department, would cause the violence, but he felt he would be right in the middle of it. "The hatred, the raging, burning hatred, is already out there in every village, town and city in this country. It is mostly disguised, and mostly denied, but it is there. I have heard its voice in too many places in too many accents not to believe it, radical as that may sound."

Crews was incorrect in his predicted decade, off by nearly forty years, but like so many writers of genius he was far ahead of his time. The America he described in 1979 is the America of 2021, a creation of Donald Trump and his supporters who have spread the hatred for decades, finally believing their time had come to re-impose slavery by denying the democratic process to Blacks.

Duke told me he also planned to come to Tallahassee, not for a rally

Mississippi Klansman / photo by Steve Gardner

but to meet with community "leaders." Intrigued by that comment I asked a few Tallahassee leaders what they thought about him visiting the city.

The director of the Tallahassee Urban League said he would not oppose Duke's visit: "If he wants to come, let him come. They do have a right to do that." The president of the Southern Christian Leadership Conference said he didn't oppose his visit, but hoped it would not create "ill will and prejudice" in the community.

I spoke to the Klan organizer for the Perry event and he said Duke would be speaking at the D&D Family Restaurant. A sheriff's deputy who worked out of Perry told me that only about one hundred people attended the last Klan rally three years earlier. "They just marched down the street. There were no problems."

BEFORE LEAVING TALLAHASSEE for a new job, I headed south one last time to St. Marks, where I had gathered so many memorable stories. I saw a sign directing me to a self-described "topless oyster bar." I followed the directions and drove up to a two-story building that had seen better days. The hand-lettered sign outside conjured up all sorts of images. My imagination was running wild. The story I wrote began this way:

Belly up to the bar, order a beer, then sit back and ogle a bevy of raw-skinned topless beauties guaranteed to make you drool.

Welcome to Posey's Topless Oyster Bar—where oysters on the half-shell, not employees, go topless. For seven years Posey's—the self-proclaimed home of the 'topless oyster'—has drawn seafood lovers to that historic port of St. Marks from as far away as California and Sweden. They come for three reasons: raw oysters, boiled shrimp and smoked mullet.

From the outside, the two-story eatery looks like a clapboard shanty bent and twisted by the Gulf winds. "They don't let you do anything to the building," says owner Bill Helson of his customers. "They yell at you if you try to paint it."[18]

Posey's Topless Bar was another one of my stories picked up by *Facing South* for national distribution. Looking, back I can see now that many of my human interest stories were easily adapted to a column format.

Another of my final Page One stories came as a result of a disaster in Pensacola, Florida. A horrific rainstorm swept into the city, seemingly from nowhere, dropping sixteen inches of rain in less than twenty-four hours. The reports coming out of Pensacola painted a picture of a desperate community that felt helpless by the unrelenting bombardment of rain. It was the worst storm that had hit Pensacola in forty-four years. Along with the rain came four tornados.

As the storm was still raging, my editor pulled me aside and told me he wanted me to go to Pensacola to cover the storm and its aftermath—and to take with me the newspaper librarian who had some newspaper reporting experience but wanted more. Browning Brooks was a woman in her mid-to-late twenties. She was efficient as a librarian, but I had no idea how she would be as a reporter. As it turned out, it would have been a difficult assignment for one person. She proved invaluable in collecting the raw data we needed from authorities while I roamed looking for color.

By the time we got off from Tallahassee, the sun already was setting. The drive to Pensacola was among the worst of my life. Blinding rain, howling wind that rocked the car from side to side, big-rig trucks splashing water over the windows and windshield whenever they passed. Visibility was sometimes zero. We would slow down to almost nothing at times, only to hear the horn of a big rig passing us. It was an absolute nightmare.

By the time we drove into Pensacola, the winds had died down, leaving mostly light rain. It was difficult finding a place to stay, but we finally did find a motel that was still open and set up a miniature command center from which we began making telephone calls to various authorities from whom we could collect damage estimates.

The next morning the sun was shining, but its light was falling on a wrecked Pensacola. Debris was everywhere. Roof parts, shoes, children's toys—everywhere you looked you saw broken shards of once vibrant life.

I hardly recognized downtown. We would check with the sheriff's office several times during the day to get storm data, but our main task now was to drive around the city looking for damage and human interest stories that could describe the fury of the rainstorm.

One story we wrote began:

Lily Simpkins said she knew it was time to move to higher ground when she saw rats swimming past her duplex apartment. They were just churning through the water, swimming the best they could. She was among the five thousand people driven from their homes after eleven inches of rain already had flooded the city.

Mrs. Simpkins said the water damage nearly broke her heart, adding "The Lord's done slipped this past us. We'd better wake up."[19]

Besides the rats, we heard stories about home-wrecked residents pulling snakes out of their homes. If you've never done that, I can tell you from experience that it is a stressful experience, primarily because you may think the snake is nonpoisonous but you're never one hundred percent certain. The worst part of the trip was our inability to find food to eat since the restaurants were closed. We literally had to forage for food.

Our drive back to Tallahassee was uneventful, with both of us exhausted and having little to say after two days of constant talking about what we were witnessing. I promised myself I would never again head blindly into a raging storm to get a news story.

Little did I know I would soon be knee-deep in a record-breaking flood, followed by a category four hurricane, floating out to sea in the cramped backseat of a water-borne VW Beetle, clutching a reporter's notebook with white knuckles while insisting that the driver explain why his car was floating away with us trapped inside.

Chapter 9

Jackson, Mississippi

MY EMPLOYMENT at the *Tallahassee Democrat* was unsatisfying, despite a long string of Page One stories. There were too many differences with editors who didn't seem to know where they wanted to take the newspaper. The editors fought me tooth and nail on every story I proposed. When the local PBS television station (or community television station, I forget which) showed up in the newsroom to do a documentary on me because of the success of my human interest stories, the interviewer commented on tape, "I bet you will get tons of new leads on people in need of help after this piece airs." I responded that my editors had told me before they arrived and set up their bright lights—"no more stories helping people." When that comment aired, it was the nail in the coffin. They couldn't exactly fire me for being honest with the media, or for writing too many Page One stories, but they could make life miserable for me in the newsroom because they didn't like my opinions or attitude.

It took a couple of months to plan and execute my escape.

Out of frustration, I wrote a letter to Jimmy Ward, editor of the *Jackson Daily News*, Mississippi's largest circulation afternoon newspaper, and asked if he had any job openings. Ward was a favorite of radio's Paul Harvey, who quoted him all the time as "Jackson Jimmy." Ward returned the favor and made Paul Harvey a frequent visitor to his Page One column, "Covering the Crossroads." Growing up, my family hadn't subscribed to the *Jackson Daily News,* but my best friend, Jimmy Patterson, delivered the newspaper on his motor scooter and I was a frequent backseat passenger when he made his deliveries. It was during that time I became familiar with Ward's column.

In 1960, Jimmy Ward had a national reputation as the most conservative newspaper editor in America. *Time* magazine said it, so how could it not be true? That year I was given a high school project to write a report on Major Frederick Sullens, the first editor of the *Jackson Daily News.* I wrote Ward a letter and asked him questions about his predecessor. Ward was only the second editor in the newspaper's history. He responded to my letter and proved to be most helpful with my school project.

In my more recent letter from Tallahassee, I told him I had worked for the *Delta Democrat-Times* (his arch enemy) and the *Greenwood Commonwealth,* edited by a legendary moderate editor, John Emmerich, with whom he was not on the closest terms. Amazingly, I received a friendly response inviting me to visit him in Jackson. About two weeks later, I walked into his office and met him for the first time. He looked nothing like the image I had of him in my mind. His appearance was gaunt, due to a recent diagnosis of throat cancer, but he shot out his hand with a big grin and welcomed me with a hearty admonition to "pull up a chair." As soon as we were seated, I showed him the letter he had sent me in 1960. He seemed touched that I had held onto it all those years.

I learned two things during my interview. First, he had a nephew in my hometown, which could be bad news for me. Second, despite his harsh choice of words on the race issue, his newsroom personality was more like the funny comments he made in his columns. After an interview that lasted about an hour, he told me he had an opening for a reporter and would be in touch. I later learned he called his nephew, who just happened to be a fan of the stories I wrote for the *Delta Democrat-Times*. The nephew told him everything he knew about me—my early support of civil rights and my opposition to the Vietnam War. In summary, he told his conservative uncle, "You know, he's more liberal than you are."

Not long after I returned to Tallahassee, Ward called and offered me the reporter's position. I was stunned. Because I grew up in Mississippi, I have never expected much from its residents, but I am often flabbergasted by the ingenious means they adopt to surprise me when I least expect it. It is true that some of the worst people in the United States live in Mississippi; but it also is true that some of the best people in the United States live in Mississippi. It is one of those things that leave outsiders scratching their heads.

I wasted no time relocating my wife and son to Mississippi, moving for the third time in three years. It was a miserable trip for my son because he had a bad case of chickenpox. The sores were on his face, in his ears, and around his eyes. Ina drove the car, with Jonathan lying in the carpeted hatchback, screaming almost the entire way because of the pain he was in. I drove the truck loaded with our possessions.

In the days prior to leaving, we had been so busy packing and closing accounts here and there that we had watched no television. If we had, we would have noticed that a storm had passed through Jackson, Mississippi, dropping up to fifteen inches of rain. They called it the Easter Flood because so much rain fell that the Pearl River overflowed and flooded Jackson in the days after Easter Sunday, causing nearly $700 million in damages. More than 15,000 people were evacuated from Jackson due to rising flood waters. It was the flood of a lifetime.

Imagine our surprise when we arrived in Jackson and tried to make our way to the townhouse apartment we had rented, only to be turned back by streets still covered in flood water. We checked into a motel that was on a hill and thus not threatened by the flooding. With Jonathan constantly screaming from his chickenpox sores, it was a miserable existence. Within a couple of days, the water receded from the streets, allowing us to drive to the apartment complex where our apartment was located. The downstairs was almost totally destroyed and the floors were covered with debris. Upstairs was untouched by the storm. The apartment manager promised to make the downstairs livable as soon as possible.

I reported for work a few days later, leaving Ina and Jonathan at the motel. Because she could not take him into a restaurant or leave him alone in the room, they had to live on the meals put together from things I could purchase that did not have to be cooked. After work I stopped at restaurants and picked up take-out dinners and took them to the motel room so that they would have hot meals to enjoy.

Once the debris and carpeting had been removed downstairs, we decided to move into the upstairs quarters of our apartment while they continued to work on installing new sheetrock and kitchen appliances, then painting the downstairs kitchen, living room and bath.

The first thing I noticed when I reported for work was that there was only one Black person working in the newsroom, a graphic artist by the name of Earnest Hart. Of course, they seated me in the desk next to him. Where else would you seat the only moderate or liberal except next to the only Black person? That worked out well because he had a good sense of humor and we ended up sharing a lot of laughs at the folly that seemed to surround us in the newsroom.

There is a wing of journalism that believes that it is the job of the reporter to rewrite press releases pertaining to his or her assigned beat. I was greeted by several weeks of press releases from public schools, private schools and universities. Believe me, you can squander an entire day reworking press releases and calling the individuals who sent them for clarification. That is a necessary part of informing readers about what is going on with schools. However, that was not a part of journalism that interested me.

After a month or two of writing "shorts" for the newspaper about education, I began using the press releases as starting points for investigative features. One such story was a Page One series on sex

172

discrimination among the coaching staffs in Jackson public and private schools. A recent survey had found that only eighteen of 124 coaching jobs in the city schools were filled by women. None of the three majority white high schools in Jackson, which made up more than 60 percent of the total white high school enrollment in the city, had female coaches. In the private schools only three of sixteen jobs were filled with women. Clearly, if a woman wanted to coach athletics in Jackson she was out of luck. There were no women basketball, track or softball coaches.

The first story in my series, which had artwork done by Earnest Hart and occupied three of the five columns above the fold, began with a couple of shocking examples:

When Leah Reed, the basketball coach at Manhattan Academy, was fired from her job last April, she was stunned. Under her leadership, the girls' basketball team had risen to second place in the state.

Ms. Reed, a six-foot-tall graduate of Mississippi College, was told she would be replaced by a man. No reason, she said, was given for her dismissal. While Ms. Reed was being told she no longer had a job, Anna Woodson, the volleyball coach at Murrah High School, also was being relieved of her job.

Sex discrimination? School officials say no, but statistics released by the Jackson Public School system show that women coaches have a subordinate status to their male counterparts in almost every area.[20]

W. C. "Pops" Allen, head of the Jackson schools' athletic department, told me that qualified women were just not all that interested in coaching as a profession. He said he had a difficult time finding women to hire. "The interest hasn't been there," he said.

Diane Upton, a basketball coach, said that wasn't necessarily so. "I don't think they would have any trouble getting women coaches in high school." What really bothered her was that male coaches were paid more than women coaches. "We don't have the opportunity to make the kind of money they make."

My investigation showed that while the average salary of male and female coaches differed by less than four hundred dollars (favoring males), the real discrepancy occurred in the coaching supplements that coaches received. At one school I investigated, there was a male coach and a female coach performing essentially the same duties, but the male received a supplement of $4,000 a year while the female received only $655 a year.

The issue of women's rights and equal pay in coaching struck a nerve in Jackson, spurred along by the series. For once, women coaches and wannabe women coaches had facts and figures upon which to tailor their demands. The series provided women coaches with the ammunition they needed to win public support for both higher pay and more coaching options. Today it is not unusual to see a woman coaching boys' teams.

ONE DAY I WENT TO WORK and was told that I was going to the Gulf Coast to cover a hurricane. I thought I was far enough away from coastal waters to ever have to do that sort of thing again. But here I was in Jackson, Mississippi, saying goodbye to my wife and son to strike out with fellow reporter Joe Rogers to welcome incoming hurricane Frederic, a category four storm with winds of up to 130 miles-per-hour.

We arrived in Gulfport in time to scout the surrounding terrain to familiarize ourselves with existing landmarks so that we would have a better understanding of what to look for after the storm had passed. I was in the cramped backseat with my knees pushed up almost to my chest, and a photographer was riding shotgun in the front seat. The wind was already gusting with strong bursts when we drove along the coastal highway, shocked to see waves washing up onto the pavement, only to retreat long enough to regroup and flow back to the highway. The sky was different shades of gray and presented an ominous threat that was unmistakable.

Up ahead I noticed the highway was completely covered with water. "Should we be driving into that?" I asked.

"I think it is just an inch or two," answered the driver.

Then we were in the water, slip-sliding back and forth, the engine whining as the wheels spun faster and faster.

"I can't get traction!" called out the driver. The wind was howling through the VW Beetle and our voices got louder and louder in order to be heard over the roar of the unrelenting winds.

Suddenly, I noticed that the sound of the engine subsided.

"What's going on?" I asked the driver.

"I'm just spinning the wheels. We're not touching the ground. That's why I can't get traction. We're several yards out in the gulf."

"Keep spinning the wheels. Maybe it will create a waterwheel effect and propel us forward."

"What good would that do?"

"If we are already in motion it will be easier for the wind gust to push us back to dry land."

I didn't know much about VW Beetles, but I concluded they must be highly compartmentalized, a process that would have given us buoyancy.

This nightmare went on for perhaps another thirty minutes.

What if it springs a leak? I thought. *We would sink like a rock!*

Finally, there was a distinct bump as one of the wheels found solid ground. The gusts were going inland now pretty hard and that put us back over the highway. It was still covered in water, but now our wheels had traction. The driver kept steering left until we spotted higher ground and were able to drive back onto solid land. We kept going until we found a secondary road that was not covered in water. It eventually took us back to Gulfport and the county courthouse where the civil defense team had assembled in its basement headquarters to do battle with the storm.

The first thing we saw when we entered the room was a buffet that officials had put out for their workers and any journalists who had not been smart enough to pack food to sustain themselves over the next day or so. That would be us!

Joe and I each picked up a plate of sandwiches and chips, and grabbed a soft drink out of the ice chest before sitting in chairs along the wall. I

175

removed the waxed paper from my sandwich and peeked inside. To my horror, I saw a discolored circle on the processed meat.

"Damn!" I exclaimed. "This meat's gone bad."

"Let me see."

Joe examined the piece of what turned out to be salami and laughed.

"There's nothing wrong with that meat. That's a pepper."

I leaned over and looked closer.

In my defense, I said, "Mother never let us eat processed meat. This is the first salami I've ever seen." I took a bite. "Not bad."

Joe didn't hear my explanation. He was too busy laughing.

Over the next several hours we killed time by getting up every so often to go outside and look at the sky. Each time we went out, we had to push harder to open the door. The wind grew stronger and the sky became darker. By the time nightfall arrived we could hear the storm outside. At one point, a civil defense official announced that we were experiencing the full fury of the storm:

"We've got winds that are well over 100 miles-per-hour. Soon we will be In the eye of the storm and it will get very quiet outside. That's when you can go outside and look around. Just don't overstay your welcome out there. As we move out of the eye, the winds will hit again like a sledgehammer."

Joe and I listened for the winds to go down. Then we stepped outside and looked around. The sky was a spooky pinkish color even though it was around midnight. We ventured out beyond the courthouse and watched other people emerging outside to check the damage to their buildings. The air smelled wet and had a copper-like odor to it. We kept walking, long past when we should have stopped.

Suddenly, we saw a small metal building rolling down the center of the street like tumbleweed. Then the wind hit our faces like a strong bitch slap and we ran back to the courthouse, the wind howling at that point. Joe pulled out ahead of me and managed to pull the door open enough to get inside the building. I was right behind him, but a sudden gust of hard-driving wind slammed into me and moved me away from a straight line to the door and knocked me up against the wall, where the winds pressed against me and lifted me so that my feet no longer touched the ground. The rain peppered against my face as I inched my way toward the door using my fingers to claw myself forward while pushing with my feet as my heels dug in against the brick wall.

Once I got to the door and started pulling on the handle, the door opened slightly and then fully as Joe pushed from the other side. Joe and I returned to where we had eaten our processed meat and collapsed into the chairs. The civil defense workers constantly worked their radios and telephones, creating a hum that eventually lulled us to sleep in our chairs. When we awoke the storm had passed and there was an easy banter in the room. Frederic had dumped twelve inches of rain in Jackson County and devastated sixteen counties that later were classified disaster areas. The bill for the damages came to $1.77 billion.

Joe and I did interviews with different people and wrote our stories and said goodbye to Gulfport and headed back to Jackson, thoroughly exhausted. Neither of us said a word during the two-hour drive and, in fact, did not speak again for nearly twenty years.

ONE DAY I RECEIVED a tip that a male nursing student who lived in a dormitory at the University of Southern Mississippi had applied for a room in the women's dormitory because he had scheduled an operation that would change him from male to female. Well, that was enough for me to saddle up my Mustang hatchback and head south to the university.

I arranged an appointment with the student, who asked to be called Barnett X, to meet him at his dormitory. When I walked into the lobby I did not have to ask around to find him. I was greeted by a muscular Black man wearing blues jeans and a sweater. He probably weighed 225 to 250 pounds, about the size of a linebacker in football. We picked a quiet corner of the lobby and sat in overstuffed chairs to talk. Because he had been undergoing hormone treatments to prepare him for the surgery, which he said would be performed sometime next year in Colorado Springs, Colorado, at a cost of $3,589, he had the physical appearance of a woman. His hips were full, rounded, and his hair was worn short and professionally styled. He explained he had wanted to be female since the age of ten. Because he was only midway through his treatments, he looked to be part male and part female. It was disconcerting to talk to him, not because of that, but because he was very angry and it showed on his face.

I could not help but reflect on the terrifying scene in Hitchcock's *Psycho* when Norman Bates, dressed as his deceased mother, is shown with a rather large butcher knife in his hand. I asked him if he owned a knife. He answered no, but said he owned a pistol that he kept loaded in his dorm room.

"What are you afraid of?" I asked.

"I'm afraid of what I don't know."

As a psychology major at the University of Mississippi, I was familiar with transgender case studies (at that time it was classified as a mental illness; that had been changed by the time I met Barnett X), so I was not disturbed by his decision to become a woman, but rather by the bullying he had been subjected to at the university. His anger at being singled out at the university, for what he viewed as a life choice, was not far from developing into rage.

"Everyone in the world has something to hide," he explained in a woman's voice. "I just have a different set of norms."

As a Baptist, he had strong beliefs about the morality of a sex-change operation. "The Bible says it is wrong for a person to change his body. You're supposed to keep the body that God gave you. But my need to become a woman is so great I am willing to risk going to Hell for my decision."

After I concluded my interview, I walked about the campus, stopping female students at random to get their perspective. I found their answers very surprising.

"I believe he has a right to have his sex changed," said Cindie

Campbell, a third-year student. "I know I enjoy being a female. More power to him."

"It's not wrong for him to want to become a woman, but if it will cause problems for him (to move to a female dormitory) he should not," said Yvonne Leggett, a freshman. "I wouldn't tell my parents. They'd be terribly shocked."

Before leaving the campus, I returned to the male dormitory to talk to male students on the floor where he lived. They explained they had a "live-and-let-live" truce with Barnett. Whenever Barnett heads for the shower wearing bikini panties and a bra, the other students shout a signal to clear the room. Interestingly, at the time of my visit none of the students on his floor had asked to be transferred.

When I returned to Jackson, I called Attorney General A. F. Summer to ask if there were any laws pertaining to transgender issues in the state: "The Legislature has never felt it necessary to define who is male or female," he said. "That's a question that will have to be answered when we reach that point."

I found a wire service printout on my desk about a civilian clerk-typist at Kessler Air Force Base named James Gootee who had been sent home for wearing women's clothing to work. Air Force officials told him he would have to dress like a man when he returns to work before they would even consider his request to dress like a woman.

By then he had retained the services of a lawyer, who said, "There is no way he will go to work as a man."

I got in touch with Gootee by telephone and he told me it would make him very tense to go to work dressed as a man. He explained he planned to undergo surgery to change his gender and doctors had told him he must dress like a woman for a year before they would agree to do the surgery.

"I'm not an activist," Gootee said. "But this is nothing more than a human rights issue."[21]

I had returned to Mississippi to find a new gender war underway.

I wrote both stories and both appeared on Page One in one package.

It is quite amazing when you think about it. The stories were written forty years ago, the point being transgender issues have been around a long time. In many ways, people were more understanding forty years ago than they are today. Our collective IQ has dropped considerably in recent years.

My next investigative feature involved the Mississippi Institutions of Higher Learning (College Board). In going over their reporting data, I saw something that surprised me. In recent years there had been a marked decline in white males entering Mississippi universities. Enrollment for African Americans, both genders, and white females was up.

I found it surprising that white males in Mississippi no longer considered a university degree essential for success. For over one hundred years, Mississippi universities had been dominated by white males. In recent years that had changed. Although I didn't know it at the time, white males "dropping out" of higher education in Mississippi is part of a national trend that has culminated in a generation of white males who were displaced from their jobs by women of all colors and Black men.

Instead of adjusting and learning new job skills, they retreated into hurtful right-wing politics characterized by racism and a passion for violence. Outwardly, they were identifiable by their bushy Civil War-era beards and an obsession with military-style weapons they often displayed in public while citing their Second Amendment rights.

Although we didn't clearly understand it at the time, America was fracturing into two distinct cultures. One defined itself by the words "all men are created equal." The other by the belief that America is defined by Second Amendment rights that give citizens the right to use armed force to overthrow governments of which they do not approve.

IN NOVEMBER 1979, I put together yet another investigative feature, only this time it would change the trajectory of my journalism career. In going over College Board minutes, I learned that the board members had allocated themselves up to 10,000 free football game tickets per season. It was a transparent abuse of power that everyone could understand. The story ran on Page One of a Saturday joint *Clarion-Ledger/Jackson Daily News* edition. It turned out to be quite the scandal.

On Monday I heard from one of the board members who said that they had been plagued by callers demanding their fair share of the tickets.

"It's not fair," the board member said. "I didn't get 10,000 tickets. I get only a handful of those tickets."

The board member was visibly upset over the newspaper story and said he had considered resigning because of the controversy. "If you can't stand the heat," he said, quoting a favorite phrase of President Harry Truman, "maybe you should get out of the kitchen."

He decided not to resign because he felt the College Board, overall, was making a valuable contribution to the improvement of higher education in Mississippi.

The story hit a sore spot with the public, who collectively were of the mind that public officials should not receive anything free, certainly not at the public's expense.

To my surprise, Jimmy Ward asked me to write an editorial.

Because there was an upcoming College Board meeting, I suggested I write the editorial after I attended the meeting. That was fine with Ward. The resulting editorial, which, like the story, ran in a combined *Clarion-Ledger/Jackson Daily News* Sunday edition, at the top of the page I might add, above the *Clarion-Ledger* editorial, began with:

"There's a reporter out there."
"Who is it?"
"I forget his name . . . but he's the one who did us in."
"Oh, you must mean the one from the Jackson Daily News."
"Yeah, he's the one."
The above conversation did not happen in a back alley on a Saturday night. It happened in broad daylight at a recent meeting of the state College Board.
The secretary who began the exchange obviously is guilty of nothing

more ominous than saying what was on the minds of many board members: Namely, that the reporter—James L. Dickerson—had injured the board's prestige by writing an article for a recent Saturday edition of the Clarion-Ledger/Jackson Daily News *pointing out that board members had made themselves eligible for up to 10,000 free football tickets per season.*[22]

The investigative article pointed out that the state College Board was stealing bushels of college football tickets, which they were free to give away or sell. It was quite the scandal. Within days of the publication of the editorial, Jimmy Ward called me into his office and closed the door.

Here it comes, I thought. *Nice knowing you!*

Ward got right to the point. He was transferring me to the editorial page, where I would write editorials each day for the *Daily News* and for the Sunday newspaper, a joint edition put out by the *Daily News'* sister publication, the *Clarion-Ledger*.

At first I could not believe my good fortune. Reality set in when he explained I would be in charge of both the editorial and op-ed pages, along with the cartoon produced each day by cartoonist Jimmy Johnson (who subsequently left newspapers to produce a cartoon strip called *Arlo & Janis*). This is something I had wanted to do for as long as I could remember. I did not major in journalism at the University of Mississippi, but I did take a semester's worth of journalism courses, one of which was in editorial writing.

One day, the professor gave a class assignment to write an editorial on the China-India War of 1962 over a disputed border that was part of Kashmir. India asserted it belonged to India. China claimed it was part of Xinjiang. The war ended with thousands of casualties and was unresolved in 1967, when I was taking the class. I wrote an editorial and turned it in.

When the class next met, the professor handed out the editorials that had been turned in, each marked with a grade from A to F. My editorial had an oversized "F" in bright red ink. I vociferously objected, prompting my professor's face to redden.

"Why," I asked, "Would I deserve an F for such a well-thought-out opinion?"

"Because it's the wrong opinion," he replied, practically shouting. "You will never make it as an editorial writer."

There wasn't much to say after that. My professor wasn't supposed to inject his personal political opinions into his classroom, but he did. It was too late in the semester to drop the class and I didn't want to sabotage my Bobbie Gentry story that I had turned in to *Mississippi Magazine*, but I had two of five classes with this professor and I knew I would get an "F" in both. So, I stopped going to all five classes and went to talk to my dean about my situation. Apparently, he had received other complaints. After doing a little math, he determined that I could take an "F" in all five classes and still have a grade point average high enough to graduate. He couldn't erase my grades but he could reinstate me for the next semester.

My Bobbie Gentry interview story was published in the winter 1968 edition of *Mississippi Magazine*. I had been told it would be the cover story because my interview was the only one she had granted since her hit record "Ode to Billie Joe" had reached Number 1 on the charts. Instead of Bobbie Gentry on the cover, however, was the image of three redneck deer hunters riding in a boat in a cypress swamp, two dead deer displayed on the bow. My professor had allowed a personal grievance to override the professionalism of a university publication.

Now that I was editorial page editor of the *Jackson Daily News* I had to develop an editorial philosophy for the editorial page and the op-ed page. I looked around me and this is what I saw: A family drama as powerful, passionate, poignant, and complicated as anything Shakespeare ever conceived. *The Clarion-Ledger* (morning newspaper) and the *Jackson Daily News* (afternoon newspaper) were owned by the Hederman brothers—Robert, Henry and Zack. Robert "Bob" Hederman was the publisher of both newspapers and his cousin Tom Hederman was the editor of the *Clarion-Ledger*. On an organizational chart, Jimmy Ward reported to Bob Hederman, but in reality he also reported to Tom Hederman.

When I arrived on the scene in 1979, Rea Hederman, who was my exact same age, was the managing editor of the *Clarion-Ledger*. Rea became executive editor of the *Clarion-Ledger* the following year and established an office on the floor above the newsroom. Rea did not control the *Clarion-Ledger* newsroom or editorial page. Tom Hederman supervised both. Rea supervised a staff of reporters who mainly did investigative reporting. He was known to be a person of liberal disposition, but since he had no control over the editorial pages he assigned investigative stories that exposed excesses of racism and police brutality.

For decades the two newspapers were best known for the vigor with which they fought school integration and voting rights for Black citizens. The Hederman family was hard-core Baptist, a denomination that was the last in the state to accept human rights for African Americans. The Hedermans were generous in their contributions to the Baptist Church and the Baptist Hospital. Although all Hederman families were stockholders in the newspaper, only Tom and Bob were involved with the day-to-day activities of the newspapers. That meant they were under constant pressure to ensure that the newspapers reflect their "family values" on racial integration and other conservative issues.

On the *Jackson Daily News,* Jimmy Ward was the undisputed editor, but before I arrived the Hederman's had hired a managing editor named Bob Gordon to supervise the newsroom staff. Gordon had no control over the editorial and op-ed pages, but he desperately wanted to have control. Ward knew that and he knew that Gordon wanted his job as editor. It would take time to figure out how I fit into that equation, but for the moment I had to create a plan for the editorial page.

Fully understanding that the editorial page was not there to reflect my opinions, but rather the opinions of the newspaper, I felt the editorial page needed to move to the center, away from the hard right where it had been for decades. I decided I could write editorials that were left of center in the areas of the arts, education, child abuse and women's rights, but slightly right of center on business, religion and politics. Comments on racial issues were confined to dead center. From a centrist position, the newspaper could not show strong leadership, but it could embrace progressive leadership on key issues as they arose.

I had no power to make political endorsements. That was Ward's responsibility in consultation with Tom Hederman. It was a high wire act for certain, because I could be fired on the spot for moving too fast. Ward frequently sent me written memos such as this one: "Our past position editorially has deplored the rape of the CIA and the FBI as a spinoff of Watergate and allied events, the emotionally-passed "Freedom of Information Act" (yes, a newspaper thought this legislation unwise—and more and more newspapers are taking a second thought at the damage this has done to national security). You may want to keep this info handy when your delightful editorial bug bites you again. Thanks to you and an appreciation of our growing alliance in this field."

I appreciated the diplomatic approach he took to giving me direction. If you ask me, he was thankful that I was moving the page away from the far right. With Rea Hederman installed as the executive editor of the *Clarion-Ledger,* that told him that the morning newspaper was already moving away from the hard right. I think he correctly assessed the support that the Hederman's involved in journalism gave to Rea, but he misjudged the willingness of the non-journalism Hedermans to go along with change. Because of the change taking place at the *Clarion-Ledger*, Ward thought that my editorials would help him keep his job in the midst of such change. That was the "alliance" he referred to in his memo: He would watch my back from conservatives, and I would watch his back from the newspaper's emerging liberalism under the leadership of Rea.

My first editorial carried the headline:

SOUTH TOWARD HOME FOR WILLIE MORRIS

Morris, the former editor of *Harper's Magazine*, was a leading proponent for racial integration and opposition to the Vietnam War. A native-born Mississippian, he had lived in New York for a number of years and had announced his decision to return to Mississippi to be guest lecturer at the University of Mississippi. The editorial put the *Daily News* on record as welcoming Morris back to the state.

When I turned the editorial in to Ward I half-expected him to reject it. To my surprise, he emerged from his office and walked across the newsroom to my desk and dropped the editorial onto my typewriter.

"How's it going, hoss?" he asked, giving me a thumbs-up before returning to his office. He used the word 'hoss' as a term of endearment for individuals he liked.

I must admit his "thumbs up" left me feeling somewhat empowered. My next controversial decision was to create a "man on the street" feature for the op-ed page. Each week I sent out a reporter and photographer to ask passersby on the street their opinion about issues in the news. Nothing radical about that, right?

Actually, the newspaper had a history of publishing as few images of Black individuals as possible. I instructed the reporter to interview both white and Black individuals.

When the first "man in the street" feature was published there was an uproar over the Black faces on the op-ed page. Within days I was receiving hate mail and death threats.

"What do you want me to do?" asked the reporter when next week's deadline rolled around.

I thought a minute and said, "More Black people." I had learned from dealing with racists in the Delta that you had to stand up to them.

"If you say so," was her response.

As I expected, we survived having photographs of Black individuals on the editorial pages.

Not a word from Jimmy Ward.

AS TIME WENT BY, it became apparent that Bob Gordon was becoming jealous of the attention I was getting with my editorials. I had become a barrier to his goal of replacing Jimmy Ward as editor. He began making suggestions to me for editorials. Topics that I knew would anger Jimmy Ward if I wrote them. Bob Gordon knew that, too. That's why he made the suggestions. He was the supervisor of the news side. I owed it to him to listen to his suggestions, but I wrote what I felt was called for.

Finally, I made an appointment to meet with Tom Hederman.

On my way downstairs to his office, I began to second guess my reason for asking for a meeting. There was enough drama on the *Clarion-Ledger* side of the building. I did not want to add drama to the *Jackson Daily News* side. Still, I had a problem that needed a resolution.

Once I was in his office, he asked me to close the door.

I told him about the situation in the newsroom and he nodded knowingly throughout my presentation. Then I asked the question that was on my mind.

"I am being pulled in two different directions," I explained. "What should I do?"

Tom Hederman lowered his head in thought for a moment. Then he looked at me and smiled.

"I think you should dance with the one that brought you," he said.

"By that you mean I should only take direction from Mr. Ward?"

"Correct."

Problem solved.

* * *

I pressed on with editorials on a variety of subjects, including one on Mississippi's lack of focus on treatment for emotionally disturbed children. A crisis was generated by Rankin General Hospital when it decided to close its treatment center for emotionally disturbed children because the hospital did not find the center to be cost effective. Because it was the only treatment center for older children and adolescents in the state, it left a gaping void in the mental health system. In June 1980, in an editorial headlined **WINTER'S HAND**, I called upon Governor William Winter to do something about what had become a crisis.

Within weeks, Winter responded by appointing a special task force to look into the needs of Mississippi's forgotten citizens, its children. In an editorial for the combined *Clarion-Ledger/Jackson Daily News* weekend edition, titled **FORGOTTEN CHILDREN**, I applauded Winter's decision and acknowledged immediate action by Mental Health Director Jan Duker to recruit a staff member to work fulltime on developing programs tailored exclusively for the needs of children and her announcement that she was working to establish state-operated residential treatment centers for emotionally disturbed children as well as making ten beds available for the treatment of adolescents at East Mississippi Hospital in Meridian. The editorial ended with the words: "By establishing a task force to study the problem Gov. Winter has shown genuine leadership in meeting the challenge. We hope that leadership will be heeded in the months ahead."[23]

Children's issues were one area where I felt I could go full throttle because there is only one issue in which there is a conservative-liberal divide and that is on whether government has the right to intervene in how parents raise their children. Of course, there is consensus when it comes to whether parents have a right to abuse their children—they do not. The number of Mississippians who would claim the right to abuse their children is troubling but miniscule.

In 1980, I wrote an editorial in response to a series of articles on the news side that dealt with the growing problem of child prostitution in Jackson. Headlined **CHILD MOLESTERS,** it was critical of the city's unwillingness to tackle what was a big problem in Mississippi. The editorial applauded progress in recent years in the state's efforts to tackle physical abuse and mental cruelty inflicted on children, but it was critical of the state's lack of concern about child sexual abuse, which is what child prostitution is all about. Said the editorial: "As incredible as it may seem, Mississippi is a dream come true for child molesters. While the age of consent (that age at which individuals are considered legally free to consent to sexual activity) is eighteen, any child between the ages of twelve and eighteen is considered fair game for child molesters if it can be proved that the child had a "previously unchaste character." In other words, children were fair game if they previously had been molested. The editorial concluded with:

"The time has come to get tough with child molesters and those who profit financially from the sexual exploitation of children. The longer state lawmakers wait to face up to the problem, the more difficult it will become to find a workable solution."[24]

Unknown to me at the time, managing editor Bob Gordon included that editorial, along with others I had written, in the newspaper's submission to the Associated Press's annual awards competition at which the winners would be announced at a dinner in New Orleans. He didn't tell me my editorial had been submitted for a very good reason: If the editorials won, he planned to accept the award and take credit for writing them because the editorial cited a series of news stories on child prostitution that had been edited by him. Somehow Jimmy Ward got wind of his plans and encouraged me to attend the ceremony. I did and sat at the table with Gordon and others who had been nominated for awards. Gordon was surprised to see me at the dinner.

The presenter that evening was my former editor at the *Greenwood Commonwealth*, John Emmerich, who was president of the Mississippi Associated Press Association. He announced the category—editorial writing—and then began announcing the winners. First place goes to . . . "The *Jackson Daily News*." I was shocked, first of all, because my editorials won first place, and secondly, because Gordon had not attached my name to them, part of his plan to take credit for writing them. That was infuriating because the winner of every other award had a name attached, including the second place winner, Thomas Suddes at the *Clarion-Ledger*.

I glared at Gordon across the table, as the room grew restless for someone to stand up and accept the award, but Gordon made no effort to stand. After about a thirty-second standoff, I stood and walked toward the lectern. By that time, John Emmerich had realized I was the winner. When

I reached the lectern he announced my name and then cupped his hand over the microphone and said, "Why didn't you do this for me?"

"I tried, remember?" I said, smiling.

He smiled back and nodded.

I returned to the table and gazed at the award I had won that didn't bear my name. I did take pleasure out of the fact that my editorial won first place while the news stories did not. It was a dirty thing for Gordon to do to me, but at least I now understood what kind of man he was. As important as the honor was to me, it was even more important for the newspaper, which had never, in its eighty-something years, won an award for editorial writing.

The next morning shortly after I sat down at my desk in the newsroom, Jimmy Ward strolled out of his office and walked over to my desk. "Congratulations," he said, smiling broadly while giving me a thumbs-up as he spoke. The award had justified his decision to put me in charge of the editorial and op-ed pages.

THE MOST INTRIGUING STORY I *never* wrote involved the Shah of Iran. In January 1979, he and his wife had fled Iran after Ayatollah Khomeini seized power in that country. The Shah travelled to several countries in search of a place to live in exile. Not far behind him in each case were Iranian militants who sought to assassinate the former Iranian leader, or kidnap him so that he could be returned to Iran and put on trial.

In 1979, the Shah came to the United States to receive medical treatment for cancer. His first stop was New York City, where he was greeted by protestors. In response to his entry into the United States, Iranian militants stormed the American Embassy in Tehran and seized fifty-two American hostages. It developed into a major crisis for President Jimmy Carter. He ordered the Secret Service, the agency that usually protects foreign dignitaries, to step back to allow the FBI to provide security for the Shah until such time as he could turn the Shah over to the U.S. Air Force. When that occurred, the Shah and his wife were flown to the Air

Force base in San Antonio so that his cancer would be treated there.

Around that time, Jimmy Ward called me into his office and told me that one of his reliable sources had informed him that the Shah of Iran had been flown aboard an Air Force plane to Jackson so he could be treated by cancer specialists at Baptist Hospital. He asked me to look into it. What I discovered was that the Shah and his wife were staying with a prominent Jackson family while he traveled back and forth to the hospital for treatment. That was a huge international story and I was eager to flesh it out. I was able to locate a friend of the Jackson family hosting him and I was in the process of approaching the family, when Jimmy Ward called me into his office with a grim look on his face. He told me that the FBI had contacted him in response to my inquiries about the Shah.

"The FBI asked us not to write anything about the Shah because of national security concerns," said Ward. "They are concerned that a story giving the Shah's location would result in the hostages being abused by their captors."

Ward agreed that we both were aware of the pros of pursuing the story. Then, without stating his opinion, he asked me to define the cons of doing the story. I told him I would be concerned with the ethics of doing a story that resulted in the abuse or deaths of any hostages in Iran. I then pointed out that there were a number of Iranian students attending Jackson State University and I was concerned that I did not know the politics of the individual students. "What if one of the students was able to assassinate the Shah based on the information in my story," I said. "In that case, we could have a dead Shah in addition to dead hostages in Iran."

Ward said he agreed with me and he asked me not to tell the managing editor Bob Gordon or anyone else. I did as he asked. So, the Shah came and left without anyone ever knowing he was in the Magnolia State. I didn't like being put in a position to keep secrets, especially when it meant I would be losing the byline of an important international story, but as my journalism career advanced, I learned that keeping some secrets is an unwelcome and sometimes necessary part of being an ethical journalist.

Years later, I asked a FBI contact if the local Jackson office had a file on the Shah's visit. He reported back that there was no file in existence. That did not surprise me because the FBI had a long history, especially during the 1960s and 1970s, of compartmentalizing assignments from the national office so that the local office would have no knowledge of their clandestine activities. That told me that Ward was approached by the agents assigned to the Shah, not by agents from the local office.

CORONER REFORM WAS ANOTHER ISSUE I tackled on the editorial page. In the first of two editorials I pointed out that Mississippi's coroner system was a "dead-end street plagued by corruption, ignorance and simple neglect." Backing that assessment was Dr. Faye Spruill, the state's first medical examiner and the only forensic pathologist in the state. As proof there was a problem, she stated that in 1977 there were 4,043 violent deaths in the state and of that number 1,800 were classified by coroners as resulting from unknown causes.

That should not come as a surprise if you consider that most coroners have had no medical training. But there is more to the problem than incompetence. Over the years, sheriffs have corrupted the coroner's office by buying off or otherwise "taking care of" coroners who rule the way they want them to. Sheriffs don't have the power to rule whether someone was murdered or died of natural causes. Only coroners can do that. Coroners have another unique responsibility: They are the only official in the state who has the power to arrest a county sheriff and place him or her in jail. That's a lot of power for an unemployed plumber or fishing bait operator to have and it opens the door to corruption.

In a signed column that ran under the headline **STATE CORONER SYSTEM 'LUDICROUS'** I began with "Our problem is that you can come into Mississippi and commit murder—and get away with it," another right-to-the-point comment by Dr. Spruill. There are only two requirements for being a coroner in Mississippi: First, the candidate must be a registered voter; second, the candidate must never have denied the existence of a Supreme Being. I kid you not. That's all it takes.

Edgar Little, Harrison County coroner, told me that a coroner in North Mississippi recently was convicted of fraud because it was learned he had a habit of roaming through graveyards at night searching for names to put on nonexistent death investigations, which he undertook for twenty dollars a case. I ended the column with a quote from Edgar Little: "There are a whole lot more people being murdered in Mississippi than we have any idea of. And there're more dying of industrial poisoning than we realize." All Spruill and Little asked was that Mississippi create a standard of excellence for coroners so they no longer would be regarded as a joke.

* * *

Another "first" I did for the editorial pages was to add a weekly political column written by the reporter that covered the Legislature, David Hampton. He was an individual with liberal sensibilities. Gordon did ask Ward if David's column could appear on the editorial page. Ward said no. I let a few weeks go by, then I asked Ward the same question. He did a thumps-up gesture and said, "Sure." But there was one condition: It would be my responsibility if Hampton stepped too far over the line. He never did. For years Hampton thought his benefactor was Bob Gordon, primarily because Gordon told him that was the case. I flourished in anonymity.

WORKING FOR AN AFTERNOON NEWSPAPER presents an entirely different rhythm from working for a morning newspaper. When you work for a morning newspaper you don't see the finished product until you return to the newsroom the next day. When you work for an afternoon newspaper, you see the finished product before you leave for the day.

When I reported to the newsroom on May 12, 1980, there was a buzz in the room, but I had no idea what was going on. Reporters and editors were hurrying here and there, speaking in hushed voices. Finally, it became evident what was going on. Reporter Gary McElroy had written a two-part series about the Nazi Party in Mississippi. The story included an interview with the then current commander of the National Socialist White People's Party, Matt Koehl, the heir of Lincoln Rockwell's Neo-Nazi

Americans.

"Ours is a simple philosophy, with simple problems, simple solutions," Koehl said. He went on to explain that America under Nazism would be a world of idealism and moralistic behavior, in which crime would be nonexistent and food would be available to everyone. About African Americans, he said: "There is this fundamental understanding. There must and will be total geographical separation of the races. We see no future where the races are artificially amalgamated. Resolving these questions will be difficult, but not be insoluble."[25]

McElroy also interviewed a local leader of the Christian Identity Church, a so-called denomination that is closely linked to the Nazi Party in its beliefs. It is a religion that believes that whites are the true chosen people of God. It is a belief that excludes Blacks and Jews (sons of the Devil himself, according to the Christian Identity Church). He proudly listed as members in good standing Sam Bowers, former leader of the White Knights of the Ku Klux Klan and Byron De La Beckwith, who at this point had been tried and found not guilty of the 1963 murder of civil rights leader Medgar Evers (Beckwith was retried in 1994 based on new evidence and he was found guilty and sentenced to life in prison).

Of course, stories like this had run before. What made them relevant in 1980 was the existence of the Nazi Party in Mississippi. McElroy interviewed a local member about the beliefs of the organization. After describing Klan members as "stupid and lazy," the Nazi Party member said. "The Klan will have an upsurge in membership for a few years, just like they did in the 1960s, and then they will die off for a while. They have no program; they are for apple pie and motherhood. We are for destroying the United States government as it now exists."

It was at his point that the reporter's journeyman look at the subject took an explosive turn. McElroy had interviewed the leader of the Nazi Party in Mississippi with the promise that his identity be protected. In good faith, the Nazi leader told McElroy: "I was invited to attend a leadership conference with David Duke's group (the Louisiana-based Knights of the

Ku Klux Klan) recently, and I went. Yet, in one of their newspapers right after that they wrote that they would have nothing to do officially with us. They said we made them look bad. I don't know. You ask ten Klan members and you'll get ten different answers, but basically we are just too far apart philosophically."[26]

McElroy turned in the story with the Nazi leader's identity withheld.

Then the story took a bizarre turn. Managing editor Bob Gordon demanded to know the identity of the Nazi leader. The reporter told him he had promised to protect his identity in exchange for an interview that could provide insight into the Nazi movement in Mississippi.

Gordon insisted on knowing the man's identity.

Finally, McElroy relented and told him.

The leader of the Nazi Party in Mississippi was none other than the national news editor at the *Jackson Daily News*. His name was James Quinn and Gordon was his supervisor. Quinn was responsible for pulling national stories from the news wire, writing headlines for them, and editing the stories for publication. Before the series ran, Gordon stripped away Quinn's anonymity and published his quotes under his name, breaking the promise that his reporter had made to Quinn. Because my desk was close to Gordon's cubicle, I overheard McElroy tell him that if he did that he would have to resign.

"That's up to you," said Gordon.

When the series began there was a sidebar that bore the headline:

DN STAFFER LIVED DUAL NAZI ROLE

The story went on to identify Quinn by name and to announce to the world that Quinn's employment at the newspaper had been terminated. The sidebar also contained Quinn's reaction to being fired: "I love my people. I love my race. If they find that to be a crime, then that's their belief. And I have mine." He appealed to the ACLU for help, but he was turned down on the grounds that there is no statute concerning protection of political beliefs in the private sector.

I didn't talk to Jimmy Ward about the incident, but because it was

Ward who had hired Quinn, I knew he would have felt a sense of betrayal. Ward was proud of being a journalist. However, he was also proud of being a heralded World War II bomber pilot in the European theater. In that capacity, he had flown fifty missions to drop bombs on heavily defended Nazi troop concentrations. Before leaving the U.S. Army Air Corps. he was promoted to Captain. It was a rank he held on the day of Quinn's firing as a member of the Air Force reserve.

Ironically, while Ward was dropping bombs on Nazis in Germany, Mississippi was providing living quarters for German Nazis captured during the war. There were four such prison camps in Mississippi—Camp Clinton was located in Clinton, just outside Jackson; Camp Como was located in the Delta; Camp Shelby, near Hattiesburg, was an existing U.S. military camp; and Camp McCain was located near Grenada.

Incredibly, Camp Clinton allowed thirty-one German generals to live in a village of individual houses furnished with chairs and sofas upholstered in red leather. Their orderlies were also provided special housing. As a show of respect, the generals were allowed to put on their dress uniforms and travel unaccompanied to Jackson to do personal shopping. General Hans-Jurgen von Arnim, who had commanded the Afrika Korps, was among the generals allowed to freely walk about downtown Jackson at the same time that Jimmy Ward was flying bombing runs over Nazi military camps in Germany.

I didn't write an editorial about Quinn's firing because Bob Gordon wrote an editorial that appeared on the news pages with the story and an announcement of Quinn's termination.

I did not agree with the way in which Gordon handled the situation for two reasons: First, because reporters have an obligation to protect their sources if the information was given with a promise of anonymity. There are exceptions to that, of course. If an unrevealed source proceeded to use that anonymity to commit a crime I believe the reporter has an obligation to step forward. McElroy should not have been put in a position where he would have to resign to protect his source. Second, because in recent years, three to be exact, the courts had upheld the rights of the Nazi Party to participate in marches and to display the swastika.

I found Quinn's opinions repugnant, but I realized there were editors and reporters at the newspaper who found my opinions in support of voting rights for Blacks and equal rights for women equally repugnant. I felt Gordon should have supported the reporter's pledge to his source. A better way to go, I think, would have been to quietly terminate Quinn, exerting the newspaper's right to fire any employee "at will," thus preserving Quinn's First Amendment rights and the reporter's journalistic ethics to protect his sources. Regardless of my feelings about the way the incident was handled, it gave me the creeps to know I had been working alongside the commander of the local Nazi Party, even if he was a somewhat shy man who was never heard to raise his voice in the newsroom.

One of Quinn's friends and co-workers, who asked not to be identified, told me Quinn was a card-carrying Nazi, literally. He actually had a card in his wallet that identified him as a Nazi. Said the friend: "Two or three days [after his firing], I looked out the window of my apartment and saw him walking up the steps, carrying a six-pack of beer, just like old times. We shook hands and were glad to see each other. We sat in my living room, drank beer and just bullshitted like always. Then he got very serious. 'I want you to know that I'll never forget how you came up to me in the breakroom that day and in front of everybody sat down and talked to me like always. Everybody ran out on me but you and I won't ever forget that.' Then he said something that stunned me. 'I want you to know that when we come to power, I'm going to see to it that you have a high position in the government.'"

SEXUAL MISBEHAVIOR was a common theme in Mississippi in 1981. There was the Page One story about a Jackson woman who was arrested for having sex with her pit bull dog. That didn't happen every day in a city dominated by the Baptist Church, that was for sure. The woman's husband had come home early and found his wife naked on the bed being humped with wild abandon by the pit bull, with her screaming out, "Don't stop! Don't stop! Don't stop!"

When confronted by her shocked husband, the wife claimed the dog had raped her. The astonished husband called the police.

Uncertain of what they should do, the police officers arrested both the husband and the wife and transported them downtown to the police station, along with the pit bulldog. I wondered if the pit bull sat between the man and woman in the booking area. I pictured a stylish *New Yorker* cartoon with the dog dragging on a weed. Understandably, the husband protested that he shouldn't be arrested because he was the one who called for police assistance. In the police report, officers noted that the pit bull was "black," a distinction that had psychological implications in a city so fearful of Black men "corrupting" white women.

Of course, the pit bull story ran on Page One above the fold in the first afternoon edition, affectionately known by journalists as the bulldog edition. The reporter who wrote the story went on to become a valued Gannett editor and after that a Christian missionary in Africa.

Another sex scandal that rocked Jackson that year was news that Republican Congressman Jon Hinson had been arrested in February 1981 by Capitol Police and charged with sodomy, a felony. Arrested with him was a male library assistant at the Library of Congress. According to a story in *The New York Times,* authorities began surveillance of the isolated men's room through a peephole a week earlier after receiving a tip that homosexuals had been using the room as a meeting place.

News of his arrest shocked Mississippi voters, but it should not have come as a surprise. During his 1980 campaign for re-election, Hinson called a press conference to make an astonishing series of confessions, beginning with his admission that he had been charged in 1976 of "committing an obscene act" and had paid a one hundred dollar fine for creating a public nuisance. He confessed to being a survivor of a 1977 fire in a Washington, D.C., movie theater frequented by homosexuals. Nine of the moviegoers died in the fire.

After making his confessions, he walked away from the press conference without answering questions. People were left scratching their heads. To some it seemed like he might have given someone the finger while sowing a few wild oats and gotten arrested for it. Regarding his comments about the movie theater frequented by homosexuals, some felt he probably had been tricked into going into the theater by some of his old fraternity brothers from college.

Then the following week, he called another press conference to announce that he was not a homosexual and had no intentions of withdrawing from the race. He didn't address the fact that no one had publicly called him a homosexual, nor had anyone publicly asked him to withdraw from the race. He did take one reporter's question about why he was confessing to the incidents. Hinson's response: "I'm simply sick and tired of worrying about it."

I wrote an editorial because his confessions had sailed right over the heads of most Mississippians who felt the congressman looked like a Republican and talked like a Republican and could not possibly be a homosexual because he just denied it. In an editorial, I wrote: "Hinson has pretty well eliminated himself as a viable candidate in this year's election. To say that is not to pass judgment on Hinson's personal conduct (which he admitted occurred during a period of great personal frustration), it is merely a recognition of cold, hard political fact: Mississippi voters aren't ready—nor will they be ready anytime in the near future—to elect a candidate who has made disclosures of the type made by Hinson."

I would have felt the same way if Hinson had been arrested having sex with a woman in a public restroom. Sexual orientation was not an issue. Public sex by a member of Congress was the issue. It was reckless and forecast even more reckless behavior in the future.

Hinson proved me wrong, of course. He was re-elected to serve a second term in the House of Representatives. If I had really been astute, I would have picked up on a massive change in the attitudes of Republican voters toward sexual indiscretions. Power at any cost was the issue, not morality that considered public sex wrong. Forty years later, those changes became obvious with the election of Donald Trump. Not only could he, in his own twisted mind, shoot a man in the street in full view of passersby without being arrested, he could talk about grabbing women by their "pussies," all with impunity because he possessed the right racial politics.

Two months after the restroom arrest, Hinson resigned and became a LGBT activist in the Washington, D.C. area. By all accounts his reckless behavior ceased once he could be honest about his sexual orientation. He died in 1995 of complications from AIDS.

IN EARLY DECEMBER 1980, I sent an employment inquiry to *The Commercial Appeal,* the largest circulation newspaper in the Mid-South. I loved my job at the *Daily News*, but I was working for an editor who was dying of throat cancer and I knew my job would be in jeopardy when he was gone. Besides that, I had a feeling that both the morning and evening newspapers were at risk of not surviving. In addition to my career concerns, my son was experiencing health problems, for which treatment was costly, and I desperately needed more income. I didn't know for sure, but I felt *The Commercial Appeal* would likely give me a nice raise to relocate to Memphis.

On the day I drove to Memphis to meet with Mike Grehl, editor of *The Commercial Appeal*, I had an upset stomach and was swigging over-the-counter medicine as if I were an alcoholic nursing a silver-plated flask. We had a very pleasant talk during which he discussed the newspaper's longstanding policy of not commenting on or making electoral endorsements in Mississippi politics. If I joined the staff, he explained, that policy would change. I would be in charge of overseeing the editorial page coverage of Mississippi elections, along with other duties such as commenting on city and state matters of interest in Tennessee.

Before we left for lunch, Grehl called in one of the three existing editorial writers on staff to join us. Norm Brewer was a well-dressed, urbane man who resembled actor Cary Grant. Prior to joining the editorial board he was a well-known Memphis television news anchor and commentator. I would soon learn that his opinions varied from moderate to liberal. Grehl explained that Brewer usually focused on Memphis matters. I noted with interest that E.W. Kiekhefer, the editorial page editor, was not invited to lunch. Kiekhefer, as everyone called him, was the most liberal member of the editorial board. The third editorial writer was David Vincent. He was the most conservative member of the board.

Rounding out the team was the design and copy editor, Richard McFalls, and the cartoonist Bill Garner, who left shortly after I arrived to work for the *Washington Times*. He was later replaced by Bill Day. During our lunch, Grehl talked about *The Commercial Appeal's* history, with me informing him that I had been a reader of the newspaper since the age of eight because my grandfather, who lived next door, was a subscriber and I had poured over the newspaper every day until I went off to college at the age of seventeen.

I felt good about the interview, but because that was before the era of cell phones I could not report back to Ina until I returned to Jackson. I gave her a play-by-play description of the interview and told her that if *The Commercial Appeal* offered me a position it would involve a significant raise and I needed to accept it. She voiced concerns about pulling Jonathan out of school for such a move and I agreed with her and suggested that the best option would be for her and Jonathan to remain in Jackson until school was out. Meanwhile, I would be able to commute to Jackson on weekends.

Sure enough, about a week after my interview I received a letter from Grehl offering me a position as an editorial writer at twice the salary I received in Jackson. I accepted by return mail and then gave Jimmy Ward two weeks' notice. Within days I returned to Memphis and made a deposit on a one-bedroom apartment in a high-rise close to the newspaper that I could rent month-to-month until Ina and Jonathan were able to move to Memphis at the end of the school year. That would give me time to research the schools and determine which apartments were in good school districts. That way, they could make a smooth transition.

Ina was somewhat subdued about the entire matter, but voiced no opposition other than unhappiness about moving yet again. I suppose there was more opposition expressed between the lines of what she said, but I have never been good at reading between the lines, especially when communicating with women.

* * *

One of my last columns and editorials at the *Jackson Daily News* was about a track sensation named Teresa Harmon. Sometimes you witness a fight that you just have jump into. This was such a fight. Although she was the defending girls' state cross-country runner and a nationally ranked high school distance runner, Teresa Harmon ran into a brick wall named the Mississippi High School Activities Association (MHSAA) when it came to them honoring her request to provide the same races for girls that are offered for boys. The organization had refused to allow girls to run mile and two-mile races, although girls in other states are allowed to run in those races. Teresa may be the best mile runner in the state, possibly better than any of the boys who are allowed to run in mile and two-mile races. Mississippi's restriction on Teresa and other girls her age means they can't be competitive.

"It makes me mad they don't have to," Teresa said. "They're just old-fashioned. They just think that girls can't run."

As a result of the stubbornness of the MHSAA, Teresa's family turned to the ACLU for help. Said an ACLU spokesperson: "The only reason these events aren't offered is sex discrimination. We have filed this complaint in behalf of Teresa and all other girls interested in running high school track."

After going out to watch Teresa compete in a race, I wrote an editorial that made the case that MHSAA "erred in not responding to an appeal from Teresa's parents to include the event in its activities. As long as the MHSAA is going to sanction mile and two-mile events for boys, it is only fair that the same events be offered to girls. Mississippi has always been very supportive of those male students who show talents of an athletic nature. Just because female students in the past have been slow to show an interest in sports is no reason for the state to now relegate them to a second class status. Run for it, Teresa."[27]

MY FINAL SURPRISE at the *Daily News* came when it was announced that I was leaving to accept a position at *The Commercial Appeal* in Memphis. Jimmy Ward, without being asked, wrote a letter of recommendation to the editor at the Memphis newspaper and then posted the letter in the newsroom for everyone to read. In part, the letter read: "I have been associated with the *Jackson Daily News* since 1938 and editor for over 24 years. Please consider this the highest recommendation I have ever prepared for a departing employee and co-worker." He described our relationship as one based on "mutual respect and confidence."

I nearly fainted when I read the letter. I never understood why Jimmy Ward took such a liking to me. I was for civil rights and he led the opposition against civil rights. I was an early opponent of the Vietnam War, and he flew combat missions in Vietnam as a member of the Mississippi Air National Guard. I was stunned by his comments, but the more I thought about it, the more I realized that I liked him very much as a person and, while I didn't respect his leadership of the newspaper during the civil rights era, I had immense respect for his capacity to turn loose of that past and demonstrate a newfound willingness to accept alternative points of view.

A week or so later, he again surprised me. Because Bob Gordon controlled the newsroom checkbook, I asked him if he would put through a memo to advance me my vacation pay (which I was taking for my last week at the newspaper) and my final paycheck for the week of January 4 to January 8. Gordon said he would be happy to do that for me, but he left for New York without doing so.

I appealed to Jimmy Ward, who promptly put through a memo requesting I be issued my two final checks. I was set to leave at noon on January 8th after completing forty hours of work. It did not surprise me that

JACKSON DAILY NEWS

EDITORIAL DEPARTMENT

P. O. BOX 160

JACKSON, MISS. 39205

JAMES M. WARD
EDITOR

January 7, 1982

TO WHOM IT MAY CONCERN:

James Dickerson was employed by the Jackson Daily News in May of 1979 as a general assignments reporter. Soon he was given the important task as education writer. After excelling in this capacity, he was appointed an editorial writer and proved himself by hard work, devotion to duty, accepting responsibility and demonstrating a high degree of opinion writing based on logical thought and thorough research.

His performance was so much appreciated until he became, in effect, editor of the editorial page and supervisor of the opposite editorial page, certainly a signal of mutual respect and confidence.

Mr. Dickerson's personal appearance, demeanor and integrity served as a positive influence on fellow workers and for this newspaper in general.

I have been associated with the Jackson Daily News since 1938 and editor for over 24 years. Please consider this the highest recommendation I have ever prepared for a departing employee and co-worker.

Sincerely,

James M. Ward

James M. Ward

cc: R. M. Hederman, Jr.
    T. M. Hederman, Jr.
    Personnel file

Reference letter for the author when he left the Jackson Daily News

he stepped in to help me because he was always considerate of the employees. What did shock me was the final sentence in his memo: "Mr. Dickerson has been one of the most valued employees I ever hired and I would appreciate your consideration of these requests." The requests were honored.

My final column for the *Jackson Daily News* ran under the headline:

HELLO CREATIONISM! GOODBYE DICKERSON

It was written in response to the Mississippi Senate passing a bill mandating the teaching of creationism in the state's public schools. I wrote: "Hopefully, the Mississippi House will not fall victim to the political yahoo-ism that prompted the Senate to call for the mixing of religion and public education. If it's one thing Mississippi does not need now it is yet another expensive, unconstitutional law designed to cause conflict in the state's public schools." A couple of weeks after I left, I received a tear sheet of the op-ed page from the newspaper that contained a letter to the editor that ran under the headline:

DICKERSON'S PARTING SHOT AT STATE'S
CREATIONISM BILL 'DISRESPECTFUL, DISHONEST'

Oh boy, did that make my day! Disrespectful? Of course it was. Science teachers can't teach creationism in their classes. They haven't been taught creationism. So who's going to teach it? Baptists? Methodists? Moslems? Jews? Backwoods snake handlers? Everyone would have a different view because creationism is not based on science, it is based on faith and no faith ever invented has been able to prove a basis for that faith. You don't teach science in Sunday school and you don't teach creationism in a science class. Dishonest? Hardly. Too honest is closer to the point.

THE MORNING OF MY LAST DAY of work, while still basking in the glow of my unusual send-off letter from Ward, I received word that the editor of both the *Clarion-Ledger* and the *Jackson Daily News*, Tom Hederman, wanted to see me in his office. I couldn't imagine why. Did he want to give me a going away present? A gold watch would have been nice, I thought. I hurried downstairs to his first-floor office, where his secretary informed me he was waiting. The first thing I saw when I entered his office was a deputy sheriff sheepishly looking down at his scuffed brown shoes. Not a good sign.

Tom Hederman spoke first.

"I brought you down here so you would not be embarrassed in the newsroom."

My heart raced. This had all the markings of a nightmare.

Hederman nodded at the deputy and he stepped forward as if on cue and handed me a folded piece of paper, adding, "You have been served."

There was a long pause as I reached for the document, during which the deputy said in a quiet voice, almost a whisper, "I am so sorry." Then he respectfully nodded at Mr. Hederman and left the office.

I unfolded the document and saw that Ina had filed for divorce.

"I'm sorry this had to happen on your last day of work," said Mr. Hederman, and by the pained expression on his face I knew he meant it. "I want to thank you for what you have done for us. Good luck to you."

I nodded, my eyes uncomfortably numb.

I took the document back to the newsroom and sat at my desk to read it. At first I was so angry you could have cooked an egg on top of my head. Then I started thinking … about the day in 1967 we ran away from Ole Miss to Alabama to get married because we were too young in Mississippi and Alabama would marry you at just about any age. Because Ina attended the Episcopal Church, we scoured the state and found an Episcopal priest at a church camp several miles out from Jasper. His name was Ben Scott Eppes. He was digging a ditch for a new sewer, so we couldn't shake his hand because it was dirty. No, it wasn't very romantic, but we liked him very much. His face radiated goodness.

We talked for a while, and then he gave us the bad news. The church had a six-month waiting period and he would have to get permission from a Higher Authority to overlook that technicality. The last time that had happened in Alabama, he explained, was during World War II and the husband-to-be was about to be shipped overseas.

"Your case is not quite the same," he said as Ina reached out for his hand and said, "Please." His resolve melted to the point that he added, after pausing for a long moment, "But it is close enough."

He told us to get a marriage license and come back the following week. We did as he asked and returned with my friend Martin Kilpatrick to serve as best man. His wife, Jean, served as Ina's maid of honor.

St. Mary's was small and rustic, and looked just like we pictured it would. We stood at the altar of an empty church, except for the priest and the attendants, and we recited our vows.

"Good luck to you," said the Rev. B. Scott Eppes, who stood in the church doorway as we hurried down the sidewalk, with Martin and Jean throwing white rice in our general direction.

"God be with you."

So now she wanted a divorce. The stress over the years had been too much for her. I thought of her bravely accompanying me to Canada, standing at my side as we navigated one challenge after another—and I forgave her with a deep sense of sadness, and followed the North Star to my next adventure, traveling alone this time.

* * *

My last conversation with an editor that day was with city editor Bob Hardison, a hard drinking but likeable, man who met me at my car on the street outside the building. I popped my hatchback and pulled out a lever-action 30-30 Marlin carbine, similar to the rifle used by TV's *The Rifleman*. I handed it to Bob and he drew a bead on a bicyclist at the other end of the street. He turned it from side to side, examining it. Then he worked the lever action. We were doing a gun deal in full view of passersby, a transaction not illegal in Mississippi, but entirely out of place in the city. He put on his business face and asked, "How much?"

"Fifty dollars."

"You sure you want to sell it?"

"I need the money for moving expenses."

Bob tucked the rifle under his arm and fished out his wallet, counting out five ten dollar bills. We shook hands and he wished me well in Memphis. Then he looked befuddled for a moment, trying to figure out what to do with the rifle now that it belonged to him.

"Why don't you take it to your car?" I suggested.

"Yeah," he said, laughing, and then started down the street to his car, the rifle slung back over his shoulder, leaving me with an unanswered question, *where are the photographers when you need them?*

I had no idea Ina was *that* opposed to the idea of moving until I was served with divorce papers in Tom Hederman's office. When I went home after receiving the divorce papers, I was too angry to even discuss it with Ina. I simply loaded up a truck with my things, with the help of friends Brown Burnett and cartoonist Jimmy Johnson, who lived just around the corner from me. As we walked in and out of the house with boxes of books and personal items, my marriage was burning down all around me. In a way it was like entering a burning house. You rushed in, and saved what you could, and then ran for your life.

Once the truck was loaded I said goodbye to my tearful son and headed out for Memphis, with Brown Burnett riding shotgun while nursing a bottle of whiskey and joyfully singing songs appropriate for the journey. When we reached Grenada, about halfway to Memphis, we turned off the Interstate to detour to Greenwood to visit my Aunt Marcie and Uncle George.

Aunt Marcie greeted me in the driveway, her eyes tearful over my divorce. She was like a second mother to me. I backed the truck up to a small storage building behind the house where she had some furniture in storage. I had called her before leaving Jackson and she asked if I needed anything. I told her all I had was a mattress, springs, and bed frame, a 12-inch television, boxes and boxes of books, and other odds and ends, including clothing. We walked through the storage room and she picked out a dining table and chairs, a couple of living room chairs, some pots and pans, and a coffee pot. We loaded up the truck and struck out for Memphis. It was around 11 p.m. and there was a forecast of snow.

When we pulled into Memphis, it was past midnight and the temperature was well below freezing. Snowflakes peppered our faces after we backed the truck up to the loading dock and stepped out of the truck and contemplated our bleak surroundings. While I went inside to unlock the apartment, Brown opened the back of the truck. When I returned I had some bad news. The building had two elevators and both were out of order. We would have to carry everything in the truck up four flights of stairs to my fourth-floor apartment. Once we finished unloading, I left Brown in the apartment and went downstairs to park the truck. When I returned he was curled up on the floor, sound asleep. I was too exhausted to fool with assembling the bed, so I, too, went to sleep on the carpeted floor.

Early the next morning, I stepped out on the balcony and surveyed the neighborhood. It was pretty bleak. Every other building was either a pawn shop or a liquor store. There was a line of homeless men leaning against the buildings across the street.

Without unpacking anything at my new apartment, we drove the truck back to Jackson. I dropped Brown off at his apartment and I turned in the truck at the rental office and drove my car back to Memphis. When I arrived, I parked my car and got out, only to be mugged by a grinning Black man with a rusty tire tool that he rhythmically slapped against the palm of his hand as if keeping time to music that only he could hear.

UNKNOWN TO ME, there was a horrific storm brewing within the Hederman family. While Bob and Tom Hederman seemed to be proud of Rea's work at the *Clarion-Ledger*, the remaining members of the Hederman family were of the opinion that Rea Hederman's aggressive style of journalism, especially as it applied to remedying past injustices against the state's Black residents, presented a threat to their standing in the ultra-conservative white community.

In 1979, when the *Clarion-Ledger* was awarded the Robert F. Kennedy Memorial Award in two categories, grand prize and print prize, for a series of articles published under the title "North Mississippi

Justice," it caused a rift in the Hederman family. Rea, who was responsible for the articles, was informed by the non-journalism members of the family that there was a family history of opposition to anything associated with the Kennedy family. The majority stockholders insisted that no money be spent on travel expenses to accept the award. Rea paid for those expenses out of his own pocket and sent the staffers responsible for the the stories to Washington, D.C. to collect the award.

It was two years after the Kennedy award that Rea dropped another "bombshell" on his extended family. He told his family he planned to divorce his wife and marry his new love interest. The Southern Baptist Church considered divorce a sin. It was only permissible in instances of sexual immorality, but even in that instance, Southern Baptists are instructed to seek reconciliation. If that is impossible, the church expects the divorcing members to remain permanently unmarried and seek forgiveness for the remainder of their lives.

The majority stockholder Hedermans, that is the non-journalism ones, let it be known they could no longer support Rea working at the newspapers. To put it in today's political atmosphere, the anti-Rea Hedermans represented the views of Republicans and Rea represented the views of Democrats. There was no room for compromise. The only solution was to simply blow the whole damn thing up. They didn't have to fire Rea Hederman from his job. They made family board meetings for him so unpleasant that he simply came to work less and less. There was a time while I worked there that no one knew exactly where Rea Hederman was. Some staffers reported "ghost" sightings, but they were never documented.

In 1982, just a few months after I left the *Jackson Daily News* to work for *The Commercial Appeal*, the majority stockholder Hedermans sold the *Clarion-Ledger* and *Jackson Daily News*, along with about a half dozen other smaller newspapers in the state, to the Gannett Company. The message was clear: If there was going to be any enlightened thinking at the *Clarion-Ledger* and *Jackson Daily News*, it would not occur under

Hederman leadership. Gannett waited a decent amount of time before merging the *Jackson Daily News* with the *Clarion-Ledger*, thus killing the afternoon newspaper.

Rea Hederman followed through with his divorce and married his new love interest, and moved to New York within months after I moved to Memphis. In 1984 Rea, his brother and two sisters, purchased *The New York Review of Books*, probably the most enlightened publication in the United States, for a reported five million dollars. In a 2016 interview with globaljournalist.org, Rea explained his purchase of the publication: "The one thread through *The New York Review* and the thread I feel like through my life has always been a respect for human rights and to be a defender of human rights and *The New York Review* has always done that. That's what drew me to it."

Jimmy Ward retired in January 1984, citing health problems. He was only sixty-five, and died shortly after announcing his retirement. I never saw him again after leaving Jackson, but I did receive letters from him on occasion. One letter chastised me for not visiting with him on one of my trips to Jackson to spend time with my son.

James L. Dickerson in a corduroy suit that mystified co-workers. It was
a tailored suit purchased in Toronto by the city's finest tailor.
Photo courtesy of James L. Dickerson

Chapter 10

The Commercial Appeal
Part I

IF YOU LIVE IN THE MID-SOUTH, Memphis is where you go when you run out of options where you are and don't have enough money to go to California or New York. As a result, the first thing you realize upon arrival in Memphis is that the city streets are littered with shards of broken dreams. Long labelled the "Murder Capital of the United States,"[28] Memphis also has a reputation for creative innovation—Home of the Blues and Birthplace of Rock 'n' Roll—and adventuresome women who have benefited from Beale Street's national reputation as the only entertainment district in the United States that historically has welcomed women. To live in the city, you have to be willing to succumb to impulse because that is the only salve that gives you hope for a better tomorrow.

Within minutes of reporting for work at *The Commercial Appeal*, I was sitting inside my own private office. It was quite cozy. There was nothing on my desk but an envelope containing employment papers I needed to sign. I didn't have a window, but I did have a door. Days later there would be a brass plaque with my name and engraved image on it attached outside my door. Finally, after years of hard work, I had made the Big Time.

The editorial board, of which I was now a member, met in Grehl's office at 10 A.M. each day to pitch ideas for editorials. The meeting usually lasted one hour. After the meeting, you could leave for lunch if you wanted to; but regardless of whether you went to a restaurant for lunch or ate from the food machine downstairs, your editorial had to be turned in to the editor by 3 p.m. It was a hectic schedule, but I loved working under deadline. If your editorial required changes, you were generously given an hour to make them before you resubmitted the editorial.

On my first day, I spent an hour reading the newspaper, wrote out notes for an editorial, and then went to the meeting. Before anyone else spoke, Grehl asked me what I wanted to write about. *Oh, great*, I thought—*he started with me*. I had hoped he would start with one of the veterans, thus giving me an idea of how the process worked.

"I see in today's newspaper that Tennessee is considering relaxing trucking regulations to allow eighteen-wheelers to pull two cargo trailers on the Interstates," I said. "I am really opposed to that. I think those rigs are dangerous and pose a danger to families traveling in cars. There is a lot of data available to make a case for stricter regulation."

Grehl jumped to attention and barked, "Write me an editorial!"

After the meeting, the editorial page editor pulled me aside and asked, "How did you know?"

"Know what?"

"That Grehl hates those double rigs with a passion. Are you going to tell me that on your first day, you hit on his pet peeve by accident? Someone must have tipped you off."

"No, I just thought it would make a good editorial."

He grinned. "You are one lucky son of a bitch. You've got him in your pocket now. If you can keep from falling out of that pocket, you've got it made here."

At the *Jackson Daily News*, I decided what I would write for the editorial page, usually without prior discussion with anyone. By contrast, at *The Commercial Appeal*, I was part of a team headed up first by the editorial page editor and then ultimately by Grehl himself. Each topic I wrote about had to be approved in advance in a meeting, not just on the topic itself, but also on the position the editorial would take. I learned to forge friendships on the board and I learned not to be strident in opposition to another writer's idea and position. What goes around, comes around.

My first alliance was with Norm Brewer, with whom I often agreed. When someone else on the board disagreed with a position I advocated, Norm was usually quick to rise to my defense. I typically seconded his suggestions for editorials. My opposite on the editorial board was David Vincent, who liked to write about public education although he home-schooled his own children, state government, and anything of a conservative bent he could sell to the editorial board. Personally, David and I got along well, but not so much on policy issues.

My first year on the editorial board I tried to stay out of trouble by avoiding conflicts with David and not encroaching on Norm's territory. Grehl could see what I was doing, but he let it ride for most of the year, although he sometimes nudged me to tackle themes favored by Norm. I assume that was to keep Norm on his toes, but I felt like someone in a chicken fight that was being thrust into the face of the other fowl for the purpose of challenging it. Norm calmly peered over the top of his glasses at me and continued puffing on his pipe without comment.

Grehl was aware that I had been sued for divorce on the same day I had moved to Memphis, so he tended to cut me some slack whenever I came into a meeting obviously distracted either by family matters or my living arrangements. I got into the habit of stopping by Norm's office prior to our meetings to ask what subject he planned to bring up. That way I could avoid bringing up the same subject.

Generally, speaking our editorial board meetings were sacrosanct, with one of the two secretaries outside the door standing guard, but occasionally there were intrusions into our deliberations. Once one of the secretaries stuck her head inside the door during an editorial meeting and said that Grehl had a call from Congressman Harold Ford, the city's first African-American sent to Congress.

"Please tell him I will call him back," said Grehl.

"He's upset about an editorial and he's crying uncontrollably."

Grehl shook his head in dismay and took a deep breath. "Tell him I promise I will call him back in a few minutes."

The most startling thing about that telephone message was not that Grehl refused to stop the editorial meeting to take a call from a Black congressman, but that the Black congressman felt comfortable enough calling the editor to complain about an editorial. That would not have happened prior to Michael Grehl's arrival in Memphis.

What most caught my eye when I first arrived at the newspaper was that I had gone to Memphis from a newsroom that had only one Black staffer to a newspaper that had numerous Black staffers. There was Leroy Williams, Jr., who subsequently changed his name to Karanja A. Ajanaku in order to embrace his African heritage (he actually had to go to court to do that and he argued his case eloquently); he covered City Hall. Then there was Otis Sanford, who covered federal courts, and Jerome Wright, who covered police. Together, they were "Three Amigos," holding down the three most important news beats on any newspaper. I never got to know Otis too well because he was always at the courthouse, but I did get to know Jerome and especially Karanja, and I valued those friendships. Karanja could make me laugh and think at the same time.

THE THING ABOUT A JOB is that at some point during the day you have to go home. In my case, it was not so much a home as it was a kinky culture war zone. The elevator at my apartment was often filled with prostitutes, transvestites, drug dealers and non-English speaking people who glared at me the entire time I was on the elevator. Often when I got off the elevator and headed toward the door to my apartment, I could look back over my shoulder and see someone leaning from the elevator, watching to see which apartment I lived in. I began to wonder if the apartment building might be a halfway house for mental health clients.

I had not felt lonely in a long time, not since high school when I saw my girlfriend climb into the backseat of a car in the parking lot on prom night with an out-of-town boy. In many respects, loneliness is not a thing in and of itself. It is a by-product of broken male and female relationships. I have never felt lonely in the woods, or hiking alone on a mountain trail. Only around other people.

Ina and I had shared a lot together. We had rebelled against the advice of family and friends. We had fled everything in life we knew and cared about to enter a world that was unknown to us. Throughout it all, we had each other when we had nothing else. Now that safety net was gone.

My lawyer advised me not to date anyone until my divorce was final, so I pretty much hunkered down in my apartment until that happened. Mostly I watched television, although there were frequent interruptions when gunfire erupted on the street below my balcony. Because I didn't know how to cook much of anything, I always dined out at Midtown restaurants. Returning home was always a little nerve racking because of the ever-present threat of muggers when I exited my car.

Housing in downtown Memphis was of two types. The upscale apartments overlooked the Mississippi River or were located within a couple of blocks from the river. Within that area were several hotels and lots of restaurants. Time in that part of downtown was always well spent. It was that stretch between downtown and midtown that was filled with vacant buildings and broken lives. That was where I lived.

Eventually, I found a Midtown apartment on Union Avenue that had hardwood floors, brass fixtures, and extra-large rooms. My entire war zone apartment would have fit inside the living room of the new apartment. I was quite pleased with the apartment until I discovered it had a severe insect infestation. That prompted me to move to another midtown apartment building, where I sometimes rode the elevator with television personality Wink Martindale and his wife, who was usually clutching a toy poodle every time I saw them. One day she stared at the elevator buttons a moment before asking, "Don't they light up?"

"It's not that kind of building," I answered, dryly.

She giggled.

On another day, a well-dressed man wearing expensive shoes said to me, "Someone has been stealing my newspaper."

I felt certain he had no idea I worked at a newspaper. Or did he?

"I'm going to catch the bastard," he continued, an irate look on his face. "Sunday morning I get up early and sit down beside the door with my pistol on the ready. If I hear the thief I plan to swing open the door and catch him red-handed."

"Pistol?" I asked, not certain I had heard him correctly.

"Yeah," he answered, opening his coat so that I could see the pistol holster strapped to his belt.

MISSISSIPPI WAS A GOOD source of editorial material for me because no one else on the editorial board could grasp the subtleties and absurdities of Mississippi politics. My third month on the job, I received a letter from Mississippi Governor William Winter inviting me to attend his second annual Colloquium on Science, Engineering and Technology, which was being held in Jackson. I showed the letter to Grehl and he suggested I attend the event. It was my first overnight road trip for *The Commercial Appeal*. The banquet was pleasant enough, but it really wasn't my cup of tea. The dinner was tasty enough, but the speeches were a little dry.

When I returned to Memphis I wrote about the event. Today, looking back, I have no idea what, but I am sure it was very pleasant. A few weeks later I wrote an editorial about Winter's effort to bring about education reform. Under the headline **WINTER'S VOICE**, I wrote: "Like the biblical voice crying out in the wilderness, Governor William Winter of Mississippi has been pleading his case for higher education standards with all the fervor of one who believes that time is running out . . . (ending with) If you listen close enough you can hear that solitary voice—a voice of reason, compassion and intellect. Winter's voice."

Governor Winter responded to the editorial with a letter addressed to me personally: "This is just a note to thank you for the most generous editorial yesterday about my efforts in prompting education in Mississippi. Such an editorial statement by *The Commercial Appeal* will be of inestimable benefit to us in helping create the kind of public support necessary to the enactment of an adequate legislative program. As a long-time subscriber to and reader of your fine newspaper, I remain grateful for its leadership and for your own splendid role in that leadership."

The year 1983 was an election year in Mississippi. That opened the door for me to get involved in the gubernatorial race between Democrat Bill Allain and Republican Leon Bramlett. It was about as dirty as a campaign can get. Under the headline **POLITICS OF SQUALOR**, my editorial addressed accusations by Bramlett supporters that Allain had frequented male prostitutes. "Allain has denied that he is a homosexual, but there is little he can do to prove it," I wrote. "Mississippi has made significant progress in a number of areas in recent years. Bramlett clearly has a lot of explaining to do."[29] Bramlett was unable to justify, or even explain, the charges leveled by his supporters—and he lost the race.

In 1983, the sitting governor was William Winter, who was easily the most progressive of the state's governors. For two years, he had tried to guide a statewide system of kindergartens and compulsory school attendance through Mississippi's ultra-right Legislature, only to be rebuffed. He felt if he could meet those goals it would help boost the state's low-wage economy. His favorite phrase was, "The road out of the poor house runs past the school house." Not until his third year in office was he able to get the legislation passed. I was very supportive of those education reforms on the pages of *The Commercial Appeal,* prompting a January 3, 1983 letter from the governor in response to a letter from me:

> **Dear Jim:**
> **Let me thank you for your very kind and thoughtful letter**

and more than that for the editorial support and
encouragement which you have given us, particularly in the
passage of what I think is a very significant educational
program. As a long-time reader of and subscriber to the
Commercial Appeal, I do not underestimate the
tremendous influence which you have in Mississippi and to
have your editorial support is a major contributing factor
to such successes as we have had on various issues. I hope
that you will pay us a visit sometime and in the meantime I
want to wish for you a very satisfying and fulfilling new
year.

William Winter.

One of the reasons for Winter's success was a staff of bright-eyed young men a House member nicknamed "the Boys of Spring." Essentially, the group was composed of Dick Molpus, who later would be elected secretary of state, John Henegan, Andy Mullins, and Ray Mabus, an Ole Miss-educated attorney who went on to obtain a master's in political science from Johns Hopkins, and a law degree from Harvard. Before returning to Mississippi, he had served as a legal counsel to a subcommittee of the House Agriculture Committee. I never met Mabus while I was working at the *Jackson Daily News*, so imagine my surprise when I received a telephone call from him in 1983, early in my second year at *The Commercial Appeal.*

Mabus told me he was running for the office of state auditor as a Democrat and would like to meet with me at my office. That was fine with me. It was my first interview for a potential election endorsement. Before he arrived I checked out his background and discovered that he was a student at Ole Miss while I was there. When he arrived I was immediately surprised at how young he looked. He was thirty-four, but he could have passed for twenty-five.

On the issues, I was delighted to learn he had played a role in drafting Governor Winter's education package. As far as being state auditor, he explained he wanted to hold state officials accountable for their expenditures of state funds. Corruption has always been a huge problem in Mississippi, past and present. His past positions on education and his vision of the state auditor's office as a watchdog agency were issues that had been dear to the heart of past editorials at the newspaper. I knew before he left that I was going to recommend the newspaper endorse him in the state auditor's race, but I did not tip my hand.

The next day I followed through and suggested to the editorial board that I write an endorsement editorial. If approved, it would be the first Mississippi endorsement in decades, if ever. Everyone agreed his positions on the issues were in sync with positions previously taken by the newspaper in Tennessee elections. We discussed the fact that newspaper endorsements were usually very influential in races in which neither candidate had a great deal of name recognition. At that time, *The Commercial Appeal* was beloved and trusted by its readers.

During our meeting, I learned that I had a connection to Mabus that neither of us realized when we first began our conversation. Talking about our days at Ole Miss, we realized his roommate was my cousin, John Waits of Washington County, whose father, Hilton, had served in the Mississippi House of Representatives for years, rising to the post of speaker pro tem. It was Hilton who introduced me to the politics of lawmaking and sparked a lifelong passion in me for the study of politics and public service. Because of Hilton, I had minored in political science at Ole Miss.

On Election Day I followed the results with great interest. Once the votes were tabulated, Ray Mabus was declared the winner. I looked closer at the returns and saw that his margin of victory had come from north Mississippi, within the circulation area of the newspaper. It was a great feeling to be part of an election victory. Grehl was ecstatic, though you couldn't necessarily tell by looking at his heavily bearded face.

Sometimes I wrote unsigned editorials; other times I wrote signed columns. My first column at the newspaper was about Mississippi's most wretched racist and would-be dictator, Theodore Bilbo.

Bilbo was a Great Depression-era governor and subsequent U.S. Senator who was an ardent supporter of President Roosevelt. He was in the news in 1982 because of his statue, which had been removed from the capitol rotunda on orders of then Governor William Winter while decorators renovated the building, recalls former Governor Ray Mabus, who was then on Winter's staff. Winter made it clear he did not want the statue returned. However, once the renovations were completed, the statue was secretly returned to the rotunda. Winter did not know that his orders were not followed until he happened to escort a delegation of people from out of town around the renovated capitol and saw that the statue was back in its place of prominence. That very day Winter called in workers to remove the statue from the rotunda and place it in a committee room on the ground floor of the building. Black legislators praised the second removal of the statue—during Bilbo's lifetime he was once described as a "pert little monster, glib and shameless"—because Bilbo was an unrepentant racist to the day he took his dying breath.[30] Today, if you want to see the statue, you really have to look to find it.

In my column, I wrote about how Bilbo won over Black voters by supporting the New Deal and won over white voters by giving them the racism they desperately wanted him to embrace:

Surely, Bilbo, were he alive, would look at what is happening in the Great Statue Debate and smile . . . . He made a career out of using race to hide the real issue. That's how he managed to slip through the cracks of history and find immortality in a statue..[31]

* * *

In March 1983 editor Mike Grehl received a letter from U.S. District Judge William C. Keady in Greenville, Mississippi, in praise of an editorial I had written, although Keady did not know I had written it because it was unsigned. Grehl gave me a copy of the letter, along with his reply. When I saw the recipient's address, I was immediately struck by the irony of it all. If I had been kidnapped in Canada by U.S. black ops and returned to Mississippi, it would have been Judge Keady who would have heard my case. He was known as one of the most liberal judges in Mississippi. It was in his courtroom that a deputy sheriff identified my draft board member as a member of the KKK. There was also irony in that my college friend from Hollandale, Martin Kilpatrick who once told me he was going to Canada if he passed the draft physical (he did not), served as the judge's law clerk.

The real cherry on this magnificent cake was Grehl's characterization of me as a "son of Mississippi" in his response, and his comment that I was "making a splendid record for himself in Memphis."

Grehl hand-delivered the letter to me and stood in the doorway, grinning proudly as he watched me read it.

IN EARLY 1983, Grehl gave me an assignment during one of the editorial meetings. He wanted the editorial board to decide whether the newspaper should support the rebirth of historic Beale Street—or allow the troubled street to die a quiet death. At one time, Beale Street had been the epicenter for blues and Black culture in the South, but during the late 1960s and 1970s, the music left town and the street became a focus of urban blight. Very few businesses remained open. The development of Beale Street was a major political issue with city and county government officials. Many white residents were fearful of subsidizing a Black entertainment district that might attract the "wrong" class of people. Many Black residents saw redevelopment as an economic and cultural benefit to the entire city.

Because Grehl knew that I had paid my way through college playing in rock and R&B bands, he asked me to take my girlfriend and spend some time at the street's only nightclub (Club Handy) and at the other businesses on the street or adjacent to it and report back to the editorial board. I did as requested and suggested that the newspaper support development of the street, citing the arguments made by Black business executives and community leaders. As a result, I was given a green light to begin writing editorials in support of that position.

In those days *The Commercial Appeal*, thanks to the leadership of Grehl, had a lot of influence in the community. That is no longer the case today, but in the 1980s the newspaper was an important player in defining and resolving community and political issues. After only a few editorials,

Beale Street, circa late 1970s
Photo courtesy of the Mississippi Valley Collection,
University of Memphis, University Libraries

the political holdouts on redevelopment changed their votes and the city made a commitment to rebuild the historic street. Grehl deserves credit for that. Today Beale Street is a thriving tourist destination that has provided opportunities to Black musicians and business investors and, in the process, preserved important aspects of Black cultural history. The entire city has benefited as a result.

As the months went by I wrote more and more editorials that supported not just Beale Street, but the city's music industry as a whole. Around this time it became known that the National Academy of Recording Arts and Sciences (NARS), the organization that gave out Grammys each year, had narrowed its selection for a Grammy museum to Memphis and Atlanta. NARAS president William Ivey and Steve Schwartz, a member of the selection committee, came to Memphis to meet with Memphis songwriter David Porter, recording artist Charlie Rich, an Arkansas native who got his start at Sam Phillips' Sun Records, and Tennessee Lt. Governor John Wilder. Of course, I wrote an editorial endorsing Memphis as the site for the museum, but it was to no avail. In March 1983 the NARAS selection committee announced it had chosen Atlanta as the site of the Grammy museum. In response, I wrote an editorial with the headline **MEMPHIS MELODIES**—and editorial cartoonist Bill Day later drew a splendid cartoon with the image of a truck loaded up with Memphis music history on its way to Atlanta—that encouraged the city to proceed with plans of its own to build a music museum in Memphis

"Memphis has an opportunity to do something original," I wrote. "A museum that focuses on the five elements of Memphis music—rock 'n' roll, blues, jazz, country and gospel—has the potential to become a major national attraction. The important thing is for Memphians to think big."

Ironically, Atlanta was unable to get its act together. After an embarrassing delay of several years, NARAS took back the offer and ended up building museums in Los Angeles, Nashville and Mississippi, literally surrounding Memphis with museums. In 2020, NARAS went back to Atlanta and gave them a second chance by awarding the city yet another contract for a museum.

Memphis was left to fend for itself. It is a curious attitude for NARAS to have. Think about it. Without Memphis, there would have been no rock 'n' roll and no home for the blues.

IN BETWEEN a series of music-related editorials during 1983, I delved into more serious matters in my editorials and signed columns. I was in attendance when Arkansas Governor Bill Clinton met with the editorial board in 1983 to ask for our support on several issues as he began his second term of office. He proved himself to be a charismatic spokesman for the issues he embraced. Needless to say, he obtained the support of the editorial board.

Then there was the day former astronaut John Glenn met with the editorial board to solicit our support for his presidential campaign. At the time, he was a Democratic U.S. Senator from Ohio. In the early days of space exploration, it took real courage to ride those massive rockets into the unknown. For that reason, he was one of my personal heroes. To the surprise of the other board members, at the conclusion of our interview with Glenn, I asked if he could stick around a while longer so that I could interview him in more detail about his candidacy. He readily agreed and everyone left us alone in the conference room.

We discussed his positions on the economy, Soviet-American relationships, Central America, the draft, arms control, and school prayer, but the main thrust of the interview was to determine whether he was a liberal Democrat, as the Republicans proclaimed at every opportunity, or whether he was a centrist. On issues such as abortion, the Equal Rights Amendment, and tuition tax credits, he had voted pro-choice, in favor of the Equal Rights Amendment, and against tuition tax credits because he felt it would do damage to the public school system. However, on some issues dear to the hearts of conservative Republicans—construction of the B1 bomber and the continuation of nerve gas production—he voted with the conservatives.

"Does that make Glenn a confusing candidate?" I wrote in the column. "It shouldn't. As remarkable as it seems, Glenn is pretty much what he says he is—a centrist."[32]

My writing output in 1982 and 1983 was considerable, with me adding more signed columns to the mix. I missed the adrenalin rush of Page One stories, such as the ones I wrote for the *Tallahassee Democrat*, but I was in my element writing editorials.

One day Grehl pulled me aside and told me that when I read stories from the news side about subjects I wanted to write about, not to be shy about following up on the news stories by interviewing individuals mentioned in the stories, or individuals who could be important sources, but were not interviewed by the reporters.

"But won't that piss off the reporters?" I asked.

"Indeed, it will," he answered. "But it will make me happy—and that's more important."

What he was introducing me to was his concept of investigative opinion writing. It was based on the belief that good opinion writing was not necessarily opinionated. A good editorial writer will use facts, science and direct interviews to shape the final product. I loved the concept and vowed to follow it in my future writings. I was sympathetic to news reporters because I had been one and I understood that as a news reporter I was no better than my sources. Beat reporters build up sources over a period of time. Sometimes that means that reporters, without meaning to, adopt the beliefs of their sources. Reporters receive pats on the back when the reporter accurately quotes their opinions. But when opinion writers at the newspaper use the same facts to reach different opinions than those held by a reporter's sources, it creates problems for the reporter.

It did not take long for me to butt heads with the news reporters at the newspaper. Whenever I walked into the newsroom, it was not uncommon for me to hear the phrase, "Look out everyone, here comes Dickerson!" Honestly, I didn't give a damn. I had a job to do. Of course, the result was in the form of blowback to editorial page editor, E.W. Kiekhefer. I liked Kiekhefer as a person, but as an editor he was hell on wheels. He possessed that quality that individuals sometimes acquire later in life that is characterized by incessant nagging, arm waving, and ill-tempered vocalizations that sometimes sounded like screeches.

One day Kiekhefer came into my office all worked up over a reporter's criticisms of me, spit flying out of his mouth as he urged me to "leave the reporters alone!" The longer he continued, the angrier I became. Finally, I jumped to my feet, grinned broadly, and shouted, "Kiekhefer, if you don't get out of my office, I'm going have to kill you!"

I admit I do have a temper. And I can generate a Sam Spade persona on short notice. But everyone has their limits. Of course, I had no intention of killing my immediate boss—and he saw the grin and knew I was not serious—but I was still telling him to leave my office. He froze like a deer in the headlights of an oncoming truck, blinked several times, and bolted out the door. I was concerned he might trip over his shoe laces.

Within the editorial board, we worked well together. Typically, we shared the same opinions. I supported his liberal leanings, and he supported mine. But outside the meetings, he continued to be abrasive in that way that older men sometimes do as a salve for their frustration. After one annoying encounter too many, I asked Grehl if I could transfer to the news side to get away from an editor I felt was becoming unhinged.

Grehl's answer was a brief, "No."

I continued on as always.

One day I came across a news story about the New Madrid Fault, which is centered in New Madrid, Missouri. It was along this fault that the greatest earthquake in U.S. history occurred, causing destruction that sent aftershocks through Memphis to New Orleans, north to Detroit, and east to New England. It caused the Mississippi River to rise in giant waves fifteen to twenty feet high.

Experts point out today that an earthquake of similar violence is long overdue and could level Memphis and divert the river into north

Mississippi. To write an editorial on the subject, I did some research at the Memphis State University Center for Earthquake Research. During one of my visits to the center, they said they were fans of my writing and they asked me to serve on their board.

I thought Grehl would be happy for me to get more involved in the community with such an important organization, but he said no because he felt the organization just wanted to use me for public relation purposes. I explained that I would be in a position to obtain information other news media would not. Still, the answer was no.

Later, because of my research, I discovered that *The Commercial Appeal* building did not comply with earthquake construction regulations that would require an investment of millions of dollars to remedy. If there was a major earthquake, the building would be a very dangerous place to be. Without meaning to do so, I had put Grehl in a position in which he either had to make a recommendation to Scripps Howard to spend millions on repairs to the building to bring it up to code, or relocate the newspaper to another building for the safety of the employees.

Grehl's solution was to deny me a seat on the board. If I was on the board, and a severe earthquake hit Memphis, levelling the newspaper's building, possibly killing many employees, the company would be in no position to deny advance knowledge of the risks involved with doing nothing to bring the building up to code. The lesson for me was that idealism suits reporters better than it does editors and their corporate bosses. Grehl did what he had to do. It was yet another secret I would have to keep. Not once in my tenure at the newspaper did we have another editorial on earthquakes.

THE MOST AMBITIOUS PROJECT to date for me was a three-part series of editorials about a directive issued by President Ronald Reagan that promoted government secrecy in the name of national security. It required all federal employees with access to classified information to sign a non-disclosure pledge and submit to polygraph tests if asked. In addition it required former government officials, whether a vice president or a secretary of state, to clear their speeches and writings with the sitting administration. It required former government officials-turned-teachers to submit their lectures to the government for prior approval. And it required former government officials-turned-journalists to get approval of their stories from the very people they were writing about.

Scripps Howard, which owned *The Commercial Appeal* at that time, had its own team of editorial writers at the corporate headquarters. It submitted an editorial to us that was fairly meek in its criticism of Reagan's directive—and we all knew Scripps Howard supported Reagan at every opportunity. Grehl gave the editorial to me to read and said he planned to use it on the editorial page. However, he asked me to write a more in-depth response to the directive that more energetically criticized the directive as an attack on free speech. Could I do a better job than they had done? Of course I could. Handing this project off to me was a gutsy thing for Grehl to do, but he knew my opinions on the issue and decided to walk on the wild side with me.

Not far into the project, I went to Grehl and told him I needed to do two editorials on the subject. He agreed. Once I finished the editorials—one headlined "One View of History"[33] and the other headlined "Weak Leadership"—the three editorials ran on consecutive days. The final editorial ran the full depth of the page, leaving no room for additional editorials. It began, "Almost every president since George Washington has been concerned about government leaks. But when they have succumbed to the temptation to wrap their administrations in cloaks of secrecy, they have done so with the knowledge that it was wrong. Historically, government secrecy, other than that directly related to immediate national security, can be traced to a weakness of leadership whose sole purpose has been to cover up mistakes."

* * *

My final editorial of 1983 about music ran under the headline, **SECOND CHANCE**."[34] Beale Street was open for business now. Strides were being made in opening new bars and restaurants. The editorial dealt with the disturbing trend displayed by businesses on the street of ignoring local blues bands, booking instead out-of-town groups or young white rock artists. I wrote that club owners would be foolish to ignore the wishes of their patrons, but pointed out that most club owners have attempted to influence, not just follow, the tastes of their patrons. As an example, the editorial cited a club named Blues Alley, which was downtown, but not on Beale Street. It featured Black performers almost exclusively.

In addition, the editorial stated that club owners had a responsibility to "give blues a chance," citing the demise of the city as a recording center. In words that would prove prophetic, I wrote, "The reasons for the demise of the recording industry in the city are many and complicated, but the roadblocks to its resurrection are simpler to understand. There's no money available. It would probably be easier for an enterprising businessman to get a loan for a hockey team franchise than for a recording studio."

NOT FAR INTO 1984, E.W. Kiekhefer resigned his position as editorial page editor. I hated to hear that. Even though I found it difficult to deal with him on a personal basis, his opinions were aligned with my own and at that point in my life that was more important than his abrasive personality. If you recall, when I had my job interview with Grehl we talked a while and then went to lunch.
Joining us was Norm Brewer, not the editorial page editor. I assumed that Norm might be in line to succeed
Kiekhefer. Naturally, when Kiekhefer left, I figured he would be replaced by Norm. A native of Memphis, he was an urbane, well-spoken man about ten years older than myself and I considered him perfect for the job.

I was shocked when Grehl chose David Vincent because he was such an unlikely choice. David was native to New England and had little understanding of Southern culture. He was the editorial board's "expert" on public and higher education, yet he and his wife home schooled their children. He was center-right politically, while the newspaper's long tradition was left of center, where it showed leadership on social issues such as civil rights, voter registration, and equal opportunity, issues, none of which, I could envision David embracing. *The Commercial Appeal's* only Pulitzer Prize was won because of editorial cartoons and editorials attacking the KKK. Despite misgivings, I promised myself I would keep an open mind, but co-existence between me and David Vincent was at best fragile and at worst potentially volcanic.

Not long after the announcement about David, Norm came into my office, closed the door, and sat down in the chair across from my desk. He released a long sigh, a sadness in his eyes I had never before seen, and he told me that he had handed in his resignation. He didn't feel like he would be able to follow David's leadership. He told me he and his wife Carol Coletta, planned to open a public relations company and get a fresh start. I told him how sorry I was that he was leaving. Not only was I losing an ally on the board, I was losing my best friend at the newspaper.

Norm and Carol put together a high-profile public relations agency that became very successful. Carole was a beautiful, socially adept woman, and Norm remained a good-looking, slowly aging man in that button-down-tie news anchor vein. In no time, they became Memphis' favorite power couple. Things went well for Norm for a number of years, and then one day he went home and discovered Carol with another man. The resulting divorce was brutal and Norm ended up writing a book about the ordeal. It took a lawsuit to break up their business partnership. It was during the lawsuit that revelations about the infidelity were made, along with Carol's admission, after publication of the book, she went to a costume party dressed as Hester Prynne, the scorned adulteress in *The Scarlet Letter*. She always did have a delightful sense of humor.

With Norm's position open, Grehl called in various reporters so that they could try out for the position. One of them was Jeffrey Katz from the Little Rock bureau. He did a great job, but it turned out he liked reporting more than he did writing opinions that were not necessarily his own.

In 1982, Grehl hired Rheta Grimsley Johnson as a columnist.

Previously she had been a bureau reporter for the newspaper, living in Tupelo, Mississippi. If you recall, she was married at the time to editorial cartoonist Jimmy Johnson, who worked at the *Jackson Daily News* while I was editorial page editor. A striking woman, with dark hair and greenish- blue eyes, she was a talented writer who went on to bigger things. However, when she was asked by Grehl to put in some time on the editorial board she found that kind of writing intimidating. Often I visited her office to find her nearly in tears. Once, while commenting on how nice she looked and how well her editorial read (it was a double suck-up moment), she said, "Oh, Jim, you always know exactly what to say."

Rheta and I went to dinner several times while she was in Memphis. On one occasion, we returned to the apartment she shared with a young, twenty-something female television reporter. She was pretty in that way that twenty-something women typically are pretty and she was full of herself, but she was no Rheta Grimsley Johnson, either in the journalism or looks departments. I asked the young television reporter a lot of questions, a habit I picked up as a social worker, about her career path, only for her to blurt out, "I was never interested in newspapers. All the attractive people go into television."

Rheta was sitting three feet away, but the woman never made eye contact with her. I glanced at Rheta with an amused look on my face, just in time to see her eyes roll back in her head. I could tell she was more than ready to leave Memphis and head back to Mississippi, where insulting comments are typically made behind your back.

WHEN KIEKHEFER vacated his office, he asked me if I wanted to move into it. That was an easy yes because it was larger and had a window that overlooked Beale Street. My current office was windowless. It was a generous gesture from an individual with whom I frequently had disagreements. I could not help but wonder if the office was haunted.

I had not been in my new office long when Grehl told me that I would be taking over editorial coverage from Kiekhefer of State Representative

Pam Gaia, one of the first women to be elected to the Tennessee General Assembly. A progressive Democrat, she represented the Midtown district in the House of Representatives. She was a real firebrand, pushing for nursing home reform and for the right of Tennesseans to have access to generic prescription drugs. I was passionate about the same issues, so supporting her efforts at reform would pose no problem for me.

Meanwhile, David Vincent met with me to inform me of the changes he planned for the editorial page. None of it was good news, except for his decision to allow me to write more signed columns for the op-ed page. He confirmed that he planned to move the editorial page to the political right. I couldn't, no, make that wouldn't, go to the right, so the question in my mind was whether he would allow me to write from the center. I gave it a great deal of thought and then wrote Grehl a note requesting that I be allowed to transfer to the newsroom to write the sort of Page One features and investigative stories I had done at other newspapers. I explained that I feared becoming a thorn in everyone's side if I remained on the editorial board.

I didn't hear back from Grehl right away, but when I did it was in the form of a letter that was delivered by his secretary. Just reading it sucked the air out of my office. He paid me a compliment by writing, "You have a fine mind, integrity and the ability to write clearly and well," but from there he pivoted to explain that I had been a disappointment because of my reluctance to get involved in writing about city and state issues. He concluded by stating that a change of assignment was not in the cards.

I never bothered to explain to him that I veered away from city and state issues because Norm and David considered those issues to be their editorial beat. It is not unheard of for journalists to ask for a change in assignment, so the only conclusion I could draw was that Grehl had viewed my request as a slap in the face. I had hurt his feelings without meaning to. I felt badly about that, but I could see that I had dug a hole for myself that would not be easy to climb out of. With Norm gone, I began a campaign to get more involved in local stories. Little did I know that I was about to dive into an even deeper hole that would considerably ratchet up my involvement with local politics.

One morning Representative Pam Gaia called me and said she had been told I was her new contact at the newspaper. Would I mind if she dropped by later that morning to introduce herself? Of course, I told her that would be fine. I had no idea what she looked like, how old she was or what kind of personality she possessed. I was working at my computer, with my back to the opened door, when I heard a knock and turned to see a very attractive brunette standing in my doorway.

"Hi," she said, smiling. "I'm Pam Gaia."

"Come in," I said, rising to my feet.

"So you're the one who will be writing about my hopes and dreams for the people of Memphis?"

"Yes," I said. "I'm afraid you're stuck with me."`

We talked for about an hour. Clearly, we were on the same page on the issues. So I knew I was going to enjoy following her career. She was a very attractive woman who seemed to possess endless energy. I was mighty impressed. As she was leaving, I reminded her to keep me in the loop on her political activities. She promised she would.

From that meeting, I went to the editorial board meeting, where I informed them of my meeting with Gaia. Grehl nodded approvingly. After the meeting he pulled me aside and asked me if I would like to attend a football game with him and his wife Audrey. I told him I'd love to. He encouraged me to bring my girlfriend along.

The twenty-something woman I was dating at the time had a history of embarrassing me in public. Once we were spending a weekend in the mountains when we decided to take a drive on a winding country road. Up and down the mountain we went, through forests and farm fields. Suddenly, without explanation, she suddenly slipped off her shirt (she was not wearing a bra) and stuck her head and upper body out the window to take in the magnificent fall scenery. This was the woman I was taking to a football game with my boss. What could possibly go wrong?

The Showboats were Memphis' most recent venture into professional sports. A football team that entered the USFL (United States Football League) in 1984, the Showboats were attendance leaders in the short-lived league. Grehl saw the Showboats as a racial and economic unifying force in the city and his invitation to join him at the stadium was another attempt to get me more involved in the city. I was already knee-deep into the city's efforts to make Beale Street a success, but he wanted me to branch out into sports because he wanted the newspaper to encourage the fledging team. That was fine with me. I was happy to carry the ball on that issue.

The morning of the game I gave my girlfriend a ticket and arranged for her to meet me at the stadium. She wasn't there at kickoff or even by the end of the first quarter. Grehl and his lovely wife Audrey asked several times if I needed to go look for her (this was in the pre-cell phone era), but I told them I felt certain she would arrive any minute now.

It was not until midway through the second quarter that she arrived, wearing a shirt that was a little too tight for her chest, and drunk as a sailor on leave in a foreign port. Just as she reached our row she stumbled and almost tumbled down the stadium's concrete steps. I don't think you need any more details. Suffice it to say she slurred her cheers and spilled her drink on everyone each time she threw her arms up to cheer. Audrey was polite and sympathetic, while Grehl was visibly amused at my uncomfortable predicament and barked out a steady stream of comments to her in that deep, growly voice of his that sometimes sounded like distant thunder. I was the only one there who was not entertained by the spectacle.

After the game I asked her what in the hell had happened. She apologized by giving me an excuse that only made matters worse. It seems that shortly before she was supposed to be at the stadium she entered a store and ran into her old boyfriend, who happened to be with his wife. She told me she was so upset by the experience that she drank herself silly, forgetting all about the game until she heard something about it on her car radio. Things like that are hard on a relationship. In her emotional state, she blamed me for putting her in that situation. I blamed her for being a horse's ass in front of my employer. We had no way to go but separate directions. Now that I was single again, I pondered the possibilities.

Ever since my office meeting with Pam Gaia I could not get her out of my mind. I was intensely attracted to her, but I couldn't just call her up and ask her out on a date. That would be too presumptuous. Instead, I called her and asked if we could meet at a restaurant, where we wouldn't be interrupted, to discuss her long-range agenda. She liked the idea. I suggested we meet at a Mid-Town restaurant named Giovanni's. It was one of my favorite eateries. Italian to the core, it had subdued lighting, cozy booths and tables with white tablecloths, not to mention some of the best Italian cuisine in Memphis.

I arrived early and sat just inside the door to wait for her. When she arrived, the first words out of her mouth when she saw me were, "How did you know this is my favorite restaurant?"

Indeed! Score one for studious editorial writers.

Our meeting began at seven and ended at ten. During the intervening hours, we talked about her background. She was born in Boston, but grew up in Memphis. She was elected to the Tennessee House of Representatives in 1974, shortly before I returned from Canada. At the time she was elected, she was a twenty-eight-year-old student at what was then called Memphis State University (now University of Memphis), working on her master's degree. We sat in a booth and ordered a bottle of Chianti in a basket. As a progressive lawmaker her issues centered on issues such as environmental protections, consumer issues, and safety nets for the elderly. At the end of the first hour, we both realized we had cross-ed over from attending a meeting to participating in a date. After dinner, we stood in the parking lot, talking for a long time. Before we parted, I asked if we could get together again on Friday.

"Sure," she said, smiling.

Clearly, she was not surprised by the question.

I wanted to kiss her, but a journalist can't kiss a member of the House of Representatives, can they? Seriously. Can you do that? What in the hell

Rep. Pam Gaia, circa 1981 / courtesy Special Collections, University of Memphis

was wrong with me?

The next day she called me early at the office, before our board meeting began, and gave me directions to her apartment. I was surprised that she lived in a fringe area of Midtown. It was not necessarily a great neighborhood. That evening I parked my car and walked up a steel staircase to her second floor, one-bedroom apartment. Because Pam was totally dedicated to her position as a lawmaker, she did not hold down a second job like most lawmakers. That meant she had to live on her meager salary as a lawmaker. But she was passionate about social issues and totally disinterested in acquiring personal wealth. As I write this, I realize she was a female Bernie Sanders, only much, much prettier.

For dinner, we went to another Italian restaurant, Pete & Sam's. If Giovanni's was her favorite place to visit, Pet & Sam's was her favorite place to eat. The restaurant opened soon after Sam Bomarito returned home in 1948 after a stint in the U.S. Army Air Corps. He recruited his cousin Pete Romero as a partner. Their goal was to offer unpretentious homemade Italian food such as ravioli, lasagna, spaghetti and pizza. Unlike Giovanni's, where children seldom roamed the aisles, Pete & Sam's maintained a family atmosphere that sometimes included screaming children. The entrance was splattered with photographs of famous people who dined at the restaurant, everyone from Elvis Presley to Wink Martindale, not that he occupied a low rung on the celebrity ladder.

While we were eating, one of the owners stopped at our booth to greet Pam. Clearly, he was quite fond of her. Her eyes sparkled when she spoke to him. That instantly made him fond of me, too. We had a delightful time that evening, with a wonderful dinner.

Conversationally, we veered from politics to life experiences, family and otherwise. I loved the way she often reached across the table to gently touch my arm while making a point. Later that evening, when we arrived at her apartment, she invited me inside. I ended up spending the night. Early in the morning, while she slept, I looked out a window on the other side of the apartment from where I parked. To my surprise, there was a fried chicken franchise next door to her apartment. I could not help but think this would make a nice scene in a noir movie.

The following Monday at work I thought about her throughout the editorial board meeting. After the meeting, as everyone was leaving the office, I asked Grehl if I could talk to him.

"What's on your mind?" he asked.

I stalled, waiting until everyone else left the room.

"I need to let you know that Pam Gaia and I are dating," I said.

"Well, suck me dry," barked Grehl, a slight smile emerging from his beard. He paused a moment looking at me as if I was a space alien.

"If you think it would be a conflict of interest for me to continue to write about her projects, I will understand if you want someone else to do that from now on," I continued.

"I don't think that will be necessary," he said, finally. "We have supported her political positions for years. I appreciate you telling me."

Again, another pause. I figured he was thinking I was the only journalist he had ever known who had dated a member of the Tennessee legislature.

"We'll play it by ear and see how it goes. Of course, if you got married or something that would change things."

Married! Grehl would be my best man!

Grehl had hoped I would get more involved in the community. For him, my relationship with Pam was a wish come true. After that conversation he stopped hounding me about community involvement. Neither did he ever again invite me to go to a ball game, but that was for an entirely different reason.

Pam and I saw each other often throughout 1984. I loved hearing her war stories about serving in the General Assembly. Sometimes she told me stories on the condition that I not share them with co-workers at the newspaper. I agreed. Most journalists hear stories off the record that they ethically feel they cannot use.

One such story that Pam told me was about the time a Memphis FBI agent approached her and asked her to wear a hidden microphone while attending an upcoming party hosted by state senator John Ford. The agent explained he had been told that Ford offered cocaine at such parties. He wanted Pam to get the goods on Ford. She turned them down. The Ford family was one of the most prominent African-American families in the United States. There was absolutely zero chance she would be a spy for the FBI, at least not in this lifetime.

In 1974, the same year that Pam was first elected to the House of Representatives, John's brother Harold, was elected to Congress, becoming the first African-American elected to Congress from Tennessee. Pam was disturbed by the FBI request because she felt it was an improper role for the FBI and because she feared her refusal would open the door to FBI harassment of herself. It bothered me greatly for the same reasons. But there was another reason that I never told her about. If you recall, one of the families in my hometown that posed a threat to myself and my family had a son that was a FBI agent in Memphis. I was unable to determine if he was one of the agents involved, but it concerned me greatly that someone at the FBI had attempted to put her in the middle of such a nefarious scheme. I couldn't help but wonder if Pam had told me everything. What if they had threatened to expose her relationship with me if she did not work with them?

Pam and I were Memphis' Number One power couple, only no one knew that but us (and Grehl, but his lips were sealed unless he told his wife Audrey). For Thanksgiving that year, Pam and I cooked a delicious meal. She handled the turkey and dressing, and I called my mother to get her recipes for sweet potato and green-bean casseroles. By the time we got through, the table was covered with food and looked like a restaurant buffet. Never mind the excess food, the sun was shining brightly and the air was nippy and her eyes sparkled like never before. A perfect day.

THE YEAR I MOVED to Memphis the city unveiled its newest downtown attraction, Mud Island. The name sounds bleak, I know, but it sort of grows on you with time. The major features include a Mississippi River Museum; the Riverwalk, a scale replica of the Lower Mississippi River from Cairo, Illinois, to just south of New Orleans, Louisiana; several very good restaurants, and a monorail that stretches from the shore across water to the island. The monorail was later used in a movie, *The Firm*, starring Tom Cruise. There is also a 5,000-seat amphitheater with seating that faces the Memphis skyline, a great view at night. Many top-rated recording artists in blues, jazz, and rock 'n' roll regularly performed at the amphitheater.

Mud Island was slow to catch on with local residents. No one liked the name. Everyone was scared of the monorail, and the museum was tailored mainly for tourists, so it was natural that I take it on after Norm left. In August 1984, I wrote a column for the op-ed page that stressed the importance of Mud Island to the city's economy.

"Mud Island should not be viewed as a river playground," I wrote. "It is an important piece of a complex puzzle that could have a significant impact on the lives of all Memphians, whether they live 'out east,' downtown or in between. Experiment with Mud Island and you experiment with the taxes, jobs and income of just about everyone in the city."[35]

Later, I certainly attended my share of concerts at the amphitheater, where I photographed and interviewed luminaries such as Stevie Ray Vaughan, David Sanborn, and the Bangles.

* * *

One of my first friends in the newsroom at the newspaper was Dan Henderson, who at that time was a feature writer, mainly for the newspaper's weekly magazine named *Mid-South*. He and I shared a great deal of admiration for Michael Grehl and a love of great writing.

One weekend, we decided to go to Heber Springs, Arkansas, to camp on the bank of the Little Red River to do some trout fishing. We erected a small tent on high ground not far from the river, and immediately broke out the fishing tackle and hit the river, even though we only had about a hour's worth of light left. The water was cool and clear enough to reflect

Stevie Ray Vaughan during sound check on Mud Island.
Photo by James L. Dickerson

light from the bottom of the rock-filled river. We stood about twenty or thirty feet apart and carried on a conversation as we cast our fishing lines in opposite directions, one upriver and the other downriver, not having much luck. We kept trying until the sun set, and then some.

Suddenly, something of a dark complexion darted out of the moonlit sky and flew between us.

"What was that?" I asked.

Before Dan could answer, the creature returned, zigzagging like crazy as it flew three or four tight circles around my head, and then paused in mid-air no more than six inches from my face, fanning the tip of my nose with its fluttering wings as it tried to make eye contact with me.

It was a ferocious bat.

"After making a shrill noise—or maybe the shrill noise came from me—the bat darted away into the night as quickly as it had come," I later wrote in a newspaper column.[36] "I don't know if you have ever stared a bat in the eye on a moonlit night, but if you have you know there are few things in life more unsettling." It's the sort of experience that sticks with you, the memory of which often returns late at night when all you can hear is the clock ticking.[37]

That night we lay in our sleeping bags with the lantern flickering and discussed the bats. Dan professed that never in all his years of fishing the Little Red had he ever seen a bat behave so peculiarly. He wondered aloud if some sort of witchcraft might be afoot.

"Maybe it has rabies," I said.

We got up early the next morning and fished until mid-afternoon and then drove back to Memphis. The next day, I did a little research and learned that Heber Springs had a cave that housed 15,000 bats. My encounter with that solitary bat was a mystery I was never able to solve.

Dan, who had published a science fiction novel, had a few unexplained mysteries of his own. He lived in downtown Memphis in the Lowenstein Towers, overlooking the Mississippi River. One day after receiving devastating news that his mother had passed away, he sat on his balcony alone with his cat, no doubt explaining his grief to his feline friend. Like most people he was granted a childhood without the death of a parent, but when his mother's death came, it hit him hard. Dan's mother died of Ehlers-Danlos syndrome, which causes curvature of the spine and a hump back. Dan had the same disease and realized that he had lost more than a parent. He had lost the belief that he would somehow live into old age. Now that he knew that wasn't going to happen, he found himself grappling with his own mortality.

Suddenly, without any warning, the cat leaped from his lap, soaring over the balcony railing. As Dan looked on in stunned horror, his beloved cat fell to its death. The incident troubled Dan greatly because he could make no sense of it. Why on earth would a cat do such a thing? Was it possessed? Crazy? Obviously, it was suicidal. But why?

Life went on for Dan. He got more cats.

Several years later, Dan awoke one morning and fed his cats, and lay on his couch to rest before going to the newsroom. Later that morning, the maid arrived to clean his apartment and found him stretched out on his couch. He was dead. When I heard the news I thought of a story he once told me about Michael Grehl. While I was at the newspaper and afterward, Dan rose rapidly up the management ranks, finally reaching the position of managing editor. We were having lunch one day on Beale Street when he told me about an experience he had with Grehl, who had told me on occasion what a high opinion he had of Dan.

The way Dan told the story, Grehl called him into his office to offer him a promotion. After Dan accepted the new position, Grehl asked him to kneel in prayer with him there in his office. To me, that said a lot about both Grehl and Dan. One can only imagine the eddying chaos of the knees-on-the-floor energy in the room during that spiritual moment. Dan didn't comment on the length of the prayer, nor did he attempt to justify it to me. He just told me the facts and left it lying on the table. After Dan died I recalled that story, confident that Dan most likely had landed himself a good gig in Heaven thanks to Grehl's foresight.

NINETEEN EIGHTY-FOUR wrapped with my last Memphis music-related editorial of the year. It was written the week before Christmas. With the headline **BRING IT HOME**, it pointed out, yet once again, how Memphis was the home of the blues and the birthplace of rock 'n' roll, and was negligent in not promoting that heritage.

"Music is critical to Memphis' development," I wrote. "It is what has made Memphis unlike any other city in the world. Some way must be found to preserve the city's music heritage."

The editorial suggested that the city and county mayors appoint a "blue ribbon" commission made up of people knowledgeable about the music industry, to determine what could be done to get Memphis "back on the right music track."

After Christmas, I again brought up the subject of Memphis music.

"I've been thinking about that editorial I wrote before Christmas about Memphis music, how the city and county mayors ought to do something," I told the editorial board. "The more I think about it, the more I realize they aren't going to do anything on their own. We will have to provide them with the ammo to go out on a limb for Memphis music."

I proposed that I do a series of Q & A's about Memphis music.

"It is how we could do our own 'blue ribbon' commission," I explained. "Instead of assembling a group of experts, I would interview experts such as Johnny Cash and Jerry Lee Lewis and B.B. King for the purpose of asking them how *they* would go about bringing back the music."

I suggested the interviews run on the op-ed page. To my surprise, Grehl said that if they ran on the editorial page, next to the editorials, readers would know how serious the newspaper was about tackling the subject. That was music to my ears.

NINETEEN EIGHTY-FIVE began with me purchasing a mini-cassette tape recorder that could be connected to my telephone so that I could record interviews. Then I began making a list of people to interview for the series. At the top of my list were B.B. King, Johnny Cash, Jerry Lee Lewis, producer Willie Mitchell, jazz legend Miles Davis, and RCA Records executive Gregg Geller. Others had suggestions as well. Grehl suggested I interview Ron Terry, board chairman of First Tennessee Bank, the largest in Tennessee. Our copy and page design editor Richard Mcfalls suggested I interview record producer Chips Moman. I didn't know who he was, so Richard had to explain to me that he was the most important producer in Memphis music history.

The more I looked into Moman's background, the more impressed I became. The Georgia native had dropped out of school in the eighth grade and hitchhiked to Memphis as a teenager to make a name for himself. He played in several bands and then got married and went to the West Coast to pursue opportunities in music. For a time, he worked as a session player in Los Angeles at the legendary Gold Star studio, where he learned how to be a producer by watching the pros there. After he returned to Memphis, he played an important role in the creation of the legendary Memphis rhythm & blues record label, Stax Records. He recorded their first hits before launching his own studio, American Sound Studios, where he recorded everyone from Petula Clark and Dionne Warwick to B.J. Thomas. In 1968 he rescued Elvis Presley's nearly dormant career with sessions that produced hits such as "Suspicious Minds," "In the Ghetto," and "Kentucky Rain." For a period of almost a decade he was the most successful hit maker in the nation.

In the early 1970s, Moman relocated to Nashville, where he created the super group named the Highwaymen (Willie Nelson, Waylon Jennings, Johnny Cash, and Kris Kristofferson) and produced hit solo albums with each of the artists, except Kristofferson. He was the first country music producer to record a Platinum album with a solo artist (it was with Waylon Jennings). Songs he co-wrote include "Do Right Woman," recorded by Aretha Franklin, "Luckenbach, Texas," recorded with Waylon Jennings and Willie Nelson, and "Another Somebody Done Somebody Wrong Song," recorded with B.J. Thomas.

If there was anyone who could advise Memphis on reviving its music industry it was one of the individuals who established it, Chips Moman. I wasted no time setting up an interview with him in Nashville. When I arrived at the studio I discovered Chips was in a recording session with Johnny Cash, whose wife, June Carter Cash, also was present. I couldn't believe my good luck. Not only was I able to watch Cash record in the studio, I was able to interview Johnny and June for my music series.

My interview with Moman was lengthy, primarily because he was involved in so much of Memphis music history. He had lots of ideas about how the city could revive its music. At one point in the interview, I asked him if he would ever consider returning to Memphis.

"Yes, under the right circumstances, I would," he said. "I'd like to have the opportunity to try to educate Memphis about its own music."

The morning after I returned to Memphis, I gave a report to the editorial board. At that time there was very little music industry left in Memphis, other than vanity recording studios that were in business to sell studio time to hopeful artists. The success of my Nashville trip prompted Grehl to encourage me to proceed full speed ahead with my interviews.

It was at this point that I saw the potential of Grehl's vision for investigative opinion writing. The legwork I was doing to assemble a series of Q & A's was the investigative part of the process. If I had been writing a traditional feature on the Memphis music industry I would have used only small parts of my interviews in a series of news stories. This way, using interviews that would be published on the editorial page, it allowed the transcripts of my conversations to be read in an unfiltered format. When the time came for the editorial board to take a position on reviving the music industry in the city, the reasons for our opinions would be based on transparent information. Grehl's concept of investigative opinion writing was one I would use as a journalist long past my newspaper career and into a new career as a non-fiction journalist writing 100,000-word investigative histories and biographies.

Following Grehl's guidance, I interviewed Ron Terry at his office at

First Tennessee Bank. I asked how he ranked music now as an asset to the city? "It's a contributor to the image. It is part and parcel of the self-image of a Memphian and that's an important part of the message we have to send about Memphis."

Terry said he thought Memphis was prepared to embrace "anything that is recognized as a potential contributor to economic growth and a better self-image." But he cautioned that a revived music industry could not successfully be built on live entertainment. He explained that studios run by smart business people were essential to a revived industry. "The key is a half dozen Chips Momans and Al Bells or Cy Leslies [founder of Pickwick Records]. Those are the people who build a music industry. What we need is management."

Before I left First Tennessee, Terry suggested I interview Mayor Dick Hackett for the series because he felt business could not do it alone. Success depended on the support of local government. When I returned to my office, I called the mayor's office and set up an appointment.

In Hackett, the youngest mayor in the city's history, I found an enthusiastic supporter of Memphis music. He said he would be willing to go to Nashville to talk to Moman about relocating to Memphis. Then he said something totally unexpected. "For the right producer or studio, listen, I can make them a bargain on some land, and I'm talking about like one dollar, if they will contribute toward creating that atmosphere or climate in the city . . . But it will have to be someone with a track record, someone who can produce."

As I was leaving the mayor's office, Hackett asked me if I thought Ron Terry (he had read his interview) would go with him to Nashville.

"I would think so. He's the one who suggested I talk to you."

In mid-February 1985, Mayor Hackett and Ron Terry boarded a plane at the Memphis airport to fly to Nashville's Berry Field airport on a secret mission. They only told their staffs and families about the trip—and, of course, yours truly. After spending several hours with Moman and his wife, Toni, they returned to Memphis and spent the next two months putting together a package they felt would bring Moman home to Memphis.

As negotiations got underway, I continued with the Q&A interviews. B.B. King had begun his career in Memphis, but had not recorded there in many years. In his interview, he said that he was making plans to return to Memphis to record. Said King: "People talk about the blues in Chicago. Well, don't get me wrong, but when I hear that I get a little bit jealous because Memphis had it long before Chicago did."

Bonnie Raitt said in her interview that she often has thought about recording in Memphis. "I have wanted to record with Willie Mitchell for a long time (the producer who discovered and recorded Al Green). Advised Raitt: "Create a museum, a place where young musicians can learn about the music. An archives where people could listen to tapes and see videos . . . a place to learn where the music came from."

Another important interview was with the surviving members of Booker T. and the MGs, who had begun their careers in Memphis with the hit instrumental, "Green Onions." I interviewed bassist Duck Dunn and guitarist Steve Cropper in a joint interview, and Booker T. separately. Dunn said, "I read your interview with Chips Moman. I think what he said just about wraps it up. It was strange coming from Chips, but it is true. Somebody there needs to be a boss. Just putting a bunch of musicians together and letting them try to do it never works out. You have to have someone you look up to."

By far, my favorite interview was with jazz legend Miles Davis. He was not from Memphis (born in Illinois, he was raised in St. Louis), but his knowledge of Memphis' often underrated jazz history helped throw light on that fact. The best part of the interview was the way it came about. I telephoned his manager, who lived in New England, and asked if he would set up an interview. He was cordial but pointed out that Davis had done few interviews in recent years.

"Don't get your hopes up," he said. "I will let him know and the rest is up to him."

With that in the works, I resumed my editorial duties.

About a hour after my conversation with Davis's manager, the telephone rang.

"Hello," I answered.

"Jim," came the raspy voice. There was a pause. "This is Miles. I hear you're looking for me."

I was speechless. He said his manager had told him I was trying to revive Memphis music. He wanted to be a part of that, so he called without the red tape of his manager setting up the interview. The interview began with him correcting me. I had asked, "When most Americans think of jazz, they think of . . . (he interrupted me).

"Try not to use jazz."

"Why is that?"

"Because it means Uncle Tom and stuff like that. To me, it does. Do you know what I'm saying . . . I say social music . . . What you call jazz is an old Negro thing . . . We don't use that term, jazz, because of its image."

Truthfully, Davis helped me understand something I needed to understand to be effective in writing about Memphis music. Moman had essentially said the same thing when he explained why he left Memphis in the early 1970s to go to Georgia and then Nashville. His American Sound Studio recorded all types of music—pop, rock, rhythm & blues and even jazz—but music promoters tended to refer to the individual music types instead of simply saying "Memphis music."

Miles Davis and Chips Moman were correct, arriving at the same intersection from different directions. The best way to revitalize Memphis music was to refer to it as simply that—Memphis music—because the whole was greater than the individual parts. In all, there were twenty-one interviews that ran on the editorial page from January 12 to March 17, 1985. Subsequently, they were published by Scripps Howard in August 1985 as a paperback book titled *Coming Home: 21 Conversations About Memphis Music*.

About a month after the series ended, Moman and his wife Toni drove to Memphis to meet with Hackett and sign a letter of intent. Following the meeting they held a press conference to announce Moman's relocation. Hackett attributed his involvement in the project to reading the series of Q & A's that ran in *The Commercial Appeal*. The tentative agreement provided for the sale, for one dollar, of an old fire station at Third and Linden about a block from Beale Street. Additional plans called for the Center City Commission to arrange for Moman to get a loan from First Tennessee Bank for $750,000, with the money earmarked for renovating the firehouse into a state-of-the-art recording studio.

As plans for the studio advanced, Moman turned his attention to recording his first album in Memphis. His studio would not be completed in time, so he made arrangements to record most of the songs in Sam Phillips's Sun Records studio and the remaining songs at his old American Sound Studio. The recording project would be a reunion of former Sun Records greats Johnny Cash, Carl Perkins, Jerry Lee Lewis, and Roy Orbison. The sessions were scheduled for September 1985.

Soon after Moman arrived in Memphis, Grehl asked me to invite him to one of our editorial board meetings so that everyone could become acquainted. By that time the newspaper had a new executive editor, David Wayne Brown, who had been transferred to Memphis in 1984 by Scripps Howard from their Birmingham newspaper. Brown attended the meeting and later spoke to Chips privately. The meeting went well. Moman was asked a lot of questions and answered with both enthusiasm and appreciation for the role the newspaper had played in his return to Memphis. Grehl said he was hopeful the music revival would be successful because if that was the case it would benefit the entire city.

BY SUMMER, Mike Grehl had retired and David Wayne Brown had taken on his duties. I asked him if I could leave the editorial page to transfer to the newsroom so that I could cover as a reporter the events *The Commercial Appeal* had helped set in motion to revive Memphis music. Although Grehl had previously refused to reassign me to the newsroom,

Brown readily honored my request.

Pam was not happy to hear about that because she had always considered our working together for the benefit of the elderly as part of the relationship. Pam became ill that summer. Although she assured me it was nothing serious, looking back now I think it must have been cancer. After one of my visits to her home I received a card from her with the following note written on it:

> I have been trying to find the right words to properly thank you for all the wonderful editorials that you have written on nursing home reform. They helped keep a handle on the whole matter by serving as a tremendous stabilizing force when all but you and I appeared to represent chaos. The words are coming harder now. I felt that we were partners working good on the world. I liked that feeling a lot. Thank you for giving the issue one hundred percent. I won't ever forget. I hope that you still care what happens about the nursing homes and that we'll always be making progress together. I appreciate you taking the time to visit me when I was sick, particularly since it really took my mind off what was ailing me. It's good when you suspect what might work works. You work…..Pam.

We continued to see each other, though not as often. In retrospect, our relationship was winding down, though it was something we never talked about. In August I underwent hernia surgery. There were complications and I was pretty much bed-ridden for a week with an open wound in my side, left open to allow blood to drain from the botched surgery. Pam brought me meals during that time. If she hadn't, I don't know what I would have done.

BY THE TIME Chips Moman's recording sessions began in mid-September, I had recovered enough from my surgery to attend the sessions and turn in stories each evening for the morning newspaper. For the reunion album he had Johnny Cash, Roy Orbison, Jerry Lee Lewis and Carl Perkins. The sessions lasted a week and I was there the entire time.

Also present at the sessions was a production team from Dick Clark Productions which had come to Memphis to film the entire project for an upcoming television special. The final session attracted luminaries such as Rick Nelson, Sam Phillips, the Judds, John Fogerty and others.

Each day after that I checked with Moman for news of a contract with a major label. Each day there was no news. In late fall, as fears grew that the album would be rejected by all the major labels, Mayor Hackett showed up with the finalized agreement for the studio. The financing for a loan to renovate and equip the studio with modern equipment was finally in place, but there was a catch. Under pressure from the vanity studio owners in town, Hackett stepped back from his original offer that had brought Moman back to Memphis.

The final agreement was not for the sale of the building for one dollar as promised, but instead a one dollar a year lease purchase agreement. If accepted by Moman, it would put him in a real bind. The one dollar a year lease/purchase agreement would have been a good deal if the lease was for a fully equipped studio. However, the building was in disrepair and required extensive renovations to make it into a functional studio.

Moman accepted the deal knowing he was screwed. He didn't want to let the city down by walking away. The only solution he saw was to launch a record label of his own, soliciting investments from the city's wealthy elite. If the record label was successful, there would be plenty of money for everyone involved, even the vanity studios.

I continued to cover the business of music for *The Commercial Appeal,* although I had a sinking feeling I had ruined a legendary producer's career by inviting him to return to Memphis. Clearly, the local music industry was on the warpath to block his success and had no interest in working with him or anyone else to revive the city's music reputation.

* * *

In late December I took a few days off to drive to Mississippi to spend Christmas with my mother. Before leaving, I sent flowers to Pam as a Christmas gift. When I returned I had a note from her thanking me for the flowers which she placed "on the dining room table reminding me of you. I loved my sexy Christmas card above all others. It gave me such a laugh. Hope that your holidays were filled with warm and precious moments ....Pam."

IN EARLY FEBRUARY 1986, I decided to write a story about the new music talent emerging in Nashville. I contacted all the record labels and told them I wanted to select three or four of the top new acts in Nashville and write a story about them. Everyone sent me tapes and press releases of the new entertainers that the record labels felt would be the stars of tomorrow. I listened to the tapes, some not yet released as records or CDs, and chose four acts to interview: Vince Gill, Lisa Angelle, Sweethearts of the Rodeo, and Marty Stuart.

On a bitterly cold day, I drove to Nashville with photographer Dave Darnell, who had shot the great photos during the Class of '55 sessions. Of the four acts, I previously had met only Marty Stuart, who came to the Class of '55 sessions with Johnny Cash. He was signed to CBS Records, as were the Sweethearts of the Rodeo," a sister act composed of Kristine Arnold and Janice Gill, who was married to Vince Gill. In 1984, when RCA Records released his first country album, *Turn Me Loose,* Vince Gill was new to country music. Previously he had performed as a bluegrass musician with the Blue Grass Alliance, Ricky Skaggs, and Pure Prairie League. Rounding out the selection was Lisa Angelle, a New Orleans native who was signed to EMI-Capitol Records and had recently released her first single, "Love—It's the Pitts."

I interviewed the Sweethearts of the Rodeo at the suburban home Janice shared with her husband Vince and their three year old daughter, Jennifer. The sisters are from California, which shaped their western style of dress—Kristine wore black boots, purple tights and a black sweater to the interview, while Janice had on pink anklets with bangles.

People think we are rodeo queens," said Janis. "But I think once they have heard us they'll start to get the right image in their minds." Added

Kristine, "We used to be called Sweethearts of the Rodeo and their Handsome Band, but we dropped the Handsome Band."

Later, when I interviewed Vince, I asked if he found it a problem living in a two-label household. "I don't feel any competition," he said. "In fact, what I try to do is stay completely clear of her career. I left town when they made their record. I took my daughter and went to Oklahoma . . . I've been a supporter of Janice and Kristine forever."

Vince is considered by his label to be part of the "New Wave" in country music. He acknowledges that the music he is making is different from the old music Nashville has released, but he does not feel it is radically different. "I think regardless of how modern my records might sound, there is more traditional country music in them than 67 percent of the acts that make records here."

Mississippian Marty Stuart began his career as a thirteen-year-old when he joined the Lester Flatt and Earl Scruggs band to play guitar and mandolin. By the time CBS Records signed him as a solo artist at the age of twenty-seven he had spent a lifetime on the road, at least in teenage years. When I interviewed him, he had recently released his first single, a rockabilly song called "Arlene." He explained: "You have a real traditional line here in Nashville—Ricky Scaggs, Reba McIntire, that set of folks. Then there is a group of young mavericks who have had a lot of stuff bottled up inside them for years. They are dying to turn it loose. I'm afraid I qualify for that group."

Dave Darnell shot photographs of Vince Gill, Marty Stuart, and the Sweethearts of the Rodeo separately from where I interviewed them— either inside a record label or on a Nashville street—but when I interviewed Lisa Angelle, he accompanied me to meet her at her song publisher's office. I had been told she had been in bed with pneumonia, but wanted to come into town to do the interview. For that reason, Dave and I felt we should get her photograph during the interview in case she was unable to go on location for the group photograph.

Before moving to Nashville, she performed in rowdy beer joints

Lisa Angelle with the author on the day of their interview.
Photo by David Darnell / The Commercial Appeal

along the Gulf Coast during the summer, sitting in with country bands that performed behind wire screens put up to catch the beer bottles patrons tossed at the bands when they didn't like the music. "It is very difficult singing behind chicken wire" she said. "I don't drink and I don't smoke. I'm very straight, so it was entertaining."

Lisa wouldn't tell me her age, but she looked to be around twenty, the youngest of my interviewees that day. You could not tell by looking at her that she had risen out of bed to do the interview because she looked very attractive in a white dress that gave her an angelic countenance. Of course, she probably knew that when she chose it to wear.

I sat on the piano bench with her while I did the interview. At one point she smiled broadly and inexplicably took my chin in her hand and squeezed it, and then she abruptly stopped my questions by asking a question of her own.

"Would you marry me?" she asked sweetly. "I don't mean today . . . or tomorrow . . . but someday. Will you do it?"

I told her I would be happy to marry her.

"Just give me fifteen minutes notice, please."

Nodding agreement to that, she added, "Would you also write my biography?"

"Absolutely."

Dave got a gorgeous photograph of her sitting alone at the piano. Now that I had concluded the interviews, we needed a group photograph of them at a central location. She told us to just let her know when we were ready. She would be available despite the pneumonia.

Over time, Lisa and I became close friends and whenever I traveled from Memphis to Nashville over the years she always made time to have lunch or dinner with me. Her career at EMI-Capitol fizzled after recording an album at Muscle Shoals that the suits at the label felt wasn't country enough, but she later signed a record deal with Dreamworks. Over time she became an outstanding songwriter, generating a Number One hit for Wynonna Judd with "I Saw the Light." In the late 1980s she did the vocals for CBS Television's "Beauty and the Beast." Today I look back and consider her to be one of the most talented individuals I got to know in Nashville.

After Dave and I left Lisa at her publisher's office, we struggled to find just the right location for the group photograph. There was an office building nearby on Music Row so we went through it floor by floor, knocking on doors and asking strangers for suggestions. We knocked on the door of one office and walked inside without being invited. Standing across the room, near a window, was recording artist Ricky Skaggs. He looked surprised to see us enter his space, but recovered quickly and smiled. Using his downhome country voice, he said, "Come on in."

We quickly apologized for the intrusion and explained our dilemma.

"Oh," said Scaggs. wheels turning inside his head. "The perfect place would be on the Shelby Street Bridge, where you could have the Nashville skyline in the background."

"Thank you," we said in unison, knowing it was the perfect place when we heard his description.

As we made our exit, Scaggs called out, "Come back—you hear?"

Several hours later, we stood in the grass to the side of the Shelby Street Bridge, collecting our future stars. It was very, very cold that day. Vince and Janis showed up with their young daughter, along with Kristine. Marty left a recording session to attend. Marty, Janis and Kristine wore winter coats. Vince had on an insulated vest. Then there was Lisa, who showed up without a coat, wearing only the linen-thin white dress she had on during the interview.

Dave got everyone in place and shot several photographs. Everyone was shivering, but when I later looked at the photographs I couldn't tell how miserable they were. Once Dave shouted, "Thanks!" everyone rushed to get back to their cars. Vince, Dave and I took a more leisurely stroll back to the cars, talking as we walked along.

Suddenly, Lisa, who was by then more than twenty feet away, whirled around and walked back toward us. She stepped right up to me, leaned in, and kissed me on the mouth. With that, the pneumonia patient turned and walked away without a word, moments later turning around to shout over her shoulder, with classic, twenty-year-old bravado:

"Now *you* have it, too!"

**Singer Bobby Womack, left, with producer Chips Moman in Memphis studio.
Photo by James L. Dickerson**

Chapter 11

The Commercial Appeal
Part II

AT THE END OF FEBRUARY, 1986, Chips Moman announced that America Records, his new record label, had attracted eighteen prominent Tennesseans as investors, including Fred Smith, president of Federal Express and members of the Jack Belz family that owned the Peabody Hotel and numerous real estate holdings around the country.

At last, the historic album celebrating Memphis music that no record label wanted had found a home. *Class of '55: Memphis Rock and Roll Homecoming* was revealed to be the company's first release. It would not be released in the traditional manner, wholesaled to record stores, and then promoted on radio. Instead, the business plan called for the album to be marketed and sold by mail order on television.

One evening I was at home when I received a telephone call from Moman who asked if I would meet him at the nearest all-night Waffle House to discuss a business proposition. By that time we had become very good friends. I was fascinated by the sheer genius of the man.

At the Waffle House, surrounded by waffles, eggs, grits and bacon, he informed me that the *Class of '55* would be released in May on America Records. Then he told me that the consultants told him he really needed a booklet or magazine to include in the television package for the album. Because Moman was a dealmaker, he seldom paid anyone he worked with a fee or salary. Instead, he offered them a "deal" in which the both of them could make money from a common effort. In this case, America Records would not pay me to write the text and put the magazine together—they would pay the printing costs, of course—but the benefit to me would be that I could use the magazine that would be included with each sale of the album to launch a new music magazine of my own. Inside the magazine would be coupons that record buyers could fill out to purchase a subscription to the new magazine.

I told him I would be willing to do that, but first I would have to get permission from the newspaper to use the material—and, if the permission, was granted—then I would have to resign my position at the newspaper because publishing a magazine would present a conflict of interest. With my mind made up, I asked for a meeting with Executive Editor David Wayne Brown, who had replaced Michael Grehl upon his retirement. He gave me permission to use the material and accepted my resignation, effective in two weeks.

Walking out of his office, I was aware I had left the best and most satisfying job I had ever had. It was May 1986, yet another turning point in my life. The week after I actually left the job, Michael Grehl called me at home one evening. His voice was strong, though not so gruff as it usually was coming from behind the massive desk in his office. He said he had heard I had left *The Commercial Appeal*.

"I hope it's not because of me?" he asked.

"Not at all," I answered.

"Good."

My first thought was that he was referring to the letter he had written and placed in my file, saying there were times I had been a disappointment. I didn't bring it up because I had decided he had written it out of frustration or even anger after I had asked to leave his team and move over to the newsroom. Clearly, I have a knack for hurting the feelings of my editors.

Perhaps it is the Sam Spade that resides deep within my psyche.

I told him about the magazine startup and thanked him for his support at *The Commercial Appeal.* We had a warm conversation and he said several times he hated to see me leave the newspaper. I told him he was the best editor I had ever worked with. He thanked me with an undertone of melancholy in his voice. It would prove to be the last conversation we ever had.

BECAUSE I HAD ACCESS to Dave Darnell's excellent photographs from the *Class of '55* session, I was able to put together a very attractive, 28-page magazine that bore the images of Johnny Cash, Jerry Lee Lewis, Roy Orbison, and Carl Perkins. Inside, it was filled with the story of the sessions and both color and black-and-white area code for Memphis. The name was the brainchild of Moman's wife, Toni Wine. She preferred the name in numerals, 901, but I used text because Bose Corporation had a speaker named 901 they had trademarked and they protested my use of the number for a music magazine.

I hired a top-notch Chicago attorney and he worked out a deal with Bose whereby I could use *Nine-O-One Network* as a name for the magazine and they would not charge infringement.

I had withdrawn my savings to live on, so from the beginning I heard a clock ticking in the background. Once I completed writing, designing, and editing the first issue, I got busy planning the second issue. I found distribution more difficult to arrange than I expected. For the first issue, I ended up with the circulation of the first magazine limited to Memphis.

Since my Waffle House meeting with Moman, America Records had reached a retail distribution agreement with PolyGram Records in Nashville. Once it was determined that Carl Perkins's "The Birth of Rock 'n' Roll" would be the first single, PolyGram head Steve Popovich decided to do a video. To direct it, he hired Arnold Levine, who previously had directed videos for Bruce Springsteen, Billy Joel, and Neil Diamond. He flew to Memphis from New York and hired a local film crew. His concept

The author, left, filming a video for Carl Perkins as Arnold Levine directs.

was to take a vintage 1955 blue Cadillac and make it into a time machine, depicting two kids out on a joyride. In this case the two kids would be, two fifty-year-olds, Carl Perkins and Jerry Lee Lewis.

I went to the location so that I could get interviews and photographs for *Nine-O-One*. Levine paced the first thirty minutes I was there because Lewis was late for the shoot. Finally, I was asked to put on Lewis's pants, shirt and shoes and be his stand-in. The script called for Perkins to drive the car while Lewis sat on top of the back seat with his feet on the top of the front seat. Levine explained that to me and then he told me I had to make my feet dance.

"Do what?" I asked.

"You know, make them move to the music as if your feet were playing the keys of the piano."

Well, I gave it everything I had. They left my scenes in the video, though you can't see my face, only my dancing feet.

A few days after work was completed and the video was edited, I was in a riverfront office with Perkins sitting in front of me, viewing the

264

finished video. After my dancing feet segment, he turned around and looked at me, grinning and said, "You don't keep bad time for a writer."

* * *

The first thing to go wrong with the album was the failure of the television marketing plan. Long before they told me it was struggling, I knew because of the lack of magazine subscriptions that came into the *Nine-O-One* office. To my surprise, the first subscription order I received was from Johnny Cash. I still have a photocopy of the check. Two years later, when I interviewed Rosanne Cash for the magazine, she told me her father kept a stack of the magazines on his nightstand table and read from them before going to sleep at night. A few weeks after I received Johnny Cash's subscription, I received a check from Jerry Lee Lewis for a subscription. By the time the television marketing campaign was over, I only had received about a dozen subscription orders. According to my formula, that put television sales at around a couple hundred.

Realizing I was not going to make enough money from the America Records magazine promotion to even pay for a post office box, I got busy organizing an effort to sell stock in the magazine in the hope that would sustain it until advertising revenues started coming in. Once I had the paperwork for a stock offering, I began selling shares in the company in Memphis, while my then brother-in-law James McCaskill sold shares in Mississippi. It did not take long to round up almost twenty investors. My next task was to convince a national magazine distribution company to take on the magazine.

As I gathered text and photographs for the first regular edition, I took time off to attend Chips Moman's first recording session in his new studio. It was with rhythm and blues artist Bobby Womack. Moman and Womack had worked together in the late 1960s, recording several hits. Of all the choices he had for a first session at the studio, Moman calculated he had the best odds of recording a commercial hit with Womack.

I took a lot of photographs in the studio while Womack recorded, but I never got one good enough to use on the cover. I wanted to use the story for the second regular issue, which would go on newsstands in November, around the time Womack's album would be released. With the interview with Womack out of the way, I focused on the September edition of the magazine. Because I did an interview with Ron Wood and he was still in town, I asked Dave Darnell to get a cover shot of him. The image was terrific. I supplemented the Wood interview with interviews and photographs of Belinda Carlisle, The Fabulous Thunderbirds, country artist Steve Wariner, and the Sweethearts of the Rodeo.

The Ron Wood issue was enough to land us a contract for national newsstand distribution with a major company. Now we were off and running. The November/December issue (we were a bimonthly then) was our first to garner national exposure. Because the Womack photographs were not good enough for a cover, I did an extensive layout on the inside of the session. For the cover, I used a pensive shot of Memphis-born country artist Deborah Allen, who had scored hits with RCA Records. She was very photogenic and had a good backstory.

Shortly after the release of the November/December issue, *Variety* published a story that gave the magazine staff, as tiny as it was, a big boost: "Jim Dickerson split the music beat at *The Commercial Appeal* to publish Nine-O-One (named for the Memphis area code). It's the first southern-based music mag to do well on northern newsstands, says Memphis State University professor Samir Husni." Everything was correct except Husni's educational affiliation. He was, and still is, a respected journalism professor at the University of Mississippi.

By 1987 we were the third largest circulation music magazine in the United States, with a circulation of 100,000, right behind *Spin* and *Rolling Stone*. The January/February issue was noteworthy not so much for the cover story, which featured an interview with Aimee Mann, lead singer of 'Til Tuesday, but because of a story that bore the headline "Memphis Women Rockers." It featured several popular local female performers. None of the women had recording contracts, but all had a local following. What I viewed as a salute to local Memphis talent, became a crisis that

The legendary Memphis Horns—Wayne Jackson, left, and Andrew Love with latest issue of Nine-O-One. Photo by Greg Campbell

came close to sinking the magazine.

There was an early warning from one of my star writers, a twenty-year-old woman who dropped a story off and caught a glimpse of the layout for the next issue. She protested that one of the photographs was too revealing. I disagreed and ignored her advice to use another photograph and proceeded to drop the content off at the printer's facility. She always argued that I listened to her, but did not hear what she said. By that she meant I did not give consideration to what she said. As it turns out, I discovered years later, after having my hearing tested, that I literally do not hear women's higher-pitched voices. That is due to my playing in loud rock and R&B bands during my college years.

Several days later I got a call from the printer informing me that the men working the press refused to print the magazine because of the photograph my writer had protested. I tried to reason with the back shop, but got nowhere. There was no time to find another printer. I was on deadline with the distributer. If I missed the deadline, the issue would not go to newsstands all across the country. Finally, I relented and told them to crop the photograph and proceed with the printing. When the issue went onto the newsstand, I received a telephone call from an advertiser who cancelled all future advertisements because he didn't think the photograph had been cropped enough. Sometimes you just can't win. My new definition of compromise became *"an accommodation in which neither side is happy."*

Perhaps the most consequential issue of the magazine ever published was the February 1988 issue. With a cover story on Heart's Ann and Nancy Wilson, along with interviews with Waylon Jennings and Jackson Browne, it contained a retrospective on Otis Redding and the current survivors of Stax Records and an investigative article on BMI, the performance organization that collects royalties for songwriters.

All of the above made for great reading, but it was the investigative story on sexual harassment in the music industry that attracted the most attention. The idea for the story began when a distraught woman came into our office one day to speak to me. She told me she had been held down on the floor and sexually assaulted by a studio owner. Dazed, she confronted the man the next day, only to have her outrage rejected as unreasonable. When she pushed back against subsequent advances and complained about him walking around the office with his penis dangling from his fly, she was terminated.

"Is that normal?" she asked, tears streaming down her cheeks.

"Hell, no, it's not normal," I answered.

"Nancy," I called out to my assistant, "I have a women here I want you to talk to."

Nancy Randle, who ended up writing the story, took it from there. The article created quite a stir not just in Memphis but in other music cities where the subject simmered beneath the surface of day-to-day business.

ANGRY SONGWRITERS TAKE ON A GIANT

Nine-O-One
NETWORK™

February 1988

$2.50 USA
$3 Canada

SEXUAL HARASSMENT
in the music industry —
How to fight back

OTIS REDDING
Stax survivors
look back 20 years

JACKSON BROWNE
Is Nicaragua
the new Vietnam?

PLATINUM BLONDE
Canada's answer
to white funk

**WHO'S
HIP IN '88**
Julie Brown
Little John Chrisley
The Insiders
John Kilzer
Gary Moore
Vienna

A Hoss
Named
WAYLON

**HEART'S
ANN and NANCY
WILSON**
Broken Heart
until 1990?

BY THE TIME the April 1988 issue of *Nine-O-One* hit the stands, we knew the magazine was in serious trouble. Newsstand sales varied from month to month, depending on the race and gender of the cover story, something I had to learn from experience; but advertising revenue, although remaining constant, was not enough to cover printing and office payroll. Record labels remained loyal to the magazine with full-page ads, as well as a number of local Memphis advertisers such as Graceland and other music-related businesses. At one time we had as many as three advertising reps working at one time. Sadly, our best efforts were not enough. Also, there was a constant struggle with organized crime.

Once, while we were up against a critical deadline, the driver of the 18-wheeler taking our magazines to Chicago for distribution, pulled off the road and abandoned his truck and our magazines. That man had to be awfully afraid to do something like that. He just got out of the truck cab and started running along the highway, a target of mob intimidation.

The April issue, which featured Dan Fogelberg as the cover story, also contained interviews and photographs of Willie Nelson, the pop group YES, Kenny G, a look back at teen star Rick Nelson, Ry Cooder, Tanya Tucker, Kathy Mattea, and Sweethearts of the Rodeo. It was a great issue that would become known as the magazine's last.

AFTER *NINE-O-ONE CLOSED* its doors, I returned to *The Commercial Appeal* in mid-1990 to work twenty-four to thirty-two hours a week at the newspaper as a night copyeditor. About three months before I returned to the newspaper former editor Michael Grehl passed away. Since retiring from the newspaper, he had suffered from various ailments and was in and out of the hospital on a regular basis. He entered the hospital in late January with chronic kidney disease. Doctors could have extended his life with kidney dialysis, but he waved them away once it became clear to him that there was no hope for full recovery, or even much improvement.

When he passed away, his wife, Audrey, was at his bedside. His official cause of death was cardiac/respiratory arrest. Upon hearing of

Grehl's death, William R. Burleigh, executive vice present of the E.W. Scripps Company, which owned the newspaper at that time, said that Grehl was "simply the best newspaper editor I ever knew."

I would second that assessment. As an editor, Michael Grehl was a giant. His vision for Memphis was a positive force for change during an era when change was fiercely resisted by some elements of the city. He oversaw the newspaper as if he were a maestro, drawing masterful performances from the news and editorial staff that exceeded individual capabilities, making the whole stronger than any individual effort. There were plenty of good reporters, writers, photographers, and editors who served under him, but none who could measure up to him as a leader. Because of his forceful integrity, the newspaper's readership trusted the newspaper as a major institution that was devoted to the city's betterment.

I thank God I was able to work under his supervision for as long as I did. What he taught me was the equivalent of a Ph.D. education in journalism. We are not likely to see his like again, ever. He was only sixty-one at the time he died, much too young for a brilliant newspaperman.

Working on the night desk was an entirely different animal from working days in the editorial or news departments. Newspaper copyeditors are not terribly verbal, so it was not unusual to work several hours on the night shift without ever hearing a human voice, even though you are surrounded by people. Also, copyeditors tend to dress like field workers, unconcerned with how they looked. One of my co-workers always reported to work carrying a briefcase. One night I asked him what kind of paperwork he was carrying around. He twirled a twisted smile at me and opened the briefcase. Inside was a fully loaded 9mm automatic. Without saying a word, he closed the lid and walked away, placing the briefcase within reach of the computer at which he sat for eight hours a night.

Meanwhile, I broadened my free-lance reach to include moonlighting in music as well as editing copy at the newspaper. Through an unlikely series of events, I was approached in 1990 by a delegation of Russian Communists who had come to the United States from Moscow to network with music executives. They wanted to know if I would represent a rockabilly band named Mister Twister. They had talked to a Los Angeles producer, Richard Podolor, best known for his work with Three Dog Night, Alice Cooper and Black Oak Arkansas, about working with a hard-rock group, Galaxy. I spoke to Podolor. He said he had heard Galaxy perform in Los Angeles and was very interested in working with them.

I asked the Russians why they had contacted me. It was because of *Nine-O-One* magazine, they explained, which had been read, word for word, on underground radio in Moscow. I asked what they liked about it. "It represents everything we don't have but want," was the response. I was intrigued, so I asked the Russians to send tapes and photos of the band.

Trust me, I don't think *Nine-O-One* toppled Communism in Russia, but I think it played an important role in educating freedom-hungry Russians about the role of a free press in a democracy. The magazine also highlighted what foreigners have always loved best about America, its greatest contributions to the world—a free press, and rock 'n' roll, blues, jazz, and country music. Combined with a free press, all four music genres speak to the power of democracy and personal freedom.

Visually, Mister Twister was a throwback to the Fifties: black leather jackets, tattoos, lots of redneck biker attitude. Musically, they were a Russian version of the Stray Cats. They sent me a videotape of "Blue Suede Shoes." Valery Lysenko, the drummer, played standing up, rockabilly style, and bassist Oleg Usamov, a former English student at Moscow University, sang in decent enough English. I thought they might be salable to an American audience. Their spokesman was Erkin Touzmuhammad, a Moscow-based journalist. After a long series of telephone conversations, Erkin and I became friends.

Politically, the situation appealed to me very much, so I agreed to represent them. This was before the Second Revolution. The Soviet Union was still in place. Mister Twister and a number of other groups were under the direction of Ovanes Melik-Pashayev, one of the top record producers in the Soviet Union. His production company, the Moscow Rock

Organization, had created controversy in 1989 when it held a "Rock Fest" at the nuclear test site at Semipolatsinsk to protest nuclear testing. Not only were they playing Memphis music in Moscow nightclubs, they were duplicating American peace marches.

The Nashville *Tennessean* ran an item about Mister Twister in June 1990 that credited me with becoming "the first American music mogul to bring a Russian band to the U.S. to record." To pitch Mister Twister, I had to overcome the fact that Russia was still a Communist country and the band I was pitching played a form of music that was uniquely American and not the style of music that was at the top of the charts.

Russians singing rockabilly! The executives on Music Row, even the ones I had known for years, just didn't get it. They all passed on the group. I kept in touch with Erkin by fax and that Christmas he phoned from Moscow to wish me happy holidays. I told Erkin the prospects didn't look good for Mister Twister, but I promised to continue to look for openings for them.

ONE OF THE FIRST THINGS you realize when you are out on your own as an independent journalist is that you have to keep up with current events. On occasion you might interest an editor in an article that has a historical foundation, or perhaps a thoughtful analysis, but that doesn't happen often enough to fill up the grocery cart. Magazines and newspapers want today's news and tomorrow's trends.

In 1991 Memphis had a nationwide reputation that few local residents were aware of. Once labeled the "buckle" of the Bible Belt, Memphis had sucked in its economic gut, reluctantly tucked its Bibles into the nightstand drawer, and gone after a new label certain to make ripples all up and down the Mississippi River: Memphis had become the topless dancing capital of America.

This was both a news and a trend story that could perhaps become a book. In the 1970s I had received a review copy of a book titled *. . . a kind of life: Conversations in the Combat Zone* by photographer Roswell

Angier. It was a book of black-and-white photographs and text about Boston strippers in the district locals called the Combat Zone. It was interesting because of the fly-on-the-wall photography and gritty text.

First, I gathered relevant information for my pitch, beginning with Memphis' new reputation as the topless dancing capital of America. I spoke to Dr. Columbus Hopper, a sociology professor at the University of Mississippi, who had conducted research on the subject, and he told me that only San Francisco could compete with Memphis as a topless center. Assistant City Attorney Robert Rolwing agreed. "There's nowhere else that compares to Memphis, especially when it comes to openness—not even New Orleans or Las Vegas."

Memphis' newfound prominence as a topless center is reflected in sales figures reported to the county clerk's office. The previous year, seven clubs—Danny's, Gigi's Angels, Super Chics, Tiffany's Cabaret, Club Playboy, Doll house and Club Playhouse—reported gross sales of $3.6 million, making them second only to Graceland in tourism dollars generated in the city. Hopper explained it this way: "You can't make it as a tourist center unless you offer things people can't get at home. Tourists are the people most attracted to that sort of thing [adult entertainment]." They also are attracted to the willingness of Southern belles to give of themselves; that is, to allow their breasts to be fondled at bargain prices, twenty dollars a song to be exact.

I submitted the feature idea to a female editor at *The Commercial Appeal* and explained that I would tell the story through the eyes of the women, individuals I knew from my career as a social worker were most likely abused as children. She gave me a go-ahead and I began my interviews. If the story was as good as I thought, I figured I could parlay the feature into a book deal.

For the purpose of the interviews, I assumed the identity of Humphrey Bogart's character in *Maltese Falcon*, Sam Spade. At that time there were two rivalries involving topless clubs in the city. The owner of Danny's was Danny Owens and he also owned several other clubs. He was a complex man who donated lavishly to the arts in Memphis, especially the little theater, while operating one of the roughest clubs in the city. If you are familiar with the movie *Walking Tall*, he was the Buford Pusser of nightclub owners. He carried a big stick and he didn't take crap from anyone. In the early 1980s he was convicted of assault against half a dozen members of a motorcycle gang. Some people said he used a baseball bat. Most people would say it was a job well done, but not Memphis. Officials felt they had to take a stand to make the city safe for biker gangs, the overwhelming majority of whom were white.

I decided to start with Danny Owens. I went to the club one afternoon To meet him and was told that he would not be in until the evening. I returned that night around eight in full Sam Spade mode. I spotted the manager, a middle-aged woman with a pleasant personality, and waded through dozens of nimble women giving lap dances to a rather large contingent of Asian businessmen. The manager smiled when she saw me and walked toward me, her eyes telling me she had good news.

"He's in the back office," she said. "I'll take you to him."

We made our way back through a writhing mass of humanity to a door, which she rapped on and then said, "It's me."

Without hearing a response, she turned the knob and we walked into an office that had a desk and a couple of chairs, all surrounded by crates of liquor.

"This is the writer I told you about," she said.

Owens rose from behind the desk but did not offer his hand. I later learned he did not shake hands because of a gnarled thumb and forefinger. Because it embarrassed him when people fumbled to try to gripe his misshaped hand, he usually refrained from being the first to offer his hand.

I sat and then he sat.

"So what can I do for you?" he asked.

Despite his reputation, Owens was a pleasant man women probably found attractive. He had obviously built up his upper body, and the reason why was not hard to figure out, considering his occupation. Newspapers and district attorneys had labeled him a "kingpin' of the topless industry. He always denied that, and to me he looked more like a tough high school football coach. I told him I was writing a story about the clubs and their influence on tourism in the city, but I wanted to provide an inside look at the clubs by interviewing the dancers as well. They were a major part of the city's economy and yet no one knew much about them.

What I did not tell him or others who would be interviewed, mainly because it was none of their business and did not directly involve the clubs, was that I had a second goal that involved looking for a killer that might be known by the nickname of Helter Skelter.

A friend of mine, a twenty-something blonde with a pretty face and a big heart, once asked me what Helter Skelter meant. I told her it was an adverb that was associated with acting in a haphazard or confused manner. The question puzzled me, but I didn't ask why she wanted to know. She rebounded with, "What else does it mean?"

"It was the name of a Beatles album."

That wasn't the answer she wanted, either. I could tell by the frown on her face. "Doesn't it have something to do with death?"

"Charles Manson, you know who he was, don't you? He thought the Beatles song named 'Helter Skelter' forecast an interracial war in America. Yes, it is associated with death. His cult members wrote it in blood when they killed people. Why are you asking me this?"

"Because someone wrote it on a wall outside the window where I work so I would see it."

I told her it probably was just a coincidence; the sort of phrase that inspires graffiti artists, and she shouldn't worry about it. She started to respond, but then thought better of it and looked out the side window of the car, a look of sadness on her face. Within weeks she was dead, after allegedly falling to her death from a high rise building. The police declared it accidental. You can imagine what I thought about that.

In the months after her death, I became a believer in her premonition about death. She didn't know I knew she dated Black men, not Black men with professional jobs, but men who had street-level professions, certainly a motive for murder in race-obsessed Memphis. She was evicted from more than one apartment for entertaining Black men in her home.

She was a friend, not a partner in a serious relationship. There was a romantic beginning, but once she told me she had been sexually abused as a child—and I saw a framed photograph of her abuser, and he looked remarkably like me—I ended that part of our relationship and eased into the role of an abuse counselor. It would be an understatement to say she was trouble prone. Once I received a telephone call from her at the city jail, asking if I would pick her up. She had been taken in for a traffic violation and locked up for forty-eight hours and she didn't want her family to know. So she called me.

"Thank you," she said once I arrived, getting into the car only to ride in total silence until I stopped outside her apartment complex, at which time she got out of the car, closed the door and said, "Thank you," once again, and walked away, deep in thought.

On another occasion, the intercom buzzed at my apartment complex late one night. She had been out on a date, but decided she wanted to end the date. She told him she had a headache and wanted to go home. Instead, she asked him to drop her off at my complex. I buzzed her inside and she took the elevator up to my apartment and we talked until she felt it was safe to go home without being followed.

After her fall, I went to the hospital to see her. She was in a coma, but still alive. Her face was serene, unmarked by the violence of the fall, but her brow was somewhat wrinkled, as if she was experiencing thoughts and sensations that puzzled her. Her hand was still warm, but soon it would be icy. There was an open incision beneath her left ribcage so doctors could work on her spleen. She had broken arms and broken legs. Two nearby doctors argued over whether her broken bones should be set or left alone.

In a quiet voice, almost a whisper, I told her the pain she had experienced in life would soon be over and she would find herself in a world in which there was no remembrance of pain. She had gone through so much as a child of abuse, she had every right to withdraw into a dark view of life; but she chose to do the opposite, so much so that others often took advantage of her big-hearted approach to life. The visit left me with a feeling of dark desolation. I recalled a letter she had written me, thanking me for helping her understand her past. "You have seen me though some of the most sad, embarrassing times of my life," she wrote. "Yet I am so confused, scared inside . . . I want to get on with my life. The realization of this has been so long coming to me and accepting it so hard."

After she died, I spoke to her therapist, who told me that my advice and support about her traumatic childhood had helped her come to terms with her abuse. Well, good for me, but now I wanted to find her killer. The way I figured it, the killer was either a white racist male who was upset about her views on race, or it was a Black man, perhaps married, who had received money from her and did not want the transfer ever tracked back to him. Or the vengeful wife of a Black man she had dated.

As long as I was going to be hanging out at topless clubs for the story, I thought I would keep my eyes and ears open in the clubs for any reference to Helter Skelter. It could be a customer nicknamed Helter Skelter. Or it could be words in a tattoo. The dancers all considered me a "brainy" person because I wrote for a living. They often approached me for explanations for things they did not understand. I didn't suspect anyone associated with the clubs, but I knew there was no more culturally mobile group of people in Memphis than topless dancers. They showed up wherever the action was. They overheard conversations they shouldn't have on a regular basis.

Every good investigative reporter who works In an urban environment, if he knows what the hell he is doing, has a topless dancer or two on his confidential source list. I was hoping that at some point some cute little, half-naked thing would get in my face with a question and ask in a pouty, sing-song voice: "What does Helter Skelter mean?"

* * *

Owens and I talked a little while and then he called in his bookkeeper and asked her to make copies of any filings related to sales tax and liquor taxes, and she readily agreed. Before she left the room, he stopped her and asked me, "How many years you need that for? One, two, three?"

"One will be fine," I answered.

Owens nodded, telling her to send in the woman they called the housemother. Within minutes, the housemother was in the office.

"This man is going to be writing about us and he wants to talk to the girls. So why don't you set him up a table just inside the dressing room door and give him two chairs.

"Sure," she said.

"You can go with her," he said to me, then added, "Why don't you come out to the house early tomorrow afternoon, say one o'clock?"

I nodded.

"They'll give you directions before you leave today."

As I recall Owen's house was in a blue collar neighborhood. There was a metal gate and cinderblock walls inside the gate. I knocked on the door and Danny invited me into a large room, ostensibly the living room.

Every wall in the room was lined with mirrors. We sat on a couch and talked. As Owens explained the economics of his clubs to me, the clubs don't pay the dancers who work there a penny. The dancers pay the clubs a percentage of their earnings. Patrons don't pay a club cashier for table and lap dances. They give the money directly to the women, who at the end of the night settle up with the club owner. Dancers do not get paid for dancing on stage unless they are tipped by customers. The stage dancing is considered advertising for table dances, the real source of revenue for the dancers and income that was second to liquor sales for club owners. The average price for a table dance at the seven clubs then operating in Memphis was twenty dollars. The economics are impressive. Because the average length of a song is three minutes, dancers who do lap dances sit out the next song to look for a new customer. Then they perform another dance, talking in about $200 an hour.

Owens denies his girls turn tricks outside the club. "If a girl goes out to turn a trick, they may get $200 or even $300, and I don't hear from them for two or three days," explained Owens. "I'm against it anyway . . . Also, where would I get my percentage on that? Its economics . . . granted, I'm not stupid. You'll find one girl out of twenty who will try to beat the system. I'm not saying it doesn't happen every once in a while, but not like what they [the police] say."

Owens said he tries not to be bitter about the police raids on his clubs. "There's nothing illegal in what I do," he explained. "There may be something immoral in other peoples' minds, but I don't think so. The girls are human beings like anyone else, and they're there to make a living. The industry is not real bad like people think it is."

The tax statements and receipts Owens had copied for me showed that he paid $102,493 in sales tax the previous year on sales at Danny's, Gigi Angels, and Super Chics, which he managed but did not own. That figure represents reported sales of $1.3 million. Owens also paid $11,339 that year in state bar taxes.

Like the locker room of a college football team, the dressing room at Danny's ripples with bare, game-worthy flesh and half-time bravado. About a dozen women in varying stages of undress crowd the small room. The contrast between the stark metal lockers and the undulating stream of female pulchritude was startling.

"I can't believe it! I've only been here for an hour and a half and I've already made two hundred and fifty dollars. Not bad for a high schooler." *What! Did I hear that correctly?* The dark-eyed, eighteen-year-old with alabaster skin is wearing only a G-string. Waving a fistful of dollars at me, she leans against a locker, and then slides to the floor in a sitting position. She counts her money, slapping out the wrinkled wad of bills with the methodical motion of a veteran front porch whittler. I am seated nearby at a table, an island in a stream of sequins and broken promises.

"I didn't know you were in high school," says another dancer.

"Me and Heather both are in high school," answers Rachael without looking up from counting her money. Later, Rachel confides she and her best friend, Heather, are students at the same high school. They are part of the new breed of dancers who are filling the clubs in increasing numbers— young, middle-class suburbanites desensitized to public nudity by a lifetime of R-rated movies on cable TV. Rachel's father is a commercial airline pilot. When she is not dancing topless, Rachael is cruising the malls like most other teenagers, scoping out the shops, her pockets filled with wrinkled ten and twenty dollar bills.

Later, I talked to Owens about the high schoolers. He confirmed it and said he was proud to be helping the school find jobs for the girls. "The girls actually get classroom credit for working here," he said, beaming. He genuinely believed he was performing a civic duty.

I wasted no time stopping by the school. At the front desk, I asked where I could find the principal. She gave me directions and then picked up the phone to call him. "Yes, he's a newspaper reporter and he wants to talk to you about your work study program with Danny's."

She hung up the phone and smiled sweetly. "Just stick to that hallway and you can't miss him."

I walked down the hallway until I saw an office that was enclosed in glass. As I approached, I saw a man jump up from his desk and crouch down behind it. I tapped on the glass.

"I can see you behind the desk," I said. "Could we talk for just a minute?"

I walked over a few steps and tried the doorknob. It was locked.

"I just want to talk to you," I said again.

When I realized he had no intention of coming out from behind the desk, I left the school.

A day or two later, I pulled Rachael aside to talk to her about her after school job. I told her I didn't think it was such a good idea for a high schooler. Finally, I stopped talking because I could see she had stopped listening. She had been patiently and politely waiting for me to finish.

After a long, girlish sigh, she spoke her mind.

"You know, I'm a dancer, not a whore," she said in a monotone, smiling in a knowing way.

Class dismissed.

* * *

Next on my list of people to talk to was Steve Cooper, owner of Tiffany's Cabaret and fourteen other topless and rock clubs in Florida, Texas and Arizona. His manager, a man named Skinny, set up an appointment for me at Cooper's house, an East Memphis mansion with Greek columns. I never knew what his real name was, only that they called him Skinny because he once had been obese and lost a lot of weight. I was greeted in the driveway by Cooper's bodyguard, a tall, dark-haired man who clearly had once put in time as a bouncer.

Because Cooper was on the telephone, the bodyguard gave me a tour of the house, politely narrating the tour with comments he obviously felt would be of interest to a writer. Cooper had an extensive library, the shelves of which were constructed of aged oak.

"Every book on those shelves is a first edition," said the bodyguard, with considerable pride. "Ain't nothing's too good for the boss. He likes everything to be top quality. He's the classiest boss I ever had."

Then he showed me the gym, which was filled with expensive equipment.

"The boss likes to keep in shape," he said. "So do I. In my line of work you've got to be the best you can be or else . . ." His voice tapered off. By the time we made it downstairs to the sitting room, Cooper was off the phone, sitting quietly with a beverage in his hand. He rose when I entered the room and offered his hand. After a few pleasantries, we got down to business. Skinny already had briefed him on the theme of my article.

Cooper said there was no doubt about where his customers in Memphis come from: Mostly they are from out of town. Recently he started a promotion offering free admission to customers who left their

Dancers at Tiffany's Cabaret / Photo by James L. Dickerson

business cards. Out of approximately 6,500 cards handed in over a two-month period, he said, 75 percent had out-of-town addresses.

"When white-collar business people come to town you don't see them on Mud Island or on Beale Street," he said. "You see them in Tiffany's Cabaret. We're in the Top 20 in the nation."

Cooper said city officials understand the importance of the clubs to tourism and tax revenues, but don't want to admit it for fear of voters' wrath. "It's a good ole dog for the politicians to pick on. I don't blame them from the standpoint it keeps them in office. It helps bring in the votes of the 50-to-60 year old men and women. The closer you get to meeting God, the closer you come to voting to put them [clubs] out of business." Even so, said Cooper, the clubs are legal and should not be harassed simply because they are 'good ole dogs' to pick on."

One of the things I walked away with from the interview was Cooper's awareness of the miserable home lives most dancers experienced before ever showing up on his doorsteps. It was something he brought up himself. He showed convincing sensitivity to their abusive backgrounds.

283

I'm going out on a limb and say I think he really cares about his dancers. There was this one dancer that I witnessed him wooing in the club. One day I met the dancer and her young daughter at the Memphis Botanical Gardens to take pictures of them together. The dancer was dressed in her Sunday best and the little girl was dressed like the little girls I remembered being dressed for Easter in my childhood. Afterward, I received a call from Skinny asking if Steve could please see the pictures. I was happy to give him some photos of this beautiful mother and daughter. I told the mother and she shrugged and said, "Well, OK."

IN AUGUST 1977, U.S. Attorney Hickman Ewing was in a Memphis court trying Arthur Baldwin, the godfather of the Memphis topless industry at the time, on cocaine possession charges. At about 3 o'clock one afternoon while the court was in recess, someone came into the courtroom and dramatically announced that Elvis Presley had been taken to the hospital and had died.

"Baldwin, who had never said a word to me in his life, came over to me and said, 'Well, Mr. Ewing, I hate to wish ole Elvis any bad luck, but at least it will take the publicity off of me for a few days," Ewing recalled "And it did . . . but a few days later the jury convicted him."[38]

Subsequently, Baldwin offered to assist the government in exchange for leniency, and Ewing, a career prosecutor, literally went door to door trying to locate a federal agency willing to work with Baldwin. The FBI turned him down. So did the DEA. Ewing grew frustrated.

Then one day Ewing received a call from Baldwin. Two city electrical inspectors were at his new club, and they wanted money, payoffs, to approve the club. "What should I do?" asked Baldwin. It was the opening Ewing had been hoping for. He went to the FBI office, picked up the supervisor and took him to meet with Baldwin. As a result of that meeting, Baldwin started wearing a hidden tape recorder. It wasn't long before Ewing got another call from Baldwin. This time he reported that a man had offered to get a man out of prison for a price. The government supplied

Baldwin with a chauffeur, a man Baldwin knew was an undercover FBI special agent.

"Between August and December 1978 we started meeting with Fred Taylor, who was head of security for Governor Ray Blanton," said Ewing. "He's a Tennessee Highway Patrolman and sits at a desk in Blanton's office. He flies to Memphis on several occasions and was picked up by Baldwin's chauffeur, who took him to [Baldwin's club] and in that atmosphere they talked about getting people out of prison."

As a result of the Memphis topless nightclub connection, a legal counsel to Blanton was arrested with bribe money on him, leading to the hasty swearing in of Governor-elect Lamar Alexander three days early. "It is not the clubs themselves that are illegal," explained Ewing, "It is the activities the owners sometimes get into to protect their businesses that sometimes turn out to be illegal."

"Baldwin said, 'In Seattle, we took care of the beat cop and it worked its way up,'" said Ewing. "But in Memphis, a local lawyer says the way you do it, you take care of public officials and it works its way down. Meaning you contribute to their political campaigns."

Baldwin played a dangerous game with the U.S. Justice Department. Although it would take years for all the pieces to fall in place, investigators in Hamilton Country, Tennessee, an area that includes Chattanooga, disclosed in 2021 that Blanton's administration funded a contract murder of a witness cooperating with the feds. His name was Samuel Pettyjohn and he was a trusted ally of union boss Jimmy Hoffa. He was shot down by a gunman wearing blackface and a wig. Investigators attribute at least five murders associated with the investigation of Governor Blanton.[39]

Among those working with the feds in the late 1970s was a controversial Black Memphis family that got cold feet before they ever reached the testimony phase. It was with a member of this family, more than a decade after the investigation, that my Helter Skelter friend had a relationship that could have put her life at risk.

* * *

Tiffany, the saucy door girl at Tiffany's Cabaret
Photo by James L. Dickerson

I spent the entire summer alternating between Danny's and Tiffany's Cabaret. At Danny's I had my little table just inside the dressing room where dancers would sit and talk to me after making their rounds of the dance floor. You could always tell when they didn't sell many dances because they would enter the dressing room with their costume on. When they were selling dances right and left, they would come in wearing next to nothing, or sometimes nothing at all. I always regretted never getting someone to take a photograph of them seated at my tiny table, with me in a suit and tie, taking notes.

Once a dancer came in and plopped down at my table and said, "Now, where were we . . ." Suddenly, she looked down and gasped. Her breasts were covered with blood. "Oh my God, that last dance was for a man I think must have been stabbed."

She jumped up and grabbed a towel to wipe the blood from her chest.

"When you go out there you just never know what you're gonna get. Maybe he wanted to get one more dance before he croaked."

After she removed the blood from her chest, she looked up at me and smiled. She was pale as virgin butter.

"I'm ready now," she said, batting her eyes for dramatic effect.

After we spoke, we went out into the club together to find the man who had been stabbed. He was nowhere to be found. We followed the blood drops to the club entrance and then out into the parking lot where the trail ended.

"Oh, well," she said. "I guess he went somewhere else to die. I'll say this for him, he was a big tipper."

I suppose a lonely man could do worse in life than be comforted in his final hours by a lap dancer. It all depends on your perspective.

* * *

When you enter Tiffany's Cabaret, the first person you encounter is the door girl. She is the person who decides who gets into the club and who does not. There is a bouncer not too far away who has her back. On most days the door girl will be a tall, striking blonde with a Marilyn

Monroe vibe about her. Her voice is like a shot of fine whiskey, filled with promise in its smooth warmth. Her name is Tiffany, as in the club, or at least that is her name on this day. Tomorrow it could be something else. If you meet her approval, she will ask you for the five dollar admission fee or for one of the courtesy cards that the owner hands out to his friends.

Before going into the club I always amiably chatted with her for a while to get the latest news—and, believe me, in an establishment in which 99 percent of the staff was female, there was *always* news. One of the things that set Tiffany apart from the dancers and waitresses, who showed up for work in jeans or shorts before they changed into their glitzy costumes, was her penchant for wearing sun dresses, even in the winter.

In some ways Tiffany's Cabaret was like a church. There was music and a deep-seated longing for redemption and a laying on of hands and a pulpit from which promises were made to sinners who passed the collection plate from table to table. Many a man left in the wee hours of the morning feeling he had found salvation in the arms of a stranger who cared not one bit that he had failed in life at everything he had ever attempted—except this! In this he could buy his way to success!

I usually sat at the rear of the room with my back to the wall, the better to see everyone. Once Skinny took me into a room just off the dance floor to show me their surveillance system. There were twenty-five or thirty television screens on the wall catching images of everything taking place in the club. It was fascinating. It was so tech heavy you would think they were launching rockets to space from that room. Watching human behavior in that context, moving from screen to screen, was a surreal experience.

On another night I asked Skinny if I could get some screen time.

"Sure," he said, without hesitation. "You know the way."

The office had one desk behind which was a swivel chair. There were two or three additional chairs scattered about the room. Dominating the room was an entire wall of TV screens, all flickering with activity on the dance floor. I watched the screen for a while, looking for celebrities, then returned to the main room and sat down. Soon after that a big-eyed blonde dancer I had befriended walked by and stopped right in front of me, hands on hips.

"What were you doing in there?" she demanded, looking at me with Betty Davis eyes that grew even larger in the passion lights of the club.

"Just watching TV," I said matter-of-factly.

She leaned over close enough for me to smell her perfume and whispered with a surprising sense of urgency. "Don't ever, ever do that again," she said. "They keep things in there and if anything comes up missing they will blame you."

"Thanks," I said as she walked away, pausing to smile at a grey-haired man with a cane who, with a shaky hand, slipped ten dollars into her garter belt and slapped her on the ass, almost losing his balance. She kissed him on the cheek, helped steady him, and walked away.

Another night I was in the club, around midnight, when Skinny sauntered over to where I was seated, scanning the crowd for celebrities—the other night Frank Beard, the drummer for ZZ Top came in for an hour or so—and asked me if I would go with him someplace.

"Sure."

When we got outside, instead of going to his massive black Lincoln, Skinny walked over to a battered, nondescript late-model pickup truck that had been amateurishly painted mint green. He motioned for me to get in the truck; then he backed up to drive out of the parking lot. I didn't like the look of that, but what was I going to do? Tell him to let me out? That I'd rather walk? Not hardly. Whatever it was I knew I was in for a damned good adventure. I wasn't too concerned, though. I had a five-shot, .380 Bulldog automatic strapped to my left leg where I could get to it in a hurry.

We drove down a deserted industrial street where the flickering street lights became fewer and fewer and human beings were nowhere in sight. Then I realized where we were going. He was driving to Danny's, the main competition for Tiffany's Cabaret. As we approached the well-lighted club, he slowed down to check out the parking lot. The club entrance door opened and threw a swatch of bright light into the parking lot while releasing a blast of music. Skinny floored the slow-to-react accelerator and the truck sputtered and picked up speed and shimmied back into the dark end of the street.

"What in the hell was that all about?" I asked.

Skinny grinned like he had put something over on me, but said nothing.

"Why did you come here?" I asked.

"Because the boss wanted me to see how much business they were doing," he said. "And I knew they wouldn't kill me if they saw that you were with me."

"Skinny, you've got you some brains."

"I tell you what. You got to in this business."

Skinny laughed about that all the way back to the club. When we walked in the door I could tell the blonde dancer was relieved to see me come back again. She approached me rubbing the back of her neck. "Would you rub the back of my neck, please," she said in a voice loud enough for others to hear. "Must have twisted it on the pole."

"Sure," I said, half expecting some kind of setup. She wasn't *that* good of a friend. She viewed me as a puppy that had showed up on the front porch. Puppy pity would only get me so far. I looked around to see who was watching. Plenty of people had their eyes on us.

She pulled a chair over and sat in it with her back to me. A waitress brought her a soft drink in a glass. In between sips, she crushed ice with her molars, while under the illusion no one could hear her. Suddenly, she flicked back her hair, exposing her neck. As I began massaging her neck, she whispered so that no one could hear but me, "I worry about you sometimes. You think you know everything, but you don't."

"Baby, I know it is an unfriendly world."

"Just don't get smart with anybody. The boss likes you. Just keep it so he keeps on liking you. Got it?" She cut her pretty face around to look at me. She wore sincerity the way some women wear holiday makeup.

I smiled and nodded.

She raised her hand for a high five and I smacked it.

When I left that night, I walked around the building to the back parking lot, followed by two men from inside the club. I turned around just as they approached me. They were both young, late twenties. One of the men wore cowboy boots that were scuffed on the inside, leading me to believe he worked on a ranch.

"Excuse me, sir," the cowboy said.

"Yeah, what is it?"

"My buddy and me, we was just wondering if you are the boss of all these girls?"

"Why do you ask?"

"Because all the girls stop by to say hello to you. They don't do that for anyone else. We been watching you."

"Well, you got me there. You boys are plenty sharp."

The one who asked the question looked at the other man, grinning. "I told you."

Finally, the other man, who squinted one eye so it was nearly shut, said, "Man, you're the luckiest son of a bitch I know. Would you mind shaking my hand?"

I shook hands with both of them and they turned and staggered away, bickering as they talked over what they would do if they were the boss of the dancers. Before they got into their pickup truck they paused to wave one last goodbye.

I probably should explain that when you do investigative work like this, you pick up a survival instinct that you never knew you had. Most times you can size up a man in an instant. Something about the way he walks. The level of eye contact he makes. Whether he smiles or the way his face darkens. You've either got it or you don't. If you don't have it, maybe you should pick another profession, maybe see if you have the skills to be a florist.

* * *

By the time I finished writing the article on Memphis topless clubs, the editor who assigned the story to me had left the newspaper. I turned it in to another editor and he refused to honor the assignment. I looked into his background. What I learned from my sources was that the editor had a family member who was a dancer and the editor felt the story might displease someone in her profession. It is rare to encounter a corrupt editor, but they do exist. It is neither here nor there, but suffice it to say I had never cared for that particular person.

Surprisingly, neither Danny Owens nor Steve Cooper ever asked to read my article when I finished it. However, something interesting happened during this time. It was late at night and I was outside at the rear of the club talking to Skinny about something related to the article.

Suddenly, while we were talking, Skinny's head turned sharply and we saw Steve's limo pull into the parking lot and stop, headlights remaining on bright. We continued talking and then Skinny's head again turned to see a second limo turn into the parking lot.

"I've got to go," he said abruptly, turning toward the lights.

I left without looking back.

The following day, I received a call from Skinny. He asked if I would do him a favor.

"Sure, if I can," I said.

"We've got someone from out of town visiting us, and Steve wanted me to ask you if you minded meeting with him."

I paused a moment, going over in my mind all the possibilities. Finally, I figured the odds were in my favor on this, and I said, "I'd be glad to. Just tell me where to go and when."

Later that day I drove to an office off Poplar Avenue in Memphis. It was essentially a square concrete building with a drop chute built into the wall so that, I later learned, club managers could drop off each night's proceeds. The building was solid with very few windows. It reminded me of a bank, which, in fact, it was at one time. The door was locked, so I pushed the buzzer. Moments later I was asked who I was and then buzzed inside. I was greeted by a man in an expensive business suit. He was probably in his mid-to-late forties. He had a stern countenance, but he was affable enough in the way he shook hands with me. The more I looked at him, the more he looked like an accountant. We sat down and talked, first about Memphis, and then about the story I had written. He asked me questions and I told him what I had told Owens and Cooper. The story was not accusatory in any way. It was written to explain the business and the lifestyles of the women who worked in them, and, not unimportantly, what the businesses meant to tourism in the city.

The man in the suit asked if he could read it. Ordinarily, I would never entertain such a request, but in this case, because I gathered Steve Cooper must have had some out-of-town backers, the last thing I wanted to do was to get him in any trouble with his investors, who may have figured he gave me too much access to the clubs.

So, I pulled a copy of the story, which had been folded in two, from inside my jacket and handed it to him. He read the story all the way through, then carefully folded it back the way it was when I handed it to him, and he gave it back to me.

"Good story," he said, "But they'll never publish it."

"Why do you say that?"

He shook his head. "I'm just telling you it won't be published."

I stood up and we shook hands and he walked me to the door. Driving away, I concluded there were two possibilities. One, the man in the suit thought the story was not critical enough of the industry to be published by a local newspaper, or second, the editor who turned down the story had been influenced in some way, probably financially, not to publish it. I don't think it was the former, but you can decide for yourself.

I put a lot of work into a story that was not published by a newspaper, and I was unable to find a book publisher interested in taking it on. Nor was I ever able to locate the mysterious Helter Skelter. That was a big disappointment. Now it has been over thirty years since the murder. If the killer is still alive it is possible he will contact me and confess to ease the dark pain he must be feeling during the long nights of his wretched soul. He is my one-armed man, a fugitive still on the run.

I need to make it clear that neither Danny Owens nor Steve Cooper, both of whom gave me unrestricted access to their businesses, were in any way involved with what happened to my friend, nor did I see any evidence they operated their clubs in any way other than advertised. They made fortunes by selling large quantities of alcohol and by inviting beautiful women to come into their clubs to dance as independent contractors, happily accepting half of what they earned. They have very little overhead, and don't offer pensions or health insurance. They offer the two commodities that surveys show that Americans, male and female, most desire—booze and sexual fantasy. If you can't make money off that business model, there is no hope for you as a capitalist.

As far as stories that fall between the cracks, those are the breaks. To be a successful independent journalist, you have to take it on the chin from time to time. One thing about it. Life is never dull. About a year after I finished the project, my telephone rang at two in the morning. I looked at my clock and realized I was on dancer time.

"Hello."

"Hi, Jim, this is Desiree," a female voice said. "Do you remember me?"

She was one of the dancers I had interviewed.

"Of, course, how are you doing?"

"I'm good. I live in Las Vegas now and I work at the Crazy Horse Saloon."

I could hear loud music and crowd noises in the background.

"The reason I called is to ask your advice. I met this man in the club who says he is a famous photographer. He thinks I'm beautiful and he wants to take me out on the desert and take pictures of me. What should I do?"

"Are you crazy? Run like hell!"

"Really?"

"As fast as you can."

"OK. Thanks a lot, Jim. I knew you would know what to do."

EARLY IN 1992, I pitched an idea to *Playboy* magazine. I wondered if they would be interested in a Q & A interview with Democratic presidential candidate Bill Clinton. If you recall, I met him while he was governor of Arkansas. They were very interested. They had obtained a great deal of publicity out of their 1976 Q & A interview with Democratic candidate Jimmy Carter. In the interview Carter stated he had "looked upon a lot of women with lust." Then he went on to say, "I've committed adultery in my heart many times. This is something God recognizes I will do—and I have done it—and God forgives me for it."

Carter's presidential campaign imploded and exploded at the same moment once his comments were published. His office was flooded with calls from irate voters. The negative fallout almost sank his campaign. However, he obviously recovered from it because he was subsequently elected president. Politicians all over America learned a lesson from Carter's interview. Namely, to never do an interview with a men's magazine during an election campaign. After the election, perhaps; but definitely not during the campaign. What happened to Carter was every candidate's nightmare.

I figured Clinton, at some point in his life, probably was a *Playboy* subscriber and would try to talk himself into doing the interview. *Playboy* sent me a contract for the interview that offered more money than many journalists receive for book advances. I began by calling Clinton's campaign headquarters in Little Rock. I asked to speak to his campaign manager, David Wilhelm. I identified myself and explained that I had written editorials that supported several of Clinton's initiatives as governor. Then I made a request that I am certain he never expected to hear. Would Bill Clinton do a Q & A interview for *Playboy?*

There was a long pause.

"I don't know," he said, finally.

"I know what you're thinking," I said. "You're thinking Jimmy Carter. But because I would be responsible for asking the questions, I can tell you now that I have absolutely no interest in knowing if Bill Clinton has ever lusted in his heart for a woman other than Hillary."

Wilhelm laughed.

"I also might add that *Playboy* readership is composed mostly of white males, an audience your campaign will need to target. They have been trending Republican, you know."

"Tell you what," he said. "I'll talk to him and we will get back in touch with you."

Two or three days later, I received a telephone call from George Stephanopoulos, who was the chief strategist and spokesperson for the campaign. He told me that Clinton was interested in thinking about it, but they wanted to get deeper into the campaign before saying yes or no.

"I'll check with you in a few weeks."

"Fine," he said.

MEMPHIS IN MAY is the city's showcase festival. It is a month-long affair that celebrates a different country each year. Toward the end of the month, the festival culminates with an outdoor festival that features dozens of big-name blues and rock artists. The honored country for 1993 was Russia. Not all Memphians were happy with the choice—there were rumblings of displeasure from the political right—but most Memphians were eager to learn more about Russia.

At the time I signed Mister Twister in 1990, Mikhail Gorbachev was president of the Russian Federation and the General Secretary of the Communist Party. I have always been curious about Russia. In the late 1950s or early 1960s, the American and Soviet governments entered into an agreement whereby citizens in both countries could receive picture magazines depicting everyday life in the other country. The American magazine, which was translated into Russian, was named *American Life* and the Soviet magazine, which was translated into English, was named

Soviet Life.

As a high school student in Mississippi, I subscribed to *Soviet Life*, no doubt causing apoplexy among local postal workers. However, I balanced that subscription with subscriptions to *Progressive Farmer*, *Sports Afield*, *Field and Stream*, *Ammo*, *Life* magazine, and *Look* magazine. I was a prolific reader. By the end of my first year in college, I was also subscribing to the *New Republic* and the *Progressive*.

I tell you all that to let you know I was smart enough to ask my Russian contact exactly where my faxes to Russia were ending up. There was a long pause. I heard whispers in the background. Finally, my contact said, "the Russian White House."

"The White House!" I said.

I knew the White House was the seat of government for the Russian Federation, which was to say the Communist Party.

"Really?" I asked.

"Yes. We could not communicate with you outside of our government."

I wanted to ask if President Gorbachev was in the vicinity, but I didn't for obvious reasons.

"That's fine," I told him, realizing rock 'n' roll transcended political ideologies.

We exchanged faxes and telephone calls into early 1991.

Then in June 1991 an amazing thing happened. Boris Yeltsin was elected president of Russia. He promptly dismantled communism and replaced it with capitalism. In the blink of an eye, the Soviet Union was dissolved and members of the Communist Party were no longer given reserved parking spaces at the White House.

The next time my fax machine rang and printed out a letter, I promptly faxed my contact back, "Where the hell is the fax machine now?"

The answer came quickly. "We are still at the White House."

That was good news the way I saw it. I could not help but wonder what role my magazine and rock 'n' roll had played in this new Russian revolution.

It was not long before Memphis In May officials called to ask if I could book a Russian band for the festival. I considered Mister Twister until I learned from Erkin that Galaxy was recording in New York under a new name, Red Rage. In Moscow, the band had sold an unprecedented 1.2 million albums. Erkin said the earlier deal with Podolor had fallen through and they now were working with a New York production company. The band did not have a work visa and could not be compensated for their performance in Memphis, but they agreed to perform in exchange for transportation and expenses.

Erkin told me the band members were getting stir crazy in Brighton Beach and were eager to get out of town. After hearing that, I got busy arranging their travel plans. When they arrived at the Memphis airport, I was there to greet them, along with van drivers from Memphis In May. After two years of telephone conversations, it was my first face-to-face meeting with Erkin. Physically, he was the opposite of what I had envisioned. He had dark hair and a full beard. He didn't look like the Russians you saw in James Bond movies. He more accurately resembled the rugged mountain fighters we came to know in subsequent years during the war in Afghanistan. It was nice to finally match a face to a voice. With him, to my delight, were the producer Ovanes and his lovely wife and their pretty nineteen-year-old daughter. They had flown in from Moscow to attend the festival. Five band members and a brooding delegation from Ovanes's Brighton Beach organization rounded out the group.

Ovanes fascinated me. He was heavy set, with his dark, thinning hair pulled back into a ponytail; he was probably in his mid-forties. He began as a record producer, at a time when it was a rarity, and through the years had developed a Quincy Jones-type of reputation. After the second revolution, when the walls of communism toppled, Ovanes became an entrepreneur. He took advantage of the changing economics of Russia to become a world-class trader of consumer goods.

Moscow Rock Organization had several bands and solo artists on its

Russia's Red Rage

roster; I was told I could represent any of them I wished. I considered the possibility of using Memphis as a headquarters for new Russian talent. Red Rage performed on both days of the festival. It was hot and the band members were miserable, but they gave a solid performance and the crowd loved their high-energy act. Because none of the band members spoke English, all communications with the Memphis sound crew had to go through Ovanes or Erkin.

Slava Sintchouk, the lead vocalist, had given up a career as a boxer for rock 'n' roll. He was well over six-feet tall, weighed about 220, and, on stage, showed the aggressive posturing of a professional fighter. Before joining Red Rage, Oleg Hovrin, the drummer, played drums in a folk group while serving in the Red Army in East Germany. Guitarist Dmitri Sharayev was a top-ranked session player in Moscow. All the band members had long, shoulder-length hair, like their American counterparts, and they constantly asked me the same question, using one of the few English phrases they knew: "Where's the women?"

299

Everyone in the group was outgoing, with the exception of the Brighton Beach delegation. They remained in the background and complained about the heat. I stayed with the group when they performed and traveled with them in the Memphis in May van from the hotel to the festival grounds. All the van drivers were local volunteers, and, as the trips back and forth increased, I noticed more of the drivers were female.

One perky young driver, a university student with bright-blue eyes and a cover-girl face, sent a hormonal tremor through the van when she turned around and asked Erkin, in that syrupy voice indigenous to Southern womanhood: "*Honey, how do you say fuck in Russian?*"

"*Ebat*," he answered, smiling.

Hearing that, one of the non-English speaking band members looked at Erkin in horror, thinking he had propositioned the driver in the crudest way possible. Erkin explained and he relaxed.

On their last night in Memphis, I asked the boys in the band how they had fared with Memphis belles. They laughed. As they told it, several young women showed up at the hotel during their stay to exchange sex for the Russian words for each sex act they performed. When it came to sex, the Russians proved they had a genius for manipulating naïve Americans. Apparently, everyone got what they wanted and deserved. With Red Rage, Memphis coeds had forged their own "hands on" style of Russian *détente*.

IN JUNE 1993, I began looking for more free-lance opportunities. I was intrigued by an article I read about a new entertainment magazine named *CoverStory*. It was owned by the Thomson newspaper chain, a Canadian family-owned company that began with the purchase of a newspaper in Timmins, Ontario and grew into a large media company. At one time the company owned fifteen newspapers in the United Kingdom including the *Times of London*. They also purchased the *Vancouver Sun*, the *Winnipeg Free Press*, and the Toronto *Globe and Mail*, the major morning newspaper in Canada and one of my favorites even though I was a book critic for the *Toronto Star*. By the time I approached them, they owned about 100 newspapers in the United States.

CoverStory was a weekly newsprint entertainment magazine that was carried by the newspapers in the Thomson chain. Each week it was sent to the newspapers as a magazine which could be inserted into the newspaper or broken up into individual stories that could be inserted around advertising if the newspaper wanted to use the stories in that manner. I thought it was a brilliant concept. It was the sort of magazine that I probably could get a lot of assignments from.

I wrote a letter to the editor, Joe Yanarella, who called me when he received the letter. After our conversation, I knew I would be doing a lot of work for them. At the time, the IRS had seized the possessions of Jerry Lee Lewis for nonpayment of taxes. They were scheduled to be auctioned off in a few days. I told him that Lewis's wife would be there and I could try to talk to her. "The Killer" was living in exile in Ireland, putting as much distance as he could from himself and the IRS.

Yanarella was ecstatic, his voice indicating he felt he had pulled the slot machine lever and won the jackpot. There are few things an editor likes more than a well-connected writer who makes them look good. I was given the assignment for the Lewis story, along with assignments for interviews with Dian Parkinson, the co-star of "The Price is Right," who had sued host Bob Barker for sexual harassment, and Carroll O'Connor, whose television show "In the Heat of the Night," was a big hit at the time.

I arrived early at the IRS auction for items seized at the home of Jerry Lee Lewis and ran into his wife Kerrie Lewis, whom I had met several times before. The Lewis household items were stored in a vacant building that looked like it might have been a former grocery store. I walked up and down the aisles with her as she surveyed her seized belongings. I couldn't even imagine what it must have felt like to see cherished items she had used every day for practical purposes, all on display to be sold by the government.

At one point, she spotted a toy that had belonged to their six-year-old son, Jerry Lee Lewis III. Suddenly, she burst into tears. She called one of the auction officers over and tearfully explained that it was Little Jerry's favorite toy. Could she please have it to give to him? All these years later, I don't recall if the man gave her the toy. I doubt it since he would have had no authority to release what was then IRS property, other than to sell it at the auction. It goes without saying that my *CoverStory* article was sympathetic to Jerry Lee Lewis.

From the Killer I moved on to Dian Parkinson, the gorgeous blonde on "The Price is Right." She had made headlines after she resigned and filed a sexual harassment lawsuit against host Bob Barker, accusing him of making her his personal sex slave. The things he made her do were unspeakable, she claimed. Neither she nor her attorney specified the particular sex acts, but from their descriptions of some of the acts as having endangered her health, I take it he had demanded unprotected sex in general.

Not surprisingly, Barker denied everything. After a two-year legal battle the lawsuit was dropped because of her mounting legal expenses. It is very difficult to win a lawsuit against someone who has more money than you do. She helped finance her lawsuit by appearing in a nude spread in *Playboy* and by filming a nude video that was sold by the magazine.

Almost thirty years after the interview, I recall that she had a great voice. It was sexy without being overtly so. I asked her if she would record a voicemail greeting for my answering machine. She said she would be happy to. It went something like this:

Hello, this is Dian Parkinson. James is very, very busy at the moment. If you would like to leave a message, please do so at the beep.

You wouldn't believe how many hang-up calls I received because people liked her voice so much they called over and over again.

Up to that point I think my favorite interview was with Carroll O'Connor, because of his role as Archie Bunker in "All in the Family," and more recently because of his role as the police chief in the television hit, "In the Heat of the Night." I still try to catch re-runs whenever I can.

The series began with a racially motivated joust between a white police chief and a Black chief of detectives in the fictitious town of Sparta, Mississippi. It was a do-over from the movie of the same name starring Sidney Poitier and Rod Steiger. It was a powerful movie that created a demand for the television series. However, producers quickly learned that it could not sustain that narrow premise year after year.

"You couldn't go week in, week out, having a racial bone of contention between the chief and the Black chief of investigators, so some accommodation had to be made," O'Connor explained to me. "That was an untenable series idea. It had to change. How it was going to change nobody really knew. My first producers seemed not to know; they seemed to want to write the racial strain into every episode."

That strain was the reason O'Connor took over as executive producer of the series. Under his direction the show added a subplot that involved his character's romantic relationship with a Black woman, the first black member of the city council. O'Connor's view of racial harmony carried over to off-camera personnel as well.

"I think we may be the only film producing unit that has nearly as many Black people behind the camera as white. Our cameraman is Black. We have a Black assistant director. People say, 'What does that have to do with the nature of the work you do on screen?' Nothing direct. And yet there is some kind of feeling that permeates the whole operation."

Because I had lived in two Mississippi towns similar to the fictional Sparta, we talked about that and the experiences O'Connor had filming the show in Georgia. He said he experienced for himself many of the changes, positive and negative, that had taken place in the South during that time.

"It's the difference between night and day," he explained. "I've seen it happen myself. I didn't have to read about it. I wanted to make the show the real South. I wasn't going to sugar coat anything."

Another thing that interested me about "In the Heat of the Night," besides Carroll O'Connor, was writer/co-producer Mitch Schneider. One of the things that helped my magazine, *Nine-O-One*, be successful editorially was the great interviews and cover stories, many of which were obtained through the efforts of Mitch Schneider who was at that time a Hollywood publicist in partnership with legendary Hollywood publicist Michael Levine, who helped as well with the magazine. Levine later became a friend of mine, one of the few people who called on a regular basis to check on me during a health crisis in the mid-2010s. Those telephone calls were greatly appreciated.

LATE IN 1992 I PITCHED an investigative story idea to the editors at *Omni* magazine. I wanted to investigate the murders or suspected murders of several historical figures whose deaths were cloaked in mystery—U.S. President Zachary Taylor (was he poisoned?), explorer Meriwether Lewis (was it suicide or murder?), Texas outlaw Wild Bill Longley (did he escape the hangman's noose and live out his life in obscurity?). Written early in 1993 and published in the August 1993 issue of *Omni*, the story began:

An electric saw buzzed through a lead container that had been sealed for 150 years. Slowly, the liner lid was removed, exposing the remains of Zachary Taylor, the twelfth president of the United States. Face to face with the former president, a blue-ribbon panel of investigators was surprised to see a thick mass of dark hair and a large cloth bow under the chin. Since the president's visit was meant to be brief, his hosts went to work immediately.

University of Florida forensic anthropologist Bill Maples method-ically cut away the president's clothing, finding abundant body hair beneath the one-piece, pleated shroud. Then he took hair, nail, and tissue samples, hoping they would prove whether the president had succumbed to arsenic poisoning or died of natural causes.

Ghoulish? Perhaps to most. But to a forensic sleuth like Maples, who focuses on murders and other mysteries a century or more old, exhuming and examining the remains of celebrities from presidents to political assassins is business as usual.

Interestingly, shortly after it was published, Professor Starrs made an appeal to the superintendent of the Natchez Trace Parkway in Tupelo, Mississippi, for permission to exhume the remains of Meriwether Lewis. In the package of data he submitted was a copy of the *Omni* magazine article that contained my story. He was not given permission to exhume the body, but he was given permission to use ground penetrating radar to find the explorer's remains since it was non-invasive to the gravesite.

When I learned Starrs was going to the Meriwether Lewis Monument, which was located near the Grinder's Stand area, about twenty-five miles from Nashville, I asked *The Commercial Appeal* if they wanted a story about the visit. I was told they already had given the assignment to one of their feature writers, Bill Thomas. I offered to go along as the photographer and that was agreeable. When I mentioned my involvement with this story to Thomas, he invited me to accompany him in his camper. That way we could spend the night in a camping area near the monument. If there was going to be any grave robbing, we would be right there on the scene.

When we arrived, Professor Stars was already at the monument, sizing it up. We introduced ourselves and he was surprised to see me there as the photographer. I had interviewed him for the *Omni* story over the telephone, so we had never met. He was pleasant enough, and bubbling with excitement over being able to use the ground penetrating radar device. I was a little disappointed in the actual device because it looked sort of like a 1950s-style lawn mower. The technician pushed and pulled the device back and forth in predetermined quadrants that resembled nothing quite so much as it did a teenager mowing his parents' lawn. It was anti-climactic, to say the least.

From what I understood, the radar detected human remains beneath the slab that supported the monument. I may have heard him wrong, but it was my understanding the famous explorer's feet and legs were protruding from the slab like the legs of a mechanic who had slid beneath a car.

Bill got the story; I got the photographs.

A couple of months after that, one of my friends at the newspaper, Brown Burnett, sent me a printout of a story that had run on the Associated Press wire. It was my *Omni* article that the magazine was offering to sell to newspapers as a Sunday feature. They could purchase the entire article or parts of it. They were selling it as if it was a frosted cake in a deli they were selling by the piece. Of course, I didn't earn a penny from any of those sales, but they did pay me handsomely for the original.

THE NINE-O-ONE NETWORK suite of offices had been on the ground floor of a high rise building that had apartments on the upper floors and offices on the ground floors. One of the offices next to ours was a beauty shop owned by Vikki Rollins. Over the months and then years, we became close friends. At one point, her future husband, Emmo Hein, worked for me as the marketing director for a radio syndication I owned. He was a great guy whose quirky sense of humor allowed him to fit in well with everyone else. I had known Vikki for a long time before I learned that her father was the legendary Scotty Moore, Elvis Presley's first guitarist.

In the beginning, Elvis was a revolutionary, a threat to the world order. He wasn't the genius behind the music—Scotty Moore was responsible for that—but he had a velvety voice, an unforgettable face, and charisma in spades. When Elvis first recorded at Sun Records Studio in Memphis, it was Scotty who breathed musical life into their first recordings. He was one of the founders of rock 'n' roll. It was Scotty Moore who did the delicate guitar picking on the earliest records and then contributed the throbbing power chords on "Jailhouse Rock" that transformed American music. In reality, Scotty built the Wonder Horse that Elvis rode until its heart gave out. What were the odds that the daughter of rock royalty worked next door?

One day in 1993 Vikki asked me if I had ever written about her father, who had lived in Nashville for the past several decades. I replied that I had not. Like everyone else, I assumed he had passed away years ago.

"Why don't I call him and see if he'll talk to you?"

To my surprise, Scotty Moore agreed to talk to me, even though he had turned down interview requests for years. He made it clear he was only doing it because his daughter had pressured him into doing it. Once I set up the date for the interview, I contacted *CoverStory* and asked if they were interested in publishing the first interview with Scotty Moore in twenty years. Of course, they were interested.

At first I thought it odd that Scotty wanted to meet at a tape duplication business not far from Music Row. It was not until after I arrived that I learned he owned the business in partnership with Gail Pollock, the woman I met when I arrived at the business. She walked me over to the plant that was just next door.

Scotty was inside tossing tape cassettes to a Lab named Miss Babe that promptly retrieved them and returned them to Scotty and then patiently waited for the next toss. I knew right away I was going to like this guy. He was friendly, unpretentious, and open to any excuse for a good laugh. *So, this is the guy*, I thought, *who was Elvis' right-hand man in the early days of rock 'n' roll!*

Scotty explained to me that he had done no interviews or photographs in twenty-four years, at least none related to Elvis Presley. He had found a rock to crawl under and saw no reason to leave it. "When Elvis died, the phone started ringing off the wall," he explained. "Everyone came out of the woodwork wanting interviews. So for years I didn't do any."

All that had changed recently when he returned to the famed Sun Records studio in Memphis to record an album with his old friend Carl Perkins. They titled the album *706 Reunion. A Sentimental Journey*. Recording in the studio again, he explained, "got the juices flowing."

At sixty-one, he looked trim and healthy. We went outside and I took photographs of him playing one of the Gibson guitars he had made famous. In between songs, we talked about Elvis.

If Elvis' movie career had been better managed, he said, the

Scotty Moore on the day the author first met him in Nashville
Photo by James L Dickerson

entertainer might be alive today. "That was something he could have done, even when he got fat," said Scotty, who had appeared in four of Elvis' movies, including *Jailhouse Rock* and *G.I. Blues*. "Elvis was vain and I don't think he could have grown old gracefully just doing the concert thing. Movies would have given him another avenue."

I wondered if he had followed music during the years he had hung up his guitar. Not surprisingly, the answer was yes. "There is some of it I like. One of my favorites is Vince Gill. He's a great guitar player."

When I returned to Memphis, I told Vikki, who I might add is a real sweetheart of a person, what a wonderful time I had with her dad.

"It's time for him to stop being a hermit," she said, beaming.

It was my interview with Scotty that made me realize it was time for me to relocate to Nashville. The opportunities for a free-lance journalist were more plentiful in Nashville than in Memphis—and the city offered a level of creative energy that simply did not exist in Memphis.

BACK IN JUNE 1992 I had pitched another idea to *Playboy* magazine. This one was for a "Girls of Country Music" pictorial for which I would write a text about how women had changed country music in recent years. In addition to the women featured in the pictorial, I explained in my pitch, "I could talk to recording artists about how women entertainers have injected sex appeal into what used to be an denim overalls and bandana image. That way the reader would get a complete package about some of his favorite entertainers."

The idea floated around the *Playboy* offices for a couple of years; then one day I heard from Jeff Cohen, a revered photography editor of the magazine, who gave me an assignment in February 1994 to go to Nashville as a talent scout to determine if such a story could be put together. My advantage at this point was that I had been around female country singers and musicians enough to know that most had private lives that were vastly different from their public personas. I knew any number of them who would not bat an eye at posing for *Playboy*, especially those who routinely showed up for interviews sleepy eyed and wearing see-through shirts. The only question was whether their corporate handlers would let them.

People become country music stars for different reasons. Men chase that dream either because they have a deep-seated love of the music, or because they think it is an easy way to become wealthy, or because they see it as a means of obtaining unlimited sex for the rest of their lives. I have encountered very few female entertainers who became country music stars to get rich or to get unlimited sex (that is usually not a problem). Instead, they either have a lifelong love of the music, or they crave the adulation that comes with stardom.

My biggest problem would be in overcoming the Nashville music industry's reputation for demanding sexual favors in exchange for auditions or meetings with important people. I will never forget the time one of my female ad reps, a very attractive, twenty-something woman, went to Nashville for a few days to sell ads to people in the music business.

When she returned to Memphis, she told me the story of calling on a music executive and being escorted into his office, where she sat across the desk from him to give her energetic pitch for why he needed to advertise in *Nine-O-One*. After giving her presentation, she asked, "So, would you be interested?"

Leaned back in his chair, he listened patiently, as she later related to me, only to respond with a question of his own.

"Have you ever fucked on a tour bus?"

"What?"

"I have access to (here he gave the name of a current female star) tour bus. We could go in there and fuck, and then we could go have lunch anyplace you like. How 'bout it, babe?"

My ad rep, who had nerves of forged steel, rose to her feet and calmly said, "Thank you for the generous offer, but I have already fucked once today and that's quite enough."

Then she let herself out of the office and crossed him off the list.

It was *that* reputation the city had that I had to be cognizant of to put together an article for *Playboy*. Before leaving for Nashville, I called a number of the publicists that I had been working with for years to tell them about the project. Some turned me down flat. Others agreed to meet with me to discuss the project. Before leaving Memphis, I reserved a room at the Vanderbilt Hotel, at the time the best in the city (subsequently, it changed hands and is now Loew's Vanderbilt Hotel).

When I arrived at the hotel to check in, I was informed by the desk clerk they had upgraded my room at no extra cost to me. I didn't ask why. I knew why. "The phone has been ringing constantly," said the bright-eyed young man. "What do you want *me* to tell the women when they call?"

I thought a moment.

"Tell them I will start interviewing at two o'clock. When they arrive, would you be kind enough to direct them to my room?"

"Sure," he said, his eyes wandering over to the lobby. "Those women over there have been waiting for you for hours."

"Thanks," I answered.

I walked across the lobby to meet a half dozen beautiful, smartly dressed women. Some were sitting. Other were standing. Those who were standing had their arms folded across their midsection the way women do when they are nervous. I introduced myself and invited them to return at two o'clock. As I turned, one of the women stopped me by reaching out to touch my arm. "I have a sound check at that time," she said, almost in a whisper. "Would it be possible for me to come up and talk to you now?"

She had enormous blue eyes and a terribly earnest look on her face.

"I'm sorry, but I'm not organized yet."

"Thanks. I'll give the band a case of beer and I'll see you later."

The first thing I had to do when I got into my room was figure out how I was going to accomplish this assignment. Luckily, the room layout proved to be assignment friendly. As I entered the room, there was a wall to the right and an open door to the bathroom to the left. The bathroom was three times the size of a normal hotel bathroom and it was furnished with a padded bench and a vanity counter that was surrounded by mirrors.

Beyond the bathroom was a bedroom three times the size of a normal hotel bedroom, well furnished with snacks and beverages, and a rather large couch. The layout was perfect. I now had a plan.

At five after two o'clock I realized no one had knocked on my door.

I opened the door and looked out into the hallway. I was shocked to see a line of beautiful women that stretched from my door all the way down the hall, and then around the corner for an indeterminate distance.

"Hi," said the woman who was first in line. "Looks like I got here first."

I smiled and called out down the line, "Are there any of you ladies who would be able to stay for a couple of hours?"

Three women raised their well-manicured hands.

"Come with me," I said, escorting them into the room.

Once inside I explained I would interview the candidates and then take some test photographs. I asked the chosen three if they would mind sticking around a while so that the other women would be comfortable doing their interviews and photos. That was agreeable to all three women.

Yes, I wanted the women to be comfortable, but I also wanted witnesses present while I carried out this assignment. Because I didn't ask any personal questions, none of the interviews needed to be private. All I asked for was their name, contact information and their involvement in the music industry. Once I did that, I asked if they would be kind enough to pose for a test photograph, following up with the final question, "Would you be comfortable with nudity?"

"We all have seen *Playboy*," one woman smirked. "None of us fell off a turnip truck, you know."

With my volunteers in place, I proceeded to interview and then photograph the Chosen Three, after which they made themselves comfortable as I proceeded to open the door to the masses. Waiting outside in the hallway were singers, guitarists, female trios, background singers, fiddle players, country music video stars, and even a Ph.D. in education who was pursuing a new career as a vocalist.

The protocol was this: I interviewed each woman, notepad in hand, and then invited them into my "studio" (provided they were agreeable to being photographed), after which they entered the bathroom and undressed (I never instructed them on how much to undress). My camera was set up on a tripod in the hallway. I never entered the bathroom. I only gave verbal instructions from the hallway.

At all times I was visible to the women waiting in the bedroom and at no time was the privacy of the women in the bathroom ever violated by the others in the room. They were all calm, cool and collected, undressing as if I were not even there, hanging their articles of clothing on a hook, only to then ask the same question: "Now what do you want me to do?"

During the session, the hotel phone rang. I asked the woman on the counter top to sit tight while I answered the phone. "No problem," said the woman, who had the patience of an angel. "I'm good."

The caller was Jeff Cohen himself. He called to say he was going to catch a plane for Nashville and would see me tonight. He suggested I plan on having dinner with him that night. He explained he had never left the office to go on an assignment before, but this one was so interesting he had to see it for himself. I certainly could understand that.

As I hung up, I glanced out the window and saw that it was snowing quite heavily.

"How long has that been going on?" I asked no one in particular.

"Ever since we started," said one of my volunteer assistants. "You didn't know that?"

I nodded, no.

"The hotel is the only place downtown that has electrical power. They must have a generator."

Once I finished the session and everyone was leaving the room, a set of twins I had interviewed asked if they could stay a while to watch their favorite soap opera since they couldn't do it at home because of the power outage.

"We only want TV," one of the twins explained. "No funny

business."

So, I sat on the edge of the bed, between the twins, watching a soap opera I had never before seen. It was an interesting experience. When it was over, the twins gave me a high-five and left and I took a nice nap.

* * *

Jeff Cohen called me when he checked into the hotel and we left to go to dinner. I suggested an Italian restaurant that was within walking distance of the hotel. The legendary editor wasn't at all what I expected. He was unpretentious, highly intelligent, and soft-spoken. With his dark beard, he looked more like a rabbi than any photographer I had ever known. His specialty at the magazine was the "Girls of …" features that focused on non-professional models, usually women of college age.

Over dinner, he told me he had two reasons for coming to Nashville. The first was to check on the progress of the country music feature. The other was to look for talent among the women I had interviewed for an upcoming feature on older women. He was looking for women in their forties and fifties. Had I encountered any he needed to meet? In fact, I had interviewed a forty-year-old redhead with blue eyes, I thought he might be interested in. He asked me to call her the next day to ask if she would come to the hotel to meet him. No problem.

After the main course, he ordered dessert and asked me to share the ultra-fancy chocolate dish with him. I readily agreed, though with some discomfort. Up until that point the only thing I had ever shared with another man was a bottle of scotch. So there we sat, each person with a spoon in hand, alternating dips into a six-inch pile of something chocolate. It is something I don't think I will ever forget. I was sharing dessert with a man who probably had seen more naked women than any other male in recorded history.

When we returned to the hotel, we hung out in the bar for several hours, talking. Every time an attractive woman entered the bar, I found myself watching his eyes to determine if he was evaluating her as *Playboy* material. He noticed every woman who walked into the bar, but never once did he ever comment on any of them.

The following morning I called the woman I had described to him for his "seniors" project and asked her to stop by the hotel because my editor was there and wanted to meet her. She said she would be happy to. Later, when I heard the knock at the door, I noticed that Cohen walked over to the window. It was overcast from the snow and he could see the entrance door in the reflection from the window.

I opened the door and invited her inside. As we walked through the hallway, Cohen stayed glued to the window, evaluating the woman in her reflection. I said, "Jeff, this is the woman I told you about."

With that he turned and began a conversation with her. She was a 40-year-old redhead with blues eyes. He was friendly, but I could tell by his facial expression and his questions that he was not all that interested. After she left, he merely said she was not what he was looking for. I felt badly for her, but there was nothing I could do. I thought she was attractive. She just wasn't in the Pamela Anderson mold.

Later, I ran into her at a music event and she told me she had told a photographer friend of hers about meeting Jeff Cohen. At, first he didn't believe her. He asked her to describe him. She did and he said, "Yes, that's him. I can't believe you got to meet him. He is a legendary photo editor and photographer. I would give my right arm just to shake his hand. I can't believe he came to Nashville. From what I hear, he hardly ever leaves Chicago. You don't know how lucky you are."

For lunch, I had an appointment with Ronna Reeves' manager. Ronna was a very attractive, twenty-six-year-old brunette who had been signed to Mercury Records for several years. After the release of her first album, she was nominated—but did not win in the new talent category of the Academy of Country Music Awards. I met her manager at a steak house near Music Row. I think Jeff Cohen went with me, but I am not sure.

At that time in her career Reeves was struggling for relevance. Competition among female artists was fierce. Her manager felt that *Playboy* exposure might be just the thing she needed to boost her career.

We talked and I explained that as far as photos were concerned she would have a choice about what she would feel comfortable doing. He agreed to discuss it with her, but she must have nixed the idea because I never heard back from him. The following year, she was dropped from her record label and was unable to sign with another major. In music, an artist's talent is always going to be secondary to his/her hunger for success.

After Jeff left that afternoon to return to Chicago, I had meetings with Tanya Tucker's publicist, who had discussed the project with her but had not yet received a firm yes or no. I was to consider her still a possibility.

Then I met with Nikki Nelson, the new lead singer of Highway 101. It was a surreal experience because we sat on a couch, side-by-side with a *Playboy* opened across our combined laps so that she could go through it and point out photos she might be willing to do.

"I would do this one."

"I would never do anything like that."

"This one has possibilities."

And so it went.

At the conclusion of our meeting, I went to meet with the original singer for Highway 101, Paulette Carlson, whom I considered one of the most beautiful women in country music. If she agreed, it would help pull the whole project together. However, the meeting was for me to interview her for *Cover Story* magazine and to take photographs of her for the feature. It was during the photo session that I brought up the subject of *Playboy* with Paulette and her manager, John Bumgardner, who was present for the interview.

"I might do that," she said, looking at John.

I suggested she go through magazines and clip photos she would be comfortable duplicating. She accepted that as a good alternative to a potentially embarrassing conversation about body parts.

Before leaving Nashville, I heard rumors that the country music establishment was outraged at my plans for a *Playboy* pictorial. The Nashville suits didn't much care for Gonzo journalism. Because of that, I

Country recording artist Paulette Carlson
Photo by James L. Dickerson

set up a meeting with longtime friend Rick Blackburn, formerly the head of CBS Records, but now the president of Atlantic Records in Nashville. He had gone home for the day, but generously returned to his office to see me. As a former president of the Country Music Association, he had a lot of clout in the music industry. I explained my situation to him and he made some suggestions that I followed. Before leaving, I told him I had one more request. "If the record labels are in the process of lynching me, would you mind rescuing me?" He promised he would.

After I returned to Memphis, I received a letter from Bumgardner with clippings Paulette had selected for me. Yes, she would be in *Playboy* if the poses depicted in the clippings were agreeable to the editors. The clippings depicted tasteful nudity, only without clear views of private parts. Glory be, that worked for me!

Although I had left Nashville behind, the uproar among the suits there continued unabated in my absence. Not long after my return, I received a telephone call from Jeff Cohen who informed me that the project had been cancelled. Sony Records had appealed to its parent company for help. As a result, *Playboy* received a telephone call from Sony threatening to cancel all advertising of its electronic products if *Playboy* proceeded with the country music pictorial. So much for the First Amendment and the rights of women to make their own decisions. It was a good example of how multi-national corporations that operate in the United States can have a negative influence on free speech.

EMPOWERED by my grand adventure in Nashville, I got back in touch with George Stephanopoules about the *Playboy* interview with Bill Clinton. At the time of my first conversation with the campaign, rumors were circulating that a wannabe singer named Gennifer Flowers was going to go public about an alleged twelve-year sexual relationship with Bill Clinton. By the time I returned to Memphis from the "Girls of Country Music" feature, Flowers had given interviews on the subject. Nonetheless, Stephanopoules was still reluctant to say no. He suggested I give it more time to see how things developed. We talked around Flowers, without mentioning her name, but we both understood we were talking about the same situation.

After concluding the conversation, I pondered my increasingly bleak situation. I lost an opportunity to do the country music feature because of Japanese fears that naked women would devalue their investment in the music industry. Now I realized that same fear of naked women was likely to torpedo my interview with Bill Clinton. I never realized naked women were such a threat to established order.

Clearly, I needed a bold plan to have any chance of putting Bill Clinton into a magazine with naked women. I decided to confront the situation head-on with a visit to the campaign headquarters to give performance journalism an opportunity to save the day. I would do what Gonzo journalist Hunter S. Thompson had become famous for doing. I didn't want to become famous. I just wanted the interview.

If I was going to roleplay, I needed a role model. I narrowed it down between Clint Eastwood and Johnny Cash. Eastwood had that boyish smile, but he also could be pretty intimidating when the role called for it. Johnny Cash had the same smile-thing going for him, but he was intimidating in a different way. When he mustered an intimidating countenance he conjured up more of a wrathful God than a back alley roustabout. I decided to go with Cash.

I put on black jeans, black boots, a black overcoat I had brought back from Canada, and topped all that off with a black fedora. Then I drove to Little Rock from Memphis, my fedora riding shotgun on the car seat next to me. I had no problem finding the campaign office. I parked outside and fitted the fedora atop my head, nudging the brim first to the left, then down, so that it would cover my eyes, allowing only my lips and my black moustache to be visible. I remembered Johnny had done that once on an album cover. I took a deep breath and breezed inside the front office, stepping up to the receptionist's desk.

"Honey, is George in today?" I asked. I don't ordinarily talk like that, but in Gonzo journalism you have to be true to the role you are playing.

She was a bright-eyed young thing that I bet Bill Clinton himself had picked out.

"Yes, he is," she answered.

"He's expecting me. Which office is he in?"

"Just down that hall over there, third door on the right."

"Thank you, honey."

My boots had solid heels and leather soles, and I worked that as I walked the hallway, the sound of my footsteps clearly audible all over the building, my overcoat flowing behind me as if I were walking into a strong wind. When I got to the third door, I didn't bother to knock. I just walked right in. Two men were standing next to a desk, looking at a piece of paper rolled out on the desk.

"How you boys doing?" I asked, closing the door behind me. "I'm James L. Dickerson. I've been talking to a fellow named George about a *Playboy* interview with Mr. Clinton."

"I'm George," he said, turning to face me.

"I just thought maybe we might could make some progress if we spoke face to face."

"'Sure" he said, looking at the other man. "This is David Wilhelm, the campaign manager."

As I approached the desk, both men extended their arms to shake hands. "Why don't you pull up a chair?"

I sat in a chair across from the desk, lifting my hat brim enough for them to see my eyes. I was hoping to create a spaghetti western atmosphere.

"I'm sure you have been following the problem that we are dealing with now," said George.

"Yes, I have, but I can't conceive of your closing up shop just because of that."

"So, why don't you tell us why Bill should do the interview," said Wilhelm.

I went over the demographic issue in more detail, and I pointed out that American society had changed a great deal since the mid-1970s when Jimmy Carter did his interview. Appearing in the magazine was not so much a stigma now. I pointed out some of my favorite *Playboy* interviews: Albert Schweitzer, Princess Grace, George McGovern, Martin Luther King, and Johnny Carson, to name a few.

"I think it would put him in pretty good company," said George.

George looked at David, who said, "James doesn't impress me as the type to do ambush journalism."

"I agree," said George. "Tell you what, James, keep in touch and we'll just play this by ear."

I promised to stay in touch.

As I was headed out, David said, "Very impressive entrance."

I turned and waved good-bye with a farewell twirl of my hand and a Johnny Cash grin. I was the only one hearing the spaghetti western music as I made my exit, but that was all right. The fantasy added a certain outlaw deliberation to my step. Hell, I had once been the target of a right-wing, black ops abduction scheme—if that doesn't give me the right to have spaghetti western music in my soundtrack, what does?

Shania Twain-Mercury Records-photo by Albert Sanchez

Chapter 12

Nashville, Tennessee

When I relocated to Nashville in the spring of 1994, I leased a two-story townhouse on top of a towering, heavily treed hill. If I turned to the left after leaving the complex, I entered Bellevue, where Vince Gill and his wife Janice had lived when I did the feature article on them. If I turned to the right, I encountered a spectacular Buddhist Temple and beyond it a countryside of gently rolling hills. I had a screened porch off the living room, peering into a wily forest teeming with wildlife. Upstairs in the master bedroom was a bathroom with a tub the size of a small automobile.

By that time I owned a white Miata. Driving around Memphis with the top down was not much of a thrill. But driving on the hilly roads that surrounded Nashville, with the wind blowing into my face, was a really nice experience. I did it whenever I could. I had visited Nashville a lot over the years, but I soon found out that living there full-time offered new adventures.

One day I drove to a copy center to make copies of some proposals. I wasn't there long, when a beautiful woman walked over to the machine next to mine. Right away, I knew it was Jennifer O'Neill, who had starred in the movie *Summer of '42*. I couldn't believe it. I had loved that movie. I love most coming-of-age movies. At that point in my life, I was still coming of age myself.

"Pardon me," it all began. "Should this go face up or face down?"

"Face down," I replied authoritatively, thinking *I can't believe I told Jennifer O'Neill to do anything face down.*

She was friendly and approachable, and we made small talk that was often punctuated with laughter. She was forty-six at that time, but she was every bit as beautiful as she was at twenty-six when she made the movie. Because she was making copies of a children's book in manuscript, we talked about it. It was not until she left that I realized I had the perfect excuse to invite her to lunch—to talk about her book for *CoverStory*. But I froze in my tracks and merely babbled, "Good luck."

Not to worry. I would soon have another beautiful woman reaching out to shake my hand. Once I was settled in Nashville I wasted no time getting into the swing of things. Now when I wanted to interview an artist in person I didn't have to drive 200 miles to do it. I simply drove downtown and walked into the room.

One day I received a press release in the mail about a Canadian singer who had driven from Ontario to Nashville to find a career as a country music recording artist. She had the unusual name of Shania Twain. Because she had signed with Mercury Records, I called their publicist Sandy Neese, a very likeable woman who worked overtime to help the artists assigned to her. She set up an interview for me with Shania Twain to take place in their office.

From the photos I had received, I knew Shania Twain was very attractive, but I was totally unprepared for what I saw when I was introduced to her at the Mercury Records office. The photos didn't do her justice. Hands down, she was the most stunning woman I had ever met in my life. Her skin was flawless, and her smile was totally engaging. Some

324

women shake hands with their elbow at their side. Shania reached out strongly with a straightened arm to grasp my hand. I held her hand a moment or two longer than I should have to establish an interview rhythm.

After pleasantries, we went to the board room and re-arranged chairs from the massive table so that we would be facing each other on the same side. I told her how pleased I was to see someone from Canada because I had lived there, and she told me how relieved she was to talk to someone who knew what "back home" was like for her.

I couldn't wait to hear her answer to my first question: "So, what was your biggest cultural shock about moving to Nashville?"

"When I first moved here, going into the grocery and everything was real different because of the labelling and things like that," she said, eyes sparkling. "You've got thirty or fifty different types of beans here."

Now she is relaxed, laughing aloud, probably because I am a "home boy" of sorts.

She continues with her story of adjusting to life in Nashville.

"It was, 'Where do I start? What kind of butter do I buy? Just going to a restaurant was different. If you order a tea and you don't specify you want a hot tea, they give you iced tea. I'm not used to that, you know. I ordered a country steak one time. At home country fried steak would be a piece of ham. Here it's deep-fried beefsteak that's battered. I couldn't believe it. I said, 'I can't eat this!' What is it? And it had white gravy on it."

She continued laughing, practically slapping her thigh. The laughter made her complexion glow. It was at that precise moment that something happened I had never before seen during an interview. Suddenly, she looked startled and gently pushed her chair away from me, a stricken look on her face. All conversation came to an abrupt halt. Seconds went by. She lost eye contact with me, and turned her head to the side, exhaling several deep breaths. The social worker in me knew that she was having a panic attack. She had let her guard down with me by making fun of Southern food and it frightened her that she had done it. She felt vulnerable. I slowly pushed my chair back as well so there would be more space between us. I never wrote about her panic attack, but later on, as her career soared, I read stories about how uncomfortable she was doing interviews with radio DJs in cramped sound booths.

When I moved the conversation along to her newly released album, she immediately settled down. She confessed that she had written only one song on the album, but hoped to do more writing on her second album.

"I'm a serious writer," she explained. "This deal came together quite quickly, so I didn't really have a lot of time to write for it. You've got to concentrate on those things. You can't just throw them together.'"

Shania's first single did not attract a lot of attention, but her second single, "Dance With the One Who Brought You," attracted attention as much for the video as for the song itself. The video was directed by actor Sean Penn. She went to Los Angeles to shoot the video, but it only took one day to complete. Shania loved the experience of doing something so different from what she was used to doing.

"Everyone expects me to say that Sean Penn has a really bad temper and is aggressive, but he's actually just a very easygoing guy and I've made a good friend out of it all. He wasn't intimidating', the way I thought he'd be. He is a great director. He just makes you feel comfortable."

Now that she felt she was back in control of her surroundings, she returned to the point where she had lost control in an attempt to make things right. She desperately did not want to come across as ungrateful for her success. That was not who she was.

"I certainly appreciate what's happening to me," she said, re-establishing strong eye contact with me, and broadcasting a radiant smile that danced on tip-toe across the three-foot divide between us. "If you go through hardships growing up, you really learn to appreciate the good things in life. Sometimes I wore rubber boots at 40 below through the winter. When you live your life only worrying about the necessities, and not about the extras, your priorities change."

When that first interview concluded, I had no doubt she was going to be a superstar. It was not so much because of her first album. I was unimpressed by the songs, but blown over by her voice and her personality. When I interview someone who is destined for greatness I can usually feel it in the force of their personality. Facial and conversational energy speak volumes to me, thanks to a previous social work career in which the lives of homeless children depended on my ability to correctly decipher body language.

True to her word, when her second album came out she had written or co-written (with the man she eventually would marry) all of the songs. The album was a huge success and made her the most successful female country artist in history. I did several more interviews with her, but she didn't remain in Nashville long, soon moving to a farm in St. Regis Falls, New York. By then we had developed a rapport that enabled her to give me her telephone number at the farm so that I could call her whenever I had questions. Perhaps she was so kind and generous because I had backed away when I saw her in emotional distress.

* * *

On another assignment for *CoverStory*, I arrived at the Music Row office of country artist Lari White whose single, "Wishes," had recently reached Number 1 on *Billboard's* "Heatseekers Chart."

I walked in on Lari and a photographer trying their best to get a good photograph of the T-shirt *Billboard* had sent her in recognition of her achievement. She kept holding the T-shirt up to her chest, and the photographer kept giving instructions to her on how to turn this way and that way, but nothing was working out. Holding up a T-shirt is not the same as wearing it.

Finally, Lari took matters into her own hands and hurried into the adjacent kitchen to boldly slip off her shirt and pull on the T-shirt. She returned with a big smile on her face that flashed in sync with the strobe lights of the camera. The photographer also smiled because now a T-shirt photograph made sense to him, especially braless. After the photo shoot, Lari and I retreated to the dining room to talk about her career. There had been nothing sudden about her brush with instant stardom.

"I had seen *Coal Miner's Daughter*, so I thought, shoot, I'll just get in my car and go traipsing around the country. Of course, I was naïve."

Everyone was nice to her, but there was no way they were going to play her song just because she walked in the door. Of course, by the time Lari hit the road, playlists were made by "experts" who lived in the big cities. Local radio stations had little control over what they played.

It was not until earlier in the year in which we spoke that she knew she had made it. That happened when she was booked for an appearance on *The Late Show with David Letterman*. "I was really nervous. Much more for that performance than any show I had ever done. It was one of those 'you've been preparing your whole life to be there' things."

Greatly to her relief, Letterman only flubbed her name once. "He said it beautifully, except for the one time. If he had said Lorrie, everyone in the country would have called me Lorrie for the rest of my life. I was so thrilled I could have kissed him on the mouth."

After that initial brush with success, Lari's music career, at least with the major record labels, faltered four years later and she explored other opportunities, this time in acting. In 1999 she landed the role of Bettina in the 2000 film *Cast Away*. She was the vivacious and irresistible welder of angel wings who sent the FedEx package that Tom Hanks held onto while stranded on an island. Lari appeared in the first and the final scenes of the movie. She died eight years later of peritoneal cancer.

* * *

I didn't limit myself to country artists when writing for *CoverStory*. Sometimes I ventured into television. One of the television shows that year that I enjoyed was "Lois and Clark: The New Adventures of Superman," which starred Dean Cain as Superman and Teri Hatcher as Lois Lane.

I was delighted to get the assignment to interview Teri Hatcher. I found her to be personable and flirtatious, two qualities that can give energy to an interview. In addition it would give me the opportunity to slip into my Clark Kent persona, a transition I knew would increase her comfort level during the interview.

To research her role as a newspaper reporter, she told me she spent the day with a female reporter at the *Los Angeles Times*. What she saw was not exactly what she expected.

"She was really terrific. She was sort of young and worked on the metro section, which is hard news. One of the things that surprised me was that her desk was so messy. I was surprised there was mold growing out of her coffee cup. Files were everywhere. So I guess I brought some of those qualities to Lois. I don't know if anyone ever notices, but there's a dead plant on Lois' desk. I love it that she has no time to water the plant."

In addition to high ratings, "Lois & Clark" garnered talk among television observers about, for lack of a better phrase, the liberation of Lois Lane's chest. At the beginning of the season, Lois was dressed so conservatively she almost presented a unisex image. Recent episodes show Lois to be quite well endowed.

"What gives?" I asked.

You had to know I would ask.

Hatcher burst into laughter because the question was so unexpected.

Afraid I had crossed the fragile line of good taste, I pleaded insanity and blamed my lapse in judgment on a faulty imagination.

"No, no," Hatcher said with a laugh. "It's not your imagination. You're not crazy. I don't think it was anything purposeful. You know, like show Teri Hatcher's chest—there was no note that came down from the network—but you're right, there were a couple of episodes where . . ." Hatcher's voice trailed off. "You know, where it was appropriate."

Does that mean there will be even more liberation in future episodes, I asked, the hope in my voice obvious.

"I think Lois is back to dressing the way she was in the beginning," Hatcher lectured, with just a hint of devilment in her voice.

The resulting article was so titillating it was used as the cover story.

ANOTHER COVER STORY article written for *CoverStory* was my interview with supermodel Claudia Schiffer. By now, you must be concluding that I only interview beautiful women. In the 1980s I found myself interviewing mostly male entertainers. But by the 1990s, female recording artists were surging on the charts. By the mid-1990s they had out-charted males for the first time in history. Naturally, I wanted to write about a trend that was on the cutting age. Women were hot in the 2000s.

As far as Teri Hatcher and Claudia Schiffer are concerned, what magazine writer would not want to talk to them? Because Claudia was in Paris when I needed to talk to her—and the magazine was not inclined to fly me there—the interview took place via telephone, with her in her Paris apartment and me sitting atop the highest hill in Nashville. At the time she was twenty-three and easily one of the highest paid models in history.

Interestingly, she has avoided scandal by living a squeaky-clean private life. She doesn't drink, smoke or keep late hours. Her first steady boyfriend was aspiring screenwriter Bill Goins and they dated for four years. More recently she was linked to Prince Albert of Monaco. At the time of our interview she was engaged to master illusionist David Copperfield. About him, she said: "For me the most important thing in a relationship is that you have two people who understand each other. If there is a problem, the most important thing is to sit down and talk about it and find a solution."

Claudia met Copperfield when she attended one of his performances. He spotted her in the audience and invited her to participate in an illusion. She did not hesitate to join him onstage.

"I was impressed by his sense of humor and by his charm," she explained to me. "He is a very romantic person. He's very sensual, and very passionate in that when we both like something—and I'm the same way—we want to know everything about it. We want to know the most we can do with it."

Claudia described herself as being a very shy person, and then tried to walk it back, perhaps feeling she had misrepresented herself. "I'm not as shy as I used to be. Over the years, with all the experience of traveling,

I am almost over it."

One aspect of her success she still has a difficult time getting used to is the necessity of travelling with bodyguards. "You can't just do [spontaneous] things when you want to. You have to make a schedule. You always have to tell somebody what you are going to do."

At the end of the interview, I decided to test her sense of humor.

"Tell me, Claudia," I said, "What are you wearing? Enquiring minds want to know."

She laughed, paused a minute to think it over, and then said, her voice quite flirtatious and somewhat breathy, "I am wearing a very soft, V-neck, black sweater (by her tone I knew she was cuddling herself), ballerinas . . . and tight, tight, tight black pants." Then she giggled. "And, oh yes, my hair is in a ponytail." It was her G-rated version of phone sex.

"Thank you, Claudia," I said. "You have made my day. Now I will go take a cold shower."

"And you have made mine as well (pause)," she said, her voice softening. "Goodnight." There was just a lingering whisper of seduction in her voice as the line went dead.

I DON'T RECALL how I ever found out about Lt. Colonel Sarah Deal, the first female pilot to fly for the U.S. Marine Corps, but I do know I was intrigued enough to get an assignment from *CoverStory* to travel to Florida in 1994 to write an article about her. I went through channels to get in touch with her at the Naval Air Station in Pensacola. Being in a magazine feature article is one of those things that Marines cannot decide for themselves. They can say no, of course, without prior permission, but if they want to say yes, it goes up the chain of command, all the way to the Pentagon, where it has to be approved at the U.S. Navy office. After going in circles for days, I got the go-ahead from the top brass at the Pentagon and struck out for the cornerstone of the infamous Florida Panhandle.

When I pulled up at the guard station at the entrance to the Pensacola naval base, I identified myself and told them who I was there to see. The guard, who looked young enough to be a First Class Boy Scout, said, "Just follow this road to the water and park your vehicle."

"Thanks," I answered. "But where will I find Miss Deal?"

"Second Lieutenant Deal," he corrected in a staccato voice. Then with a smile, continued, "Don't worry. She'll find you."

I was struggling to find the right persona. Johnny Cash or Clint Eastwood would not work in this situation. Neither would my old standby, Humphrey Bogart's Sam Spade. I kept driving until I saw water. Then I parked my car and looked out at the gulf. It was a sunny day that seemed filled with promise. I briefly considered adopting the persona of John Wayne in 1942's *Flying Tigers*. But then I considered that she was way too young to appreciate that and it would fall flat. I decided to go with mild-mannered newspaper reporter Clark Kent. More than one woman in my life has sent me greeting cards addressed to Clark Kent.

Suddenly, I heard a female voice.

I turned and saw a 24-year-old woman running in my direction. She had on a USMC T-shirt, shorts, and running shoes. I was amazed at how young and fit she was. She had a familiar and confident aura about her. She was without makeup, yet her skin seemed glamor-magazine flawless. Almost any Hollywood director worth his salt would have picked her for the girl next door. But she wasn't the girl next door; she was at a naval base being trained in the T-34C Turbo Mentor, something that had never before happened for a female. Prior to that she was stationed at the U.S. naval base at Millington, just north of Memphis, where she was enrolled in air traffic control school. While there, she learned the defense department had decided to accept women for pilot training by the U. S. Marines. She raised her hand and then packed her bags for Florida.

Face to face, she made strong eye contact and reached out to shake hands. We stood in the parking lot for a while, talking and taking photographs of her doing her exercises. Then I asked if she minded changing into her dress uniform so I could get some photographs of her with the planes she flew. She wasn't gone long. When she returned, I saw

Sarah Deal- Photo by James L. Dickerson

that there was nothing remotely out of place on her uniform. Nor was there a single wrinkle. She was perfection.

During our conversation, I asked about her tastes in music and she said her favorite group was Diamond Rio, a country music band that was playing in Pensacola that night at the county fair. I recently had interviewed them for *CoverStory*. I made a mental note to call the band's manager when I returned to the hotel.

With the interviewed wrapped up, I asked if she would like to attend the fair that night.

"Sure," she said without hesitation.

For some reason I was not surprised.

We made a date for me to pick her up at seven. I returned to my hotel, eager to talk to Diamond Rio's manager. I told him about Deal and he said to just bring her backstage before they performed so they could meet her. The manager was as excited about the meeting as I was.

I picked her up at the appointed time and as we drove past the gate I noticed the guards were grinning ear to ear. Because we had time to kill before the performance—she still had no idea of the surprise I had planned for her—we walked about the fairgrounds, eating fair food and playing the games in the booths.

We arrived at the performance venue early and sat in the grandstand for a while, until I saw some activity backstage. Then I took her by the hand and said, "Let's go."

'Where?" she asked, standing but not resisting my gentle tug.

I led her down to the stage and knocked on the back door. The manager opened the door and smiled when he saw me.

"Come on in," he said. "Everybody's here."

We were greeted by the entire band.

Sarah was barely able to contain her excitement as they introduced themselves, one by one.

"You guys are my heroes," she told them, to which the lead singer responded, "No, you are *our* hero."

I snapped a picture and we returned to the stands to listen to the show.

On the way back to the naval base, we pulled over to get ice cream at what appeared to be a teen hangout. Leaning against my vehicle on a balmy night, with a juke box playing an Eagles song in the background, we talked about music, flying, and how proud she was to be the first woman to earn wings in the U. S. Marine Corps.

To bystanders, it was just a guy and a younger woman, eating ice cream, only the girl was a navy pilot. I took her back to the naval base and asked if she would like for me to pick her up in the morning to take her back to my hotel so that I could get some photographs on the balcony of the Gulf in the background.

Again, to my surprise, she said, "Sure."

The next day when I picked her up, she was back in her shorts, looking comfortable, with her flowing blonde hair falling to her shoulders. She looked like a million bucks. When we arrived at the hotel, I noticed her give several furtive glances as we got out of the car.

"Is anything wrong?" I asked.

"Those two men over there getting out of the car are from base security. They followed us here."

"Oh," I said.

We were sitting out on the balcony, watching the waves crash, when I noticed two burly men across the way on the balcony of a unit that appeared to be on the same floor. Although they were at the beach, they were dressed in civilian suits. One of the men looked at us through binoculars.

"Look," I said. "Those two gay men are looking at us."

She laughed. "Those aren't gay men. They're from NCIS. They are here to keep an eye on me . . . and you! Not too subtle, are they?"

Within two years Sarah would earn her wings, becoming the Marine Corps' first female aviator. She was subsequently assigned to Marine Heavy Helicopter Squadron 466 as a CH-53E pilot and deployed to Afghanistan during Operation Enduring Freedom, providing support to the troops on the ground. She turned out to be one bad-ass pilot.

AFTER COVERSTORY MAGAZINE underwent editorial changes, trimmed back its freelance material, and finally ceased publication, I pondered my choices. I could prepare a stack of resumes and send them to newspapers around the country. Or I could target several magazines that could provide me with a living wage. Because my *Playboy* assignment for an interview with Bill Clinton, now President Bill Clinton, was ongoing, I wrote to George Stephanopoulos at the White House to see if Clinton and his advisors had warmed up yet to doing the interview.

Clinton was about to begin the third year of his first term. Certainly he had nothing at this point to fear from a right-wing backlash over answering a few questions for the world's leading men's magazine. George responded that he had brought the request up again, but everyone was still apprehensive about doing the interview. He promised to keep me updated on any progress.

I corresponded with my editor at *Playboy* and he said for me to just keep him updated. I thought about that for a while and then pitched my editor an alternative interview. Why not do the *Playboy* interview with the president's chief domestic advisor, George Stephanopoulos?

My editor thought that was a splendid idea. George had himself become something of a media sensation as a presidential advisor. His comments would be of interest to most readers of the magazine. *Playboy* sent me a separate contract for that interview and I wrote a letter to George, addressed to the White House, notifying him of the new assignment. Would he be interested in answering 100 or so questions for *Playboy*?

After a couple of weeks with no response, I was getting discouraged when the telephone rang one morning. On the other end of the line was George Stephanopoulos. He explained that although he wanted very much to do the interview, the consensus at the White House was that no one close to the president should appear in the magazine. We had a nice conversation. George is a very media-friendly guy. And when he turned me down I could tell he felt badly about it. The telephone call from George was just one of several surprise callers I had while living in that townhouse. Another call that caught me off guard was one from Rolling Stone Keith Richards. More about that call later.

For a long time I sat in my favorite chair, gazing out the window while listening to one Beatles album after another. I distinctly remember listening to their *Rubber Soul* album, when an idea popped into my head that would change my life. *Why not write a non-fiction book? Why not boost my journalism career to the next level?* As a journalist my list of possibilities was unlimited.

A good journalist can write a book on any topic that can be researched for factual information. When I thought about the advice I had most often heard from successful writers, it was to write about something you already know from personal experience. That led me to conclude the best book I could write would be a history of Memphis music.

Long before I went through that baptism of fire in Memphis over *The Commercial Appeal's* efforts to revitalize the music industry in the city, I had played in bands of my own while a student at Ole Miss, even becoming part of Memphis music history as a member of the first white group to perform at a Black nightclub in Memphis at a time while racial segregation was still strictly enforced.

I began listing potential book titles and sub-titles. In between coffee breaks, frequent pacing, and a walk around the apartment complex during which I slipped on the ice and fell flat on my back, I came up with the title I felt I could do justice to: *Goin' Back to Memphis: A Century of Blues, Rock 'n' Roll, and Glorious Soul.* I would write about the city's music history, beginning with W.C. Handy and the blues of Beale Street to the invention of rock 'n' roll at Sam Phillips' Sun Records studio, all the way up to the present day.

What I didn't want to write was a geeky adoration of music styles, brands of guitars, and chord progressions. I wanted to write about the emotional and intellectual energy of the music. I wanted to investigate the effect cultural influences had on the development of the music.

I knew how to submit fiction to publishers. All you needed was a finished manuscript and a brief summary of the book. Editors would make up their mind based on that information. Non-fiction books were different. I understood that from many years of reviewing non-fiction books. What I needed now was a sample chapter and descriptions of each chapter I planned to write for the book. The best chapter I could submit, I concluded, would be a rewritten version of what I wrote for *The Commercial Appeal* and *Nine-O-One* about the *Class of '55* Sun Records reunion.

With a sample chapter and chapter outlines of my proposed book in hand, I proceeded to research the publishing industry to determine which companies published music titles. As it turned out there were not all that many. The publisher that caught my eye was Simon & Schuster. They had an imprint that published only music titles, Schirmer Books. The editor was Richard Carlin. On a Friday afternoon in mid-January 1995, I sent my proposal via Federal Express to only one publisher, Simon & Schuster. I had no idea I had broken every rule in the book. Editors don't like to receive special courier proposals because they have to sign for them and they don't like to sign for things from writers they don't know. Truthfully, they prefer to work with agents.

On Monday after the Friday I had shipped the proposal, I received a telephone call from Richard Carlin. He told me he liked what I had sent him and was prepared to offer me a contract to write the book I described. Richard quoted an amount for the advance against royalties and it was more than fair. He would pay me half when I signed the contract and the other half when I finished the book. There are no words to express the elation I felt. Half of my advance would provide me with the biggest single check I'd ever had in my life . . . *and it was to fulfill my lifelong dream of becoming an author.*

Schirmer Books gave me seven months to write an 80,000-word book and gather seventy-five photographs. All of the newspaper stories I had written had been on a twenty-four-hour cycle. I got longer for magazine articles, up to a week. Seven months to write and turn in a project seemed so extravagant. I actually enjoyed working on deadline. My schedule called for me to interview and research until the end of spring, then to begin writing through the summer. I made numerous trips to Memphis during that period. I already had a large collection of interviews with many of the Memphis movers and shakers in that city's music industry (I may have the best Memphis music archives in existence), so most of my time was spent filling out missing links in my interviews and doing research at the University of Memphis Library.

AS A FORMER SLAVE PORT, MEMPHIS has a long history of racial tensions that continue to the present day. Although the blues was not invented in Memphis (that happened in Natchez and the Mississippi Delta) W.C. Handy brought the blues to prominence in two ways: first, by becoming the first person to musically notate the blues on sheet music, and, second, by being the first to orchestrate the blues with European instruments and song structures. Handy is also of interest because of his association with longtime Memphis Mayor E. H. Crump, or "Boss" Crump as he was known to locals, for whom he once wrote a campaign song which he performed while marching up and down Beale Street.

Boss Crump was no ordinary politician. For most of his career, he was sort of a middleman between the Memphis mob and the New Orleans Italian mob and the redneck Dixie Mafia, based in Biloxi. I know a little something about that because one of my family members worked for Crump, a red-headed Mississippi boy who had a talent for walking both sides of the street. He was equally at home dealing with the well-educated, upper-crust Memphis mob and the street-smart, poorly educated New Orleans and Biloxi mob organizations. The Memphis mob had no official name like the New York Italian mob, so I gave them the name Memphis Hoodoo Cartel and used that term throughout my book.

In early summer I received a telephone call from Richard Carlin, my editor at Schirmer Books. He wanted to fly to Nashville, along with the publisher, Paul Bolger, to meet me in person. He named a date and it was agreeable with me. I suggested Amerigo, the Italian restaurant where I had shared a chocolate dessert with the photography editor from *Playboy*.

We had an enjoyable dinner. I had lots of questions about book publishing and they patiently answered each one. After a while it became apparent why they had flown to Nashville to meet a first-time author— *me!* Bolger wanted to know what I wanted to write next.

"I'm not through with the first one," I protested.

"But you know there will be a second one."

"Sure," I answered. "Well . . . if you'd really like to know, I would like to write Scotty Moore's autobiography with him."

"Do you think he would do it?" asked Carlin.

"I'm pretty sure, yes."

With that Bolger rose to his feet and extended his hand.

"Deal," he said as we shook hands.

As I drove home that night, I thought *Damn, who knew selling books was so easy.*

NOT ONLY DID I MEET MY DEADLINE, I got the manuscript in to Richard three weeks early. The week after I turned the manuscript in, I received a second contract from Richard. This time it was for the Scotty Moore autobiography, *That's Alright, Elvis*. After our meeting at the Nashville restaurant, I called Scotty's daughter, Vikki, and talked to her about the offer. She was eager for him to receive the recognition he deserved from current generations who were not around in the early years.

Then I called Scotty and he indicated he was eager to do the book. He was tired of "living under a rock" for the past twenty or so years. I notified Richard that Scotty was on board, and Richard and publisher Paul Boger made a return trip to Nashville to meet Scotty and his longtime friend Gail Pollock, and myself, at the same downtown restaurant where we previously had met. The meeting went very well and a couple weeks later we received the contract. The manuscript was due July 1, 1996, two months before *Goin' Back to Memphis* was published.

The reviews of *Goin' Back to Memphis* were encouraging. The *Publisher's Weekly* review said, "[Dickerson's] engaging chronicle sizzles with the energies that transformed American music and popular culture."

Before I knew what had happened, I was on a plane to New York to be interviewed on CNN about the book. It was my first trip, ever, to New York City and I was very impressed. I was picked up at the airport by a Schirmer Books employee and taken to my hotel, and then to the offices of the publisher, where I was introduced to everyone in the office.

All in all, it was an exciting trip, although I was startled when the plane landed in Nashville and I walked past the cockpit while departing and glanced inside, and saw the curly-headed pilot, still seated, leaning over to make out with his twenty-something, blonde co-pilot. It was a rock 'n' roll ending to a great adventure in the big city.

That October I participated in the 1996 Southern Festival of Books in Nashville, where I was a panelist on the discussion titled "The Glory of Southern Blues." Also on the panel were Paul Garon the Chicago-based author of *The Glory of Southern Blues*," and Paul Kingsbury, editor of the *Journal of Country Music*. The best part of the event, for me at least, was when I arrived early and was greeted by a delightful couple who had driven down from Massachusetts to hear me speak. I was deeply humbled by their love of books and music.

The following year I received an invitation to attend the Ralph Gleason Music Book Awards because *Goin' Back to Memphis* had been nominated as a finalist. The award was named after Gleason, a gifted music critic and co-founder of *Rolling Stone* magazine. *Rolling Stone* sponsored the award along with BMI and New York University. I didn't attend because the Scotty Moore manuscript was due that month.

SCOTTY MOORE lived several miles from Nashville on a winding, country road named Blueberry Hill. If Robert Frost had ever seen it he would have written a poem about it. The first time I saw it was when I took

A photo of my maternal grandfather Audie Turner taken
during his first trip to New York City at the age of eighteen.
His father had helped write the Mississippi Constitution of 1890.
It was Audie who taught me how to shoot instinctively and
accurately by pointing instead of aiming.

Scotty the contract to sign for his autobiography. He lived in a two-story, cinder block home with lots of rustic wood trim. It was nestled between two stands of high-timber woods. For that reason, it was easy to drive past it if you didn't know exactly where you were going. On the ground floor was a large kitchen that also served as his den. Off that room were two rooms he had converted into a recording studio. His bedroom was upstairs. Over the next five years I visited this house many times.

Scotty allowed me full access to his financial and personal records, his friends and relatives, his ex-wives, his letters and photographs, and, most importantly, his memories of a most remarkable life. All he asked in return was that I not write the book in the first person. He felt it would be pretentious of him to say "I did this" and "I did that." He didn't want people to think he had gotten the "big head"—and he certainly didn't want people to think he was cashing in on his close association with Elvis.

My only question at that point was, "What do we do if one or more of your ex-wives sees things differently than you do?" His response was that if that happened I should use what they say, whether good, bad or indifferent. That told me a lot about his character that he would allow his ex-wives to speak in an uncensored manner.

Because it is not my routine to research and interview, and then write it up before proceeding, I do all of my research and interviews before I write a single word. I tried doing it the other way, but what invariably happened was that new evidence would come to light, whether through research or interviews, and it changed what I had written before. After Scotty had gathered together all the physical evidence of his relationship with Elvis Presley—contracts, letters, magazine and newspaper articles, etc.—he made a list, complete with telephone numbers, of people he felt I should interview. Some of the people were relatives, childhood friends, business associates, ex-wives, musicians, performers, and others.

Once I began taping interviews with Scotty, the list he had made for me proved to be helpful in stimulating his memories of certain events he had shared with others. For example he would give me his recollection of an important event; then I would talk to individuals who were present at the event and they would offer their recollections, which in turn stimulated more of Scotty's memories. Sometimes the truth is best discovered by piecing recollections together as if they were a patchwork quilt.

My list of people to interview about shared experiences with Scotty was pretty impressive: D.J. Fontana, the drummer who played with Scotty and Elvis for so many years; country star Tammy Wynette, record producer Billy Sherill, who produced Scotty's heralded instrumental album; singer Tracy Nelson, musicians Lee Rocker, Ronnie McDowell, guitarist Reggie Young, the Jordanaires, and Rolling Stone Keith Richards, to name a few. For the latter individual, I left messages with people all over the country who knew Keith in the hopes he would learn of the book and give me a call. That call came one Saturday morning with no advance warning.

"Hello," I said.

"Is this Jim?"

"Yes, it is."

"This is Keith. I hear you've been looking for me."

I told him all about the book, and he said he was excited that Scotty was finally going to do a book. By 1996 everyone and their cousin had written a book about Elvis Presley. That was one reason Scotty had turned a deaf ear to offers to do a book. He didn't want to join that crowd.

Keith said that after he received my message he spent several days doing nothing but listening to those early Elvis Presley records with Scotty on electric guitar.

"To me, and it's a sad thing to say, but without Scotty, Elvis wouldn't have been as big," says Keith Richards. "It was Scotty and Bill Black's rapport—and Scotty's ability to understand the space he was working in. Elvis got big so quick, he overshadowed the band. Parker, the beloved Colonel, being the man he was, saw no percentage in the band. It is really scandalous what Parker did to Elvis. I'm sure the Colonel told him [Scotty and Bill] were being paid a fortune. Knowing this business—and knowing

The author, left, and Scotty Moore at his Nashville home.
Photo by James L. Dickerson (taken with time exposure)

the Colonel—I would put money on it."

Another interview for the book I greatly enjoyed was with Tammy Wynette. One of Scotty's job's after he was discharged from the Navy was in his brother's dry cleaning shop in Memphis. Scotty worked there as a hatter. His job was to dissemble men's hats for cleaning. He had to remove the lining and the band and then put the hat back together after it had been cleaned. Sometimes he made hats for men and women of his own design. Also working at the dry cleaners was Tammy Wynette's mother. Tammy was twelve at the time. In the summer, Tammy was accustomed to hanging out at the dry cleaners. It was there she met Scotty, Bill Black and Elvis Presley. During the lunch hour and after work the trio rehearsed in an upstairs room, creating music that Tammy clearly heard downstairs.

Because Tammy Wynette was on my list of interviews I got in touch with her publicist and told her about the book. The following day the publicist called to let me know that Tammy was on the road out West and would call me at such and such time.

On the day she was supposed to call, I attached my tape recorder to the telephone and waited for it to ring. After fifteen or twenty minutes passed without a call, I became concerned. Finally it rang and it was Tammy. She began by apologizing for being late. She explained that her tour bus had entered a stretch where there was no cell phone service. At the next town they came to, they drove around until they spotted a telephone booth in a small strip mall.

As we spoke, her tour bus attracted a crowd. Then all hell broke loose once the fans realized she was only twenty or so yards away in the telephone booth. Tammy laughed as they surrounded the booth, holding out pads and pieces of paper for her to sign. Every few minutes, as we spoke, the conversation was interrupted by Tammy's laughter as the crowd became more and more rowdy. She told me she had never felt so vulnerable in her life. She was literally trapped inside a box. I could hear some of the crowd noise on the other end of the line. Shortly before we finished talking, a member of her crew approached the booth and broke up the crowd long enough for her to sign a few fan books and make a mad dash for her tour bus.

* * *

The week after Christmas 1996, Scotty and I, along with Gail Pollock, went to a Nashville nightclub to listen to Tracy Nelson perform. Scotty doesn't often go to nightclubs, but he was a staunch Tracy Nelson fan—and he wanted to show me why he enjoyed her music. Scotty and Gail met me in the parking lot of the tape plant, located just off Music Row. I left my car—a white Miata convertible—in the parking lot and rode in the car with Scotty and Gail to the nightclub.

"Do you think my car will be safe there?" I asked.

"As safe as it would be anywhere," Scotty said.

It was a great performance by Tracy Nelson, and she was very attentive to Scotty, both from the stage and during breaks when she sat at the table with us. Later that night—it was after midnight—Scotty and Gail drove me back to my car. The downtown streets were deserted at that time of the night and I saw no one in the vicinity of the parking lot.

After talking a few minutes, I got out of the car and watched Scotty and Gail drive away. Once inside my car, I realized someone had cut a hole in the roof and stolen items from inside, most notably a chrome-plated, 44-magnum revolver. It was a discovery that sent chills racing up my spine. As I pulled out of the parking lot and drove onto Music Row, a late model car with mismatched headlights pulled up behind me, following me through the deserted city streets—past the old RCA building and the current address for Mercury Records. As I increased speed, they increased speed. I could not see any faces in the rearview mirror, just several shadowy heads that kept bobbing around inside the car. It was a late-model vehicle, what people are fond of calling land barges. The further I got from downtown, the faster I drove.

At one point I was speeding sixty miles-per-hour on Nashville's long avenues. I didn't care because I wanted to attract the attention of the police. I didn't have a cell phone then and I wasn't about to stop to place a call from a telephone booth. The chase lasted for several miles and I was able to lose my pursuers only because my smaller, faster car was more maneuverable than the land barge that stayed on my tail.

Finally, I made it to Bellevue and up the hill to my apartment complex. I parked my car and just sat in it for a few minutes, allowing my adrenalin to tap down. The lights were out in most of the townhouses. After a while, I got out of the car and walked to the front door. It was then that I spotted the land barge inching toward me. It was like something out of a Stephen King novel. The land barge had assumed a hellish life of its own. I rushed inside and called the police and reported what had happened. They said it sounded like a carjacking attempt.

After I gave them descriptions of my car and the gun, I grabbed my father's 20-gauge, Remington automatic shotgun and pumped four buckshot shells into the magazine and then yanked one into the chamber. On my way out the door I snatched up a wooden chair and took it with me. Outside, I sat in the chair under the light at the entrance of my apartment,

347

the shotgun resting on my lap. When that happened, the land barge stopped moving forward and just sat there, the engine idling, with me staring at it, determined to unload the shotgun into the windshield if I saw a hand clutching a .44 magnum come out of the driver's window. I wasn't about to go inside and wait for them to kick in the door. What they wanted were the keys to my car—and anything else of value I had inside the apartment.

I starred at the mismatched headlights for a while, the toxic clouds of exhaust ominously drifting beneath and over the car; then the land barge began slowly backing away. When the car reached a cross-street, it backed into the cross-street, turned, and sped away. Of course, the police never came. I slept with the shotgun leaned against the wall by my bed, wondering if that pistol with my fingerprints on it would someday be used to kill someone who didn't need killing.

* * *

After the interviews and research were completed, the process of writing the book seemed to go by very quickly. I would write a chapter, print it out, and take it to Scotty. When I arrived with the next chapter for him to read, I picked up the previous chapter he had read and marked up with notes. Sometimes he wrote comical notes in the margins of the manuscript pages that dealt with his three former wives.

Soon we developed a system. He would give me a memory. I would talk to others who were there to flesh it out with more details—and he would add a nugget to put on top, like cake frosting. Once that process was finished, I shipped the final draft and photographs off to Richard who proofed it, asked questions, and made suggestions.

When the book was published in the fall of 1997, we hit the road to promote it. We began our book tour with a train ride to New York City, a re-creation of the ride that Elvis, Bill and Scotty made on their first trip to New York, only this time around, there were two major differences: The first was that since Scotty now lived in Nashville, and Memphis no longer had direct train service to New York, we had to go all the way to Alabama

Scotty Moore on the train to New York to promote *That's Alright, Elvis*
(Photo by James L. Dickerson)

to board the train in Birmingham—and the second was that nearly fifty years after Scotty's first trip, train service had gone downhill. Scotty thought the modern trains, especially the Pullman cars, would really be knockouts, but the old ones were much better the way he remembered it.

On the first leg of our trip, from Birmingham to Atlanta, a TNN camera crew accompanied us on the train, recording everything we did. That wasn't too bad. The interviewer did a good job dealing with the stress of conducting an interview on a moving train and patiently dealing with fans as they interrupted to shake Scotty's hand or ask for an autograph. We said goodbye to the camera crew in Atlanta, and stayed there a day or two doing interviews and attending a book signing at Chapter 11 that attracted an Elvis impersonator or two.

From Atlanta, we travelled to Washington, DC, where we did more interviews—Scotty appeared on NPR's "Fresh Air" with Terry Gross— and did book signings, and then on to Philadelphia for more of the same. I became somewhat concerned when I noticed that Scotty was frequently breaking out in a cold sweat whenever he had to walk more than a few steps at a time. Whenever I asked Scotty if he was feeling all right, he always said yes, except for being more tired than usual. As it turned out, he was experiencing heart failure, something he did not realize until he returned to Nashville and then took a road trip with Gail to Paducah, Kentucky, to surprise his friend Ronnie McDowell at one of his performances. While backstage he collapsed and was driven back to Nashville. Two weeks later he had triple-bypass heart surgery.

Meanwhile, despite Scotty showing early signs of heart failure on the train, we continued on to New York City, where we had signings planned; unfortunately, they had to be canceled because the publisher ran out of books. The best part of the trip was playing a concert in Central Park with Ike Turner, Joe Louis Walker, and Matt "Guitar" Murphy. The fans were disappointed we didn't have books to sign, but they were very enthusiastic about the concert. We ended the tour back in Birmingham, but had to cancel a scheduled book signing there because the store was unable to get books. Gail Pollock picked us up at the train station and drove us back to Nashville. We had dinner along the way and Gail said she was shocked we sat at the same table.

"I figured you two wouldn't be speaking after that trip," she laughed.

She had travelled with Scotty for almost twenty years and was well aware of his many moods. Sure, cooped up the way we were, we grew tired of each other at times, but never a cross word was uttered.

The reviews and comments pouring in about the book were encouraging and filled with admiration of Scotty. Wrote the reviewer for the *Los Angeles Times*: "Scotty Moore also knows what it's like to sit by the phone waiting for Elvis to call. His as-told-to biography by James Dickerson has an air of forgiveness, clearly indicated by the title ... Presley's first (and best) guitarist, Moore's the cool genius behind all those gripping Sun sessions licks as well as the unassuming shy guy on the 'Comeback' stage. If Elvis was the pelvis then Moore and bassist Bill Black were his first great kicks in the pants . . . [Scotty's] voice is modest, point-blank and disdainful of myth."

We actively promoted the book for about a year, culminating in 1998 with news that the book was a finalist for the now-defunct Ralph J. Gleason Award for best music book of the year. This made me a two-time nominee, in consecutive years, for the prestigious honor. However, by that time I had already finished a third book, and I was hard at work on two additional books.

GROWING UP IN THE DELTA, I was acutely aware of the many ways in which blacks were mistreated. I loved Black music, and I loved fitting entire families of Blacks into shoes, from toddlers on up to senior citizens, in my grandfather's department store in Hollandale, the population of which was 50 percent black. My use of the word "citizens" caused me a lot of grief because while I was growing up Blacks were not considered citizens who had the right to vote. Most of the whites in the Delta at that time didn't even consider Blacks to be human beings.

For much of the early 1990s, I encountered news stories on a regular basis about efforts by the ACLU to force the State of Mississippi to open the secret files of the Mississippi State Sovereignty Commission, a super-secret, white-supremacist state agency that had spied on individuals who had spoken out in favor of full citizenship for Mississippi Black residents. In 1994, four years after he had issued a ruling that the secret files should be opened and made public, Judge William Barbour issued a ruling, finally, on how the files should be opened. Of course, the court fight continued on *how* the files should be opened. If there was anything Mississippi valued above all else, it was secrecy.

In 1996, before the release of *Goin' Back to Memphis*, I decided to write an investigative book about the Sovereignty Commission. In describing the crimes committed by the commission, many reporters had used bootleg copies of commission files. I was not interested in using material that could perhaps later prove to be false, so I used my old sources in Mississippi to locate files that would hold up under intense scrutiny. I found those files in the papers of Mississippi Governor Paul B. Johnson which had been donated to the University of Southern Mississippi Library.

I visited the library and went through the files, discovering countless instances of wrongdoing by the Commission.

Using that information as a foundation, I wrote a book proposal that a literary agent in New York used to sell the book to Turner Publishing in Atlanta. The company was owned by Ted Turner and was part of the CNN family. As I recall, the contract was not the largest contract I had received—the Scotty Moore contract was the largest—but in 1990s dollars it was quite substantial. The book would be titled *Dixie's Dirty Secret: The True Story of How the Government, the Media, and the Mob Conspired to Combat Integration and the Vietnam Antiwar Movement.*

I did tons of interviews, utilized the Sovereignty Commission files that had not yet been made public, but which I had in my possession, requested FBI and Selective Service files under the Freedom of Information Act, and read every book about the civil rights movement I could get my hands on—all to piece together an investigative true account of the horrors committed by white supremacists in partnership with the State of Mississippi during the 1950s, 1960s, and 1970s.

* * *

James Meredith was the first Black to successfully enroll at the University of Mississippi, prompting a bloody riot during which two men were killed. My first semester at Ole Miss in 1963 was Meredith's final semester. I recalled seeing him on campus, shadowed by armed U.S. Marshalls walking shoulder to shoulder behind him.

The second Black to enter the university was Cleve McDowell. Recalling the day I was eating in the school cafeteria when McDowell entered with his tray and sat not far from me, only to see every student in the room get up and leave rather than eat with him, I called him to set up an interview for my book. I reminded him of that day in the cafeteria that only I stayed to eat with him; he laughed and said he did indeed remember that day, saying "So that was *you* that stayed?"

On the day of our interview, I drove 350 miles from Nashville to Indianola, Mississippi to meet with him, only to learn he was nowhere to be found. I waited a couple hours, then returned to Nashville. Not long after that, McDowell was shot to death by an alleged robber who took his year-old Cadillac. Authorities arrested someone for the crime who was convicted and sent to prison, but I still have a hard time believing it was unrelated to my scheduled visit with him. I think word got out he would be meeting with me, prompting threats that if he did, something bad would happen. One thing about the Delta: *someone* is always charged.

Three of my most memorable interviews for the book were with former Mississippi Governor William Waller, FBI special agent Joe Sullivan, and George Rogers, one of only two members of the Mississippi House of Representatives to vote against the formation of the Sovereignty Commission.

First, Governor Waller. In the summer of 1996, I met with Waller in his Jackson law office to talk about the Commission. I was shown to his office and found him seated behind his desk. He was affable, friendly as one Ole Miss Graduate is to another. Moments after I arrived, his telephone rang. It was from his secretary who told him he had a call on line one. He turned sort of sideways to take the call, speaking almost in a whisper into the telephone.

"Yes," he said, "He's here now."

The "he" in question was myself. The call only lasted another few seconds, at the end of which he turned around and said, "Now where were we?" He made no attempt to explain the call. Clearly, my investigation was rattling cages in Mississippi.

Before we began with my questions, he had one of his own.

"When you get through with it, will you give me a chance to rebut any charges?"

I responded that I had nothing but praise for him because of his decision to shut down the Commission and did not anticipate there would be anything in the book he would feel personally compelled to rebut.

"As far as rebutting charges against the Commission," I said. "I do not feel it would be your place to defend an agency you single-handedly destroyed."

He studied me with eyes that weighed my words. I looked at his expressionless face, wondering what he was thinking.

After we discussed his reasons for abolishing the Commission, I notified him of one of my discoveries. "Did you ever know the Commission opened a private bank account, one that would allow them to handle money without its going through the state auditor?"

Waller's face dissolved into a deep frown.

"Why no," he said, his voice lowering almost to a whisper. "Did they really?"

"Yes, they did," I said, probing his face.

The governor froze, staring at me.

It is moments like that that investigative reporters live for.

FBI special agent Joe Sullivan was one of two legendary agents who was responsible for breaking the KKK in Mississippi. He was sent from Washington to Mississippi to search for the missing civil rights activists Andrew Goodman, James Chaney, and Michael Schwerner, who had disappeared while undertaking voter registration in Neshoba County. He worked with FBI special agent Jim Ingram, who was in charge of the civil rights violent crimes division based in Jackson.

Sullivan led the effort to find the three men's bodies and then pieced together the crime (it was the horrific story told in the movie *Mississippi Burning*). The two white men, Schwerner and Goodman, were each shot once, while Chaney was shot by several of the Klansmen. The FBI office in Washington helped me track down Sullivan, who by the time I started working on the book had retired and was living in New York City. He provided me with a great deal of background about the murders and the murder scene, and I provided him with information I had unearthed for the book. One of the startling documents I found with Governor Johnson's papers at the University of Southern Mississippi was proof that prior to the Neshoba County murders the Commission had spent undercover agents to Alabama to purchase guns from a dealer. Among their purchases were two

.38-caliber revolvers which were listed as inventory of the Commission.

I had been unable to determine in my research the caliber of the weapons used in the murders, so I was eager to ask Sullivan if he knew the caliber. "Sure," he answered. "Ballistics determined that four of the five bullets found in the victims were from the same caliber weapon."

"And what caliber was that?"

"They were fired from a .38-caliber pistol."

"And were the pistols ever found?"

'No," he answered.

I told him about the secret private banking account the Commission had set up. Sullivan said this was the first he had heard about that.

"We probably made a mistake of not making a more intensive probe of the Commission," he said, his voice tinged with regret. "I think that was perhaps the key to a lot of the problems. I was aware they had money. I always suspected the White Knights were funded in some fashion by the Commission. In the years that followed, I wished we had done some probing in that area."

The third individual that proved to be an important source in the book was George Rogers, the former member of the Mississippi House of Representatives who was one of the two individuals who voted against creating the Sovereignty Commission. Disillusioned with public service he did not run for re-election. Instead, he joined the Central Intelligence Agency (CIA). I knew that about him, but I had no idea how to locate him. I was pretty sure he did not live in Mississippi. In the hope of locating him, I wrote a letter to the public information office of the agency asking for help in my search. The first thing I learned about the agency was that when they call you on the telephone they don't identify the name of the agency. A couple of weeks after I wrote the letter, my telephone rang.

The caller began without identifying herself or the agency.

"I am calling regarding the letter you sent about Mr. George Rogers. He has been retired for a while, but I located him and he has agreed to talk to you for your book. Please call (this) number tomorrow at 3 p.m. and he will take your call."

Then the line went dead.

There was no goodbye or "have a nice day." Just silence.

When I called George Rogers, I found him to be most cooperative. Of course, my first question was what possessed him to vote against the Commission. "I voted against it because there was talk that public money would be used to finance the activities of the Citizens' Council [the city equivalent of the KKK]. I thought that was an improper—if not unconstitutional—use of public funds. I wasn't in sympathy with all the activities of the Citizens' Council anyway, so I voted against it."

We chatted about other issues of the era; then I asked him the question that was most on my mind. "What exactly did you do with the CIA?"

"I worked in the Intelligence Community, a division of the CIA that coordinated the intelligence-gathering activities of more than thirteen governmental agencies, including the Defense and Justice Departments. I was in the part that dealt with computers. It was fascinating work."

When I completed the book I turned it in to my editor at Turner Publishing. We went through the editing process, with me answering his questions about various items found in my research; then I was delivered devastating news. Ted Turner had decided to sell his media holdings, CNN, Turner Broadcasting System, and the publishing company, to Warner Media in New York. Warner Media expressed no interest in acquiring all the titles published by Turner because its publishing arm, Warner Books, specialized in entertainment titles.

Talks went on for several months, and then I was notified that *Dixie's Dirty Secret* was not chosen to join the Warner Books list (no surprise there). I was told someone on the Warner team remarked, "Is this guy a zealot or something over voting rights?" If I had been there, I would have answered, "Yes, pretty much. Our democracy depends on it." As a result, the rights were reverted to me so that I could place the book with another publisher. My contract with Turner Publishing specified that I would be allowed to keep the advances paid to me.

For the next publisher, I chose a publisher of serious books, M.E. Sharpe, which had offices in New York and London. The contract was signed in 1997 and I submitted the manuscript to them in January 1998. My editor there was Peter Coveney and I found him to be a great editor to work with. The book was published in February 1999, garnering these comments from Kirkus Reviews: "Dirty isn't nearly harsh enough to describe the 20-year- reign of intimidation and deceit perpetuated by the secret state agency founded to defy the Supreme Court's order for school desegregation. Dickerson, a veteran journalist and author of *Goin' Back to Memphis* (which studied the influence of organized crime and politics on Memphis music), traces the commission's genesis in 1955, its escalating use of unlawful tactics (including spying, dirty tricks, media manipulation and forced conscription of political enemies) in the 1960s, its eventual demise in the 1970s . . . It's a bizarre story, involving organized crime, presidential and congressional politics, assassination conspiracies and government corruption of sickening proportions."

During the year that elapsed between the date I submitted the manuscript for *Dixie's Dirty Secret* and the time it was published, I circulated a proposal for a new book titled *North to Canada*. It was another investigative book, this time about Americans who went to Canada rather than support or participate in what they felt was an illegal and immoral war in Vietnam. Peter made me an offer for that book as well, but his offer arrived just days after I accepted an offer from Heather Ruland, a history editor at Praeger. She was yet another terrific editor that I enjoyed working with very much.

To write this book, I began an internet and telephone search for individuals I felt would be representative of the individuals who chose to remain in Canada after President Ford's amnesty and President Carter's pardons. I began with telephone interviews during 1997 and then followed up with a visit to Canada in 1998. In one case, I chose a woman who had been the girlfriend of a war resister, but chose to accompany her boyfriend to Canada because she shared the same opinions about the war.

For nostalgia's sake, I followed the route to Canada I had taken in 1968—up through Indiana and Michigan to Sarnia, where I entered Canada. From there I drove to Toronto, shocked at how the highway lanes had multiplied from four or six lanes to what looked like twenty lanes of traffic. As quickly as I could, I exited into downtown Toronto, where I was familiar with the street names. After I emerged from the city, I found my way back to the main route, Highway 401, and it took me all the way to Brockville, Ontario. As soon as I arrived, I called my old friend David Rice, who promptly met me and took me home to meet his new wife, Debra. They graciously allowed me to use their home as a base to work from while setting up meetings in Ottawa. They also had a get-together for me to visit with people I had worked with at the Children's Aid society. Sadly, there were only a handful left because most had passed away.

The war resisters who could travel to Ottawa, met me at the home of Michael Wolfson. He had fled to Canada in 1968 from his hometown of Buffalo, New York, only days before I arrived in Canada. He married a Canadian woman and they had four children. He received his Ph.D. in economics in 1977 and held a variety of positions in central agencies of the government, including the Treasury Board Secretary, the Department of Finance, and the House of Commons. Since 1993 he had served as the director general of Institutions and Social Statistics Canada, where he was responsible for Canada's statistics on health and education.

We were joined at Michael's house by Patrick Grady, who had grown up in Danville, Illinois, and had fled to Canada in August 1968, and Richard Deaton, who had left the States in June 1968 with his entire family—his stepfather, his mother, and his three younger brothers—to find a new home in Canada, all because of their opposition to the Vietnam War. Three years before we met at Michael's home, Richard was hired as an associate professor at the Royal Military College in Kingston, Ontario. Perhaps only in Canada would a government hire an America war resister to teach a course in military ethics to young army cadets.

Patrick worked for the Bank of Canada for a number of years and then worked for the national government as an economic consultant. For a time he served as an economic advisor to Prime Minister Jean Chretien.

One of my interviewees who couldn't come to Ottawa was the woman who had fled to Canada with her draft-eligible, British-born husband. Dianne Francis was just nineteen when they crossed the border into Canada. "We knew we could not go back, maybe ever," she said. It was a big bridge to burn. Early on Diane landed a job as a reporter with the *Financial Post*. In 1991 she was named editor, a position she held until 1998 when the newspaper merged with a new national publication, the *National Post*. At the time I interviewed her she was an editor at large for the *National Post*.

IN BETWEEN THE PUBLICATION of *That's Alright, Elvis* and *Dixie's Dirty Secret*, I wrote an investigative book titled *Women on Top: The Quiet Revolution That's Rocking the American Music Industry*. During the course of writing many newspaper and magazine articles about rock, pop blues, and country music I began to sense that something important was happening with women in music. By 1996, I was writing more articles about women than about men.

With the help of a New York agent, I landed a deal with Billboard Books for a book about this phenomenon. To write the book I examined many years of Top 20 pop album charts to determine how men and women fared in record sales. In addition I interviewed both recording artists and those on the business side—female record executives, publicists, record producers, etc. The results were quite shocking.

In 1986, male solo artists made up 68 percent of the rankings, with female artists only accounting for 32 percent. That ratio pretty much held firm until 1996, when for the first time in recording history fourteen female artists accounted for 61 percent of the hit albums.

Featuring interviews with Shania Twain, Brenda Lee, the Bangles, Bonnie Raitt, Ann and Nancy Wilson, Pat Benatar and others, the book was written for a general audience. However, the publisher, Billboard

Books, reorganized the narrative-driven manuscript into a business book style with lots of headings and marketed it as a hardcover business book (unbelievably, there was no photograph of a woman on the cover, nor was there a paperback edition). It was poorly promoted by the publicist, mostly targeting radio, which is notoriously ineffective at selling books. As a result the book never received a single review that I ever saw. This was the second publishing disaster I had in two years, Turner Publishing going under being the other. Luckily *Dixie's Dirty Secret* was placed with an excellent publisher, but when books are derailed or delayed in publication it always has a negative effect on an author's income and work schedule.

With little to do promoting *Women on Top* in 1998, I ended up working on three different books: biographies on *Shania Twain* and *Dixie Chicks, and Last Suppers: If the World Ended Tomorrow, What Would Be Your Last Meal? It w*as a concept book based on approaching celebrities in different fields to ask them for recipes or menus of what they would want for their "last supper." It was published by Lebhar-Friedman Books, a company that primarily published business magazines. The book came about because Jim Barkley, who had worked in the sales department of Simon & Schuster when *That's Alright, Elvis* was published, told me about the upstart company.

The actual book wrote itself. I simply called, emailed or faxed publicists and celebrities, explained the concept, and requested they send a recipe or menu. The response was overwhelming. Most responses came in the mail, but some came by fax. A few came by telephone. *Playboy's* 1998 Playmate of the Year, Karen McDougal, telephoned me from the *Playboy* Mansion in Los Angeles. Cammi Granto, captain of the gold medal United States' hockey team, called me from an airport on her way to Finland. When I sent a request to the White House for President Bill Clinton I had no idea what to expect. He was experiencing a great deal of political turmoil at the time. To my great surprise, one of the first responses I received for my book was from Clinton. It was a terrific recipe for chicken enchiladas.

After beginning the book, I began wondering about deceased famous people. What had been their actual last meal? I added an entire section on actual last suppers. Included were Princess Diana, James Dean, Jimi Hendrix, Howard Hughes, Marilyn Monroe, and Elvis Presley, to name a few. However, my absolute favorite is Ernest Hemingway. I   researched the matter and discovered that he died in 1961 in Ketchum, Idaho. I read a couple of biographies and neither book mentioned his last supper. Ketchum is not a huge city, so I started working the telephone, calling town officials to ask if they knew the name of the restaurant Hemingway dined in the night before he died. I got a name and luckily the restaurant was still in business. I called and asked the manager if they knew the name of the waitress who had served him dinner nearly forty years ago. They knew her name because she was the waitress who always served his table. I obtained her telephone number and called her without any warning. Her name was June Mallea. She was twenty years of age at the time and she clearly remembered everything the great writer ordered for his last supper. Now, that is what you call legwork.

Last Suppers received great reviews. *Playboy* featured the book. *People* magazine wrote: "As if celebs didn't already have their plates full of strange requests from the ravenous media, now author Dickerson has gone and asked a bunch of top bananas what they would choose for their last meal . . . While some readers may find the exercise tasteless and some of the dishes cheesy (like Vanna White's cottage cheese salad, which calls for a whole cup of Cool Whip), most will relish the book's many enticing recipes." In addition to newsprint, at least one television show featured the book. *Donnie & Marie* did an entire segment on the book, while members of the audience were seated around a "last suppers" table.

* * *

While the menu gathering for *Last Suppers* was underway I received a contract for a biography on Shania Twain from a West Coast publisher by the name of Renaissance Media. The company was best known for its audio books but it also published print books. I received the contract in October 1998 and shortly thereafter the first half of the advance. Little did I know then I was about to cross the threshold of yet another publishing nightmare. Unknown to me, the publisher of Renaissance, was in negotiations with St. Martins' Press to sell his company to them. Because a biography of Twain had already been published, or was about to be published by Berkley Books, Renaissance decided the market could not handle two books, so I was notified that my contract had been cancelled. They demanded the advance be repaid. I refused. I already had spent much of the money on travel and research.

After negotiations, the book publisher agreed to issue me a contract on another book, a biography of the Dixie Chicks, with the Twain advance applied to that book. The only money I would receive would be the second half of the advance, due after the completed manuscript was received and accepted. Since I planned to travel to Texas to research the book—and my mother's home was about halfway to Dallas and Fort Worth—I spent several months working out of her house. Titled *Dixie Chicks: Down-Home and Backstage*, the book was a behind-the-scenes history of the Grammy-winning group. Especially helpful was Laura Lynch, the group's first lead singer, the one replaced by Natalie Maines.

I met with Laura at her home, where I was able to go through the group's very extensive archives and photographs. Laura was a delight and we ended up becoming good friends. Because the Chicks had an extensive online fan base, individual fans proved to be helpful in gathering information for the book. After what had happened with the Shania Twain book, it was a great relief to finally finish the book and turn it in two months early. I went through the editing process with the assigned editor and then waited for my check. It arrived on the first of September.

One week later, I received a letter from Renaissance Media, saying the following: "This is to inform you that Renaissance Books has elected not to publish the work entitled The *Dixie Chicks* at this time. We are aware of at least two other publishers who are producing similar titles that will hit the marketplace before our scheduled release date of April 2000."

Renaissance indicated they would be "pleased" to relinquish their rights to the book if I repaid the advance. I counter-offered to pay them half of any advance I received from a new publisher. Accordingly, I sold it to Taylor Trade Publishing of Dallas, which eventually sold it to Cooper Square Books. I spent a year working on two books for Renaissance Media, only to end up paying them thousands of dollars. Of course, I never received a penny from Cooper Square Books. When all the travel and other expenses were paid, I probably netted only one thousand dollars for one year's work on two well-researched books.

When I saw a finished copy of *Dixie Chicks*, I was impressed they had followed the narrative layout I wanted and had made liberal use of the color photographs I had collected. It was a very attractive paperback. Just a few months after it was published I was contacted by *Penthouse* magazine and told they were publishing in September 2000 an article titled "Nashville Nymphs: Meet the sexy no-nonsense women at the top of the charts—the new queens of country music" by Alanna Nash. The magazine asked if I would write a sidebar on the Dixie Chicks for her article. I was delighted. I had met Alanna in Lexington, Kentucky at a Joseph-Beth bookstore for a signing I did with Scotty Moore. She wanted to meet Scotty because she had written a book or two about Elvis Presley and planned to write more. When it came to information about Elvis, Scotty was the gold standard.

I enjoyed meeting Alanna because I found her to be an engaging person and an excellent writer. She had started out as a newspaper reporter, but then moved into music journalism, becoming one of the top writers on country music. *Penthouse* was the only publication in which we were ever in a publication at the same time, in this case sandwiched between a scorching pictorial featuring one of the most glamorous porn stars in the business at that time, Tera Patrick, and a girl-on-girl pictorial that left nothing to the imagination. It was a fairly unique experience for a Mississippi-born journalist. The payment from *Penthouse* thankfully helped offset the loss on the book.

* * *

Earlier that year, I sent a proposal for a biography on Faith Hill to a New York literary agent named Lori Perkins. In quick order she placed the book with St. Martin's Press. I was a little apprehensive about the book going there because the former publisher of Renaissance Books was now in charge of the audio books there. On the positive side, the editor at St. Martin's who acquired the book was Glenda Howard, a Black editor with a sterling reputation. I was looking forward to working with her.

One of the first things I did after signing the contract was to get in touch with Faith Hill's manager, Gary Borman, to see if he would provide me with some photographs for the book. A Los Angeles-based manager, he had only one other country artist, Dwight Yoakum. He liked that idea, especially after I told him I would show him the photo package in advance and allow him to replace any images he felt were not up to her standards. I also asked if Faith would do a series of interviews with me for the book.

While discussing photographs and interviews, he confided that he had turned down several offers from publishers "in the $100,000 range," but he would be willing to discuss doing an authorized book with their full cooperation if St. Martins' would match the offers they had turned down. I passed this information along to Lori, adding that I felt the book would be a bestseller with Faith participating in the promotion of the book.

The offer of an authorized biography was shot down because the St. Martin's editorial board did not feel Faith Hill was a big enough recording artist to merit star treatment (she would soon prove them wrong in the months ahead). As a result, Gorman was no longer interested in providing me photographs or setting up an interview with Faith. That put me on track to interview the people who had been instrumental in her life and career. That required an extended trip to Mississippi, where I conducted interviews at her high school and with friends. I also attended a benefit concert she gave at the Jackson Zoo, where I took photographs of her performance on stage.

It didn't take long for word to get out about the book. During this time

Alanna Nash called me or emailed me, I don't recall which, and offered me the transcript of an extended interview she did with Faith for a magazine article. That was most generous of her to offer that material. I made good use of it in the book, citing quotations as being told to Alanna.

Along the way came word from Glenda Howard that she was leaving St. Martins' Press. Ordinarily, that would mean the project would be killed. Lori and I had a few anxious days until we received word that another editor, Christina Prestia, would be taking it over. From that point on, the editing process for Faith Hill was relatively painless. Christina quickly became my favorite editor of all time. She understood how the process worked. In one instance she sent me several pages of edited manuscript with the note, "In some places I'm just being a hard-ass so, please, feel free to disagree with me . . . As I said before, the voice really works. It feels like the reader is hanging out with someone that's not only knowledgeable, but is comfortable telling a story. Good work."

Subsequently, I received an email with comments that matched my own about working with her. In it Christina wrote: "Can I just say I love working with you . . . I can't believe no one else was smart enough to do a bio on Faith. Look at how many there are on Shania and the Dixie Chicks. You're one helluva smart fellow."

Faith Hill: Piece of My Heart (subtitle contributed by Glenda Howard before she left) was not a blockbuster, but it sold well enough to attract the attention of *Good Housekeeping*, which offered me a contract to write a cover story about the singer. I sent Gorman an email to set up the interview. Being on the cover of a music magazine is a big deal, and Faith got her share of country music covers, but it does not compare to being on the cover of a large circulation women's magazine such as *Good Housekeeping*. I did not hear back from Gorman, but the magazine received a call from their publicist stating that Faith would not do the interview with me because they felt she had been "overexposed" as it was. I still don't know whether it was Faith's or Gorman's decision. Whoever made the decision, it would prove to be a fateful one for her career.

Good Housekeeping's response was not surprising. The editors decided to proceed without her participation. Wrote my editor: "Her manager, publicist, etc. informed us that Faith feels she's too 'overexposed' right now and hence, we can take a hike . . . If you could get us the new stuff by next Monday that sure would be great."

Somehow Gorman or the publicist heard that I still was on the story. The publicist called my editor and said that Faith had changed her mind and would call the magazine the very next day if they promised not to do a write-around [that is, if they included nothing from me].

As a result, Faith Hill called the magazine and talked about her new baby and Tim and wanting to be an actress. The magazine went with it, but wrote me this note: "We don't want to pay you just a kill fee, because it hardly seems fair that your story isn't running simply because Faith's people caved in. It seems obvious that a large part of why they agreed to do it is because they knew we had you on the case and it made them nervous. So we're giving you the full story fee, and I hope you will work for us again in the future." I smiled all the way to the bank with the check. I am a journalist, not a fanzine writer. My editor was correct. I sometimes make manipulative music publicists and managers nervous because I write as a journalist, not as a fan who is concerned about future favors. Frankly, I don't give a damn whether they return my calls or not.

When Faith Hill or her representatives entered into a gangsta mode to deprive me of my livelihood, they stepped onto a glide path of self-destruction that ultimately crippled her career. Otherwise, she would still be making hit records. Music pros like Dolly Parton and Shania Twain would never even consider being abusive to the press.

As the Faith Hill drama played out, my literary agent Lori Perkins sold a biography on actress Natalie Portman to ECW Press, a Canadian owned publisher, and a magazine article to *Good Housekeeping.* It was a pleasure to be working with Canadians again. The ECW book was titled *Natalie Portman: Queen of Hearts* and it was published in 2002. The magazine article was published in August 2001 under the headline "The

Author self-portrait (time exposure) for Dixie Chicks biography.

Town That's Raising Quadruplets." A sub-headline read: "When a young mother died suddenly, leaving her husband with four infants and a toddler, the folks of Mountain Home, Arkansas, reached out to help with time, money, and all their hearts."

I went on to write about the support the family received from the town. People donated their time and their money, raising more than $60,000 for a down payment for a larger home. Almost everyone in town helped in one way or another, with most pitching in to help babysit the children so that Jesse could go to work.

For the story, I also spoke to an associate professor of obstetrics and gynecology at Vanderbilt University Medical School, Cornelia Graves, M.D., to explain Julie's disease to a lay public. Called fatty liver of pregnancy, it is characterized by a buildup of fat deposits in the liver that, left untreated, can lead to total liver, kidney and heart failure, typically with no advance warning. Doctors don't know why some pregnant women develop this disease and others don't, or why some recover from it after delivery, and others die without warning.

THROUGHOUT THE DRAMA with Renaissance Media, I was in another messy situation with Billboard Books. Before I had seen the disappointing results of how *Women on Top* was edited and published, I had entered into contracts with Billboard for two additional books—a biography of Colonel Tom Parker and a biography of Lil Hardin Armstrong, the second wife of Louis Armstrong. Both those projects became endangered in the wake of the clumsy launch of *Women on Top*.

As time went by problems arose over differences of opinion about the responsibilities and duties of a book editor. Book publishing and newspaper and magazine publishing are two entirely different professional cultures. When you work on salary for a newspaper or magazine your relationship with an editor is as an employee who signed on to work for hire. You are paid a regular salary. The editor is your boss and you carry out assignments and copy edits under close supervision. Changes are made whether you agree or not. Whatever copy you turn in is copyrighted in the publication's name, not yours. Make no mistake about it, the company is your boss.

That is not the case when working with a book editor unless your manuscript is a work for hire, meaning you are paid outright for your work. Work for hire books are a rarity. The typical book contract is an agreement in which the publisher effectively leases the right to publish your manuscript under terms specified in the contract. You will be paid a royalty rate on sales. The cash advance you may or may not receive is just that—an advance against royalties. It is not a salary. You are not an employee. Once you turn in your manuscript you are assigned an editor whose job it is to guide you through the company's publishing maze. Your editor will edit your manuscript or assign it to a copyeditor, or sometimes end up doing both. They will correct typos, question your grammar, and ask you for source information if it is not footnoted or identified within the text. What they cannot do is be your boss. They cannot order you to do anything you do not feel is right for your book. The book will be copyrighted in your name, not in the name of the company. As an author, you are in control of what is published in your name. If you have a disagreement, you can always reclaim your manuscript, pay the advance back, and walk out the door and make a deal with someone else.

Once I completed my investigative biography *Colonel Tom Parker: The Curious Life of Elvis Presley's Eccentric Manager,* I knew it was one of my best works, a biography that someday would attract movie interest. It was an intensely investigative work that ultimately carried me to dark corners of the music business. Most of the individuals I sought out for information did not hesitate to cooperate with me. However, some were fearful for their life. I do not use unnamed sources in my work if the information can potentially hurt a living person, but I agreed to allow some interviewees to be unnamed because their information did not call for rebuttal from a living person.

As you might expect, my most reliable source was Scotty Moore, who knew more about Elvis and Colonel Parker than any other person alive. Lastly, the information I received from court
records and government agencies such as the FBI was invaluable.

I submitted the manuscript to my editor on April 8, 1998 and waited for feedback. Five days later, I received an email from the editor: "Am 5 chapters into the Colonel [author's note: there are 8 chapters in the book]. I think it's wonderful. I doubt your writing was ever better!"

Several weeks went by and then all hell broke loose.

Out of the blue, the editor called and asked me to package up all my notes, source material and interview recordings and ship it to them for fact checking. I refused. I suggested he simply ask questions about anything he had questions about and I would provide the source material for the text in question. I explained that some of the tapes from sources contained material that would have endangered their lives if it fell into the wrong hands. This went back and forth, with the editor yelling and shouting, so I dug in my heels. I was done. Someone had sabotaged my book. Whether it was the publicist I had complained about, or underworld connections to the publisher, or something else entirely, I did not know.

At my request, the publisher generously negotiated a payback price for me to recover both books (they get high marks for that, at least) and I ended up publishing *Colonel Tom Parker* and the biography of Lil Hardin Armstrong with Cooper Square Press, a publisher that already had published a paperback reprint of my first book, *Goin' Back to Memphis*. I liked the editor a lot and we had a great working relationship.

When Colonel Tom Parker was published by Cooper Square Press in 2001, it was to rave reviews:

"A rare glimpse into the underbelly of the music biz."
—Los Angeles Daily News

"This intriguing, meticulously researched biography of Presley's Svengali could be a manual of how *not* to take care of your client . . . Dickerson has painted a riveting portrait of an especially unsavory character."
—Billboard

"This jaw-dropping biography . . . is a model of research, assembled with crafty objectivity and humor."
—Hal Kanter, director of the Elvis film *Loving You*

The following year, *Just for a Thrill: Lil Hardin Armstrong, First Lady of Jazz* was published by Cooper Square Press—and, in time, Billboard Books reverted the rights to *Women on Top* to me and I placed it with Schirmer Trade Books for publication in 2005. This time the book was published as I had written it, but unfortunately it did not contain a single photograph. Imagine a book about women singers and musicians without photographs! I weathered the Billboard rough patch (the publishing company was subsequently sold to Random House) and I looked forward to resuming stress-free publishing.

In the year 2000, Simon & Schuster sold its music imprint, Schirmer Books, to a British publisher named Music Sales. They opened an office in New York, where they had a music and film imprint titled Omnibus Press. Once they acquired Schirmer Books, they retitled it Schirmer Trade Books. That was where *That's Alright, Elvis*, the book I wrote with Scotty

Moore, landed. As you might have gleaned by now, book publishing is a lot like other businesses concerned about the bottom line. Books and authors are moved about without discussion, and sold to the highest bidder, without any regard about the feelings or approval of the authors.

Now that I was a Schirmer Trade Book author, I pitched a proposal for a biography on Ashley Judd to its editor Larry Birnbaum. He made a nice offer which I accepted. I did a ton of interviews for the book, including one with filmmaker Victor Nunez, who directed *Ruby in Paradise*, which was Ashley's first starring role. It is still my favorite movie she ever made. Subsequently, I sent Larry a proposal for *Russell Crowe: The Unauthorized Biography*, which he accepted. Beginning with his upbringing first in New Zealand and then in Australia, it took a close look at his music career before he became an actor and continued on during his glory years as a film actor, including his masterpiece, *A Beautiful Mind*. It was before the release of that book that Larry told me his publisher was upset with him for accepting the book about Ashley Judd, an actress he apparently did not like.

The next thing I knew Larry was no longer at Schirmer Trade Books. Anyone just entering the book publishing world should be well advised to keep in mind that the editor that you hate or the editor that you love can be snatched away on the slenderest of whims of someone higher up the editorial food chain. To the executives at the top of a publishing company, editors are like paper cups that can be wadded up and tossed away.

The Chinese edition of the author's book
Nicole Kidman: A Kind of Life

Chapter 13

Jackson, Mississippi

NOT LONG AFTER RELOCATING to Mississippi in 2002, I began work on a Nicole Kidman biography that had been placed with Kensington Publishing by an agent. The idea for the book arose when I read that her father was a well-known Australian psychologist and author who had taken his daughter to peace marches in the United States during the Vietnam War, and her mother was an activist for feminist causes. The question I asked myself was what kind of child would an intriguing marriage union like that produce?

Added to the motivation of answering that question was the belief that Nicole Kidman is one of the best actresses of her generation. I didn't have the budget to travel to Australia to do my research there, but I quickly learned that most of the people I wanted to talk to were reachable by telephone. Actually, using the telephone and emails I was able to reach out across the world for interviews and insight.

One of the most enlightening and enjoyable parts of the research was tracing her early career in Australia, focusing on roles she had before she ever became a worldwide box-office sensation. One of her most important early movies was *Dead Calm* (1989) in which Kidman plays the part of a woman who loses her young son in an automobile accident and then goes on a cruise with her husband (Sam Neill) to recover from the loss. After three weeks at sea, they spot their first ship, a schooner that looms ominously ahead in the distance, dead in the water. As they stare at the schooner they see a man in a dinghy slowly rowing toward them. Played by Billy Zane, the man tells them the ship is sinking and all aboard are dead of food poisoning. At that point the plot takes a wicked twist that turns a peaceful interlude into a suspenseful psychological thriller.

Assistant director Stuart Freeman, who a few years earlier had worked on *Mad Max Beyond Thunderdome*, generously spent time with me, re-creating the movie from his perspective, with a focus on Kidman. I wanted to know what she was like to work with and what he felt was special about her acting, and I wanted anecdotes about working on the film with her. He provided all that and much more, making the filming experience come alive for me so that I could do it justice when I wrote about it. After the book was published and made its way to Australia, where it was published by an Australian publisher named 5 Mile Press I received an email from Freeman:

> **Dear James,**
> **After much searching I re-discovered your email address.**
> **I loved your book on Nicole Kidman and I was really impressed at the virtual verbatim quotes from me. Thank you for your honesty.**
> **I know this is a delayed thank you but it is nonetheless sincere.**
> **Congratulations!**
> **Stuart**

Another much sought after interview for that book was the actor who played the steamy sex scene with Kidman in *Eyes Wide Shut* (1999). The scene was important because it provided a movie-defining moment for the production and served as a reflection of Kidman's relationship with her husband Tom Cruise. It took weeks for me to locate the actor in that scene. His name was Gary Goba, and he was more of a fashion model hoping to get into show business than a card-carrying actor. That changed when a representative from Warner Bros. called Goba's agent and asked if he would like to audition for the role. The agent was advised, "Mr. Goba will be naked and engage in a sex scene with Kidman in the film." As luck would have it, I located Mr. Goba in Canada. He was happy to talk to me about his role in the film, beginning with the moment he and Kidman stood naked in front of each other with only the director Stanley Kubrick in the room with them. Kubrick's only direction was "Just go at it!"

For six days they repeated the same sex scene, over and over again. Goba estimated they probably acted out fifty different sexual positions. His recollections of the event were enthralling, not just because he was so much in awe that he was actually doing those things with a world-famous actress, but because of the insight those intimate scenes provided for an understanding of the genesis of the film itself. Goba confirmed that Cruise was in the building on those days when they filmed the sex scenes. I can't prove it, but my gut tells me that Cruise was somewhere in the dark corners of the set, watching the actual filming of the scenes. Voyeurism was very much at the core of the theme of the film.

MISSISSIPPI NATIVE SON Willie Morris, the editor of *Harper's* magazine in the 1960s and an accomplished author for the remainder of the century, once gave a description of the Mississippi Delta that merits repeating. While driving from his hometown of Yazoo City to Greenville, he came to terms, finally, with the mysterious power of the landscape near a small Delta town named Onward. He wrote:

> **This, I knew from my boyhood, was one of the most desolate and treacherous drives in the whole state. My gasoline gauge pointed to empty and I beseeched**

the Lord that I would not be stranded here in a
storm, with not even a road shoulder to drive the car
to, much less a Seven-Eleven or a Bun 'N Burger. I
drove for miles in a mindless fright until, praise
eternally be His name, there was the town of
Onward, Mississippi, with a general store plastered
with patent-medicine posters and a gas pump sitting
precariously on the edge of the swamp . . . and on this
night in a dark and relentless November storm, the
land from which I and my blood-kin had emerged
was scaring the unholy hell out of me.[40]

I made that same drive in March of 2003—with much the same
visceral reaction—though I drove much deeper into the Delta on U.S.
Highway 61 to Clarksdale, where I met with Hollywood actor Morgan
Freeman, who had been born in Memphis, but raised in the Delta near
Greenwood. Over dinner conversation at his restaurant, an upscale
establishment named Madidi (it has since closed), the actor compared
notes with me about growing up during the same era in Greenwood.

The previous week, Freeman had been in Memphis to promote a new
film, *Levity*—co-starring Billy Bob Thornton, Holly Hunter and Kirsten
Dunst. On that night, when the bright lights of publicity were on him, he
had been dressed in a black suit, with a blue shirt and a white collar, but
on this night, accompanied by his lovely wife, Myrna, and his assistant,
Samantha, he drove in from his Delta home, wearing blues jeans and a
baseball cap, the modern-day uniform of down-home, Southern leisure.

Freeman was immensely proud of his restaurant and of the chef he
had imported from out of state. I don't recall what he ordered for dinner,
but I ordered pork loin with asparagus. In the South, we prefer our pork
loin to be supple enough to be cut with a fork and the asparagus with a
little snap to it. In this case the pork loin was tough enough to require a
knife and the asparagus was soggy. I pretended it was delicious, but
Freeman could see me struggling to cut the pork loin with a butter knife
and his face could not hide his embarrassment. I felt badly about that.

Freeman is older than I am, but our lives intersected for seven years in the 1950s, when Greenwood was a town filled with contradictions. Segregation was the law. We attended the same movies in the Paramount movie theater (mostly westerns staring Roy Rogers and Gary Cooper, and World War II films starring John Wayne and James Stewart), but state law dictated that the whites sit in the seats on the floor of the theater and the Blacks sit in the seats in the balcony. We marched in the same Christmas parades, though our school bands were separated by enough mechanized floats to mark a clear boundary between the white bands and the Black bands. And we walked the same streets, seeing the same sights and hearing the same political posturing about the civil rights movement.

"Where did you live?" he asked, drawing a line on the white tablecloth to denote the railroad tracks that ran through the center of town.

I told him.

"Ah," Freeman said, picking up the salt and pepper shakers. "You lived here"—the salt shaker was placed on one side of the tracks—"and I lived here"—the pepper shaker marking his address on the other side of the tracks. What Freeman remembered most about growing up in the Delta was not the racial discord (Greenwood was where the killer of civil rights leader Medgar Evers called home), but rather that a doctor once diagnosed him as suffering from malnutrition.

"I didn't know I wasn't getting the right food," he said. "There seemed to be enough food on the table for everyone to eat."

The question I most wanted to ask Freeman was how he had grown up in such an unfriendly environment, but had then moved on to become a movie star of liberal sensitivities—someone who could live anywhere in the world he chose, but wanted to live in the Mississippi Delta. The question hung there for a moment—"How did you go through everything that everyone else went through, but turn out so differently?"—and the answer came in the form of a question from Freeman:

"How did *you* do that and turn out the way you did?"

It is a good question, for it goes to the heart of the Delta experience. It is a place where passions run deep, and the power of the land dictates

Morgan Freeman and the author in Memphis.

roads taken and not taken, and where the myth of time and place stir the creative juices, sometimes to the boiling point and other times to that point where everything in the past is frozen fast, just the way it was—and, of course, where great art grows in the soil alongside the tomatoes, snap beans, and sweet corn. Where every man, woman and child is born seemingly with an innate knowledge for playing the guitar or piano, or writing a clever verse. The Delta is the best part of Mississippi. Too bad it is the poorest and least developed.

Toward the end of the conversation, the restaurant was filled with an interracial group of high school students from Freeman's hometown. Whites and Blacks sitting at the same table. Black boys. White girls. Weren't people once lynched for doing much less? The teacher came over to speak to Freeman, and he graciously got up from the table to cross the room to speak to the students. As he walked away, leaving me alone at our table, I looked up to see Myrna looking at me from a nearby table with a knowing look.

"Now you see how I feel," she said, nodding her head and seeking understanding from a stranger. That comment was a harbinger of an inevitable divorce. I nodded in acknowledgement and smiled.

When Freeman returned to our table, he said, "Isn't that something?" He lowered his voice so the students would not hear him. "They've come to my restaurant to learn the proper etiquette for eating in a restaurant. Things have really changed since I grew up."[41]

Perhaps because I grew up in the Delta, I am acutely aware of Black sensitivities about certain words and phrases. I know every pratfall because in my youth I heard derogatory opinions directed toward people of color, whether African-American, Native American, or Asian—and I do my best to avoid those pratfalls. Despite that awareness, I occasionally blunder as I did with Freeman that evening. We had a conversation about race relations and Black culture, but then I moved on to the subject of acting, apparently without him making the transition with me.

While speaking of actors, not African-Americans, I remarked how articulate he was about his craft, "unlike the others." Well, I have interviewed my share of movie actors and I have encountered few who could be articulate about their craft. I found Freeman to be the exception. Reflecting on that conversation on the long drive home through a batshit dark night, and recalling his facial expression when I uttered that historically infamous phrase, I convinced myself that he probably thought I was referring to Blacks when I said he was "articulate, unlike the others."

Have you ever insulted someone while trying to pay them a compliment? I considered calling his assistant to explain, but the more I thought about it, the more I realized that probably would have made matters even worse because he would have stuck with his first impression. It is a reminder of why deep-rooted racism is so difficult to exterminate. Racial sensitivities are often indelibly ingrained like tattoos.

EARLY IN 2004, I put together a book proposal on a subject that had fascinated me for as long as I could remember. If you draw a straight line from New Orleans to Nashville, then over to Memphis and back down to New Orleans, you outline a triangular piece of real estate where all of America's original music was created—blues, jazz, country music, and rock 'n' roll. People have long known that those various genres of music were created in the South, but they are not fully aware of how small that piece of real estate actually is. Because it did not have a proper name, I gave it one: The Mojo Triangle.

The title of this investigative book was *Mojo Triangle: Birthplace of Country, Blues, Jazz and Rock 'n' Roll.* I sent the book proposal to Schirmer Trade Books and the new editor there Andrea Rotondo made an offer that I accepted. The book, which I think is my greatest contribution to the understanding of American music history, traced the development of each form of music and explained its significance, using interviews with the innovators who made the music, whenever possible.

The book destroyed some longstanding myths by pointing out previously unacknowledged contributions of Native Americans to the blues and by demonstrating that the blues existed on the Natchez bluffs long before the Mississippi Delta was ever cleared for farming. However, there is no doubt that the blues were *perfected* in the Mississippi Delta.

The Literary Guild proclaimed *Mojo Triangle* "a rich and rewarding book," and the Independent Publishers Association voiced its opinion by naming it the "Best New Book Out of the South in 2005," giving it a first place position in its annual IPPY award competition.

ONE DAY EARLY IN 2005, I was in conversation with one of my co-authors, Mardi Allen, when she told me my eyes looked yellow. I was taken aback because I was writing a spine-tingling and prescient history of the yellow fever epidemics of the 18th and 19th centuries. Titled *Yellow Fever: A Deadly Disease Poised to Kill Again.*, it recounted the deadly epidemic of 1793 that killed four thousand residents of Philadelphia and forced President George Washington and Thomas Jefferson to find refuge in the less-populated countryside. The narrative then expanded into the terrible yellow fever epidemics in later years that rocked New Orleans, Memphis, and large parts of Mississippi.

One of the first symptoms of yellow fever is jaundice and yellow-tinted eyes. Mardi's comment certainly sparked my paranoia about getting the disease I was writing about. What writer has not researched a particular disease only to become convinced that he has the disease as a result of writing about it? Still, I was baffled. A couple of weeks earlier, I had gone to a doctor complaining of gastric distress. She diagnosed my condition as gastritis and gave me a prescription for an antibiotic named Cipro, which bore liver failure notices in the United Kingdom but not in the United States.

With my now brightly colored yellow eyes, and even worse gastric distress, I went back to see the doctor. She ordered a urinalysis and a blood test to evaluate my liver enzymes. When the results showed that I was experiencing liver failure, she referred me to a gastroenterologist named Dr. Charles Hall, who arranged for a series of new tests: additional blood work, an ultrasound and a liver scan, a nuclear medicine test that involves the injection of radioactive particles into the bloodstream. I liked Dr. Hall right away. He asked lots of questions about my symptoms and seemed eager to get to the root of my problem. When he told me that his wife was a former newspaper reporter, I knew I was with the right doctor.

"The only way to know exactly what is going on in your liver is to do a biopsy," said Dr. Hall. "You've only got one liver. We've got to do what we can to take care of it."

The biopsy itself was uneventful. Several days later I returned to Dr. Hall's office for the results. "You don't have cancer," he said, pausing just long enough for me to savor that bit of good news, before continuing with a devastating follow-up comment, "But you do have cirrhosis of the liver."

Since I was in good health otherwise, Dr. Hall told me to start taking one-a-day vitamins, and come back to see him in three months, at which time I would be evaluated for a liver transplant. "Between now and your next visit," Dr. Hall said, "I want you to read everything you can find about cirrhosis of the liver. Some of what you will read will be encouraging. Other parts will be pretty nasty." As he was walking out of the examining room, he turned and paused a moment, his face reflecting concern. "We'll get you through this."

After I left his office, I took his advice and went online and discovered that the only books offered about cirrhosis were written for physicians and researchers, and most of them were all out of print. There are some good books on the subject of hepatitis and liver disease in general, but their focus was not on cirrhosis and they only contained a few pages of helpful information.

The more I researched cirrhosis, the more convinced I became that Cipro was the likely cause of the acute phase of my disease. British medical journals have warned doctors in that country for several years that the antibiotic can cause liver failure. Incredibly, Cipro was sold for several years in the United States under the name Baytril, a veterinary version of the antibiotic used by poultry growers whenever chickens showed signs of illness; but instead of treating individual chickens with the drug, they gave it to all the chickens in the facility as a preventative. Thankfully, the FDA reversed its position on the drug and banned it effective September 2005; but there is no way to know how many unsuspecting people developed liver disease from eating chicken and eggs tainted by the drug.

When my next round of blood tests showed no improvement in my condition, Dr. Hall referred me to Dr. Fredric Regenstein, the chief of clinical hepatology at the Tulane University Liver Transplant Center in New Orleans, and one of the top three liver experts in the nation.

Dr. Regenstein determined that I had autoimmune hepatitis, a disease that is treatable with medication. "Hopefully," he said. "You will never need a liver transplant."

All the research I did on liver disease resulted in a book proposal that was accepted by Marlow & Company of New York City. They had a series of medical books written by patient experts who walked the reader through a particular disease. My book was titled *Cirrhosis: An Essential Guide for the Newly Diagnosed* and offered advice on understanding the disease and finding the right doctor. Dr. Regenstein generously offered to write a foreword for the book.

By this time I had begun co-parenting two cocker spaniel puppies with Mardi Allen.[42] They were the two best-looking dogs I'd ever seen. Mattie, the smaller of the two, was chocolate in color and had a delicate face. Allie was multi-colored, with chocolate and white dominance, with the occasional streak of brown. Mattie had the personality of a solicitous beauty queen, while Allie was stoic and protective of everyone else. I fell in love with those girls right away.

The entire time I worked on the book Mattie sat or napped on my lap as Allie kept guard at my feet,[43] ever ready to spring into action should trouble arise. I bonded with those two pups in a way I had never before done with dogs of my own. I considered them writing assistants.

By the time I finished the book, my liver disease had gone into remission—and it's been that way ever since.

AFTER A YEAR HAD ELAPSED I reached the point when I felt I might beat the odds of my liver disease. The literature had given me three months to live, and here it was one year later and I was still alive. I felt a celebration was in order. I decided to get in touch with my old flame, Pam Gaia. I could hardly wait to tell her about my bout with liver failure. She would be amazed and horrified in the same instant. It was the sort of thing we ordinarily would talk about for hours.

I pulled out my Pam Gaia correspondence file to see where we had left off our email conversations. One email she sent me in December 1999, more than a year before I moved to Jackson, jumped out at me.

> **Dear Jim,**
> **I'm not doing politics now, but I'm going to sit on a panel for the Memphis Women's Political Caucus the first of the year. I had two losses. One to Congressman Ford and one to Carol Chumney (the person who took my place when I ran against Harold Ford). The loss to Chumney had to do with Gov. McWherter's wrath against me for my support of nursing home reform. If you remember he was in the nursing home business. I'll never forget your help with that. It was a worthy cause and I still care about it . . . Tonight I'm taking some children to dinner who used to work in my campaigns. They were just ten years old then and they are in their twenties now. I can't wait to see them again.**
>
> **Merry Christmas, Pam**

When I re-read that email it left me stunned and concerned. Obviously, I had not contacted her in a long while, probably not since I had moved to Nashville. I wasted no time responding to her, apologizing for my lapse in judgement. Truthfully, that was nothing new to me. I have a history of getting lost in my work. I once dated a woman for three years, seeing her a couple times a week, and then one day I got busy editing my magazine and forgot to call her—for almost a year.

When I realized my error, I called immediately.

There was a long silence on the other end of the line.

"Where have you been?" she asked, her voice strained. "I haven't heard from you in almost a year."

I apologized profusely and she gave me a second chance. You probably won't be surprised to learn that I blew the second chance as well. I've never been good at reading signals from women, which is why I am always in trouble with them. Pam seemed to understand that about me, which is why she never once chastised me for forgetting about the passage of time when I was writing. She understood I was living in an alternate universe when I was engaged in my work. I moved on to another email, one she wrote three weeks after the previous email, after my response to her last email. She wrote that she had heard about my book, *Dixie's Dirty Secret*, and looked forward to reading it. Then she went on to tell me a heartbreaking account of life after her election defeat.

> After I resigned my House seat, and after I ran for Congress, I couldn't get a job and I lost everything. No one would hire me. I went to Ron Terry [chairman of the board for First Tennessee Bank] to ask for a job and he asked me if I would be willing to relocate. I also asked Bill Farris [chairman of the Democratic Party in Memphis] and he pretended to be helping me get a job being a guard at the local prison. Thank goodness I didn't get it. I feel that Ned McWherter had something to do with this since I opposed him so strongly on the nursing home issue. You might say it cost me my political career.

I don't have an email record of my response to that email because I drove to Memphis to see her in person instead of sending an email. As usual, I took her to Pete & Sam's for dinner, where we talked for a good four hours. She seemed in better spirits than she had been in the email and that may have been because we were together again and talking about things that made her happy. Pam and I had almost identical political and social views, and we were equally attracted to each other physically and emotionally, but we never discussed living together or marriage. Whose fault was that? Is it something I should feel badly about? Some questions don't have answers. Her laughter was something I always looked forward to, waited for, delighted in, and recalled with precision in my dreams, no matter how many days or weeks we were apart.

After re-reading the emails, I called the last telephone number I had for her, but the line was disconnected. I sent her an email to the address she had maintained for a long time. It bounced back. Then I googled her to see if I could find a current telephone number or email address.

The first thing to pop up on my computer screen was a *Memphis Flyer* story with the headline **PAM GAIA, LONGTIME LEGISLATOR**. That grabbed my attention and I started reading and the words jumped off the screen "... died Tuesday at the Memphis home of her brother Rick Gaia."[44]

That was in September 2004, exactly one week after my birthday.

She had been dead for two years and I had no idea she was gone. No one bothered to call me because no one knew how close we were when she was still alive. It was a jarring moment. I was stunned. All I wanted was a telephone number or an email address! What I got instead was unexpected heartbreak delivered with an emotional slap across the face. I felt both loss and guilt. I could not believe she was gone.

The story went on to say that she had suffered from a recurrence of cancer. Despite her illness, the evening before she died, she had asked her brother to take her to Pete & Sam's for what would become her last supper. That last bit of information took my breath away. I feel she intended that for me, a message from the grave. Pam's passing was a stark reminder that my life was strewn with unfinished conversations. I knew it would only get worse from this point on. Most of my friends have passed away.

I asked a friend at *The Commercial Appeal* to send me whatever the newspaper had published. He sent me an obituary that provided me with more information, namely that Pam had been living with her brother during the final stages of her illness. After he took her to Pete & Sam's, she awoke the next morning experiencing difficulty breathing and died moments later.[45] I am glad she was not alone when she died, although I understand from my research being alone at the end of life can be a gift.

There was also was a tribute on the editorial page, which was entirely fitting for several reasons, not the least of which is that it was in those offices that we first met. It read, in part: "Gaia, who lived in Midtown, was charming, energetic and accessible. In another congressional district she might have been able to extend her career beyond the state legislature. But in 1990, when she left the General Assembly to pursue that course, she was considerably mismatched against then Rep. Harold Ford Sr. in the Democratic primary . . . Pam Gaia was a positive female role model for young girls during a period when there weren't as many as there are today. The inspiration she provided and the service she gave to her district and the state of Tennessee should not be forgotten."[46]

I could not have written it better myself.

FOR MY NEXT BOOK, I turned to a childhood friend that I had grown up with in Hollandale, Mississippi. Nine years older than me, Alex A. Alston, Jr. worked Saturdays in my grandfather's store from 8:00 A.M. to midnight. Because I also worked in the store on Saturdays, Alex and I became friends, with him playing the role of a mentor for me. He was the best salesman I ever saw. Like myself, he got along well with the Black customers who came into the store and they seemed to like his outgoing personality which typically exhibited itself as cackling like a demon with equally boisterous customers over a funny story.

Alex was one of our town's first Boy Scouts to achieve the rank of Eagle Scout. No one was surprised after he was graduated from high school that he joined the U.S. Marine Corps and entered into pilot training. I'll never forget the first time he walked into the store wearing his brightly colored dress uniform. I'm not sure how far along he got in his flight training before that momentous day he returned home on leave and decided to fly a crop duster that belonged to the family of a high school friend. He wanted to show off his new skills.

Because it happened on a Saturday, I was at work when someone came running into the store, screaming that Alex had been in a plane crash.

My grandfather, Audie, who had a prominent limp since the age of eighteen because of an accident in which he shot off his foot, began a wobbly run up to the visitor to find out what had happened. I could see them in animated conversation, after which my grandfather hurried wild-eyed out the door on his way to the hospital in Greenville.

After my grandfather left, I talked to the man to get the details; then I got on my bike and rode out to the field where the accident occurred. I could see the single-engine airplane from a distance, its nose stuck into the ground and its tail up in the air perpendicular to the ground. Once I got there I gently lowered my bike to the ground and stared in awe at the airplane, the engine of which was buried three to five feet in the ground. I could see oil dripping from the airplane and I could smell gasoline though I couldn't see any. How could anyone survive an impact like that?

Alex did survive and return to the Marine Corps, but I don't think he finished his flight training. He was not hurt internally, but his face was so badly cut that it was scarred for many years, causing him to look like he had been in a knife fight. After three years in the Marine Corps he entered Millsaps College in Jackson and then attended law school at the University of Mississippi. In no time at all he was known among his peers as a lawyer's lawyer.

In 2007 I approached Alex with a question: "Why don't we write a book about our experiences during the civil rights era?" Alex said yes, of course, and we put together a proposal for a book to be titled, *Devils Sanctuary: An Eyewitness History of Mississippi Hate Crimes.* Lawrence Hill Books, an imprint of Chicago Review Press, offered us a contract in July 2007. The book was published in 2009.

In a prepublication endorsement, Parham Williams, Dean Emeritus, Chapman University School of Law, wrote: "Alex Alston and James Dickerson have performed an invaluable service by unearthing painful truths … and portraying them with graphic clarity. Alston, a tenacious and able trial lawyer, and Dickerson, a gifted investigative journalist, bring to the task not only their impressive skills, but a passion born of having lived through the terrible events they describe. The result is a courageous, provocative, and sobering reminder that evil inevitably flourishes when good men fail to challenge it."

After successful book signings in Memphis, and Nashville, we had a signing in Jackson. Alex was thrilled at the response in Jackson, where he saw old friends in the long lines, but he was somewhat disheartened by the response of some friends who unfriended him over the book. In the former slave State of Mississippi, the issue of equal rights for Blacks still interfered with friendships.

I lost no friends over the book because everyone who knew me, including my high school classmates, had put up with my views against human bondage for most of my life. The generosity of my high school friends in looking the other way about my beliefs still amazes me. Most simply carried on as if there were no differences in our views. Among those people in Mississippi I did not grow up with, I have been tolerated but not always wanted. That's fine because it is a two-way street.

* * *

As Alex grieved over the loss of some old friends over his progressive views on race, I moved on to an even more controversial investigative book about American concentration camps. Titled *Inside America's Concentration Camps: Two Centuries of Internment and Torture*, it was published by the same company that brought out *Devil's Sanctuary*. The genesis of the book began with my awareness of the World War II internment camp for Japanese Americans that was built across the Mississippi River from my hometown of Greenville, Mississippi.

To write the book, I located survivors of the World War II camps and interviewed them about America's dark side, and I researched archival material and recent news articles. It is important to remember, in reading a book like this, that the victims of the American camps were, for the most, American citizens of Japanese, German, Italian, and Hispanic descent. They were voting citizens who had families and jobs and dreams for the future. The largest group of non-Americans imprisoned in the camps were

Jewish refugees from Nazi Germany. It was a shameful period of time in the evolution of American democracy.

ONE OF THE INDIVIDUALS I interviewed in 2007 for *Devil's Sanctuary* was Jim Ingram. He was a legendary FBI special agent who also had served as the head of the FBI offices in New York and Chicago before being sent to Mississippi to head up the violent crimes division of the civil rights desk, specifically to solve the infamous "Mississippi Burning" case in which three civil rights workers were murdered by the Ku Klux Klan because they were helping Blacks register to vote.

Later, he went on to become an assistant director of the FBI. After retirement, he returned to Mississippi to live with his wife and three sons. Shortly after he arrived he accepted an offer made by Mississippi's first Republican governor Kirk Fordice to head up the Mississippi Highway Patrol. By the time I met Ingram, he had retired from the highway patrol and was again working with the FBI to help Mississippi Attorney General Jim Hood with several cold-case prosecutions of individuals responsible for murders during the civil rights era.

The first time I met Jim Ingram was in the lobby of a hotel. He was a tall man with an imposing presence whose stern look could burn right through you like a welder's torch. However, when he smiled and turned on the charm, he was an engaging individual who could talk you into most anything. Both qualities he used to great advantage in finding witnesses and solving crimes. I was a little apprehensive about meeting him because he was assigned to the Jackson bureau during the time I refused to be drafted by a draft board headed by a Grand Dragon of the KKK. It didn't take long for him to put my concerns to rest.

By the time Ingram walked into the lobby, I had been there a few minutes. I stood up when I saw him approaching—I had no idea what he looked like, but I knew a confident, authoritative figure when I saw one—and he smiled and walked over and shook hands with me. As we were sitting down to talk, he said, "I just want you to know that I checked you out and we're good to go."

Well, that was certainly a relief. The past would remain in the past.

With that out of the way, we talked about the cold-case investigations he had come out of retirement to help investigate. He turned out to be a terrific source for the book. His attention to detail was a journalist's dream.

One of the things that stuck with me long after that interview was his remark that when J. Edgar Hoover ordered dozens of agents to Mississippi to solve civil rights murders, many special agents resigned rather than move to Mississippi to solve civil rights murders. There are two ways to look at those resignations: One is that some agents were too racist to investigate murders of Blacks and liberal whites, and the second, by far the largest group, were individuals who were scared shitless of the state's insanely violent reputation. One agent expressed fear that someone would put a snake in his mailbox

It didn't take long for me to decide that Jim Ingram was one of the most likeable people I ever met and one of the most knowledgeable about the violence that took place during the civil rights era in Mississippi. At the conclusion of the interview, I asked if he had ever thought about writing a book about his life as a FBI special agent. He replied he often had thought about it. We talked some more and came to an agreement to become co-authors in writing his life story.

We discussed the different ways we could proceed—with me sitting down with him and asking him questions, or me writing out a structure for the chapters and him interviewing himself by speaking into a portable tape recorder—and we decided the latter would be more convenient and would probably produce more detailed information. To be a good FBI special agent you have to have good organizational skills—and he was the best I'd ever seen at that.

Ingram asked me not to tell anyone that we were working on the book. He was still working part-time for the FBI on the cold-case murders, but he didn't feel it was any of the agency's business that he was writing a book. I readily agreed. As a result of our agreement to work in secrecy, we developed a cloak-and-dagger approach to our communications.

Sometimes I would meet him for coffee in the dining room of the hotel in which we first met. At some point during the conversation he would push a small, brown paper bag filled with cassette tapes across the table to me. I would nonchalantly take the bag without looking inside and put it in the chair next to me.

One day we were sitting at a table in the hotel dining room after making the transfer, still sipping coffee, when the manager of the hotel approached our table and suspiciously asked if we were guests at the hotel.

Ingram spoke first. "Oh no," he said. "I'm here visiting him."

She looked at me.

"You enjoying your stay?"

"Very much," I answered.

With that, she smiled and said, "Well, if you need anything just let me know."

We both thought that was a hoot. I thanked Ingram for his quick thinking, but good-naturedly chastised him for passing the buck to me. He chuckled at that.

Other times we met at a Shell filling station. I would get there early, park, and wait for him to arrive. When I saw him pull up to the pumps to get gas at a pump that had a vacancy on the other side, I would pull up into that space and insert the gas nozzle and walk around the pump to greet him. There would be a brown paper bag on the trunk of his car. After a brief conversation, I would pick up the bag and walk away.

Other times we met in the parking lot of a Walgreen's drugstore or at the post office parking lot on Airport Road. Whoever arrived last would park next to the other car. Invariably, I got out of my car and sat in his car with him to talk. A time or two he had the tapes in a Wendy's bag. When I left his car, I called out, "Thanks for the burgers," in case there were any listening devices in the vicinity.

Once I had a new tape I would transcribe it and then call him to discuss it, often asking him questions about what he said on the tapes. We spoke almost every day.   Over the course of the year that it took to gather the information for the book we became very good friends. Sometimes we met just to have breakfast. I told him that some of my writings had been used in the FBI's Bibliography Related to Crime Scene Interpretation with emphasis in Forensic geotaphonomic and Forensic Archaeological Field Techniques, compiled by Special Agent Michael J. Hochrein. He told me he thought I would have made a great FBI special agent myself. I considered that a high compliment. At one point, he confided in me that he had cancer and was dying. It was then I realized he might never see the book that I planned to write about him.

When he passed away on August 2, 2009, it saddened me greatly. Not only was he a great human being, he was a great American, a role model for all future FBI special agents. "Jim was fearless," said Billy Stokes, his partner on the cold-case murders. "Give him a case and he will run with it. That's one of the main reasons why he was a go-to guy. I'm not sure Jim Ingram was afraid of anything."

Certainly, Ingram was not afraid of death. After he was placed in hospice care, I spoke to him the day before he passed away through one of his sons because Jim was too weak to hold the phone. "Jim, you know what I want, don't you?" he said through his son.

"Yes sir, I do," I answered.

"I know you do. Thank you."

"Thank you, Jim."

One day an older man dropped by the hospice to visit. When Jim saw who it was he asked his sons to leave the room. After the man left and his sons returned to the room, he told them his visitor was a Klansman who wanted to say goodbye. No one knows whether it was someone he had arrested, or a secret source who had reported to him back in the day on Klan activities.

IN THE YEAR 2012, I called Scotty Moore to talk to him about writing a new book. This go around I wanted to tell his story in the first person, not in the third person as we had done with *That's Alright, Elvis*. At that time, he had thought readers would think he was presumptuous writing in the first person, as if he were some sort of big deal or something. The outpouring of love and respect he received about that book, helped him realize his importance to the Elvis Presley legacy. This time he readily agreed. After I spoke to Scotty, I got in touch with the University Press of Mississippi and they offered us a contract for the book to be titled *Scotty & Elvis: Aboard the Mystery Train.*

Scotty and I worked on the new book throughout 2012 and before the year was over we turned in the finished manuscript. Scotty told me he liked the first person account better than he did the third person used in the first book. That did not surprise me at all. I could capture more of his personality in a first person account. His longtime friend, Gail Pollock, confirmed that when she called to tell me she felt it captured the "real" Scotty. The book was published the following year, 2013, and Scotty and Gail drove down the Natchez Trace that July to meet me in Jackson to launch the book at Lemuria Bookstore. Scotty was not feeling well that day, but he held up for several hours signing books. We had dinner that night and the next morning he and Gail drove back up the Trace to Nashville. In the weeks that followed, I joined him for signings in Nashville and Memphis.

On August 3, 2013, I met Scotty and Gail in Memphis for a signing and party at the Gibson Guitar factory. Gibson gave the party to celebrate not only the publication of the book, but the issuance of eighty-one limited edition Scotty Moore ES295 tribute guitars, Scotty's favorite guitar while performing with Elvis. There were a lot of music celebrities at the party, including Priscilla Presley, who introduced Scotty on stage after tearfully recalling how much Scotty had meant to Elvis.

One week later, I met Scotty and Gail in Nashville for a signing at Parnassus Books. The MC for the event was recording artist Marshall Chapman who sat with Scotty, Gail and myself during the question and answer part of the event. It was the last time I saw Scotty, though I spoke

**Scotty Moore book signing at Parnassus Books in Nashville.
Left to right, Gail Pollock, Scotty Moore, Marshall Chapman, the author.**

to him fairly often after that by telephone.

Early in 2016, I tried to get in touch with Gail to ask her some questions about Scotty's recordings. After several days of no one answering the telephone, I called Scotty to ask if he knew where she was. It was the only awkward conversation I ever had with him. Immediately after asking the question, I got a bad feeling in the pit of my stomach.

Finally, after a long pause, Scotty said, "Why . . . She's dead."

For a while we talked about what a loss it was, and about how everyone had assumed she would out-live him. She lived with him for several months leading up to her death so that he could take care of her. When the time came he could no longer provide the care she needed, she was moved to a hospice facility. I asked if he had visited her there. He said he had not. They said their goodbyes at his house where they had so many happy times. Scotty's relationship with Gail was the longest he ever had with a woman, except perhaps his mother. Gail was his constant companion and former business partner, but they lived in separate homes.

395

I always wondered why they never married. They clearly adored each other and depended on each other for emotional support.

I called back to see how he was doing a couple months later and Gail's daughter Margi, one of Gail's three children, answered the telephone. She explained she had moved into Scotty's house with him to take care of him. Scotty's daughter Vikki also traveled from Memphis on a regular basis to look after him as did other children.

Margi gave the telephone to Scotty and I spoke to him until he seemed to grow tired. He said he was fine, but his voice, which I had become accustomed to in all its many nuances, told me otherwise. As his co-author, I had become acutely aware of his memory losses in recent years. At first I attributed it to his daily alcohol intake. Later I concluded he was slipping into dementia. By the time I called him about Gail, I knew he was well into dementia. He knew who I was, but he stumbled over any conversation about past events.

* * *

On June 13, 2016, I received calls from news media about Chips Moman, who had passed away that day at the age of seventy-nine. I was shocked but not surprised. He had been in failing health for more than a decade. Nonetheless, the news hit hard because I had not seen him in several years. Health issues of my own had slowed me down when it came to travel. My last face to face meeting with him had been in 1995, but I had spoken to him on the telephone several times since then. I tried to locate his ex-wife Toni Wine and his son, Casey, but they had more or less disappeared from the radar of my contacts.

Then the second shoe dropped.

Two weeks later, on June 28, 2016, I received a call from the obit writer at *The New York Times*, asking for a comment about Scotty's passing. I had not heard the news. Even though I knew in my heart that his time was running out, the news came as a shock. I got in touch with his daughter Vikki and others, including Gail's family members. It was disheartening to learn that vultures called Scotty during his final days, when he was in full-fledged dementia, in an attempt to manipulate him to sign over rights to his life. There are only two copyrighted accounts of Scotty's life and I wrote both. Never would I ever allow vultures to profit from his life.

Scotty and I had been friends for twenty-three years. We had travelled together all over the South and Northeast to book signings and interviews. Together we had visited at his family home in West Tennessee. We took the train from Birmingham to New York, stopping along the way for book signings. Once we went to a book signing in Kentucky on Reba McEntire's old tour bus. It was a loaner. There was just the driver, Scotty, his friend Gail, and myself on the bus.

Upon learning of Scotty's passing Paul McCartney may have said it best in this post on his official website: "When we were growing up in Liverpool the sound of Scotty's guitar on early Elvis records was nothing short of miraculous. It sounded to us like nothing we'd ever heard before and the gods in Valhalla couldn't have made a better sound. His technical skills, mixed with his sometimes wild abandon, set the perfect tone for Elvis's vocals. I was lucky enough to record with him and D.J. Fontana for a Sun Records tribute record that Ahmet Ertegun put together and Scotty's quiet manner and subtle sense of humour made the occasion very special for a fan like me. I saw him a few more times and spoke to him on the phone and he never ceased to be the hero he had been in my youth . . . Rest in peace, Scotty. One of the great gods of the guitar."

Scotty wasn't much for goodbyes—all the years I knew him, he never said goodbye; he simply lifted the needle of our conversation as if our visit were a phonograph record he wanted to pause—but he would have been so pleased with Paul's thoughtful words of farewell.

ALLIE AND MATTIE were the best companions I ever had, even though I only had them during the daylight hours, some weekends and most holidays. They were unbelievably bright and high spirited. They always had the best of intentions, but sometimes they succumbed to the beast inside them and exploded like popping corn whenever they saw a cat or a squirrel. Other times they were calm and deliberative. Always they were as loving as they could be.

One day when I was away from home, Allie balked at my mother's suggestion they go outside into the fenced-in backyard. Allie felt she was responsible for Mattie's safety, and she just wasn't sure Mother had the authority to tell them to go outside. At her wit's end, Mother called me and asked what she should do.

"Put your phone next to Allie's ear and hold it there a minute while I speak to her."

"OK," Mother said, never questioning the reason.

"Allie," I said into my phone. "I want you to mind Miss Juanita [the name everyone called her] and go outside . . . do you hear me? I want you to mind Miss Juanita and go outside."

Suddenly, Mother was on the phone.

"I've got to go," she said, breathlessly. "They're both running to the back door. Thank you, Son."

Allie and Mattie both endured severe health issues throughout life. As a puppy, Mattie had red mange and Allie had a stroke when she was still relatively young. Allie had to go the Mississippi State Veterinary School for treatment of her stroke. She stayed there several days, and when she returned she was back to her old self. The vets said she could live for years without having another stroke.

In January 2016, knowing that Mattie was in the throes of kidney failure I held her before she went to her other home that day and I talked to her of what was to come, explaining that I felt Heaven did not discriminate against canines. When she walked out the door, I knew I would never see her again. Sure enough, she died during the night.

I had no idea how Allie would react to losing Mattie. At first she was stoic, going about her business the way she always had done. However, as the months passed, you could see the growing sadness in her eyes; sometimes it looked as if she were silently weeping.

Mattie and Allie / Photo by James L. Dickerson

One night Allie was her usual self, but you could tell by looking at her eyes that she was ill. Shortly after eleven, we were sitting on the couch watching television, when Allie stood and began panting. Thinking that she was overheated, I lifted her off the couch and carried her outside and put her down in the grass so that she could use the bathroom. It was cooler outside and she stopped panting. The cool night air made us both sleepy.

When we went back inside, I turned out the lights and we went to the bedroom. I picked her up and gently placed her on the bed. This was no time for her to sleep in the office. I wanted to keep an eye on her.

Suddenly, she started scratching at the covers as if she were trying to make a bed. She was so energetic she tumbled back off the bed onto the floor. I walked around the bed to check on her and she was lying on her side, not moving. I wondered if she had hit her head on an air purifier that was nearby. I called out her name and gently picked her up and lowered her to the bed. She stood for a moment, eyes wide open, and then turned to look at me.

"What's wrong, Allie?"

Suddenly, she went into a seizure and collapsed, her eyes still riveted on me, pleading for help. I picked her up and placed her on the floor so she would not fall off the bed again while I called the emergency dog hospital. They said to bring her in immediately. I wrapped her in a towel and took her outside to the car and lowered her to the floor of the front seat. I did not put her on the seat because I was afraid she might fall off.

I was not eager about driving her to the vet because I have macular degeneration and have not seen well at night in a long time. Nonetheless, I made it to a four-lane highway that went directly to the vet hospital and I floored it, sometimes exceeding eighty miles per hour.

When I arrived at the hospital, I rushed Allie inside. A nurse took Allie into her arms and someone else escorted me to an office where I waited for the results. Several hours went by and finally the vet entered the room to explain what was happening. The vet was a young man with an emotionless face. Because her seizure had lasted a good thirty minutes, he said there was not much hope she would recover. In addition to the seizure her liver enzymes were sky high. In short, everything bad that could happen to her, did happen to her. I drove home that night alone, numb to the loss of Allie, who was as good a friend as I ever had.

EARLY ONE MORNING I was forced to face a grim reality. I was on my way to the front door when I glanced over my shoulder toward the back door. Through the glass in the door I saw Mother flat on her back on the grass, lying quite still. I rushed outside and asked her what had happened. She said she was picking up twigs and small branches when she stumbled and fell, landing face up. I asked if she could raise herself up. She said no, she had tried. I was afraid to try to move her without help.

I went inside and called 911. Within moments an ambulance arrived. The medics carefully lifted her onto a stretcher and drove her to the hospital, where we learned she had broken her hip. The accident required hip surgery and it took a while to recover from that. What you hear about broken hips is true if you are a senior. It is merely the first of numerous falls that eventually land you in assisted living. Subsequently, Mother fell and hit her head and twice fell and broke her wrists.

Either my sister or myself visited her every day at the facility to help feed and care for her, and to keep her company. For years Mother and I had talked about her writing down all the recipes she had compiled or simply made up herself, so they could be published in a book. In late 2018 I gathered them all together. There were a few that seemed unfinished and I took them to the assisted living facility so that she could fill in the blanks. It was during this time that she told me she had always wanted to be a writer but never had the confidence to give it a try.

Sartoris Literary published her book in 2019. I will never forget the smile on her face when I took a copy of the book to her to hold and examine. She was so proud of that book. I also gave copies of the book to employees at the facility who worked with her and they asked her to sign them. From that point on, she was treated like a celebrity, something Mother never once protested.

In February 2020, I experienced a delightful surprise when my childhood friend, Grace Mangum Crick, and I connected on social media after having had no contact for over sixty years. After suffering some bad breaks in life, the death of a son being one of them, she settled in Las Vegas, where she continued her career as a highly-regarded sculptor. Once we reconnected, she flew to Jackson and we had a wonderful reunion.

When I told Mother about the reunion, she beamed and seemed to find comfort in the knowledge I was again in contact with the person who had helped me recover from the loss of my father. I could see in her eyes that she was thinking the same thing I was thinking. Just a few weeks later, news reports about the Covid virus painted a bleak picture about the future. I went to visit Mother one day in mid-March and was told I would no longer be able to visit because the nursing home was going into lockdown.

Over the coming weeks the assistant director enabled my sister and me to have Facetime conversations with Mother and that seemed to boost her spirits. Every time the assistant director called for the Facetime visit I asked him about the Covid situation in the facility. He said they had

Mother, at 98 years of age, reading a review of her cookbook.

several cases, but he denied that Mother was ill with the virus. I also called the nursing staff for updates. They, too, denied she had Covid.

During one call they told me that Mother had commented, "Dying is so hard." That broke my heart. Mother had been with her mother and father when they died. I wanted to be with her during those moments to give her comfort.

In late April I received what would be our last Facetime conversation. We talked about various things, including my recent telephone conversation with Dionne Warwick, whom we watched on television on those occasions I visited her while living in Memphis and Nashville. She was one of Mother's favorites. Hearing me talk about the conversation with Dionne, her voice lilted up into her patented singsong expression, "Really!"

"Really!" I answered.

Then I asked her how she felt.

"I feel so bad," she answered, her voice descending into veiled agony. She uttered those same words when my father died. This time the words were a premonition of what was to come.

"Where do you hurt?" I asked.

"All over," she responded, her brow furrowed.

"Is there anything I can do?"

"No . . . no . . ."

There was a moment of silence.

Then she broke into "You Are My Sunshine," the Jimmie Davis song she had sung to me as a child, her frail voice bringing back memories of seventy-five years of motherly love:

> *You are my sunshine, my only sunshine*
> *You make me happy when skies are grey*
> *You'll never know dear, how much I love you*
> *Please don't take my sunshine away*

Just as countries have flags as a form of identity, my family had that song as a banner. Hearing the heartfelt lyrics and understanding the context of the words filled my eyes with tears.

"Goodbye, Mother—I love you."

"Goodbye, Son—I love you, too."

With that, the telephone screen went dark.

The following evening a nurse called me shortly after eight to let me know Mother had passed away at 19:45 (7:45 p.m.). The time of her death, to the minute, was the year of my birth. Coincidence? As a family, we tend not to believe in coincidence. Some events in life transcend facts.

Years before, when I was a student at Ole Miss, I stopped by the office of my favorite English professor, Dr. John Pilkington, to talk to him about a paper I was writing. As I walked in I saw him slumped over his desk, weeping profusely. As I turned to leave, I heard his voice.

"Please come in and sit down."

I did as he asked and he wiped his eyes with a tissue. "I just learned my mother died," he said. "I will give you fair warning. When your mother dies, it will be the worst day of your life." And so it was.

WHEN COLONEL TOM PARKER: *The Curious Life of Elvis Presley's Eccentric Manager* was published in 2001, I felt that of all my books it was the one most likely to attract movie interest. Sure enough, over the years, I received queries on a regular basis about movie options and gave the caller contact information for my publisher; but nothing ever came of it. Finally, after seventeen years of receiving no new royalties or any comments about movie interest, I contacted the publisher and purchased the rights to two of my books, *Colonel Tom Parker* and *Just for a Thrill*. After republishing the books under the Sartoris Literary imprint I planned to launch an energetic campaign to sell the movie rights.

Before I got too far along in re-publishing the book, my agent called. "Jim," he said after I answered an early morning call. "There is a God."

"I know, but why do you say that?"

"I just got a call from Warner Bros. They want to buy the book for Baz Luhrmann's new movie about Elvis. They want to show Elvis through the eyes of Colonel Tom Parker."

"You said buy. You mean option, right?"

"No, they said buy."

"This may be the best news I ever heard in my life, but I don't want to sell the book in totality. I am in the process of re-publishing the book."

I couldn't believe my good fortune. After nearly twenty years of waiting for a knock on the door from Hollywood about the book, it had actually happened. It is ironic that we never pitched the book to Warner. Bros. They sought me out and made an offer. A couple of days later my agent called me back and said he had worked out the details with Warner Bros. They would option the book for two years, while they put the project together; then they would purchase the rights at the end of that period if the movie was in production. I would remain the publisher of the book, but they reserved the right to use a small portion of the book for use in a coffee table book with photographs from the movie. As movie deals go, it was a good contract. I will receive a percentage of movie sales, movie soundtrack sales, merchandising rights, and, if it is made into a Broadway play, a percentage of the production's net earnings.

After the contract was signed, I put on my investigative reporter's hat to find out how and why this had all come about. As it turns out, director Baz Luhrmann began work on his Elvis movie shortly after wrapping 2013's *The Great Gatsby.* Prior to that he had successes with *Australia* (2008) and Moulin Rouge! (2001), starring Nicole Kidman.

From the beginning, Luhrmann's goal was to show Elvis through the eyes of the Colonel. Working with Luhrmann in those early years of development on an Elvis movie was his wife and frequent collaborator Catherine Martin. Out of the gate, Luhrmann and Martin were co-producers of the film. However, as the vision for the film expanded, other co-producers were added, including Gail Berman, Patrick McCormick, Schuyler Weiss, and Andrew Mittman. The grander the vision, the more producers were needed to raise money, hire personnel, and manage the operating budget.

Of primary importance was the script. Luhrmann hired British screenwriter Kelly Marcel, who had enjoyed recent successes with *Saving Mr. Banks* and *Fifty Shades of Grey*. At some point he added screenwriter Sam Bromell to the mix. It is not known how many drafts were created, but the exchanges reached a critical mass in 2017, when Luhrmann realized he was not happy with the script in hand. By then Warner Bros. had come on board the project and had secured the rights to Elvis Presley's entire song catalog for use in the movie, perhaps enticed by the decision of the Australian government to invest heavily in the project. It became clear at that point that Warner considered Luhrmann's project to be one of its major investments.

Unhappy with the script, Luhrmann asked Warner to secure the rights to my book so that he could write the script himself, along with his longtime writing partner Craig Pearce. It is not known who pointed out the obvious to the director—namely, that a biopic that is not based on the right to use copyrighted intellectual property is in perilous legal territory—but someone obviously did.

Within weeks after I signed the contract granting Warner Bros. rights to my book—it was contractually referred to as "untitled Baz Luhrmann Musical Project / James L. Dickerson / Option Purchase Agreement"—they announced that Colonel Tom Parker would be played by none other than Tom Hanks, not only my favorite male actor (favorite female actor is Nicole Kidman) but America's favorite actor as well. Certainly, any project that has Tom Hanks attached to it is assured of box office success. Not long after that it was announced that Austin Butler would be cast as Elvis Presley. I still have to be convinced that was a good choice.

For the rest of 2018, nothing said about when or where production would begin. The clock was ticking on the option agreement I signed with Warner Bros. They had until February 2020 to complete the purchase of the rights to the Colonel Tom Parker story, or risk losing the rights. I very much wanted this project to go through, but the reality is that only a small percentage of the books optioned for movies ever get past the option phase.

In the fall of 2019, pre-production of the film began in Queensland, Australia. As far as pre-production was concerned, that did not have a bearing on my contract. The key trigger phrase is "filming has begun," because that is a marker in the contract. Once filming has begun the studio only has so many days to finish out the option or the existing agreement expires and would have to be re-negotiated to resume filming. Warner Bros. didn't want that to happen. Neither did I.

As it happened, filming began in January 2020 and within weeks Warner Bros. followed through on the contract and purchased the rights of the book, thereby putting the full contract into effect. The following month disaster struck. The Covid-19 pandemic hit Australia. Work on the film was shut down while crew members and actors were tested. One of the crew members tested positive as did Tom Hanks and his wife Rita. All were put into quarantine.

With the pandemic spreading like wildfire in the United States, Australia and the rest of the world, the future looked bleak for the completion of the movie. No one had any idea if—and when—work would resume. After months of uncertainty, it was announced the movie had resumed production in September 2020 in Queensland, Australia. Production on the film ended early in 2021, but Luhrmann continued editing the film well into summer 2021. Because of all the pandemic-related delays the release date for the film was moved from November 2021 to early June 2022.

Warner Bros. spokespersons had little to say about the film, other than announcing scheduling changes related to the movie's release date. When it came to publicity, the project was put into information lockdown by Baz Luhrmann, who has said very little on the record. What little information came out was typically attributed to unnamed sources.

MEANWHILE, as the movie drama played out, I began writing another book, the biography of my late friend, Chips Moman. We had often talked about writing a book together, but the years slipped away before we could do it. After he died I knew his story had to be my next book. I possessed many hours of recorded conversations with him, and it took a while to get that together. Then I had to find and transcribe hours of taped interviews with musicians and recording artists he had worked with. After that, I had to arrange new interviews with people he had worked with. Three of my favorite new interviews for the book were with Petula Clark, Dionne Warwick, and B.J. Thomas, three of the survivors of Moman's glory years as a recording studio maestro. Sadly, Thomas died about six months after his interview with me.

After spending most of 2020 working on the book, I got in touch with Moman's son, Casey, and the woman Chips was married to while we were all good friends, the songwriter Toni Wine, and I let them know the book was in the pipeline and would be published in December 2020. I told her I was glad to finally tell Chips' story. Toni's first reaction was, "Well, it's your story, too."

Toni's New York-to-the-core voice had not changed one bit over the years. She sounded exactly the same. Casey was a different matter. The last time I saw him with his father he was a teenager. Now he was a forty-something-year-old man. It was a voice I did not know, but he had many ways of speaking that were similar to his father's. He is in many ways a chip off the old block.

Toni remains one of my favorite people in American music. The composer of hit songs such as "Groovy Kind of Love," "Candida," and "Black Pearl," and the female voice in the Archies ("Sugar, Sugar"), she had a promising career as a solo artist that she gave up to marry Chips Moman. She got a son out of the marriage that she is very proud of and one hell of a roller-coaster ride. She continued to do vocals for jingles and to go out on the road to sing background for Tony Orlando.

When *Chips Moman: The Record Producer Whose Genius Changed*

American Music was published, I knew it was the best book I had written since the Colonel Tom Parker and Scotty Moore biographies. Hopefully, it will be made into a movie, too. As I neared the ending of the book, I realized I had an obligation to not only tell the story of America's most successful record producer, but also to promote him for induction into both the Country Music Hall of Fame and the Rock 'n' Roll Hall of fame. To exclude Chips Moman from historical recognition by those august organizations would be a tragic injustice.

IN 2011 I BEGAN a book publishing company that I named Sartoris Literary Group. My goal was to publish reprints of my books in Kindle editions on Amazon. I was among the first writers to sign on to Amazon's Kindle Direct Publishing as a vehicle for reprinting books that had gone out of print with the original publishers. When I uploaded my first ebook, *Faith Hill: The Long Road Back*, Amazon's program had only been in existence for five years and few of the major publishers had non-fiction titles offered as ebooks. Because it was one of the first biographies offered on ebook, *Faith Hill* was an instant bestseller, going to Number 1 within a matter of weeks. Financially, it proved to be more lucrative for me than the original paperback published by St. Martin's Press. With money pouring in, I followed up with *Ashley Judd: Crying on the Inside* and Scotty Moore's autobiography *That's Alright, Elvis*, both of which went to Number 1 on Amazon.

Encouraged by the success of my reprints, I began soliciting manuscripts from other authors in order to become a traditional publisher. At that time, I also was teaching a night course at Millsaps College on writing and publishing books. One of my top students at that time was a former judge by the name of James Bell. I was so impressed with the synopsis of his mystery novel, *Vampire Defense*, I offered him a contract for the book. Published in 2012 the book still stands as Sartoris Literary's bestselling work of fiction. Other books followed, both fiction and non-fiction, establishing Sartoris Literary as a major publisher in the South.

My favorite books published by Sartoris Literary are *Mojo Rising: Masters of the Art* and *Mojo Rising: Contemporary Writers.* Published in 2017 and edited by myself, *Mojo Rising: Masters of the Art* is a collection of short stories and novel excerpts from Mississippi's most accomplished writers: William Faulkner, Eudora Welty, Tennessee Williams, Richard Wright, Shelby Foote, Ellen Gilchrist, Stark Young, Ellen Douglas, and Willie Morris. In order to publish the "Masters of the Art" volume I had to license, one by one, the stories used in the book. Sometimes that meant approaching the publishers, while other times it involved approaching the families or estates of the writers. My search for Richard Wright's family took me to Australia.

My second favorite book is the second volume of the series, *Mojo Rising: Contemporary Writers*, edited by Joseph B. Atkins, a journalism professor at Ole Miss with whom I had worked at the now-defunct *Jackson Daily News*. This volume features stories from contemporary writers, including bestselling author Ace Atkins, Sheree Renee Thomas, Margaret Skinner, the late Larry Brown and others. Included in the "others" group was a short story written by myself titled "The Second Coming." It is a fictional account about an encounter Scotty Moore and D.J. Fontana could have had at an Elvis festival, years after Presley's death. Also at the festival was a Toronto OBGYN who moonlighted as an Elvis impersonator. As luck would have it, the OBGYN was called upon to deliver a baby at the festival, born to a lesbian couple one of whom had been artificially inseminated at an Ohio clinic. Seeing the baby were Scotty and D.J., both of whom nearly fainted because the child was the spitting image of Elvis Presley.

Although the storyline is fictional, it is based on fact. I can at long last tell a secret that Scotty kept to his dying day. He first told me the story while we were working on his first memoir. Early on, when he and Elvis and Bill Black were on the road promoting their recordings done at Sun Studio in Memphis, Elvis often borrowed Scotty's driver's license so that he could escape the underage restrictions at bars around the country. Those were the days before photos were required on driver's licenses, so all Elvis had to remember was Scotty's birthdate and his address.

As a lark, Elvis once borrowed Scotty driver's license to donate semen at an artificial insemination clinic. Scotty thought it was somewhere in Ohio, perhaps Dayton. He thought it funny that there could be dozens, maybe hundreds of "Little Elvis" clones out there in the world. Scotty was extremely loyal to Elvis, even in the latter years of his life. He told me embarrassing stories about Elvis which appeared in his books, such as the time he and Bill waited in the hotel lobby so that Elvis could have sex with one of the young women who had showed up at their room (the three of them shared a room with two double beds; Scotty and Bill slept in one bed, Elvis in the other). All hell broke loose when Elvis came down the stairs to the lobby and told Scotty that his condom had broken during sex.

"What should I do?" he asked, perplexed.

All that Scotty and Bill could think of was to take the woman to the emergency room of a hospital so that the woman's vagina could be flushed with water by a doctor. The young woman did not seem to mind at all.

Scotty included that story in both his memoirs because he was confident Elvis would have found find it funny. He was confident Elvis would not be amused if he told the story of Elvis selling his sperm. It is the sort of thing one does when they are eighteen or nineteen and feel invincible from the repercussions of their actions. Knowing Scotty the way I do, I am confident he would not mind me spilling the beans, so to speak, now that he and Elvis both have passed on. It is incredible to think there could be sons and grandsons of Elvis out there somewhere. All I can say at this point is, "Scotty, I kept the secret for as long as I could."

✹ ✹ ✹

About the *Mojo Rising* books, Robert H. Brinkmeyer, Jr., Director, Institute for Southern Studies, University of South Carolina, wrote: "The two *Mojo Rising* anthologies showcase an extraordinarily rich group of writers from a region bordered roughly by Memphis, New Orleans, and Nashville. Volume One highlights writers who established the area's

411

rich heritage in the twentieth century, including, among others, the literary giants William Faulkner, Eudora Welty, Tennessee Williams, and Richard Wright. Volume Two, assembling fiction from a wide variety of exciting contemporary writers, testifies to the region's ongoing literary flourishing. These are superb collections—read them and get a glimpse into the mysterious depths of what James L. Dickerson calls the Mojo Triangle."

To launch the books in 2017, I inquired about the possibility of having a book signing at William Faulkner's home of Rowan Oak, a stately primitive Greek Revival house built in the 1840s and renovated   in the early 2000s. Rowan Oak curator William Griffith told me they rented the grounds out for weddings and other social events but rarely approved book signings. When I told him volume one contained a Faulkner short story, "A Rose for Emily," he generously agreed to allow us to have a signing on a side porch of the home.

On the morning of an afternoon signing, Mardi Allen and I loaded up a truck with books and refreshments for the signing, and struck out for Oxford, primed for a literary adventure. There we met Joseph B. Atkins and his lovely and energetic wife, Suzanne, along with some of the writers featured in the books—Ace Atkins, Margaret Skinner, and Renee Thomas. Because I had not seen Rowan Oak in fifty-four years, chill bumps covered my arms as the home came into view. As I opened the front door to step inside, I was overtaken by vivid memories of my last visit.

When I arrived at the University of Mississippi for the 1963 summer session, I was seventeen years of age. I would have been sixteen if my mother had allowed me to skip the seventh grade as suggested by the principal. In retrospect, I am glad that did not happen.

As a college student, I immediately accomplished two notable things: I organized a rock 'n' roll band and I placed a telephone call to William Faulkner's sister-in-law, Dorothy Oldham (her number was in the phone book). Faulkner had died the previous year and I wanted to know if I could tour his home. This was before the university took over the residence.

At the time I called, the house was still under the control of the family, specifically Dorothy Oldham. Miss Oldham was most gracious. I explained that I was a seventeen-year-old musician and writer, and seeing the house would mean a great deal to me.

When the day came for my private tour, it was pouring rain. I arrived at the gate to see Miss Oldham waiting in her car. Once we entered the house, she gestured to the left and explained that the room was his library and his writing room was connected at the far end.

"Just make yourself comfortable," she said. "Look at anything you want to. I need to go upstairs and check on a few things. I'll be back in a few minutes."

I walked around the library, looking at the books, and then hurried over to his writing room. It was about what I expected. A nondescript table and a wooden chair faced the window so he could see into the yard. There was writing on the wall where he had outlined his novel, The Fable.

I was surprised to see a single bed in the room, but since his bedroom was upstairs I supposed he used it to rest during his writing breaks.

I sat at his writing table and gazed out the window, taking in what Faulkner himself must have seen as he organized his thoughts.

After about thirty minutes Miss Oldham came down the stairs and asked if I was ready to go. By then the rain had stopped and the sun was shining again. Five years later she was dead and the legacy of Rowan Oak was entrusted to the university.

Inside the house, I was greeted by the curator William Griffith. Before he started showing me around, I told him about my last visit. That was news that greatly interested him.

"After the house was renovated, we had to work from photographs as we put everything back in place," he explained. "Since you are the only person I've met who saw the house before it was turned over to the university, please let me know if we got anything wrong."

The author visits William Faulkner's office in Rowan Oak for the first time since 1963. "Everything looks the same, except the desk chair I sat in did not have a padded seat, I don't think."—Dickerson

We began the tour in the library, where I immediately saw that some things had been added that were not there during my first visit. I told him what was different and we moved along to Faulkner's writing room. Seeing it again took my breath away because it was *exactly* as I remembered it, with his writing table and typewriter at the window looking out at the property.

There I stood, gazing into the Great Man's office. It had been fifty-four years since I had sat in that chair and pondered my future. It had been fifty-five years since the Great Man himself had sat in the chair. I felt myself sigh and I turned away, averting my eyes. Revisiting the room was like looking into the sun.

Later, a small crowd gathered outside, despite threatening weather, to hear our speeches, ask questions of the writers present, and finally to purchase books to be signed. Just as the book signings concluded, the bottom fell out of the sky, releasing torrents of warm summer rain that peppered down amid growls of thunder. Griffith shouted for us to move the refreshments onto the porch, which we did in quick order. Then, having compassion for the soaked literary gathering, he invited everyone inside the house, where he instructed us to set up our refreshments on the Faulkner dinner table. We gathered around the table two and three deep and had wine and refreshments in the very room in which the Great Man began and finished his writing days!

Driving back to Jackson that night, I was exhausted. There was just too much internally to process about the events of the day. I felt my old life slipping away. On the road from Oxford to Batesville, where we would access the Interstate back to Jackson, my thoughts flew back to that night in 1968 when I made the same journey to catch a train in Batesville.

Life is repetitive in so many different ways that we never comprehend because of the flood of emotional debris that defines our lives. Some people turn loose and float away. Others ride the wave to see where it takes them. I am compelled to wonder if life has to make sense to be of value.

Now I am at a place in the road where this story began.

I have gone full circle and I am still here, still writing.

These days I often re-read a paragraph from Willie Morris's fine book *New York Days*: "So many of my friends of those days are dead now, and others have gone their own way. In the course of an existence, people move in and out of one's life. Often we do not know the whereabouts of those once dear to us, much less what they are feeling or remembering. Close relationships oscillate between tranquility and destruction, between fire and ice. Old fidelities wither and love dies as the lovers go on living. There are a few islands of warmth and belonging if we are lucky. That is how I wish to remember the best of those times."[47]

It has been more than half a century since I boarded that train to Chicago, a trip that was destined to turn my life upside down. You might say I have remained on that train for fifty years, if you accept the train as a metaphor for a half century of reporting on American life.

Yet today as I resolutely step off onto a deserted platform under a darkened sky, memories of loved ones, and flashes of close and not-so-close relationships that have defined my life, whirl about inside my head, each a passenger with a different itinerary, and I stand next to the tracks and look for the flickering light of an incoming locomotive capable of seductively beckoning me for yet another new adventure.

I am alone.

I see nothing coming.

Perhaps I will sit on that bench over there in the shade and wait a while. The next Big Thing is probably on its way, burning up the tracks now. The only question is, will it stop for me?

THE END

Together Again: Childhood friends James and Grace were reunited
in 2020 after an absence of 60 years. Grace was there for James in the
Third Grade when his father died; she mysteriously re-appeared
just weeks before the death of his mother.

OTHER BOOKS BY JAMES L. DICKERSON

Colonel Tom Parker: The Curious Life of Elvis Presley's Eccentric Manager

Devil's Sanctuary: An Eyewitness history of Mississippi Hate Crimes (with Alex A. Alston)

Inside America's Concentration Camps: Two Centuries of Internment and Torture

Chips Moman: The Record Producer Whose Genius Changed American Music

That's Alright, Elvis: The Untold Story of Elvis's First Guitarist and Manager, Scotty Moore (by Scotty Moore with James L. Dickerson)

Scotty & Elvis: Aboard the Mystery Train by Scotty Moore (with James L. Dickerson)

Just for a Thrill: Lil Hardin Armstrong, First Lady of Jazz

Dixie's Dirty Secret: How the Government, the Media and the Mob Reshaped the Modern Republican Party into the Image of the Old Confederacy

Mojo Triangle: Birthplace of Country, Blues, Jazz and Rock 'n' Roll

Faith Hill: Piece of My Heart

Nicole Kidman: A Kind of Life

Memphis Going Down: A Century of Blues, Rock 'n' Roll and Glorious Soul

Mojo Rising: Masters of the Art (edited by James L. Dickerson). Short stories by William Faulkner, Eudora Welty, Tennessee Williams, Richard Wright, Shelby Foote, Willie Morris, and others.

ENDNOTES

[1] Dickerson, James L. "Chickasaw County Child." *Mississippi,* Winter 1968.

[2] (unsigned, but written by James L. Dickerson, "Nixon may have miscalculated Senate support," *The Recorder and Times*, Brockville, Ontario, June 19, 1974.

[3] Dickerson, James L. "Faulkner's letters — revealing." *Delta Democrat-Times,* February 20, 1977.

[4] Dickerson James L. "Stillness broken by praise to God," *Delta Democrat-Times*, May 18, 1977.

[5] Dickerson, James L. "Why the Charismatic Renewal?" *Delta Democrat-Times*, May 13, 1977,

[6] Dickerson, James L. "Finch meets the public," *Delta Democrat-Times*, May 25, 1977.

[7] Dickerson, James L. Death and Dying Series, *Delta Democrat-Times*, August 7, 1977.

[8] Moody, Jr., Dr. Raymond A., *Life After Life,* Bantam Books, 1973.

[9] Dickerson, James L. "Natural childbirth—delivery room diary," *Delta Democrat-Times*, November 23, 1977.

[10] Ironically, after her career as a fashion model she married the love of her life, David Gould, and moved to Weston, Connecticut, a small town of 10,000 that was also where my literary agent, lived. Sadly, she died in 2017 of cancer.

[11] Dickerson, James L. "Hello Big Time! Fashion world sparkles for Tallahassee models," *Tallahassee Democrat*, September 17, 1978.

[12] Dickerson, James L. "Scary sea voyage has happy ending," *Tallahassee Democrat,* October 17, 1978.

[13] Dickerson, James L. "Wakulla man kills wife, self," *Tallahassee Democrat,* December 11, 1978.

[14] Dickerson, James L. "Help scarce for orphaned Angel," *Tallahassee Democrat*, March 12, 1979.

[15] Unattributed staff writer. "Drops Charges Against Dr. Poonai," Port St. Joe *Star*, May 15, 1980

[16] Dickerson, James L. "Grand Dragon set for Big Bend visit," *Tallahassee Democrat,* December 28, 1978.

[17] Crews, Harry, "The Buttondown Terror of David Duke," *Playboy*, February 1980.

[18] Dickerson, James L. Tallahassee *Democrat* and *Facing South*.

[19] Brooks, Browning, and James L. Dickerson, *Tallahassee Democrat.*

[20] Dickerson, James L. "Women Coaches Feel Fouled by Hiring Practices," *Jackson Daily News*, July 2, 1979.

[21] Dickerson, James L. "He Wants to Live in Women's Dorm" and "Sex Change: He Wants to dress as Female as a Preparation," *Jackson Daily News*, October 30, 1979.

[22] Dickerson, James L. "Ticket Tantrum," *Clarion Ledger / Jackson Daily News*, November 25, 1979.

[23] Unsigned editorial by James L. Dickerson. "Forgotten Children," *Clarion Ledger/Jackson Daily News*, July 20, 1980.

[24] Unsigned editorial written by James L. Dickerson. "Child Molesters," *Jackson Daily News*, September 1, 1980.

[25] McElroy, Gary. "Nazi Chief Portrays His Dream World," *Jackson Daily News*, May 13, 1980.

[26] *McElroy, Gary.* "Klansman Called 'Stupid' by Nazi," *Jackson Daily News*, May 13, 1980.

[27] Unsigned editorial written by James L. Dickerson. "Running: Teresa races against tradition," *Jackson Daily News*, July 16, 1981.

[28] Prudential Insurance Company labelled Memphis the murder capital of America because of the large number of homicides that occurred in the city during the 1910s, 1920s, and 1930s.

[29] Unsigned editorial written by James L. Dickerson. "More Questions," *The Commercial Appeal,* November 2, 1983.

[30] My cousin John Waits tells me his favorite story about Bilbo is about the time he was giving a big speech while running for office and in the middle of a racist tirade pointed to two Black children sitting quietly at the edge of the crowd and said they must never be allowed to vote. The two Black children were civil rights icon Medgar Evers and his brother, Charles Evers.

[31] Dickerson, James L., *The Commercial Appeal,* September 13, 1982.

[32] Dickerson, James L. "'Centrist' tag is claim, challenge for Glenn," *The Commercial Appeal*, December 5, 1983.

[33] Unsigned editorial written by James L. Dickerson. "One view of history," *The Commercial Appeal*, October 31, 1983.

[34] Unsigned editorial written by James L. Dickerson. "Second Chance," *The Commercial Appeal,* December 9, 1983.

[35] Dickerson, James L. "Mud Island, downtown essential to city," *The Commercial Appeal*, August 21, 1984.

[36] Dickerson, James L. "Brazen bat's strange behavior flies in the face of all logic," *The Commercial Appeal,* September 19, 1984.

[37] Dickerson, James L. "Brazen bat's strange behavior flies in the face of all logic," *The Commercial Appeal*, September 19, 1984

[38] Dickerson, James. *Colonel Tom Parker: The Curious Life of Elvis Presley's Eccentric Manager*, Sartoris Literary Group, 2001.

[39] Kruesi, Kimberlee, Associated Press, June 9, 2021.

[40] Morris, Willie. *Yazoo: Integration in a Deep-South Town*, New York, Harper's Magazine Press, 1971.

[41] Portions of the Morgan Freeman story were previously published in the book, *Mojo Triangle*, by James L. Dickerson.

[42] Over a period of twenty years, Mardi Allen, who has a Ph.D. in psychology, co-authored four books with James L Dickerson: *Sons without Fathers*, *The Basics of Adoption: A Guide for Building Families in the U.S. and Canada*, *Adoptive and Foster Parent Screening: A professional Guide for Evaluations*, and *How to Screen Adoptive and Foster Parents: A Workbook for Professionals and Students*. The latter title was co-authored with Daniel Pollack, a noted Yeshiva University professor, attorney, and author on legal issues related to social work.

[43] Portions of this section were taken from my book, *Cirrhosis: An Essential Guide for the Newly Diagnosed.*

[44] Baker, Jackson. *Memphis Flyer*, September 21, 2004.

[45] (unsigned), *The Commercial Appeal,* Metro section, page B6, September 22, 2004.

[46] (unsigned), *The Commercial Appeal*, Viewpoint, section, September 24, 2004.

[47] Morris, Willie. New York Days, New York, Little Brown, 1993, p.379.

CPSIA information can be obtained
at www.ICGtesting.com
Printed in the USA
LVHW082011111021
700155LV00008B/202/J